Chinese Internal Martial Arts

BAGUAZHANG
(EMEI BAGUAZHANG)

Theory and Applications

Master Liang Shou-Yu
梁守渝

Dr. Yang Jwing-Ming
楊俊敏

and

Mr. Wu Wen-Ching
吳文慶

YMAA Publication Center
Main Office:
4354 Washington Street
Boston, Massachusetts, 02131
1-800-669-8892   www.ymaa.com   ymaa@aol.com

10   9   8

Second Edition Copyright ©1994

ISBN:0-940-871-30-0

Publisher's Cataloging in Publication
(prepared by Quality Books Inc.)

Yang, Jwing-Ming, 1946-
　　Baguazhang : emei baguazhang / Yang Jwing-Ming, Liang Shou-Yu,
Wu Wen-Ching.
　　p. cm.
　　Includes bibliographical references and index.
　　ISBN: 0-940871-30-0

　　1. Martial arts--China. I. Liang, Shou-Yu, 1943- II. Wu,
Wen-Ching, 1964- III. Title

GV1112.Y35 1993   796.8'15'5
                                        QBI93-21788

Disclaimer:
The authors and publisher of this material are NOT RESPONSIBLE in any
manner whatsoever for any injury which may occur through reading or following the instructions in this manual.
The activities, physical or otherwise, described in this material may be too
strenuous or dangerous for some people, and the reader(s) should consult a
physician before engaging in them.

Printed in Canada

This book is bound
"Otabind" to lay
flat when opened.

游龍

栗守渝題
西元一九九二年○月

ACKNOWLEDGMENTS

Thanks to A. Reza Farman-Farmaian for the photography, Jerry Leake for typesetting, Michael Wiederhold for cover design. Thanks also to Ramel Rones, James B. Phillips, David Ripianzi, and Sam Masich for general help; to Jeffrey Pratt, Jenifer Menefee, Denise Breiter, Sean Hessman, Timothy Buchannan, Tony Rousmaniere, and many other YMAA members for proofing the manuscript and for contributing many valuable suggestions and discussions. Special thanks to James O'Leary for his editing and to Yang Mei-Ling for her effort in typing the Chinese characters. Again, deepest appreciation to Dr. Thomas G. Gutheil for his continued support. A special acknowledgment to the Pa Kua Chang Journal, High View Publications, for the use of their photographs in the first chapter.

FOREWORD

Grandmaster Wang Jurong
王菊蓉教授

The origin of Chinese Wushu is far and long, and its contents are as numerous as flowers. This has resulted in hundreds of schools and styles, like hundreds of branches and thousands of vines. All of these schools, after being tested and experienced through the long seasons of history, have harvested a great abundance of fruits. Today, these schools have become known for their excellence of styles. The "Baguazhang" introduced in this book is one of the most renowned and traditional of these Chinese martial arts.

"Baguazhang" is a very interesting fist technique (i.e., martial style). If it is practiced often, it can strengthen the body and increase longevity. It can also train practical martial techniques, providing an effective method of self-defense.

In Baguazhang practice, the upper limbs use in almost all the palms. Various skills are developed from the constant changing of the palm techniques. During the palm training, the lower limbs walk along a circle, and use swaying and arcing stepping as major techniques. Baguazhang combines the theories and patterns of the Eight Trigrams of the "Zhou Yi" (Zhou's Book of Changes). Consequently, this has resulted in the possibility of changing during walking as desired. Not only that, it allows the possibility of actions such as the palm's boring, turning, sideways, and vertical maneuvers.

Baguazhang combines the maneuvers of the palms and stepping techniques, swaying and arcing stepping for walking and turning, linking each step to the next, and its variations are many. The basic palm techniques of the Baguazhang are "Lao Ba Zhang" (Old Eight Palms). These eight palms can be combined freely in practice. Therefore, they are alive and free, and can be practiced by either a single person or by two persons.

This traditional fist (i.e., martial style) has been a favorite of a great portion of Chinese people for hundreds of years. Today, Baguazhang is gradually winning many foreign friends. However, geographic limitations make it difficult for the exchange of knowledge, and the art is not currently widely known or accepted in the west. This book was written through the collaboration of Dr. Yang Jwing-Ming, Master Liang Shou-Yu, and Mr. Wu Wen-Ching. Together, they have compiled and translated documents regarding the many traditional Baguazhang theories and principles. This could help spread Baguazhang knowledge and techniques to America, Canada, and all other countries of the world. The content of this work is very abundant and profound, and includes discussion and commentary on theory, principles and basic training. Beginning with the basic training of the sixteen words and the cultivation and training of Baguazhang Qigong, it moves on to cover topics such as solo practice of the Old Eight Palms, matching of the Old Eight Palms with a partner, introduction of Gongfu, and a clear and detailed explanation of the three postures: high, middle, and low. Finally, the unique traditional Baguazhang weapon, Yuan-Yang Yue (Deer Hook Sword), is also introduced. Working with this weapon will significantly help any practitioner realize the importance of coordination, harmonious feeling and integrity of Baguazhang as presented in this book.

I am very happy to see the publication of this book, which offers a great guide to Chinese Wushu. I would like to congratulate the authors for their effort and contributions to the popularization of Chinese Wushu.

Professor Wang Jurong
Professor of Shanghai Athletic College
Chinese Wushu, National Judge of Archery
Vice Chairman of Shanghai Wushu Association and the Head of the Wushu Judging Committee
Wushu Gold Medalist – First National Athletic CompetitionTaiwan, Republic of China, 1953
Grand Guoshu Champion, Women's Division
Seventh National Athletic Competition Taiwan, Republic of China, 1946

FOREWORD

Grandmaster Jiang Hao-Quan
蔣浩泉教授

During this exciting period when Chinese Wushu is blossoming in every corner of the world, this written contribution by Master Liang Shou-Yu, Dr. Yang Jwing-Ming, and Mr. Wu Wen-Ching to the development of Chinese Wushu will definitely be both beneficial and influential.

Among the thousands of different martial styles and schools in China, Baquazhang is one of the most famous. Numerous varieties of Baguazhang schools exist today, and the contents of the art are abundant and profound, such as "Wudang Style Baguazhang,""Yin-Yang Style Baguazhang,""The Complete Technique Style Baguazhang,""Emei Style Baguazhang,""Xingyi Style Baguazhang," and "Swimming Body Style Baguazhang."

Among the numerous different styles of Baguazhang, all of them have their specific unique characteristics in technique and movement, which gives rise to thousands of variations and tens of thousands derivations. However, no matter how numerous or elaborate their variations, none can be separated from their theoretical origins. These origins (i.e., theory and principles) are walking the circle, following the strategies of four directions, four diagonal corners, and the eight trigrams - "the eight directions," "coordinating the body and hands' movements," "muddy stepping and spinning," "varying freely as wished," "the steppings are as firm as Tai Mountain," "light and agile as the goose feather," and "the shapes are like eight animals' actions." In the attacks, "the defense is hidden within and in the defense, the offense is ready to return,""use the soft to conquer the hard, and mutually support with the hard," and "once move slightly, the entire body moves."

In muddy stepping circle training, the movements often adopt the shape of animals, and coordinate with the key techniques of "striking, kicking, wrestling, and controlling." In Chinese Wushu, further advancement achieves the goal of "internally cultivate the mind and the mental body, externally strengthen the tendons and the bones, and ever-more perfectly train the techniques for defense." This is the unique characteristic of the "Baguazhang Fist Techniques." "Emei Baguazhang" also includes all of these unique characteristics. The contents of this book are abundant and profound. It is a good fist book, teaching both theoretical foundations and actual techniques.

One of the authors, Mr. Liang Shou-Yu, was born in 1943 in Sichuan, China. He was raised in a Wushu family, and trained martial techniques devotedly with his grandfather, as a child. Later in his youth he was even more infatuated with martial arts, and visited many well known Chinese martial arts mountains, learning from many talented masters. During these years of special training and practice, both his martial theory and techniques advanced rapidly. He has mastered both Shaolin and Wudang martial fists and various weapons, whether for solo practice or matching training. His expertise is especially in Shui Jiao (i.e., Chinese Wrestling). He has written numerous martial books and videotapes. Before his arrival in North America, he had taught many students in China. In 1981, he arrived in Seattle, and since then has been teaching Wushu in Washington State in America, and at Columbia University in Vancouver, Canada. He has cultivated many talented students and well known movie stars. He has earned the title "International Wushu Judge," and has orchestrated great success for the Chinese Wushu community.

The second author of this book, Dr. Yang Jwing-Ming was born in 1946, in Taiwan, Republic of China. He also loved Wushu since he was a child, and started his Wushu training at the age of fifteen. He built his Wugong (i.e., Martial Gongfu) from the Shaolin White Crane Style. Later, he received much instruction from numerous well known Wushu Masters, especially from Master Li Mao-Ching, the successful student of the well known grandmaster Han Ching-Tang. He has studied and practiced intelligently, and has specially mastered the martial techniques and their theories. He has gathered Shaolin, Xingyi, Bagua, Taiji, and various weapons knowledge in his mind, and has written many popular Wushu books. Dr. Yang obtained his Ph.D. in Mechanical Engineering from Purdue University in 1978. He and his student Mr. Jeffery Bolt founded the Yang's Shaolin Kung Fu Academy in 1980. When Dr. Yang later moved to Boston, he founded Yang's Martial Arts Association. Since then he has taught many students, and has passed down Chinese Gongfu to the public. He has visited and offered seminars and workshops in many countries such as Canada, Italy, France, Mexico, England, Ireland, Germany, Portugal, Switzerland, and Saudi Arabia. He has contributed greatly to the spread of Chinese Wushu in the world.

Master Liang, Dr. Yang, and Mr. Wu's Emei Baguazhang book is unique and special among Chinese Wushu publications, and I believe it will be favored by the public.

Professor Jiang Hao-Quan

May 25, 1993

Professor Jiang Hao-Quan is a well known older generation martial artist, professor, and doctor. Born in 1917, Jiangshu, China, he graduated with honors from Nanking Central Guoshu Institute. He specialized in Shaolin, Xingyi, Bagua, Taiji, Sparring, Wrestling, Boxing, Solo and Matching forms. He has held the title of "Chinese Fist King," defeating many challengers from around the world. He is a national level judge in China for Wushu, Water Jumping, Swimming, Gymnastics, and Boxing. He possesses an honorary doctorate from Eurotechnical Research University in Hawaii, and has authored many Wushu books. Professor Jiang is currently writing a Wushu book entitled *Jiang Hao-Quan: Wushu Gathering of the Truth*. This book will include three volumes and will include Shaolin, Wudang Fist Techniques, Qin Na, Weapons, Fast Wrestling, boxing and the most modern fighting techniques.

FOREWORD

Shifu Jerry Alan Johnson

It seems that in every decade, the eyes of the martial arts public focus their attention on a different branch of the tree. In the 1950's, attention was focused on Judo, as that particular system became more open to the public and more accessible to westerners. In the 1960's, the focus turned to Karate. In the 1970's it was Shaolin Kung Fu, and the 1980's saw a time of fascination with the Ninja and Kickboxing. Each decade unveiled a different combative approach and philosophy to the martial arts. It is only fitting that now in the 1990's, the focus of attention is being placed on the Internal Systems of martial arts training.

The increased freedom of travel and open communications between instructors has allowed concealed knowledge to grow and expand at a remarkably rapid rate. We are indeed fortunate to have access to true martial arts masters, men who are both extremely proficient in their martial ability as well as their knowledge of the internal healing systems, who are willing to share their educated insights. Both Master Liang Shou-Yu and Dr. Yang Jwing-Ming are two such men. I have admired and respected both of these men for their high level of skill, openness and honesty - which from my experience only comes through confidence developed through years of practice and training.

The Baguazhang system presented in this book is from the Emei Mountains, has been concealed from the public for centuries, and has been taught only to a discriminating few. To receive this priceless gift of insight on this esoteric Bagua system is both wonderful and rare. The martial arts community as a whole owes these two men warm, heartfelt thanks and appreciation.

Shifu Jerry Alan Johnson
May 1993

FOREWORD

Dr. John Painter

A serious medical condition almost ended my life. Medical doctors told my family that they could expect me to be frail and sickly, and that I might not live past eighteen with the hand nature had dealt me. By the time I entered grade school, my immune system was failing. Constant headaches, colds, flu, and chronic infections became the rule instead of the exception. I was weak, frail and unhappy. But I had a dream. A dream to be healthy, strong, and happy like other boys. I wanted that dream badly; I just didn't know how to go about making it come true.

Shortly before my eleventh birthday, I was introduced to and began studying Nine Dragon Baguazhang and Qigong with Dr. Frank Li. A cousin of Master Li Ching-Yuan, the famous Daoist scholar and martial arts master reputed to have lived over 200 years, Li Ching-Yuan claimed that his remarkable longevity and strength were due to his special diet and daily practice of the internal martial art and Qigong style that he devised while studying in the Emei Mountains of Sichuan. He named his style, which he passed on to Dr. Li, Jiulong Baguazhang (Nine Dragon Eight Trigram Palm). Dr. Li was a Chinese Physician, martial artist and herbalist of the old school before immigrating to America in 1945. The Li family had been respected bodyguards and Chinese traditional healers from the Emei Mountain region in China.

From 1957 to 1969, I worked mornings and evenings on a daily schedule with Dr. Li to learn this system. In the first year, my illness diminished, and my immune system grew stronger. Within three years, I found the physical health and stamina of which I had so often dreamed. Today, at the age of 47, my physical health has never been better. Baguazhang has, for me, accomplished what Western science and medicine could not. I am convinced that through dedicated practice of Baguazhang, one can enrich every aspect of daily life, cure many chronic ailments and alleviate the stress that so often shortens life span and fosters the spread of many diseases.

To profit from an internal martial art one has to emphasize and focus upon both the external forms (the bio-mechanics), as well as the internal work or Qigong that is part of that particular style. True Baguazhang skill cannot be had by copying only external forms from a teacher, video or book. Not delving deeply into the philosophy and practicing the Qigong is like having a field of dirt, some water and a hoe and believing that this is enough to grow crops. Without planting seeds, no fruit will be forth coming.

There are many styles and interpretations of Baguazhang. My style of Emei Nine Dragon Baguazhang is not precisely the same as that presented in this book. This really makes no difference, as all styles share a core truth which serves as the base for all Baguazhang practice. Every teacher has a different way of expressing his understanding of the art. While this diversity imparts the art with a unique flavor to the beginner, it is often confusing. Beginners are usually looking for some type of external stability to cling to in a Daoist art that is comprised of the ever changing principles of the Yi-Jing.

At the root of all Baguazhang practice lies the changing nature of the Universe, a concept centered in Daoist philosophy. The Baguazhang student will soon learn that life and all existence is in a state of constant flux. He learns to become one with the ever changing moment, to give up all attachment, static thought patterns and rigid postures and just go with the flow of the moment.

The Baguazhang master can express physically with his body what the mind and heart feel to be eternal truth. To do this, he must eventually go beyond external form and find his own inner freedom and power. This is the primary goal of the Baguazhang master, to be one with the Dao.

Over the years, my Emei Nine Dragon Baguazhang techniques have brought me radiant health and many friends. As a martial art, Baguazhang has also stood me in good stead in my career as a tactical trainer for police and government agents, and as a former professional body-guard. I quickly learned the hard way what really works and what doesn't on the streets. That is why I say that Baguazhang as a health system and a martial art, when properly learned and practiced, is a shinning jewel among the stones.

I thank Master Liang Shou-Yu and Dr. Yang for their many years of true friendship and support of my efforts to introduce Baguazhang to the west, but most of all for their unselfish desire to promote this wonderful art to all people - through their fine book on Emei Baguazhang - without holding anything back.

John Painter, 1993

Arlington, Texas

PREFACE

Master Liang Shou-Yu
梁守渝

I am very happy to have once again collaborated with Dr. Yang Jwing-Ming to write this book: *Emei Baguazhang*. First, I have to express my thanks for Dr. Yang's encouragement and his many forms of assistance. My contribution to this book was merely to introduce certain "Sequences" or "Practicing Routines" of Emei Baguazhang. Dr. Yang has actually contributed most of the hard work. He is a well-known Gongfu expert and a scholar. During the writing process, he always endeavored to find the deeper essence of the art and look for the best within the best. I have learned so much from him during our association. When we write a book together, neither of us have thought or concern for self-benefit or profit. We think only of how to write a good book and introduce our knowledge to the reader. From these efforts, we hope only to obtain some joy and satisfaction through the increased Western understanding of Chinese culture.

A further contributor to this book is Shifu Wu Wen-Ching whose hard work and insight enabled us to complete our task much sooner than we could otherwise. I thank him for his help and especially for his assistance to me personally. In addition, I would also like to express my appreciation to Mr. Reza Farman-Farmaian for his skillful photography.

The history of Chinese martial arts (Wushu) is very deep and long. The origin of the art can be traced back hundreds, or even a thousand years. Consequently, there exists a great number of different styles.

In China, most families know the names of Wushu styles such as Shaolin, Wudang, and Emei. Outside of China, however, and especially in the West, only Shaolin and Wudang have become popular. This is simply because Emei Gongfu has always been kept secret, conserved by its disciples. Oral instruction has been the main method of passing the art from one generation to the next. Written documents are very scarce. Because of this, there has never yet been a book competent to introduce Emei martial arts in a complete manner. Despite this, the Emei martial arts have been preserved and publicized widely in Sichuan laymen society and have generated many highly skilled and famous martial artists. Emei Wushu has thus been representative of the mysterious and secret high arts of Gongfu, and is commonly used as a subject in Chinese novels, movies, and operas.

In 1983, the Chinese government established an investigative team called:"The Martial Arts Archaeological Organization," targeting every province in order to discover, organize and systematically document all Wushu styles. According to this investigation, there are sixty-eight existing styles or schools, more than one thousand barehand sequences or practice routines, more than five hundred sequences or practice routines of various weapons, and more than three hundred ways of training Gongfu power.[1] The techniques, the fighting strategies, and even the methods of strengthening the power within each style are unique and have their own special characteristics. In fact, according to my knowledge, there is still much information about many additional styles or schools which has not yet been discovered and compiled. Some old masters have stated that there are at least seventy-two styles or schools.[1]

Baguazhang is one of the main styles in Emei Wushu history. Emei Wugong (i.e., martial Gongfu) includes both Daoist and Buddhist practices. Baguazhang has similarly divided into Daoist and Buddhist Baguazhang. Among the seventy-two Emei martial styles presently known to me, there are five styles which teach Baguazhang. Some of these train walking in a circular pattern, as do many other Baguazhang styles. However, there are also some Emei Baguazhang styles that walk in a straight line. Naturally, the names of the techniques and sequences also differ. According to one recent survey, there are more than thirty kinds of Baguazhang training which include fundamentals, barehand, weapons, and matching sets. Some of them are closely related to Master Dong Hai-Chuan and Sun Lu-Tang. The names and the movements are very similar in some respects, and very different in others. Therefore, great effort is still needed to understand and research the roots of these styles.

I started learning Emei Da Peng Gong (Emei Great Roc Gong) from my grandfather Liang Zhi-Xiang when I was six years old. Later, I also learned some other Emei Gongfu. My grandfather had many martial friends, and he always wanted me to learn other Gongfu styles from them. Among them was a man named Hong Ze. Later he was called "Hong Ze Great Master." He had been trained in a Daoist temple called: "The Temple of the Great Emperor of Martial Arts" on Zhen Wu Mountain, located on the south of Yangtze river. He also learned Emei Da Peng Gong from my grandfather. My knowledge of Swimming Body (Swift Dragon) Baguazhang, Deer Hook Sword, Bagua Crutch, and Wujiquan originated from him.

In 1960, after I entered West-South National University, I learned more Baguazhang from Master Zheng Huai-Xian. Master Zheng was a student of Grandmaster Sun Lu-Tang. He was the vice chairman of the Chinese Wushu Federation. Master Zheng represented China in the Wushu demonstration during the 1936 Olympics, held in Germany. At this time I also learned Xingyiquan and fundamental Bagua Eight Palms from Master Wang Shu-Tian. Master Wang was born on June 25, 1908 in Xincheng County, Hebei Province. In 1928, he passed the "national examination" and entered Nanking Central Guoshu Institute to further advance his martial arts career. A few of the well known teachers there at that time were: Zhu Guo-Zhen (principal), Zhu Guo-Fu (administrator), Wang Ziping (head coach of Shaolin), Sun Lu-Tang (head coach of Wudang styles), and Gao Zhen-Dong. Master Wang's classmates included Zhang Chang-Hai, Zhao Fei-Zhen, Shi Han-Zhang, Zhu Guo-Xiang, and Han Ching-Tang. Since 1980, Master Wang has held the position of Chairman of the Sichuan Wushu Federation. In addition, he has been a member of the National Wushu Federation, the president of the Sichuan Emei Gongfu Institute and Sichuan Guofu Wushu Institute, the Chairman of the Internal Martial Arts Research Institute, the Principal of the Sichuan Emei Wushu School, and the Wushu Professor of the Chengdu Athletic Institute.

The Bagua Eight Palms I learned from Master Wang is typical and representative of the style in general. In fact, almost all of the Bagua Eight Palms currently popular in China are very similar, albeit with some slight differences. In Emei Wugong training, most Baguazhang practitioners favor this style, and it is commonly used as the foundation of Baguazhang training. Furthermore, I have also been most fortunate to learn and exchange Baguazhang knowledge with other masters and friends, such as Sha Guo-Zheng and Shao Zi-Qiu. All the above sources have greatly contributed to my understanding of Baguazhang. Today in my deep heart, I do and always will appreciate the knowledge I have learned from all of them.

Chinese martial arts history extends back many thousands of years. Its contents are wide, deep and filled with treasures for the mind, body and spirit. Though I have learned and researched Chinese martial arts for over forty years, and have been involved in the study of Baguazhang for more than thirty years, I have still not yet understood all of its essence. I still need to learn continuously. There is a saying in Chinese Gongfu society: "Live until old, learn until old." In Chinese Wugong (i.e., martial Gongfu), one should never feel self-satisfied.

Finally, I would like to take this opportunity to express my personal appreciations to Madam Wang Jurong and the many others who have written forewords for this book. Madam Wang is one of the last living representatives of an entire generation of martial arts masters. She has helped me in many ways, both by inspiring courage in me and by being my teacher. Madam Wang's father, Wang Ziping was one of the most famous martial artists and teachers in recent Chinese martial arts history. He has been my idol and an inspiration to my martial arts training for many years. Thanks also to Professor Jiang Hao-Quan, for writing his eloquent foreword to this book. Professor Jiang graduated from Central Guoshu Institute in the 1940's, and is one of the few remaining representatives of the older generation of martial artists. He is also an expert in Baquazhang. He learned his Baquazhang from the very famous master Yin Fu's son, Yin Yu-Zhang. His distinguished lineage and achievements have brought him great fame in the Chinese martial arts world. Naturally, I also appreciate the contributions by Shifu Jerry Alan Johnson and Dr. John Painter.

I would like to thank my uncle, Jeffrey D. S. Liang and aunt Eva for adopting me when I was a child. Without them, I would not be where I am today. Although political turmoil in China separated us for nearly 40 years, through their effort we were reunited in 1981, in Seattle, Washington. Later, they assisted me in gaining employment at the University of British Columbia, making it possible for me to emigrate to Canada. This changed my whole life. Uncle Jeffrey, once a diplomat, an engineer, and then a cultural and social advocate, has been for years recorded as a biographee in Marquis Who's Who in the World, and several other Marquis publications. Aunt Eva has also gained recognition - in her teens as a silver medalist in Wushu fighting competition at Chongqing.

Thanks to Mr. Harry Fan for offering me my first job in Canada at the Vila Cathy Care Home during a critical time. It gave me the opportunity to make myself known to Canadian communities, and to offer my knowledge to the people of North America.

Thanks to Mr. Raymond Y. Ching, Ms. Taisun Wang, Dr. W. Robert Morford, and Mr. Arthur J. Lee - all of whom helped me when I first arrived in Canada and had a most difficult time. They assisted me in gaining employment at the UBC, and in receiving my immigration visa to Canada. Thanks also to Mr. Paul Ha, Dr. W. Robert Schutz, and Ms. Sonya Lumhoist-Smith. Because of their help, the Chinese Martial Arts in the UBC continues to develop and grow.

In addition, I would like to thank Mr. Bill Chen, Mr. L. H. Kwan, Mr. Solen Wong, Dr. James Hii, Mr. Michael Levenston, and all my friends for their continued support and concern. I am also obliged to Vancouver's "North American Tai Chi Society," "International Wushu San So-Do," "YMAA," and "SYL Wushu Institute" for their support. Finally, I would like to thank my parents, Liang Zuofeng and Huang Zhexi, for the love and education they gave me, and especially my wife, Liang Xiangyong, for her infinite support and understanding.

I am very excited that we have completed and published this book, and are once again able to share with the western public what we are privileged to know. I sincerely hope the readers enjoy this book, and I wish everybody peace and happiness.

Liang Shou-Yu
April 10, 1992

PREFACE

Mr. Wu Wen-Ching
吳文慶

It has been a decade since I came to the United States, as a proud and confident freshman studying at Northeastern University's Mechanical Engineering Department. I was ready to face the challenge of the "new world." Nothing was going to stand in my way. I was determined to be successful in anything I did. But becoming a writer, and a Chinese martial arts instructor was not in my mind. All I wanted from Kung Fu training was to learn how to fight. Like most people not involved in Kung Fu, I had the misconception that martial arts was purely a physical exercise for training one to fight. Little did I know that it contained so much wisdom and would be a humbling experience for this naive freshman.

Over the past ten years of learning from Dr. Yang and Master Liang, I have been privileged to learn several different styles of Chinese martial arts, and Qigong. My training with them has been an enriching and cultivating experience. With their continual guidance and encouragement, my love for the art grew at an "exponential" rate. They have always taught me to have an open mind, maintain a beginner's enthusiasm and attitude in learning, and always receive the "tea" with an "empty cup." This has broadened the path and perspective of my training and has opened many doors for my advancement. It is their intent to help preserve the art and to share their knowledge with the readers. Dr. Yang has told me on numerous occasions that if you do not achieve a higher level of understanding than I have, by the time you reach my age, you have not tried hard enough. My teachers have provided the guidelines for me to follow, it is my responsibility to follow them and develop them. With more and more in depth books being published, it is all the martial artists' responsibility to study them and develop the arts to a higher level. I sincerely hope that the readers will join me in preserving and developing this ancient art.

When Dr. Yang and Master Liang gave me the opportunity to help write this book, I gladly accepted. It was an important task in which I am honored to have taken part. This is another way my teachers are teaching and sharing their knowledge with me. I deeply appreciate this opportunity. From helping to write this book, I discovered many important details that I was not aware of when I was first taught. My teachers, Master Liang and Dr. Yang, have spent countless hours writing and presenting the important concepts of this style. I am sure that the readers will benefit greatly from their writing and teaching.

At this time I would like to thank Master Liang and Dr. Yang for their teaching, for allowing me to carry on their lineage, and for giving me the opportunity to co-author this book.

Wu Wen-Ching
May 27, 1993

PREFACE

Dr. Yang Jwing-Ming
楊俊敏

Since the 1960's, Chinese martial arts have become ever more popular in the Western world. This is especially true for the internal styles, such as Taiji, Xingyi, and Bagua, because people are now realizing that by practicing these arts they can not only learn effective self-defense techniques, but can also gain significant improvements in their health.

This is not surprising, given that the internal Chinese martial styles are based on Qi theory, and are considered part of Qigong (internal energy) training. Qi is the Chinese word for the natural energy of the universe. Qigong is the science of this energy, especially as it circulates in the human body. The Chinese have been studying Qi for over four thousand years, and they have learned how to apply their knowledge of this energy to meditation, and to certain types of movements designed both to improve physical and mental health, and to increase longevity. The Chinese have found that Qi theory and principles can also be used to increase muscular power to much higher than usual levels. This is done by energizing the muscles with Qi through the concentrated, meditative mind.

Although Baguazhang is classified as an internal style, its theory, principles, and applications are different from those of better-known internal styles such as Taiji and Xingyi. Taiji emphasizes power that is soft like a whip, while Xingyi's power is explosive like a cannon. Bagua's power, however, is more like an inflated beach ball: the practitioner's body becomes full of energy, which can be moved about at will and can be manifested to bounce an enemy a great distance away. While Taiji emphasizes using defense as an offense, and Xingyi emphasizes using offense as a defense, Bagua employs both defensive and offensive strategies. While Taiji focuses on middle and short range fighting techniques, and Xingyi concentrates almost exclusively on short range fighting, Bagua trains at all three fighting ranges: short, middle and long. While Xingyi is characterized by straight forward advancing and straight backward retreating movements, both Taiji and Bagua emphasize roundness and circular movements, yet Bagua manifests power in its circular movements in a way that is quite different from Taiji.

Bagua has only eight basic movements, but the variations and applications of these movements are unlimited. It is like dancing the waltz, which has only three basic steps, but hundreds of variations. Therefore, although the beginner will find Bagua easier to learn than many other arts, it will still take more than ten years of pondering and practice to reach the deeper levels of understanding and application. Because of this, it is a good style for the beginner who does not have any experience in the internal styles. It is also good as a second internal style for those who have already learned one, as it will increase their understanding of their first style. For those who are only interested in health, Bagua provides a few simple movements which promote vigor and stamina, while helping to rebalance the Qi.

Although I have practiced Taijiquan for more than 30 years, it was not until the last few years that I realized I have only just started to taste the essence and comprehend the deep theory of the internal arts. I now consider myself to be only a beginner in the Chinese internal arts. This understanding has increased my desire to explore other internal martial styles, such as Xingyi and Baguazhang, which follow theories that are different from those of Taijiquan. However, because of my busy schedule and of the difficulty in finding a qualified teacher in the United States, I have never had the chance to explore another internal martial art.

It was not until 1985, in Houston, that I was fortunate enough to meet Master Liang Shou-Yu. I learned then that he is a living repository of China's vast cultural heritage in the field of internal and external martial arts and Qigong. The emergence of any great master does not occur by mere coincidence of events. However, Master Liang does have all the advantages of having been born into a martial arts family and having had the chance to come into contact with many legendary grandmasters. Because of his love and utter devotion to martial arts, and because of his characteristic perseverance and insight, Master Liang has made himself a superbly seasoned artist, striving for nothing less than the utmost precision and perfection of the art.

When we met and realized we both shared a love for the Chinese martial arts, we felt a mutual sense of respect. This soon grew into a feeling of brotherhood, and since then we have shared our knowledge openly, without doubt or hesitation.

When I found that Master Liang is also an expert in Xingyi and Baguazhang, I asked him to teach me and my students. During this learning and teaching period, we felt that it would be a good idea to write books together on Xingyi and Baguazhang. We felt that with my experience in writing and publishing, as well as my background in the internal arts and Qigong, and also with the assistance of the many Xingyi and Bagua books which were published earlier in this century, we should be able to write a systematic, theoretical analysis of the art. Since theory is the root and the foundation of any training, we believe that a theoretical discussion of these two internal styles is necessary to help the practitioner increase his understanding and advance his training. Furthermore, in order to write a good book, I must dig into it deeply, until I really understand it. This helps me to lay out the right path for my training.

As with the Xingyi (Hsing Yi) book which we have already published, I have been responsible for writing the theoretical portion of this book, although it has all been carefully checked by Master Liang. Since the forms and the postures are very important for actual teaching, these are demonstrated primarily by Master Liang himself. We hope that our mutual effort has resulted in a worthwhile book. In order to expedite our date of publication, Mr. Wu Wen-Ching was invited to join our effort. Mr. Wu's responsibility is to describe every movement of the forms.

In addition to the theory and techniques of Baguazhang, we have also included a discussion of the martial morality which has been passed down to us. Both Master Liang and I agree that because martial morality has been widely ignored in modern martial arts society, we will begin to bring this subject to the public's attention in all the martial arts books we write.

If you plan to learn from this book, it is especially important that you study and understand Bagua's theory and principles. They will serve as a map, and provide you with clear directions leading you to your goal in the shortest possible time. If you do not understand the theory, then what you learn will be only flowers and branches, and it will have no root.

In the first chapter of this book, we will first review some important concepts of martial arts. Next, we will summarize vital martial moralities, and discuss some martial stories which are well known in China. The concept of Bagua (the Eight Trigrams) will then be introduced. In order to help you understand the cultural background of Chinese martial arts, the connection between the Chinese martial arts and Yi Jing (Book of Changes) will be summarized in the fourth section. Once these basics have been covered, we will then define the meaning of Baguazhang in the fifth section. Finally, in the last two sections the history of Baguazhang will be surveyed, and the contents of Baguazhang training will be presented.

In the second chapter, the writings of ancient Baguazhang masters will be translated and commented upon. The beginner may find it difficult to understand the deep theory of each document. However, through the course of learning and practicing, if you keep coming back to this chapter to read and ponder, soon you will realize that behind the words are the treasures of a living art, preserved for hundreds of years.

In order to help you enter the domain of the Qi sensitivity that accompanies Baguazhang, the third chapter will introduce a Qigong set, or Nei Gong (internal Gongfu) practice, which has been passed down to us. If you first practice these Qigong drills, you will build up a firm foundation of the energy aspects of Baguazhang.

In order to help you understand the movements of Baguazhang, in Chapter 4 some of the important training concepts and key words will be reviewed. This chapter will help you to better understand how Baguazhang is different from other martial arts.

In Chinese martial arts, each style's methods of conditioning a practitioner's physical and mental bodies is a very important subject. Traditionally, these training procedures were kept secret by each style. The reason for this was that, if you know the effective ways to condition yourself, you will be able to reach a higher level of fighting capability both physically and mentally. Chapter 5 will explain some of these training procedures for Baguazhang.

After you have built up a good theoretical understanding, you may then start learning the Basic Eight Palms, which is considered the most basic root of Baguazhang movement and techniques. In order to help you understand the meaning of each movement, Chapter 6 will introduce each palm and its martial applications. Furthermore, to encourage practical training with a partner, a Basic Eight Palms Fighting Set is also introduced in this chapter.

After you have mastered the Basic Eight Palms in Chapter 6, a well-known Swimming Body Baguazhang form will be presented in the seventh chapter. Naturally, the martial applications of the techniques are also included.

Since Bagauzhang has developed in China for hundreds of years, many weapons techniques have also evolved. To help you understand how weapons are used in Baguazhang, a unique Baguazhang weapon called Deer Hook Sword will be introduced in the eighth chapter. Certain martial applications of the techniques will also be discussed.

Dr. Yang Jwing-Ming

CONTENTS

Chapter 1

General Introduction
一般介紹

1-1. Introduction

The Chinese martial arts are quite new to the Western world, compared to their 4000 years of history in China. Their Western history probably began in the 1950's. Up until that time, although there had been a few masters teaching, they were virtually unknown to the general public.

After Master Cheng Man-Ching's Tai Chi book became available in the early 1960's, Tai Chi Chuan (Taijiquan) began its gradual rise to popularity in the United States. Although more and more people were experiencing the health benefits of Taijiquan practice, the enormous cultural differences between East and West kept it from being well understood, especially with regard to its internal components.

Then, in the late 1960's, the motion pictures of Master Bruce Lee brought enthusiasm for Chinese martial arts to a peak. His movies started to make the Western public aware of the potential of Chinese martial arts. Unfortunately, Bruce Lee died in the early 1970's, after only a few years in the public eye. Although his abilities increased the popularity of Chinese martial arts, his movies tended to give people a somewhat restricted view of Chinese martial knowledge.

In 1974, the American and Communist Chinese Governments established formalized relations. Since then, the concepts of acupuncture and Qi have gradually been introduced to the West. A byproduct of this is an increased understanding of the internal aspects of Qigong and the internal martial arts. In addition, cultural exchange programs have brought many Chinese martial artists and groups to the United States and Europe for demonstrations. This has resulted in many martial styles being introduced to the West for the first time. Many well known masters have since come over from mainland China, Taiwan, and Hong Kong to the United States and Europe for seminars and lessons, and many young people have traveled to Asia for training. The most significant influence in this time of great change came from the many masters who were able to immigrate to the United States and Europe.

In the last decade, the Chinese martial arts have gained widespread acceptance in the West. A variety of external and internal styles have been introduced, and the health benefits of Taiji are now so well recognized that even Western doctors have begun recommending it to their patients. Because of the popularity of Taiji, people are gradually becoming interested in other internal martial arts such as Xingyiquan, Baguazhang, and Liu He Ba Fa. Although these styles are very different from Taijiquan, they are nonetheless beneficial for health and effective for self-defense. It is very likely that these styles will become as popular as Taijiquan in the 1990's. People who are starting to learn them now will be the pioneers of these styles in the future.

Still, despite the growing popularity of Chinese internal martial arts, many people still have questions about them. The most common questions are: What are the major differences between the external and internal martial styles? How is Qi related to these different styles? What are the differences between martial and non-martial Qigong? What are the differences in both theory and techniques between the different internal styles? These general questions must be answered before you can begin to understand the role that Baguazhang plays among the Chinese internal arts. Then you will be able to ask yourself why you want to learn Baguazhang, rather than Taiji or some other internal style.

To answer these questions fully would actually require a rather large book. It is almost like trying to describe the different tastes of various Chinese foods. You can get a general idea, but unless you actually sample them, you will not really understand what you are reading about. This is especially true with the Chinese internal arts, where spiritual feeling and enlightenment are the ultimate goals.

Differences Between Internal and External Styles

Before we go into the differences between internal and external styles, you should first recognize one important point: all Chinese styles, both internal and external, come from the same root. If a style does not share this root, then it is not a Chinese martial style. This root is the Chinese culture. Throughout the world, various civilizations have created many different arts, each one based on that civilization's cultural background. Therefore, it does not matter which style you are discussing; as long as it was created in China, it must contain the essence of Chinese art, the spirit of traditional Chinese virtues, and the knowledge of traditional fighting techniques which have been passed down for thousands of years.

Martial artists of old looked at their experiences and realized that in a fight there are three factors which generally decide victory. These three factors are speed, power, and technique. Among these, speed is the most important. This is simply because, if you are fast, you can get to the opponent's vital areas more easily, and get out again before he can get you. Even if your power is weak and you only know a limited number of techniques, you still have a good chance of inflicting a serious injury on the opponent.

If you already have speed, then what you need is power. Even if you have good speed and techniques, if you don't have power, your attacks and defense will not be as effective as possible. You may have met people with great muscular strength but no martial arts training who were able to defeat skilled martial artists whose power was weak. Finally, once you have good speed and power, if you can develop good techniques and a sound strategy, then there will be no doubt that victory will be yours. Therefore, in Chinese martial arts, increasing speed, improving power and studying the techniques are the most important pursuits. In fact, speed and power training are considered the foundation of effectiveness in all Chinese martial arts styles.

Moreover, it does not matter what techniques a style creates, they all must follow certain basic principles and rules. For example, all offensive and defensive techniques must effectively protect vital areas such as the eyes, throat, and groin. Whenever you attack, you must be able to access your opponent's vital areas without exposing your own.

The same applies to speed and power training. Although each style has tried to keep their methods secret, they all follow the same general rules. For example, developing muscle power should not be detrimental to your speed, and developing speed should not decrease your muscular power. Both must be of equal concern. Finally, the training methods you use or develop should be appropriate to the techniques which characterize your style. For example, in eagle and crane styles, the speed and power of grabbing are extremely important, and should be emphasized.

It is generally understood in Chinese martial arts society that, before the Liang dynasty (540 A.D.), martial artists did not study the use of Qi to increase speed and power. After the Liang dynasty martial artists realized the value of Qi training in developing speed and power, and it became one of the major concerns in almost all styles. Because of this two part historical development, we should discuss this subject by dividing it into two eras. The dividing point should be the Liang dynasty (540 A.D.), when Da Mo was preaching in China.

It is generally believed that before Da Mo, although Qi theory and principles had been studied and widely applied in Chinese medicine, they were not used in the martial arts. Speed and power, on the other hand, were normally developed through continued training. Even though this training emphasized a concentrated mind, it did not provide the next step and link this to developing Qi. Instead, these martial artists concentrated solely on muscular power. This is why styles originating from this period are classified as external styles.

Then, the emperor Liang Wu invited the Indian monk Da Mo to China to preach Buddhism. When the emperor did not agree with Da Mo's particular Buddhist philosophy, the monk fled across the Yellow River to the Shaolin Temple. There he saw that many priests were weak, and fell asleep during his lectures. Da Mo went into meditation to discover how to help the monks. After nine years of solitary meditation, he wrote two classics –t he *Yi Jin Jing* (Muscle/Tendon Changing Classic) and the *Xi Sui Jing* (Marrow/Brain Washing Classic). After Da Mo died, the Shaolin priests continued to practice his methods, especially the *Yi Jin Jing*, to strengthen their bodies and spirits. They soon found that the training not only made them healthier, but it also made them stronger. During these times, even priests needed to know martial arts in order to protect themselves from bandits. When they combined Da Mo's Qi training with their traditional defense techniques, they became very effective fighters. As Da Mo's training methods spread out from the Shaolin Temple, many forms of martial Qigong were developed. This topic is explored more thoroughly in *Muscle/Tendon Changing and Marrow/Brain Washing Chi Kung* by Dr. Yang.

The *Yi Jin Jing* was not originally intended to be used for fighting. Nevertheless, students training the martial Qigong based on it were able to significantly increase power, and it became a mandatory course of training in the Shaolin Temple. This had a revolutionary effect on Chinese martial arts, leading to the establishment of an internal personal foundation, based on Qi training.

As time passed, several martial styles were created which emphasized a soft body, instead of the stiff muscular body developed by the Shaolin priests. These newer styles were based on the belief that, since Qi (internal energy) is the root and foundation of physical strength, a martial artist should first build up this internal root. This theory holds that when Qi is abundant and full, it can energize the physical body to a higher level, so that power can be manifested more effectively and efficiently. In order to build up Qi and circulate it smoothly, the body must be relaxed and the mind must be concentrated. We recognize at least two internal styles as having been created during this time (550-600 A.D.): Hou Tian Fa (Post-Heaven Techniques) and Xiao Jiu Tian (Small Nine Heavens). According to some documents, these two styles were the original sources of Taijiquan, the creation of which is credited to Chang San-Feng of the late Song dynasty (around 1200 A.D.).[2]

In summary: The various martial arts are divided into external and internal styles. While the external styles emphasize training techniques and building up the physical body through some martial Qigong, the internal styles emphasize the build up of Qi in the body. In fact, all styles, both internal and external, have martial Qigong training. The external styles train the physical body and hard Qigong first, and gradually become soft and train soft Qigong, while the internal styles train soft Qigong first, and later apply the built up Qi to the physical techniques. It is said that: "The external styles are from hard to soft and the internal styles are from soft to hard, the ways are different but the final goal is the same." It is also said: "External styles are from external to internal, while internal styles are from internal to external. Although the approaches are different, the final goal is the same." Again, it is said: "External styles first *Li* (muscular strength) and then Qi, while internal styles first Qi and later *Li*." The preceding discussion should have given you a general idea of how to distinguish external and internal styles. Frequently, internal and external styles are also judged by how the *Jin* is manifested. *Jin* is defined as "*Li* and *Qi*," (*Li* means muscular strength). It is how the muscles are energized by the Qi and how this manifests externally as power. It is said: "The internal styles are as soft as a whip, the soft-hard styles (half external and half internal) are like rattan, and the external styles are like a staff." If you are interested in this rather substantial subject, please refer to Dr. Yang's books *Advanced Yang Style Tai Chi Chuan, Vol. 1,* or to the future YMAA Qigong publication: *Martial Qigong*.

Qi, Health, and Martial Arts

Let us first define Qi. The original meaning of the Chinese word Qi was "universal energy." Every type of energy in this universe is called Qi. When the term was later applied to the human body, it meant the energy which the body maintains or circulates. In the last twenty years, a clearer theoretical definition of the Qi circulating in the human body has arisen: bioelectric energy. According to this model, all other types of bodily energy, such as heat or light, result from the transformation of this bioelectric energy.

In Chinese cosmology, Qi is the original energy source which keeps the entire universe alive. It is the same in the human body, where Qi keeps the cells alive and keeps the physical body functioning. Your body is like a mechanical electric fan which needs electricity to make it turn. If the electric circulation is insufficient, the fan will not work properly. Similarly, if the Qi supply in your body is insufficient or stagnant, you will become sick or even die.

In Chinese Qigong and medicine, Qi is classified as Yin because it can only be felt, while the physical body is classified as Yang because it can be seen. Yin is the root and source of the life which animates the Yang body (physical body), and manifests power or strength externally. When the Qi is strong, the physical body can function properly and be healthy, and it can manifest a lot of power or strength.

In order to have a healthy and strong body, you must learn both how to keep the Qi circulating smoothly in your body, and how to build up an abundant store of Qi. In order to reach these two goals, you need to understand the Qi circulatory and storage systems of your body.

In your body, there are twelve Qi primary channels which function like rivers and distribute Qi throughout your body. There are also eight "Extraordinary Qi vessels," which function like reservoirs, storing and regulating this Qi.[3] One end of each channel is connected to one of the twelve internal organs, while the other end is connected to either a finger or toe. These twelve Qi channels lead Qi to the twelve organs to nourish them and keep them functioning properly. The twelve channels also lead any excess Qi in the internal organs to the limbs, and finally release it outside of your body. This

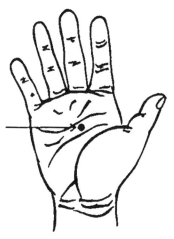

Figure 1-1. *Laogong* Cavity (P-8)

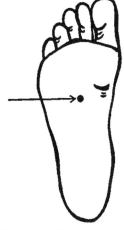

Figure 1-2. *Yongquan* Cavity (K-1)

is one of the primary methods of releasing excess Qi from the body's organs. Whenever the Qi level circulating in the channels is abnormal due to stagnation or sickness, one or several organs will not receive the proper amount of Qi nourishment, and will tend to malfunction.[4]

The eight vessels include four in the body and four in the legs.[5] These vessels store Qi, and are able to regulate the Qi flow in the twelve Qi channels. In addition, there are five major gates through which the Qi in the body communicates with the Qi in the surrounding environment, and further helps to regulate the body.[5] The main gate is the head. There are four secondary gates: a *Laogong* cavity in the center of each palm (Figure 1-1), and a *Yongquan* cavity on the bottom of each foot (Figure 1-2). Also, the tips of the fingers and toes are considered lesser gates, and help with the regulation of Qi. Finally, there are thousands of pores over the whole of your body that are considered small gates which constantly regulate the body's Qi, and therefore adjust the body's Yin and Yang.

In order to be healthy and slow down the aging process, you must learn to keep the Qi circulating smoothly in the twelve channels, and you must learn how to fill up the Qi reservoirs so that they can efficiently regulate the Qi flow. You must also understand how your body's Qi communicates with the Qi around you, so that you can adapt to natural conditions.

If you understand Qi circulation theory for the human body, then you will be able to understand how Qi relates to the martial arts. Remember that the human body is not merely a machine like the aforementioned electrical fan. It is alive, and able to improve itself. When your Qi grows stronger, your physical body will also grow stronger. If you build your Qi up to a stronger level, your organs and physical body will receive more nourishment and their condition will improve, and you will become stronger.

To make this clearer, remember that many parts of your body, such as the limbs, are governed by your conscious mind. The governing process is very simple. Your mind generates an idea, and this thought leads Qi to the appropriate muscles, energizing them to perform the desired action. The key to martial Qigong training is learning to lead your Qi more efficiently, so that you can manifest more power. This theory holds that people normally only use their muscles at no more than 40% to 50% of their maximum capacity. This is simply because you don't need any more for your daily activities. The result is that your mind has never been trained to lead the Qi as efficiently as possible.

The Chinese martial artist learns to concentrate his mind through meditation or other training so that Qi can be led efficiently. This significantly increases power and improves the effectiveness of all techniques. The martial artist also learns through meditation to use Qi to raise the spirit and elevate morality. Through correct training, the mind can reach a very calm and peaceful state. The real Dao of Chinese martial arts aims for both spirit and skills. Correct training seeks perfection in both technique and spirit, not the conquest of others.

Chinese Martial Power *(Jin)*

Jin training is a very important part of the Chinese martial arts, but there is almost nothing written on the subject in English, and very little even in Chinese. Many instructors once viewed the higher levels of *Jin* as a secret which should only be passed down to a few trusted students. Unfortunately, it is also true that many instructors don't understand *Jin* very well themselves. It is a difficult subject to explain, and even harder to express in English.

Many current martial artists do not understand what *Jin* is, or they think that it is trained only in a few particular styles. In fact, almost all Oriental martial styles train *Jin*. The differences lie only in the depth to which *Jin* is understood, the different kinds of *Jin* trained, and the range and characteristics of the Jins emphasized. For example, Tiger Claw style emphasizes hard and strong *Jin*, imitating the tiger's muscular strength; muscles predominate in most of the techniques. White Crane, Xingyi, and Bagua are softer styles, and the muscles are used relatively less. In Taijiquan, the softest style, soft *Jin* is especially emphasized and muscle usage is cut down to a minimum.

The application of *Jin* brings us to a major difference between the Oriental martial arts and those of the West. In China, martial styles and martial artists are judged by their *Jin*. How deeply is *Jin* understood and how well is it manifested? How strong and effective is it, and how is it coordinated with martial techniques? When a martial artist performs his art without *Jin* it is called *Hua Quan Xiu Tui*, which means "Flower fist and brocade leg."[6]

This is to scoff at the martial artist without *Jin*, who is weak like a flower and soft like brocade. Like dancing, his art is beautiful but not useful. It is also said: "*Lian Quan Bu Lian Gong, Dao Lao Yi Chang Kong*," which means "Train *Quan* and not *Gong*, when you get old, all emptiness".[7] This means that if a martial artist emphasizes only the beauty and smoothness of his forms and doesn't train his *Gong*, then when he gets old, he will have nothing. The "Gong" here means "Qigong," and refers to the cultivation of Qi and its coordination with *Jin* to develop the latter to its maximum, and to make the techniques effective and alive. Therefore, if a martial artist learns his art without training his *Qigong* and *Jin Gong*, once he gets old the techniques he has learned will be useless, because he will have lost his muscular strength.

Chinese martial artists say: "*Wai Lian Jin Gu Pi, Nei Lian Yi Kou Qi*", which means "Externally, train tendons, bones, and skin; and internally train one mouthful of Qi."[8] This means that it does not matter whether you are studying an external or an internal style, if you want to manifest the maximum amount of *Jin*, you have to train both externally and internally. Externally means the physical body, and internally means the Qi circulation, which is related to the breathing.

Traditionally, *Jin* was considered a secret transmission in Chinese martial arts society. This is so not only because it was not revealed to most students, but also because it cannot be passed down with words alone. *Jin* must be experienced. It is said that the master "passes down *Jin*." Once you feel *Jin* done by your master, you know what is meant and are able to work on it by yourself. Without an experienced master it is more difficult, but not impossible, to learn about *Jin*. There are general principles and training methods which an experienced martial artist can use to grasp the keys of this practice. If you are interested in a more detailed exploration of about this subject, you may refer to: *Advanced Yang Style Tai Chi Chuan, Vol. 1* by Dr. Yang Jwing-Ming.

Popular Chinese Internal Martial Arts

Because all Chinese martial styles utilize some Qigong training, it is difficult to distinguish the external styles from the internal ones. Traditionally, almost all of the Chinese martial styles were taught in secret, and it was not until the last hundred years that these secrets were gradually revealed to the general public. Even today, there are many styles that are still taught secretly. Because of this conservatism, most people (including many Chinese martial artists) simply don't have enough information to clearly distinguish between styles.

There are four generally known styles which emphasize Qi development more seriously than other styles, and are therefore considered internal. These four styles are Taijiquan, Xingyiquan, Baguazhang, and Liu He Ba Fa. Before we discuss the differences between these styles, we would first like to point out their similarities. First, they all concentrate on training the circulation of Qi and building it up to a higher level. Second, they all emphasize a calm and peaceful mind. And finally, all four styles are very effective in improving health.

1. Taijiquan:

A. In order for the Qi to move freely and smoothly in the physical body, the body must be relaxed from the skin to the bone marrow and the internal organs. In order to lead the Qi to any part of the body without stagnation, the body must be relaxed, and the movements soft, like a baby's.

B. When *Jin* is emitted for an attack, it is like a whip. Though soft, the power is strong and penetrating.

C. The fighting strategy is more defensive than offensive. This means that defense is often treated as the preparation for an attack. Because of this, training focuses on yielding, neutralizing, sticking, adhering, and coiling. The movements are always rounded. "Pushing hands" practice leads the practitioner towards this goal.

D. Strategy and techniques indicate that Taiji specializes in fighting mostly within the short and middle ranges. Almost all of the kicks trained in the Taiji sequences focus within these ranges.

2. Xingyiquan:

A. In order to enable the Qi to move freely and smoothly in the physical body, the body must be natural and comfortable. In the beginning of both attacking and defensive movements, the body remains soft so that Qi can be led to the limbs. The body is then stiffened for an instant upon striking, in order to manifest the *Jin*. Xingyi *Jin* is like rattan, soft at the beginning and hard at the end. *Jin* manifests like a cannonball exploding.

B. The fighting strategy is more active than passive. Offensive movement is usually used as a defense. Although techniques such as yielding, neutralizing, sticking, adhering, and coiling are used, the attacking mind and movement remain paramount. In order to keep up momentum, straight forward and backward movements are emphasized, although some dodging and sideward movements are used.

C. Because of the strategy and techniques emphasized, Xingyi can be very effective when fighting at short range. Though some kicks are trained, almost all of them are directed at targets below the groin.

3. Baguazhang:

A. The movements of Baguazhang are not as soft as Taijiquan, yet they are not as hard as Xingyi. The internal Qi is the main focus of the training.

B. The fighting strategy emphasizes circular movements. Generally, both the stepping and the techniques are circular. Although many techniques such as yielding, neutralizing, sticking, adhering, and coiling are used, they are mainly adopted to coordinate with the round movements. Attack and defense are equally important. Rounded defensive movements are usually used first, followed by rounded attacking movements, to uproot the opponent and make him fall.

C. Because of its strategy and techniques, Baguazhang can be effective at all ranges. Round stepping movements are constantly used in coordination with the techniques, but high kicks are seldom used. Instead, the training focuses on low kicks and firm rapid walking.

4. *Liu He Ba Fa:*

A. Liu He Ba Fa is a combination of the strategy and techniques of Taijiquan, Xingyiquan, and Baguazhang. The training contains soft within the hard and hard within the soft. Its strategy contains straight line forward and backward, as well as circular movements. It utilizes all three fighting ranges, but does not emphasize high kicking techniques. It is normally taught to people who have already learned the three previous styles, because they are more likely to understand the essence of the three and mix and apply the techniques skillfully and effectively.

Before finishing this section, we would like to mention one other point. Martial publications have gone through considerable changes in the last eighty years. When Chinese martial arts started to be revealed to the general public, through publications between 1910 and the 1940's, the authors were still very conservative and only partially revealed the secrets of their style. They emphasized martial morality, and they published some of the secret songs and poems, but gave little explanation of them.

Between 1940 and 1960, more secrets were revealed, and the songs and poems were explained by well-known masters. In addition, most books published in this period included photos of the techniques and emphasized martial morality. This made it possible for martial artists with only a limited knowledge of a styles to learn the essential theory of that style.

However, from 1960 until now, most publications have primarily emphasized the movements and the beauty of the forms. The theories and methods for reaching the higher levels of training have been widely ignored. The worst part of this new trend is that very few books even mention the moral aspect of martial arts. A person's morality is directly related to their attitude towards life. The authors of this book have always believed it is the morality of the martial artist which determines how deeply he comprehends the essence of any style. We also believe that the theory of each style is its essence and its root. Only those who have grasped the essence and the root will be able to reach the higher levels of the style.

The authors also consider that it is the understanding of theory which makes it possible for a student to reach a high level in a relatively short time. For these reasons, we have emphasized theory in this book. Almost all of the theory discussed in this book was passed down in songs and poems in publications before the 1950's.

There are still many other styles whose secrets remain hidden. For example, some of the other internal styles such as Buddha Hands and Butterfly Palms are unknown to westerners even today. The final point we would like to stress is that after several hundred years of development, there are now many different styles of Baguazhang. However, regardless of which style Baguazhang a person has learned, the basic theory and foundation remains the same. Therefore, no one should use his/her limited background and knowledge to criticize other styles. In fact, each style has its own unique characteristics and advantages.

In this chapter, after reviewing some of the important concepts of martial arts, we will summarize some vital martial moralities together with some well-known martial stories. Then, in the third section, the concept of Bagua (the Eight Trigrams) will be reviewed. In order to help you understand the cultural background of Chinese martial arts, the connection between Chinese martial arts and the *Yi Jing* (Book of Changes) will be discussed in the fourth section. In the fifth section, we will translate an ancient document to define Baguazhang. Finally, in the last two sections, the history of Baguazhang will be surveyed and the contents of Baguazhang training will be presented.

1-2. Martial Morality

Martial morality has always been a required discipline in Chinese martial society. Before you learn any martial techniques, therefore, you should first understand this subject.

In Chinese martial society, it is well known that a student's success is not determined by his external appearance, nor by how strong or weak he is, but rather by the student's way of thinking and his morality. Chinese martial artists have a saying: "A student will spend three years looking for a good teacher, and a teacher will test a student for three years." A wise student realizes that it is better to spend several years looking for a good teacher than to spend the time learning from a mediocre one. A good teacher will lead you to the right path, and will help you to build a strong foundation for your future training. A teacher who is not qualified, however, will not help you build a strong foundation, and may even teach you many bad habits. In addition, good teachers will always set a good example for their students with their spiritual and moral virtue. Good martial arts teachers do not teach only martial techniques, they also teach a way of life.

From a teacher's perspective, it is very hard to find good students. When people have just begun their studies, they are usually enthusiastic and sincere, and they are willing to accept discipline and observe proper manners. However, as time passes, you gradually get to see what they are really like, and sometimes it's quite different from how they acted in the beginning. Because of this, teachers quite frequently spend at least three years watching and testing students before they decide whether they can trust them and pass on to them the secrets of their style. This was especially so in ancient times when martial arts were used in wars, and fighting techniques were kept secret.

Martial Morality is called *Wude*. Teachers have long considered *Wude* to be the most important criterion for judging students, and they have made it the most important part of the training in the traditional Chinese martial arts. Wude includes two aspects: the morality of deed and the morality of mind. Morality of deed includes: **Humility, Respect, Righteousness, Trust, and Loyalty.** Morality of mind consists of: **Will, Endurance, Perseverance, Patience, and Courage.** Traditionally, only those students who had cultivated these standards of morality were considered to be worthy of teaching. Of the two aspects of morality, the morality of deed is more important. The reason for this is very simple. Morality of deed concerns the student's relationship with master and classmates, other martial artists, and the general public. Students who are not moral in their actions are not worthy of being taught, since they cannot be trusted or even respected. Furthermore, without morality of deed, they may abuse the art and use their fighting ability to harm innocent people. Therefore, masters will normally watch their students carefully for a long time until they are sure that the students have matched their standards of morality of deed before letting them start serious training.

Morality of mind is for the self-cultivation which is required to reach the final goal. The Chinese consider that we have two minds, an "Emotional mind" (*Xin*) and a "Wisdom mind" (*Yi*). Usually, when a person fails in something it is because the emotional mind has dominated their thinking. The five elements in the morality of mind are the keys to training, and they lead the student to the stage where the wisdom mind can dominate. This self-cultivation and discipline should be the goal of any martial arts training philosophy.

Next, we will discuss these requirements of morality.

Martial Morality (*Wude*) 武德
Morality of Deed:

1. Humility (Qian Xu) 謙虛

Humility comes from controlling your feelings of pride. In China it is said: "Satisfaction (i.e., pride) loses, humility earns benefits."[9] When you are satisfied with yourself, you will not think deeply, and you will not be willing to learn. However, if you remain humble, you will always be looking for ways to better yourself, and you will keep on learning. Remember, there is no limit to knowledge. It does not matter how deep you have reached, there is always a deeper level. Confucius said, "If three people walk by, there must be one of them who can be my teacher."[10] There is always someone who is more talented or more knowledgeable than you in some field. The Chinese say: "There is always a man beyond the man, there is a sky above the sky."[11] Since this is so, how can you be proud of yourself?

I remember a story that my White Crane master told me when I was seventeen years old. Once there was a bamboo shoot that had just popped up out of the ground. It looked at the sky and smiled, and said to itself, "Someone told me that the sky is so high that it cannot be reached. I don't believe that's true." The sprout was young and felt strong. It believed that if it kept growing, one day it could reach the sky. So it kept growing and growing. Ten years passed, twenty years passed. Again it looked at the sky. The sky was still very high, and it was still far beyond its reach. Finally, it realized something, and started to bow down. The more it grew the lower it bowed. My teacher asked me to always remember that "The taller the bamboo grows, the lower it bows."[12]

There was another story a friend told me. Once upon a time, a student came to see a Zen master. He said, "Honorable Master, I have studied for many years, and I have learned so much of the martial arts and Zen theory already that I have reached a very high level. I heard that you are a great master, and I have therefore come to see if you can teach me anything more."

The master didn't reply. Instead, he picked up a teacup and placed it in front of the student. He then picked up the teapot and poured until the tea reached the rim of the cup, and then he kept on pouring until the tea overflowed onto the table. The student stared at the master in total confusion and said, "No, No, Master! The cup is overflowing!"

The master stopped pouring, looked at him and smiled. He said, "Young man, this is you. I am sorry that I cannot accept you as a student. Like this cup, your mind is filled up and I cannot teach you any more. If you want to learn, you must first empty your cup."

In order to be humble, you must first rid yourself of false dignity. This is especially true in front of a master. A person who is really wise knows when and how to bend, and always keeps his cup empty.

2. Respect (Zun Jing) 尊敬

Respect is the foundation of your relationship with your parents, teachers, your fellow students, other martial artists, and all other people in society. Respect makes a harmonious relationship possible. However, the most important type of respect is self-respect. If you can't respect yourself, how can you respect others or expect them to respect you? Respect must be earned, you cannot request or demand it.

In China, it is said: "Those who respect themselves and others will also be respected."[13] For example, if you despise yourself and become a villain in this society, then you have lost your self-respect. Since you have abused your personality and humility as a human, why should other people respect you? Only when you have demonstrated that you are deserving of respect will respect come to you automatically and naturally.

I remember my grandmother told me a story. A long time ago a girl named Li-Li got married, and went to live with her husband and mother-in-law. In a very short time Li-Li found that she couldn't get along with her mother-in-law at all. Their personalities were very different, and Li-Li was infuriated by many of her mother-in-law's habits, the worst of which was constant criticism.

Days passed days, weeks passed weeks, but Li-Li and her mother-in-law never stopped arguing and fighting. What made the situation even worse was that, according to ancient Chinese tradition, Li-Li had to bow to her mother-in-law and obey her every wish. All the anger and unhappiness in the house caused everyone great distress.

Finally, Li-Li could not stand her mother-in-law's bad temper and dictatorship any longer, so she decided to do something about it. Li-Li went to see her father's good friend Mr. Huang, who sold herbs. She told him the problem, and asked if he would give her some poison so that she could solve the problem once and for all.

Mr. Huang thought for a while, and finally he said, "Li-Li, I will help you to solve your problem, but you must listen to me and obey what I tell you." Li-Li said, "Yes, Mr. Huang, I will do whatever you tell me to do." Mr. Huang went into the back room, and returned in a few minutes with a package of herbs. He told Li-Li, "You can't use a quick-acting poison to get rid of your mother-in-law, because that would cause people to become suspicious. Therefore, I have given you a number of herbs that will slowly build up poison in her body. Every other day prepare some pork or chicken, and put a little of these herbs in her serving. Now, in order to make sure that nobody suspects you when she dies, you must be very careful to act very friendly toward her. Don't argue with her, obey her every wish, and treat her like a queen."

Li-Li was so happy. She thanked Mr. Huang, and hurried home to start her plot of murdering her mother-in-law. Weeks went by, and months went by, and every other day Li-Li served the specially treated food to her mother-in-law. She remembered what Mr. Huang had said about avoiding suspicion, so she controlled her temper, obeyed her mother-in-law, and treated her like her own mother.

After six months had passed, the whole household had changed. Li-Li had practiced controlling her temper so much that she found that she almost never got mad or upset. She hadn't had an argument in six months with her mother-in-law, who now seemed much kinder and easier to get along with. The mother-in-law's attitude toward Li-Li had changed, and she began to love Li-Li like her own daughter. She kept telling friends and relatives that Li-Li was the best daughter-in-law one could ever find. Li-Li and her mother-in-law were now treating each other just like a real mother and daughter.

One day Li-Li came to see Mr. Huang and again asked for his help. She said, "Dear Mr. Huang, please help me to keep the poison from killing my mother-in-law! She's changed into such a nice women, and I love her like my own mother. I do not want her to die because of the poison I gave to her."

Mr. Huang smiled and nodded his head. "Li-Li," he said, "There's nothing to worry about. I never gave you any poison. All of the herbs I gave you were simply to improve her health. The only poison was in your mind and your attitude toward her, but that has been all washed away by the love which you gave to her."

From this story you can see that before anyone can respect you, you must first respect others. Remember, "The person who loves others will also be loved."

There was also another story my grandmother told me. In China, there was once a family made up of a father, a mother, a ten year old son, and a grandmother. Every mealtime they sat together around the table. The grandmother was quite old. Her hands had begun to shake all the time, and she had difficulty holding things. Whenever she ate, she couldn't hold the rice bowl steady and spilled rice all over the table.

The daughter-in-law was very upset by this. One day she complained to her husband, "My dear husband, every time your mother eats she spills her food all over the table. This makes me so sick I can't eat my own food!" The husband didn't say anything. He knew that he couldn't keep his mother's hands from shaking.

In a few days, when the husband had done nothing to solve the problem, his wife spoke to him again. "Are you going to do something about your mother or not? I cannot stand it any more." After arguing for a while, the husband sadly gave in to his wife's suggestion, and agreed that his mother should sit at a separate table, away from the rest of the family. When dinner time came, the grandmother found herself sitting alone at a separate table. And to make things worse, she had to eat from a cheap, chipped bowl because she had dropped and broken several others.

The grandmother was very sad, but she knew she couldn't do anything about it. She began to think of the past, and how much time and love she had given her son as he was growing up. She had never complained, but had always been there when he was sick or when he needed anything. Now she felt deserted by her family, and her heart was broken.

Several days passed. The grandmother was still very sad, and the smile began to disappear from her face. Her ten year old grandson had been watching everything, and he came to her and said, "Grandma, I know you are very unhappy about how my parents are treating you, but don't worry. I think I know how to get them to invite you back to the table, but I'll need your help."

Hope began to grow in the grandmother's heart. "But what do you want me to do?" she asked. The boy smiled and said, "Tonight at dinner time, break your rice bowl, but make it look like an accident." Grandmother's eyes opened wide in wonder. "But why?" she asked. "Don't worry," he said, "Leave it to me."

Dinner time came. She was curious about what her grandson was going to do, so she decided to do as he had asked. When her son and daughter-in-law were not looking, she picked up the old and chipped rice bowl that she had to eat out of, then dropped it on the floor and broke it. Immediately her daughter-in-law stood up, ready to complain. However, before she could say anything, the grandson stood up and said, "Grandma, why did you break that bowl? I wanted to save it for my mother when she gets old!"

When the mother heard this her face turned pale. She suddenly realized that everything she did was an example to her son. The way she was treating her mother-in-law was teaching her son how to devalue her when she got old. She suddenly felt very ashamed. From that day on, the whole family ate together around the same table.

From this, you can see that how we love, value and respect teachers and elders is exactly how we deserve to be treated when we are old. Real love is something that cannot be purchased. Respect your parents and love them always. Only then will you deserve the respect and love of your own children.

3. Righteousness (Zheng Yi) 正義

Righteousness is a way of life. Righteousness means that if there is something you should do, you don't hesitate to take care of it, and if there is something that you should not do, you don't get involved with it. Your wisdom mind should be the leader, not your emotional mind. If you can do this, then you will feel clear spiritually, and avoid being plagued by feelings of guilt. If you can demonstrate this kind of personality, you will be able to avoid evil influences, and you will earn the trust of others.

In the period of the Warring States (475-222 B.C.), the two neighboring states of Zhao and Qin were often fighting against each other. In Zhao's court, there were two capable and talented officers - a military commander named Lian Po, and a civilian official named Lin Xiang-Ru. Because of these two men, the state of Qin dared not launch a full-scale invasion against Zhao.

Originally, Lin Xiang-Ru's position was far lower than that of General Lian Po. But later on, when Lin Xiang-Ru was assigned as an ambassador to Qin, he won a diplomatic victory for the Zhao. This led the Zhao king to assign him to more important positions, and before too long his rank climbed higher than Lian Po's. Lian Po was very unhappy, and unwilling to accept this. He kept telling his subordinates that he would find an opportunity to humiliate Lin Xiang-Ru.

When Lin Xiang-Ru heard of this, he avoided meeting Lian Po face to face at any occasion. One day, some of Lin Xiang-Ru's officers came to see him and said, "General Lian Po has only talked about what he intends to do, yet you have already become so afraid. We feel very humiliated and would like to resign."

Lin Xiang-Ru then asked them, "If you were to compare General Lian Po and the Qin's King, who would be more prestigious?" "Of course General Lian Po cannot compare with the King of Qin!" they replied.

"Right!" he exclaimed. "And when I was an ambassador to Qin I had the courage to denounce the King of Qin right to his face. Thus, I have no fear of General Lian Po! The State of Qin dares not attack Zhao because of General Lian Po and myself. If the two of us are at odds with each other, Qin will take advantage of this opportunity to invade us. The interests of this country come first with me, and I am not going to haggle with Lian Po because of personal hostilities!"

Later, when Lian Po heard of this, he felt extremely ashamed. He tore off his shirt, and with a birch rod tied to his back, he went to Lin Xiang-Ru's home to request retribution for his own false dignity. Lin Xiang-Ru modestly helped Lian Po up from the ground and held his hand firmly. From that time on, Lian Po and Lin Xiang-Ru became close friends and served their country with the same heart.

There is another tale of events that happened during the Chinese Spring and Autumn Period (722-481 B.C.). In the state of Jin, there was a high-ranking official named Qi Xi. When he was old and ready to retire, Duke Dao of Jin asked him to recommend a candidate to replace himself. Qi Xi said, "Xie Hu is an excellent man who is most suitable to replace me."

Duke Dao was very curious and said, "Isn't Xie Hu your political enemy? Why do you recommend him?" "You asked me who I thought was most suitable and most trustworthy for the job. Therefore, I recommended who I thought was best for this position. You did not ask me who was my enemy," Qi Xi replied.

Unfortunately, before Duke Dao could assign Xie Hu the new position, Xie Hu died. Duke Dao could only ask Qi Xi to recommend another person. Qi Xi said, "Now that Xie Hu is dead, the only person who can take my place is Qi Wu."

Duke Dao was again very curious and said, "Isn't Qi Wu your son? Aren't you afraid that there may be gossip?" "You asked me only who was the most suitable for the position, and did not ask if Qi Wu was my son. I only replied with who was the best choice as a replacement."

As Qi Xi predicted, his son Qi Wu was able to contribute greatly. People believed that only a virtuous man like Qi Xi could recommend a really talented man. He would neither praise an enemy to flatter him, nor would he promote his own son out of selfishness. Instead, both his actions and his greatness eminated only from his sense of truth.

4. Trust (Xin Yong) 信用

Trust includes being trustworthy, and also trusting yourself. You must develop a personality which other people can trust. For example, you should not make promises lightly, but if you have made a promise, you should fulfill it. Trust is the key to friendship, and the best way of earning respect. The trust of a friend is hard to gain, but easy to lose. Self-trust is the root of confidence. You must learn to build up your confidence and demonstrate it externally. Only then can you earn the trust and respect of others.

There is an ancient Chinese story about Emperor You of Zhou (781-771 B.C.). When Emperor You attacked the kingdom of Bao, he won a beautiful lady named Bao Shi. However, although she was beautiful, Bao Shi never smiled. In order to make her smile, the Emperor gave her precious pearls and jewels to wear, and delicious things to eat. He tried a thousand things but still Bao Shi wouldn't smile. The Emperor was the monarch of the country and yet he couldn't win a smile from the beautiful lady. It made him very unhappy.

At that time, the country of Zhou had platforms for signal fires around its borders. If an enemy attacked the capital, the fires were lit to signal the feudal lords that their emperor was in danger, and they would immediately send out troops to help. The fires were not to be lit unless the situation was critical. However, the emperor thought of a way to use them to please Bao Shi. He ordered the signal fires lit. The feudal lords thought that the capital city was in great danger, so a vast and mighty army of soldiers soon came running.

When Bao Shi saw all the troops rushing crazily about in a nervous frenzy, she unconsciously let out a great laugh. Emperor You was so happy that he smiled and smiled, and completely forgot about the lords, standing there staring blankly. After a while the Emperor said, "It's nothing. Everyone go home."

Emperor You completely forgot about the importance of the signal fires, and went so far as to light them several times in order to win Bao Shi's smile. The lords all knew that they had been made fools of, and were furious.

Later, Emperor You dismissed his empress, Lady Shen, in favor of his concubine Bao Shi. Lady Shen's father was greatly angered, and united with a foreign tribe called the Quan Rong to attack Emperor You. When Emperor You's situation grew urgent, he ordered the signal fires lit, summoning the feudal lords to save him and the capital. Even as he died, the Emperor never understood that, because of the games he had played with the signal fires, not even one lord would come to save him.

5. Loyalty (Zhong Cheng) 忠誠

Loyalty is the root of trust. You should be loyal to your teacher and to your friends, and they should also be loyal to you. Loyalty lets mutual trust grow. In the Chinese martial arts, it is especially crucial that there be loyalty between you and your master. This loyalty is built upon a foundation of obedience to your master. Obedience is the prerequisite for learning. If you sincerely desire to learn, you should rid yourself of false dignity. You must bow to your teacher both mentally and spiritually. Only this will open the gates of trust. A teacher will not teach someone who is always concerned about his own dignity. Remember, in front of your teacher, you do not have dignity.

There was a story told to me when I was a child. A long time ago in Asia there was a king. Nobody had ever seen the king's real face, because whenever he met with his ministers and officials, and whenever he appeared in public, he always wore a mask. The face on the mask had a very stern and solemn expression. Because nobody could see the real expression on his face, all the officials and people respected him, obeyed him, and feared him. This made it possible for him to rule the country efficiently and well.

One day his wife said to him, "If you have to wear the mask in order to rule the country well, then what the people respect and show loyalty to is the mask and not you." The king wanted to prove to his wife that it was he who really ruled the country, and not the mask, so he decided to take the mask off and let the officials see his real face.

Without the mask, the officials were able to see the expression on his face and figure out what he was thinking. It wasn't long before the officials weren't afraid of him anymore.

A few months passed, and the situation got steadily worse. He had lost the solemn dignity which made people fear him, and even worse, the officials had started to lose respect for him. Not only did they argue with each other in front of him, they even began to argue with him about his decisions.

He soon realized that the unity and cooperation among his officials had disintegrated. His ability to lead the country had gradually disappeared, and the country was falling into disorder. The king realized that, in order to regain the respect of the people and his ability to rule the country, he had to do something. He therefore gave the order to behead all of the officials who had seen his face, and he then appointed new ones. He then put the mask back on his face. Soon afterward, the country was again united and under his control.

Do you have a mask on your face? Is it the mask that people are loyal to? Is what you show people on your face what you really think? Do we have to put a mask on in this masked society? How heavy and how thick is your mask? Have you ever taken your mask off and taken a good look at the real you in the mirror? If you can do this it will make you humble. Then, even if you have a mask on your face, your life will not be ruled by your mask.

Morality of Mind:
1. Will (Yi Zhi) 意志

It usually takes a while to demonstrate a strong will. This is because of the struggle between the emotional mind and the wisdom mind. If your wisdom mind governs your entire being, you will be able to suppress the disturbances that come from the emotional mind, and your will can last. A strong will depends upon the sincerity with which you commit yourself to your goal. This has to come from deep within you, and can't be just a casual, vague desire. Oftentimes, the students who show the greatest eagerness to learn in the beginning, quit the soonest, while those who hide their eagerness deep inside their hearts stay the longest.

There is a Chinese story from ancient times about a ninety year old man who lived together with his sons, daughters-in-law, and grandsons near the mountain Bei. In front of his house were two mountains, Taixing and Wangwu, which blocked the road to the county seat and made travel very inconvenient. One day he decided to remove these two mountains to the coast nearby and dump the dirt into the sea. His neighbors laughed at him when they heard of this. However, he replied, "Why is this so impossible? I will die soon, but I have sons and my sons will have grandsons without end. However, the mountain remains the same. Why can't I move it? Isn't it true that where there is a will, there is a way?"

There is another story about the famous poet Li Bai. When Li Bai was young he studied at a school far away from his home. He lacked a strong will, so before the end of his studies he gave up and decided to go home. While crossing over a mountain on the way home he passed an old lady sitting in front of her house. In her hands she held a metal pestle which she was grinding on the top of a rock. Li Bai was very curious and asked her what she was doing. She said, "I want to grind this pestle into a needle." When Li Bai heard of this he was very ashamed, and decided to return to school and finish his studies. He later became one of the greatest poets in China.

There is another well-known story which tells of a famous archer named Hou Yi. When Hou Yi heard that there was a famous archery master in the North, he decided to ask the master to take him as a student. After three months of travel, Hou Yi finally arrived in the cold Northern territory. Before long, he found the home of the famous master. He knocked on the door, and when the old master came out, Hou Yi knelt down and said, "Honorable master, would you please accept me as your disciple?" The old master replied, "Young man, I can't accept any students. I am not as good as you think, and besides, I am already old." But Hou Yi would not accept no for an answer. "Honorable master," he said, "I have made up my mind: I swear I will not get up until you promise to take me as your student."

The master closed the door without a word, leaving Hou Yi outside. Before long it got dark and started to snow, but Hou Yi remained in his kneeling position without moving. One whole day passed, but the master never appeared again. Hou Yi continued to kneel on the ground in front of the door. A second day passed, and a third day. Finally, the master opened the door and said, "Young man, if you really want to learn my archery techniques, you must first pass a few tests." "Of course, master," Hou Yi replied with great happiness.

"The first is a test of your patience and perseverance. You must go back home and every morning and evening watch three sticks of incense burn out. Do this for three years and then come back to see me."

Hou Yi went home and started to watch the incense each morning and evening. At first, he got bored and impatient very quickly. However, he was determined to keep his promise, so he continued to watch the incense. Six months later, watching the incense burn had become a habit. He started to realize that he had become patient, and even began to enjoy his morning and evening routine. He began to concentrate his mind, focusing on the head of the incense as it burned down the stick. From practicing concentration and calming his mind, he learned to distinguish between the real and the false. After the three years were up, he found that every time he concentrated and focused his eyes on something, that object would be enlarged in his mind, and all other surrounding objects would disappear. He did not realize that he had learned the most important factor in becoming a good archer - a concentrated and calm mind. After he finished this test, he was very happy and traveled to the North to see his master.

The master told him, "You have passed the first test, now you must pass a second. You must go back and day and night watch your wife weave at her loom, following the shuttle with your eyes as it moves incessantly to and fro. You must do this for three years and then come back to see me."

Hou Yi was very disappointed, because he had thought that his master would teach him now that he had completed his three years of patience training. However, because his heart was set on learning from this famous master, he left and went home. He sat by his wife's loom and focused his eyes on the shuttle as it moved to and fro. As with the incense, he didn't enjoy himself at first, but after one year passed he began to get used to the fast shuttle motion. After another two years, he found that when he concentrated on the shuttle, it would move more slowly. Without realizing it, he had learned the next important part of an archer's training - concentrating on a moving object. He returned to his master and told his master what he had found. Instead of beginning his instruction, he was asked to return home and make 10 rice baskets a day for the next three years. Chinese rice baskets were made out of rattan, and one needed to have very strong wrists and arms to make them. Even a very good basket maker could hardly make five a day, and Hou Yi was being asked to make ten a day!

Although disappointed, Hou Yi returned home to do as he was told. In the beginning he hardly slept, spending almost every hour of the day in making baskets. His hands were numb and bleeding, his shoulders were sore, and he was always tired, but he persisted in working to finish ten baskets a day. After six months he found that his hands and shoulders were no longer in pain, and he could make ten baskets a day easily. By the end of three years, he could make twenty a day. He surely had achieved the last requirement of a good archer - strong and steady arms and shoulders. Hou Yi finally realized that all his efforts for the last nine years had actually been the training for how to become a good archer. He was now able to shoot very well with his concentrated mind and strong arms.

Proud and happy, he returned to his master, who said, "You have studied hard and learned well. I can't teach you any more than what you already know." With this the master turned and walked away.

Hou Yi was thinking that all his master had taught him in the last nine years was expressed in only three sentences. He couldn't believe that this was all there was to learn. He decided to put his master, who by now was two hundred yards away, to a test. He pulled an arrow from his quiver, aimed at the tassel on his master's hat, and released. His master instantly sensed the arrow coming his way, pulled and nocked an arrow, and shot it back to meet the coming arrow in the air. Both arrows dropped to the ground. Hou Yi saw this and without stopping shot a second arrow, and this second arrow suffered the same fate. He couldn't believe that his master could shoot and meet his arrows in mid-air three times in a row, so he loosed a third arrow. He suddenly realized that his master had run out of arrows. While he was wondering what his master was going to do, his master plucked a branch from a nearby willow tree and used this branch as an arrow. Again it met Hou Yi's arrow in mid-air. This time, Hou Yi ran toward his master, knelt before him, and said, "Most respected master, now I realize one thing. The thing that I cannot learn from you is experience, which can only come from practicing by myself."

Of course, part of the story is exaggerated. However, masters in China often used this story to encourage the students to strengthen their will, to think, and to research. What the master can give you is a key to the door. To enter the door and find things inside is your own responsibility. The more experience you have, the better you will be.

2. Endurance, Perseverance, and Patience (Ren Nai, Yi Li, Heng Xin)
忍耐，毅力，恒心

Endurance, perseverance, and patience are the manifestations of a strong will. People who are successful are not always the smartest ones, but they are always the ones who are patient and who persevere. People who are really wise do not use wisdom only to guide their thinking, they also use it to govern their personalities. Through cultivating these three elements you will gradually build up a profound mind, which is the key to the deepest essence of learning. If you know how to use your mind to ponder as you train, it can lead you to a deeper stage of understanding.

If you can manifest this understanding in your actions, you will be able to surpass others.

Of all the stories that my master told me, my favorite one is about the boy who carved the Buddha. Once upon a time, there was a twelve year old boy whose parents had been killed during a war. He came to the Shaolin Temple and asked to see the Head Priest. When he was led to the Head Priest, the boy knelt down and said, "Honorable Master, would you please accept me as your Gongfu student? I will respect, obey, and serve you well, and I won't disappoint you."

As the Head Priest looked at the boy, he felt that he had to give him a test before he could accept him as a student. He said, "Boy, I would like to teach you Gongfu, but I have to leave the temple for one year to preach. Could you do me a favor while I am gone?" The boy was glad to have a chance to prove that he could be a good student, and so he said, "Certainly, honorable Master! What do you want me to do?"

The Head Priest led the boy out of the temple and pointed to a big tree. He said, "I have always wanted a good carving of the Buddha. See that tree? Could you chop it down and make a Buddha for me?" The boy replied enthusiastically, "Yes, Master! When you return, I will have finished the Buddha for you." The next morning the Head Priest departed, leaving the boy to live with the monks. A few days later the boy chopped down the tree, and got ready to make the Buddha. The boy wanted to carve a beautiful Buddha and make the Head Priest happy. He worked night and day, patiently carving as carefully as he could.

A year later the Head Priest came back from his preaching. The boy was very anxious and excited. He showed the Head Priest his Buddha, which was five feet tall. He hoped to earn the Head Priest's trust, and he eagerly waited to be praised. But the Head Priest looked at the Buddha, and he knew that the boy had sincerely done his best. However, he decided to give the boy a further test. He said, "Boy, it is well done. But it seems it is too big for me. It is not the size which I was expecting. Since I have to leave the temple again to preach for another year, could you use this time to make this Buddha smaller?"

The boy was very disappointed and unhappy. He had thought that when the Head Priest saw the Buddha, he would be accepted as a student and he could start his Gongfu training. However, in order to make the Head Priest happy he said, "Yes, Master. I will make it smaller." Even though the boy had agreed, the Head Priest could see from the boy's face that this time he did not agree willingly, from his heart. However, he knew that this time the test would be a real one.

The next morning the Head Priest left, and again the boy stayed with the monks to fulfill this promise. The boy started carving the Buddha, trying to make it smaller, but he was disappointed and very unhappy. However, he forced himself to work. After six months had gone by, he found that he had carved an ugly, unhappy Buddha.

The boy was very depressed. He found that he couldn't work on the Buddha when he was so unhappy, so he stopped working. Days passed days, weeks passed weeks. The date of the Head Priest's return was getting closer. His chances of becoming a student of the Head Priest were getting slimmer and slimmer, and his unhappiness was growing deeper and deeper.

One morning, he suddenly realized an important thing. He said to himself, "If completing the Buddha is the only way I can learn Gongfu, why don't I make it good and enjoy it?" After that, his attitude changed. Not only was he happy again, he also regained his patience and his will was stronger. Day and night he worked. The more he worked, the happier he was, and the more he enjoyed his work. Before the boy noticed it, the year was up and he had almost completed his happy and refined Buddha.

When the Head Priest came back, the boy came to see him with his new Buddha. This carving was two feet tall, and smiling. When the priest saw the Buddha, he was very pleased. He knew that the boy had accomplished one of the hardest challenges that a person can face: conquering himself. However, he decided to give the boy one final test. He said, "Boy, you have done well. But it seems it is still too big for me. In a few days I have to leave the temple again for another year of preaching. During this time, could you make this Buddha even smaller?" Surprisingly, this time the boy showed no sign of being disappointed. Instead, he said, "No problem, Master. I will make it smaller." The boy had learned how to enjoy his work.

The Head Priest left again. This time, the boy enjoyed his work. Every minute he could find he spent at his task, carefully making the carving more lifelike and refined. His sincerity, his patience, and his growing maturity became expressed in the Buddha's face.

One year later, the Head Priest returned. The boy handed him a Buddha which was only two inches tall, and which had the best artwork one could ever find. The Head Priest now believed that this boy would be a successful martial artist. The boy had passed the test. He went on to become one of the best students in the Shaolin Temple.

As mentioned earlier, we have two kinds of minds. One comes from our emotions, and the other is generated from our wisdom and clear judgement. Do you remember times when you knew you should do a certain thing, but at the same time you didn't want to do it? It was your wisdom mind telling you to do it, and your lazy emotional mind saying no. Which side won? Once you can follow your wisdom mind, you will have conquered yourself and you will surely be successful.

3. Courage (Yong Gan) 勇敢

Courage is often confused with bravery. Courage originates with the understanding that comes from the wisdom mind. Bravery is the external manifestation of courage, and can be considered to be the child of the wisdom and the emotional minds. For example, if you have the courage to accept a challenge, that means your mind has understood the situation and made a decision. Next, you must be brave enough to face the challenge. Without courage, the bravery cannot last long. Without the profound comprehension of courage, bravery can be blind and stupid.

Daring to face a challenge that you think needs to be faced is courage. But successfully manifesting courage requires more than just a decision from your wisdom mind. You also need a certain amount of psychological preparation so that you can be emotionally balanced; this will give your bravery a firm root so that it can endure. Frequently you do not have enough time to think and make a decision. A wise person always prepares, considering the possible situations that might arise, so that when something happens he will be ready and can demonstrate bravery.

There is a story from China's Spring and Autumn period (722-481 B.C.). At that time, there were many feudal lords who each controlled a part of the land, and who frequently attacked one another.

When an army from the nation of Jin attacked the nation of Zheng, the Zheng ruler sent a delegation to the Jin army to discuss conditions for their withdrawal. Duke Wen of Jin (636-627 B.C.) made two demands: first, that the young duke Lan be set up as heir apparent; second, that the high official Shu Zhan, who opposed Lan's being made heir apparent, be handed over to the Jin. The Zheng ruler refused to assent to the second condition.

Shu Zhan said, "Jin has specified that it wants me. If I do not go, the Jin armies that now surround us will certainly not withdraw. Wouldn't I then be showing myself to be afraid of death and insufficiently loyal?" "If you go," said the Zheng ruler, "You will certainly die. Thus I cannot bear to let you go."

"What is so bad about letting a minister go to save the people and secure the nation?" asked Shu Zhan. The ruler of Zheng then, with tears in his eyes, sent some men to escort Shu Zhan to the Jin encampment.

When Duke Wen of Jin saw Shu Zhan, he was furious and immediately ordered that a large tripod be prepared to cook him to death. Shu Zhan, however, was not the least bit afraid. "I hope that I can finish speaking before you kill me," he said. Duke Wen told him to speak quickly.

Relaxed, Shu Zhan said, "Before, while you were in Zheng, I often praised your virtue and wisdom in front of others, and I thought that after you returned to Jin you would definitely become the most powerful among the feudal lords. After the alliance negotiations at Wen, I also advised my lord to follow Jin. Unfortunately, he did not accept my suggestion. Now you think that I am guilty, but my lord knows that I am innocent and stubbornly refused to deliver me to you. I was the one who asked to come and save Zheng from danger. I am this kind of person; accurately forecasting events is called wisdom, loving one's country with all one's heart is called loyalty, not fleeing in the face of danger is called courage, and being willing to die to save one's country is called benevolence. I find it hard to believe that a benevolent, wise, loyal, and courageous minister can be killed in Jin!" Then, leaning against the tripod, he cried, "From now on, those who would serve their rulers should remember what happens to me!"

Duke Wen's expression changed greatly after hearing this speech. He ordered that Shu Zhan be spared and had him escorted back to Zheng.

There is another story about a famous minister, Si Ma-Guang, and his childhood during the Song dynasty (1019-1086 A.D.). When he was a child, he was playing with a few of his playmates in a garden where there was a giant cistern full of water next to a tree.

One of the children was very curious about what was in the giant cistern. Since the cistern was much taller than the child, he climbed up the tree to see inside. Unfortunately, he slipped and fell into the cistern and started to drown.

When this happened, all of the children were so scared and they did not know what to do. Some of them were so afraid that they immediately ran away. Si Ma-Guang, however, without hesitation picked up a big rock and threw it at the cistern and broke it. The water inside flowed out immediately, and the child inside was saved.

This story teaches that when a crisis occurs, in addition to wisdom and a calm mind, you must also be brave enough to execute your decision.

1-3. What is Bagua?

Baguazhang is based on the theory of the Bagua (Eight Trigrams), whose source was the *Yi Jing* (Book of Changes). It would therefore be wise to first learn about this ancient book to gain a clear picture of how Baguazhang is related to the Bagua both in its theory and applications. It is impossible to explain the entire *Yi Jing* theory in this short section. After all, the Chinese people have studied and applied it for more than four thousand years.[4] However, our aim is not to explain the *Yi Jing* and its uses, but rather to merely demonstrate the link between Baguazhang and the Bagua. Hopefully, an understanding of this will enable the reader to grasp the root and essence of Baguazhang practice.

It is said that the Bagua was first formulated in China by Fu Xi (also called Bao Xi) during The Age of The Five Rulers (2852 B.C.).[14] Later, the *Yi Jing* was explained by the first ruler of Zhou, Wen Wang (1122 B.C.), in his book called *Yi Xi Ci* (Yi's Related Metrical Composition) or *Yi Da*

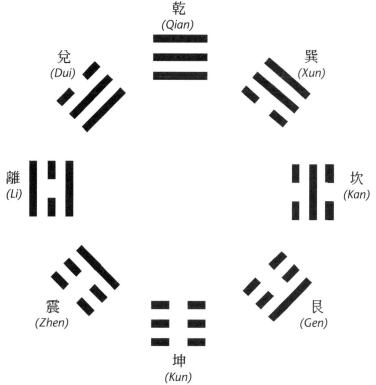

Figure 1-3. Pre-Heaven Bagua

Zhuan (Great Biography of Yi), the first written explanation of the relationship between the *Yi Jing*'s Bagua and nature.[14] This book is also commonly called *Zhou Yi* (Zhou's Book of Changes).

In this book it states: "Ancestor Bao Xi (i.e., Fu Xi) as a king under the heavens, looked upward to observe the phases of the heavens. He looked downward to perceive the rules of the earth. He viewed the inhabiting birds and animals and their connection with the earth. Close adopt our bodies and far adopt various objects (i.e., he carefully observed our body's change, which is near, and closely inspected various natural phenomenon, which are far away from us, in order to figure out the rules or patterns of nature). He then began to create the Bagua, which is to be used to collaborate the decency of the divine enlightenment and to be used to classify the effects of ten thousand objects (i.e., the Bagua he created, could be used to draw the relationship between the heavenly nature and the millions of objects)"[14] (Figure 1-3). The *Yi Jing* is actually a scientific treatise based on detailed observations and careful contemplations, which produced an understanding of the patterns and rules of nature. Since nature is always repeating itself, it is possible through careful observation to deduce the rules of the natural patterns.

The *Zhou Yi* says: "There is a Taiji (extremity) in the *Yi* (i.e., *Yi Jing*). It produces Two Poles (*Liang Yi*, i.e., Yin and Yang). Two Poles yield Four Phases (*Si Xiang*). Four Phases generate Eight Trigrams (*Bagua*).[15] It was believed that Taiji was the root and foundation of the universe. In the Xingyiquan martial style there is a song about Taiji: "Taiji was originally misty and turbid, no shape, no Yi (i.e., intention of change). But there is one Qi within. (When) this Qi circulates in the universe, all places are reached. Living things then originated. Named 'One Qi,' it is also called 'Pre-Heaven Real Sole Qi.' From this Qi, the two poles (Yin and Yang) were generated and the heaven and the earth began to divide. Since then, Yin and Yang were distinguished."[16,17] This concept of how the Two Poles derive from the Taiji was later expressed in a diagram by Lai Zhi-

Figure 1-4. Yin and Yang derived from Taiji
(Lai's Taiji Diagram)

De (1525-1604 A.D.) (Figure 1-4). The Two Poles are used to represent opposites such as heaven and earth, or any other pair of relative opposites.

The Four Phases are represented by Metal, Wood, Water, and Fire. They also assume the manifestation of four strengths: Greater Yang (*Taiyang*), Lesser Yang (*Shaoyang*), Greater Yin (*Taiyin*), and Lesser Yin (*Shaoyin*). The Four Phases yield the Eight Trigrams: *Qian* (Heaven), *Kun* (Earth), *Zhen* (Thunder), *Xun* (Wind), *Kan* (Water), *Li* (Fire), *Gen* (Mountain), and *Dui* (Lake, Ocean).[18] The *Zhou Yi* also represented the above derivation with symbols, using a straight line "—" (*Yang Yao*) to represent the Yang phase, and a broken line "--" (*Yin Yao*) to represent the Yin phase. The Four Phases are then expressed as follows: Greater Yang (☰), Lesser Yang (☲), Greater Yin (☷), and Lesser Yin (☳). This leads to the Eight Trigrams: *Qian* (☰), *Kun* (☷), *Zhen* (☳), *Xun* (☴), *Kan* (☵), *Li* (☲), *Gen* (☶), and *Dui* (☱) (Figure 1-5). To help people remember these symbols, an oral secret was passed down in ancient times: "*Qian* three linked, *Kun* six broken, *Zhen* an upward basin, *Gen* a downward bowl, *Li* the middle insubstantial, *Kan* the middle is full, *Dui* the top is incomplete, and *Xun* the bottom is broken."[19]

The Bagua is a theory (expressed in a diagram) which was used by the ancient Chinese to analyze directions, locations, causes and effects, and all the natural changes of the universe. Since nature always repeats itself, the Chinese believe that Bagua theory can be used to predict natural disasters, a country's destiny, or even an individual's fortune.

According to the *Yi Jing*, natural universal energy (Qi) is Yin, while the manifestation of this energy is Yang. These manifestations, whether in objects such as plants and animals, or in occurrences such as wind, earthquakes, or snow, are all produced by the universal Qi. Therefore, in order to comprehend the natural predilections of living things and forces, we must first study and understand natural Qi. Once we understand natural Qi, we can bring our lives into harmony with it. This will also enable us to stay healthy and even lengthen our lives.

As martial artists, if we understand and follow the natural patterns of the Qi circulating in our bodies and around us in nature, we will be able to manifest our own Qi as strength more efficiently and powerfully. If you truly understand this natural theory, then you have grasped the key to the *Dao*.

Let us now review first how the Bagua is related to the Chinese martial arts as a whole, and then how it is specifically related to Baguazhang.

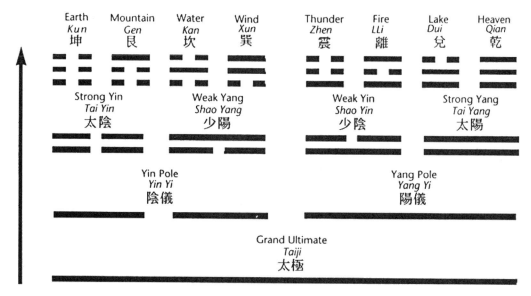

Figure 1-5. The Eight Trigrams are derived from Taiji

1-4. Chinese Martial Arts and the *Yi Jing*

Since the *Yi Jing* has been a major part of the Chinese culture and philosophy for more than four thousand years, many martial styles were created and developed under its influence; either partially, such as Xingyiquan and Taijiquan; or completely, such as Baguazhang. In this section, we will first discuss the general relationship between the Chinese martial arts and the Bagua. Then, we will summarize the concepts of Pre-Heaven and Post-Heaven in the *Yi Jing*, and their respective links with the Chinese martial arts. Next, we will discuss the theory of the unification of Heaven and Man, and finally, we will review the spiritual side of the Chinese martial arts.

1. Chinese Martial Arts and the Bagua[18]

A. Chinese martial arts imitate the Bagua pattern, described in the *Zhou Yi* (Zhou's Book of Changes), in order to express the pattern's different phases. For example, in the *Zhou Yi*, *Qian* represents the heaven (extreme Yang) and *Kun* represents the earth (extreme Yin). Between heaven and earth, Qi circulates and life is created. This is called the "Grand circulation."

In the martial arts, the human body is thought of as a "Small circulation" in which the head is considered to be the "Heaven" (extreme Yang) and the middle abdomen is considered to be the "Earth" (extreme Yin). The groin is considered to be the sea bottom. As a martial artist, you are looking for ways of circulating Qi between heaven and earth. Smooth, abundant Qi circulation maintains life, and allows power to be manifested efficiently.

B. Chinese martial arts copy the *Zhou Yi* by using animals to represent the characteristics of the phases. For example, in the *Zhou Yi*, the horse represents *Qian* and the cow represents *Kun*. Baguazhang also uses different animals to represent fighting patterns, in correspondence with the different phases of the Eight Trigrams. In his book on Baguazhang, Master Sun Lu-Tang states that, since the lion is the most ferocious animal, it should be used to represent *Qian*, which is the strongest and most powerful phase in Bagua. In Baguazhang, the "Lion palm" (*Shi Zi Zhang*) is the strongest and most powerful and so should belong to *Qian*.[16]

Also, Master Sun stated that, the *Lin* (i.e., a legendary fabulous female animal resembling a deer, which could fly and also change into various shapes) is the tamest, kindest, and softest animal, and should therefore be used to symbolize *Kun*. In Baguazhang, because the "Returning body palm" (*Fan Shen Zhang*) is the softest and can be used in many different patterns, therefore it belongs to Lin or *Kun*.[16]

C. In the *Zhou Yi*, the symbol of *Kan* (☵) is a "caved in" line (i.e., broken line) on the top and bottom, and in Baguazhang, it symbolizes the ears, which are considered hollow in the center. In Chinese martial arts, *Kan* signifies fullness and substantialness internally, and void and false externally. The words *Kan Zhong Man* (i.e., *Kan* center full) can often be seen in the martial arts secret songs and poems, especially in the internal martial styles. *Kan* here implies the abdomen, where the Qi within must be full and abundant. Since the Qi (also called original Qi or *Yuan Qi*) stored in the Lower *Dan Tian* originates with the original essence (*Yuan Jing*), which is stored and produced in the kidneys, it is believed that the kidneys should belong to *Kan*.[19]

D. In the martial arts, techniques and strategies are sometimes linked with the Eight Trigrams. For example, in Taijiquan, the eight basic techniques are compared with the Eight Post-Heaven Trigrams. In Chang San-Feng's Taijiquan Treatise, it says: "What are the thirteen postures? *Peng* (Wardoff), *Lu* (Rollback), *Ji* (Press), *An* (Push), *Cai* (Pluck), *Lie* (Split), *Zhou* (Elbow-Stroke), *Kao* (Shoulder-Stroke), these are the Eight Trigrams. *Jin Bu* (Forward), *Tui Bu* (Backward), *Zuo Gu* (Beware of the Left), *You Pan* (Look to the Right), *Zhong Ding* (Central Equilibrium), these are the Five Elements. *Peng*, *Lu*, *Ji*, and *An* are *Qian* (Heaven), *Kun* (Earth), *Kan* (Water), and *Li* (Fire), and are the four main sides. *Cai*, *Lie*, *Zhou*, and *Kao* are *Xun* (Wind), *Zhen* (Thunder), *Dui* (Lake), and *Gen* (Mountain), and are the four diagonal corners. Forward, Backward, Beware of the Left, Look to the Right, and Central Equilibrium are *Jin* (Metal), *Mu* (Wood), *Shui* (Water), *Huo* (Fire), and *Tu* (Earth). All together they are the thirteen postures."[20]

Before the *Qing* dynasty, many martial strategies, techniques, and even movements were linked with the different theories and phases of the Eight Trigrams. However, most of these correspondences were random and without a systematic organization in either theory or application. In fact, Baguazhang is the only style whose theory and applications are based entirely on the Eight Trigrams.

2. Pre-Heaven and Post-Heaven Concepts in the Chinese Martial Arts

Both Pre-Heaven and Post-Heaven (or Pre-Birth and Post-Birth) have both broad and narrow definitions. Generally speaking, Pre-Heaven refers to the time before the earth had cooled, when everything was chaotic and half-formed, like a cloud of mist. No one thing could be differentiated from another (called the state of *Wuji*, or no extremity). Pre-Heaven can also include the time when the earth was just starting to cool down, and heaven and earth were beginning to divide (called the Taiji or grand ultimate state). Once the earth had cooled, and heaven and earth were clearly distinguishable, a state of Post-Heaven arose. In this state, Yin and Yang (the two poles) were generated and discernable.

The Pre-Heaven and Post-Heaven concepts can also be more narrowly applied to human beings. Before a baby is born it is said to be in the Pre-Heaven state (or Pre-Birth, before it has seen the sky), and after birth it is in the Post-Heaven state (or Post-Birth, after the baby has seen the sky).

In Chinese martial arts and Qigong, there are three well-known expressions which refer to the concepts of Pre-Heaven and Post-Heaven. The first is: "To train the Post-Heaven to remedy the Pre-Heaven,"[21] the second is: "To train the Post-Heaven to return to the Pre-Heaven,"[22] and finally: "To train the unification of Pre-Heaven and Post-Heaven."[23]

In Qigong, the first expression is based on the belief that Qi in the Pre-Heaven (Pre-Birth) state is natural, soft, and abundant, but once the baby is born, the integrity of this Qi is compromised. For example, once you are born, instead of being nourished directly from your mother, you start to eat food and breathe air that is not completely healthy. When this air and food is converted into internal energy (Qi), the damage starts. Another example is that, after you are born, you start to be affected by emotions, and emotional disturbances can damage your Qi. You therefore need to learn how to use your Post-Heaven bodies (both mental and physical) to cultivate your Qi and repair the damage.

Sun Lu-Tang, a well known Baguazhang master, said: "Borrow the Post-Heaven shaped body to conduct the Dao of variations, then you can remedy completely (the loss of) the Pre-Heaven Qi."[24] Another well known Baguazhang master, Yan De-Hua stated in his Baguazhang book: "Whoever practices the fist techniques (i.e., martial arts), ought to train the essence and convert it into Qi, use the Qi to convert (i.e., nourish) into *Shen* (spirit), to transport and apply the internal Qi to become *Gong* (i.e., Gongfu). (Training) as ceaselessly as a river flows should be your goal and practice. Look for techniques (which can) use the Post-Heaven to remedy the Pre-Heaven."[25] The main goal in training the martial arts is to learn the method of strengthening your Qi and bringing your Qi to the abundant Pre-Heaven state.

The expression "Training the Post-Heaven to return to the Pre-Heaven" is based on the belief that when a baby is forming as an embryo - absorbing its mother's essence, Qi, and blood - it is extremely soft, natural, and comfortable. Right after birth, its movements still maintain all these instinctive virtues. But as time goes by, its blood and Qi become more and more Yang. By the time the child starts learning the martial arts, its movements and *Jin* (martial power) have gradually become stiff and awkward. The virtues of softness, naturalness, and easiness disappear with time. In order to maintain smooth Qi and blood circulation, you need to train yourself to be more like a baby. This will enable you to overcome the restrictions of stiffness and awkwardness, and reach the stage of "Fist without fist, *Yi* without *Yi*, the real *Yi* is within the no *Yi*."[26] Every movement and action has become so natural that you do not have to think about it. You are just like a baby, reacting to everything naturally and smoothly.

Finally, the expression: "To train the unification of Pre-Heaven and Post-Heaven" refers to the practices which lead you to the stage of "Training the Post-Heaven to remedy the Pre-Heaven" and "Training the Post-Heaven to return to the Pre-Heaven." Chinese martial arts masters believe that by putting yourself into a meditative state without thought or shape (i.e., the *Wuji* state), as well as into the state of thought without shape (i.e., Taiji state), then you can enter a stable and calm Pre-Heaven state. Once your body (i.e., shape) starts to move, the shapes or the postures are formed, and it is a Post-Heaven state. If you can use the Pre-Heaven mind to govern the Post-Heaven body, then gradually the actions of the body will be led into the Pre-Heaven state and enable you to move like a baby. Since your Post-Heaven body is now natural, easy, and smooth like a baby's, the Qi and blood can circulate smoothly. Consequently, the body will be natural and the *Jin* manifested will be soft and integrated. Baguazhang master Sun Lu-Tang said: "(One) should practice following the order until there is no wierd and stagnant Qi from the beginning until the end (of practice). After long practice, the four limbs of hands and feet can be controlled naturally by the *Yi*, (which) results in the connection of the top and the bottom, hands and feet mutually corresponding, internal (i.e., *Yi*) and external (act) as one; (this is) entirely in accord with the principles of Heaven."[16,27]

The goal of martial arts training is to become as soft and natural in your movements as a baby, and to unify your mind (*Yi*) and body into one. This you must do both internally and externally. It is said: "The real regulating is without regulating." This means that once you have reached the real regulating, then no more regulating is necessary. It is just like when you are learning how to drive an automobile. At first, all your attention is concentrated on the driving.

Once you become familiar with the necessary skills, you don't need to be so focused. When you are in this stage, your driving will be soft, easy, and natural.

3. The Unification of Heaven and Man

The unification of Heaven and Man is an important concept in understanding the relationship between the two. The concept includes "The similarity of Heaven and Man,"[28] "Mutual communication between Heaven and Man,"[29] "The mutual correspondence of Heaven and Man,"[30] and "The unification of the 'Heaven Dao' and 'Human Dao.'"[31] The philosophy of the unification of Heaven and Man has exerted a profound influence on Chinese culture. Consequently, it has also influenced the development of the Chinese martial arts.

Chinese martial artists and Qigong practitioners believe that the human body is like a small Heaven and Earth, while Heaven and Earth are analogous to an enormous human body. Sun Lu-Tang said, "Heaven is a great heaven (and earth) and man is a small heaven (and earth)."[16,32] Heaven (and earth) here mean the universe, which includes all natural lifeforms and objects. Both the great Heaven and the small Heaven are composed of balanced *Yin Qi* and *Yang Qi*. Just as the great Heaven is filled up with life, so too is the small Heaven filled up with living cells.

Qi always flows and communicates between the great Heaven and the small Heaven. Once you recognize that Man is part of nature, then it is not hard to comprehend that the Qi circulating in our bodies can communicate with the Qi pervading the universe. This is what is called "Mutual communication between Heaven and Man."

Furthermore, the Qi in your body is always influenced by the natural Qi around you. Sunshine, rain, wind, the moon, etc. - all of these can exert a significant influence on your Qi. Conversely, the Qi in nature can also be influenced through accumulation of human Qi. Environmental pollution is an example of the result of misunderstanding this mutual Qi influence. This mutual influence is called: "The mutual correspondence of Heaven and Man."

Through "Mutual communication" and "Mutual correspondence," the great Heaven (i.e., nature) and the small Heaven (i.e., Man) can unite. To have a healthy life, you should not struggle against the powerful Qi of nature. Instead, you should follow the natural Qi and blend your life with it smoothly and harmoniously. Thus are the "Human Dao" and the "Heaven Dao" unified. Upon this unification, you will become a pure and refined part of nature. In the Chinese martial arts and in Qigong, this is called "The body and the universe unified."[33]

In order to achieve this goal of unification, you must understand the natural rules (Dao), and then modify your thinking, lifestyle, and activities in accordance with them. When you practice martial arts or Qigong, you must look for a place where the air is fresh. The food you eat must be nutritious. The time you practice must not upset natural Qi circulation. For example, practicing hard Qigong at noontime can make your body too Yang and harm it. Only those who investigate the natural Dao and ponder carefully can bring about a harmonious unification of Heaven and Man. The well known Baguazhang master Cheng Ting-Hua believed that "Those absorbing the freshness of the heaven can be keen and those obtaining the spirit of the earth can be clever. If one obtains both, then it is the spiritual achievement of *Gong* (i.e., Gongfu)."[16,34] The implication is that natural Qi always influences your thinking and behavior.

The essence of Chinese philosophy is to follow the "Dao," that is, the way of nature. Lao Zi said: "Man patterns the Earth, the Earth patterns the Heavens, the Heavens pattern the Dao, the pattern of the Dao is natural."[18,35] This means that we should follow the natural pattern of the earth, the earth should follow the natural pattern of Heaven, and Heaven should follow the pattern of the Dao. But what, then, is the pattern of the Dao? It is simply the natural way of this universe. Following this framework, what a martial artist or a Qigong practitioner is looking for is the way to "follow" nature, to "be in accord" with nature, and finally to "be nature."

When a person reaches this stage, then his shape (i.e., physical body) and spirit become one. According to Qigong theory, this spirit must be cultivated into a high state through the process of *Jing* (essence), *Qi* (internal energy), and finally *Shen* (spirit). This cultivation is Yin, and is internal. It is the process by which the essence is converted into internal energy, and this energy is led to the brain to nourish the spirit. Through this process, the spirit can be raised to a state of enlightenment or Buddhahood.

The physical body is considered the Yang side of your being; it is the manifestation of your Qi in corporeal form. Both the Yin and Yang aspects of your being must sustain each other and be balanced. When Yin and Yang are harmoniously coordinated, then your body can be strong and your life long. In Chinese martial arts it is said: "Externally, train the tendons, bones, and skin. Internally, train the *Jing*, *Qi*, and *Shen*."[18,36] In Qigong society it is said: "Shape and *Shen* are mutually related, the external and internal mutually supported."[18,37] All of these stress the importance of coordination between the external and the internal.

1-5. What is Baguazhang?

The original name of Baguazhang was *Zhuan Zhang*, which means "Turning Palms." This refers to the way the art is practiced: "Moving around a circle turning the palms in various ways."[38] Its creation followed the process of "Gathering the fist techniques, again following the *Yi* theory, then define the Bagua, uniting the Five Phases."[39] It was developed after deep contemplation, and distributes the eight positions of the Eight Trigrams in eight locations around a circle. In addition, the eight parts of the body are also compared to the Eight Trigrams. This makes it possible to apply the *Yi* theory to the techniques and strategies. Therefore, it was eventually called "Baguazhang."

Master Sun Lu-Tang explained the relationship of Bagua and Baguazhang in his book.[16] He said:

八卦取象命名，制成拳術。近取諸身言之，則頭為乾，腹為坤，足為震，股為巽，耳為坎，目為離，手為艮，口為兌。若在拳中，則頭為乾，腹為坤，腎為坎，心為離，尾閭第一節至第七節大椎為巽，項上大椎為艮，腹左為震，腹右為兌。此身體八卦之名也。

Bagua(zhang) was named by adopting the phases (of Bagua), and compiled, becoming fist techniques (i.e., martial arts). Talking about it (in reference) to our body, the head is *Qian*, the abdomen is *Kun*, the feet are *Zhen*, the hips are *Xun*, the ears are *Kan*, the eyes are *Li*, the hands are *Gen*, and the mouth is *Dui*. If (applied) to the fist (i.e., martial arts), the head is *Qian*, the abdomen is *Kun*, the kidneys are *Kan*, the heart is *Li*, the first to the seventh vertebrae of the spine from Weilu are *Xun*, the spine on the head is (i.e., the vertebrae in the neck are) *Gen*, the left side of the abdomen is *Zhen*, the right side of the abdomen is *Dui*. These are the names of Bagua in the body.[16]

The Chinese martial arts are often called *Quanshu*, which means "fist techniques." According to the *Yi Jing*, the eight different parts of the human body were compared and related to the Eight Trigrams (Bagua). In Baguazhang, eight different portions of the body are also adopted to correspond to the Eight Trigrams (Figure 1-6). You should understand by now that when Bagua theories or patterns are applied to thoughts or to objects, their mutual correspondences can be varied depending on the timing and nature of the comparison.

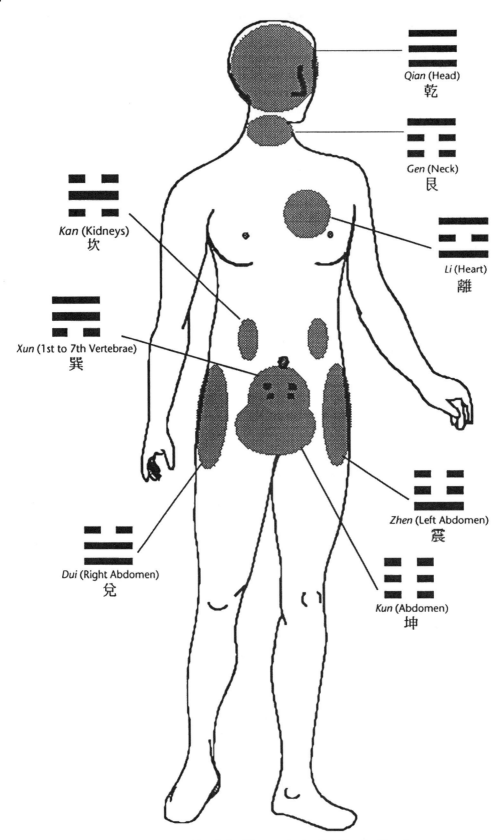

Figure 1-6. The Eight Trigrams in the Fist (Sun Lu-Tang)

自四肢言之，腹為無極，臍為太極，兩腎為兩儀，兩胳膊兩腿為四象，兩胳膊兩腿各兩節為八卦。兩手兩足共二十指也。以手足四姆指皆是兩節，共合八節。其餘十六指，每指皆三節，共合四十八節。加兩胳膊兩腿八節，與四大姆指八節，共合六十四節。合六十四卦也。此謂無極生太極，太極生兩儀，兩儀生四象。四象生八卦，八八生六十四卦之數也，此四肢八卦之名稱。以上近取諸身也。

Applied to the four limbs, the abdomen is *Wuji* (i.e., no extremity), the navel is *Taiji* (i.e., great ultimate), the two kidneys are *Liang Yi* (i.e., two poles), the two arms and two legs are *Si Xiang* (i.e., four phases), the two arms and two legs all have two sections, (which) are the Bagua (i.e., eight trigrams). Two hands and two feet, in total have twenty feelers (i.e., fingers and toes), the thumbs and big toes have two sections and total eight sections, while the other sixteen feelers have three sections each and total forty-eight sections. Adding the eight sections of the two arms and two legs, together with the eight sections of the thumbs and toes, in all they have sixty-four sections, which match the sixty-four diagrams. This is what is called *Wuji* generates Taiji, Taiji produces *Liang Yi*, *Liang Yi* yields *Si Xiang*, *Si Xiang* begets Bagua, and finally, eight times eight produces the number of sixty-four diagrams. These are the names of the limbs in Bagua. This (i.e., Bagua theory) was adopted and applied to our body.

The Lower *Dan Tian* is located in the middle of the lower abdomen. In Qigong, the Lower *Dan Tian* near the skin is called the False *Dan Tian* (*Jia Dan Tian*), while the one in the middle of the lower abdomen is called the Real *Dan Tian* (*Zhen Dan Tian*). This is because the False *Dan Tian*, which is also commonly called the Furnace of Elixir (*Dan Lu*), produces Qi (elixir) but does not store it. When the Qi is generated, it is stored in the Real *Dan Tian* (Figure 1-7).

Since the Qi stored in the *Real Dan Tian* is not divided into Yin and Yang, it is *Wuji* (no extremity). The navel is where life enters during gestation, and is Taiji (grand ultimate). It is out of this life that Yin (the Qi body) and Yang (the physical body) derive. The kidneys, it is believed, store the essence of our lives; the Qi generated out of this essence is differentiated into Yin and Yang. This is why the two kidneys are the two poles. Life is generated out of the interaction of Yin and Yang. During early development, the four limbs are formed out of Yin and Yang and become the four phases, and so on.

若遠取諸物，則乾為馬，坤為牛，震為龍，巽為雞，坎為豕，離為雉，艮為狗，兌為羊。拳中則乾為獅，坤為麟，震為龍，巽為鳳，坎為蛇，離為鷂，艮為熊，兌為猴等物。以上遠取諸物也。

If we apply it (i.e., Bagua) to objects away from us (i.e., other than the human body itself), then *Qian* is a horse, *Kun* is a cow, *Zhen* is a dragon, *Xun* is a chicken, *Kan* is a pig, *Li* is a pheasant, *Gen* is a dog, and *Dui* is a lamb. In the fist (arts), then *Qian* is a lion, *Kun* is a Lin (i.e., a fabulous deer-like animal), *Zhen* is a dragon, *Xun* is a phoenix, *Kan* is a snake, *Li* is a sparrow hawk, *Gen* is a bear, and *Dui* is a monkey. All of these objects are adopted which are away (from us).

The *Yi Jing* finds correspondences between the Eight Trigrams and animals, and Baguazhang also uses animals to represent the Eight Trigrams.

以身體八卦屬內，本也。四肢八卦屬外，用也。內者先天，外者後天。故天地生物，皆有本源。先後天而成也。內經曰：'人身皆具先後天之本。腎為先天本，脾為後天本'。本之為言根也，源也。世未有無源之流，無根之本。澄其源而流自長。灌其根而枝乃茂。自然之理也。故善為醫者，必先治本。知先天之本在腎，腎應北方之水。水為天一之源。因嬰兒未成，先成胞胎。其象中空。有一莖透起如蓮蕊。一莖即臍帶，蓮蕊即兩腎也，而命寓焉。

The Bagua of the body belongs to the internal, it is the foundation. The Bagua of the four limbs belongs to the external, it is the applications. Internal is Pre-Heaven while external is Post-

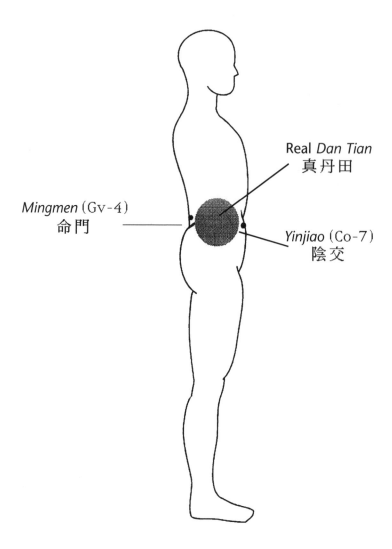

Real *Dan Tian*
真丹田

Mingmen (Gv-4)
命門

Yinjiao (Co-7)
陰交

Figure 1-7. Real *Dan Tian*

Heaven. The *Nei Jing* (Inner Classic) says: "The human body all (i.e., the entire human body) has Pre-Heaven and Post-Heaven foundations. The kidneys are the foundation of the Pre-Heaven, while the spleen is the foundation of the Post-Heaven." The foundation means the root, the origin. There is no flow which does not have its origin, and no foundation which is without its root. Purify its origin, then it can flow far; water its roots, then its branches will flourish, (this is a) natural theory (i.e., natural course). Therefore, those who are expert in healing, must first (know how to) cure its foundation. They must know that the Pre-Heaven foundation is in the kidneys. The kidneys correspond with the water in the north. Water is the source of heavenly unity. Because before a baby is formed, first formalize the embryo. It feels like it is empty in the center. There is a stem sprouting out like a lotus bud. This stem is the umbilical cord, and the lotus buds are the two kidneys, there the life resides.

When Bagua theory is applied to our bodies and limbs in Baguazhang, the body is considered internal, while the four limbs are considered external, because they manifest the decisions (applications) of the body. Following the *Nei Jing*, Chinese medicine believes that the kidneys are the root of Pre-Heaven Qi and life, while the spleen is the foundation of Post-Heaven Qi and life. This is so because our Original Essence (*Yuan Jing*) is stored in the kidneys before and after birth, and it is out of this essence that our Original Qi is created.

The spleen and bone marrow produce blood cells, and the blood cells carry oxygen, nutrition and Qi to every part of the body. This enables us to grow, replace cells, and restore the body. If the blood cells are not healthy, then all these processes will be impaired. This is why, of all the organs, the spleen is considered the foundation of Post-Heaven life.

知後天之本在脾，脾為中宮之土，土為萬物之母。蓋先生脾官，而後水火木金循環相生以成五臟。五臟成，而後六腑四肢百骸隨之以生而成全體。

Know that the foundation of the Post-Heaven is in the spleen. The spleen is the earth (or dust) in the center palace (i.e., torso) and the earth is the mother of the thousand objects. This is because the spleen organ is born first, then water (kidneys), fire (heart), wood (liver), and metal (lungs), mutually constructed into five viscera (i.e., when they are completely formed, they mutually support and relate to each other). The five viscera completed, there follows the birth of the six bowels, the four limbs, and hundreds of bones until the entire body is completed.

The five viscera of Chinese medicine (lungs, liver, kidneys, heart, and spleen) are compared to the five elements (metal, wood, water, fire, and earth), respectively. According to the theory of the five elements, the earth is able to produce millions of lifeforms. This means that the earth is the foundation for growth of the entire body. Since the spleen belongs to the earth, it forms first, and is then followed by the other four organs. When all the internal organs are completely formed, they are all related and mutually support each other. Finally, after the five viscera are born, then the six bowels (i.e., Large and Small Intestines, Stomach, Bladder, Gall Bladder, and the Triple Burner) and the rest of the body are constructed.

先天後天二者，具於人身，皆不離八卦之形體也。醫者既知形體所由生，故斷以卦體，治以卦理。無非即八卦之理，還治八卦之體也。亦猶拳術，即其卦象。教以卦拳。無非即八卦之拳，使習八卦之象也。由此觀之，按身體言，內有八卦。按四肢言，外有八卦。以八卦之數，為八卦之身。以八卦之身，練八卦之數。此八卦拳術，所以為形體之名稱也。

Pre-Heaven and Post-Heaven, the two are implemented with the human body, all cannot be separated from the figure (trigram) of Bagua. The doctors know where the shape (i.e., human body) originated, therefore they diagnose it with the figure of trigrams and cure with the theory of trigrams. It is nothing but using the theory of Bagua to treat the shape of Bagua (i.e., human body). It is the same with fist (martial) techniques. Using the variations of the trigram to teach the trigram fist. It is no more than using the fist of Bagua (i.e., Baguazhang) to study the variations of the Bagua body. From this viewpoint, in the body, there is Bagua internally. In the limbs there is Bagua externally. Apply the number (i.e., rules and theory) of Bagua to the body of Bagua, and use the body of Bagua to verify the number of Bagua (i.e., Bagua theory). This is how the Baguazhang techniques were named - by following the figures (of the Bagua).

If we summarize the concepts we have learned so far, we can say that **Baguazhang uses not only the palm techniques to compare with the Bagua diagrams, it has also borrowed the Bagua figures to symbolize the different parts of the body. From these fundamental linkages, the keys of the techniques were created and developed.**

Master Sun Lu-Tang explains the general concepts of how Baguazhang is named. In order to make this clearer and more specific, let us analyze the subject further.

The traditional eight basic palms, which are also called the "old eight palms" (*Lao Ba Zhang*),

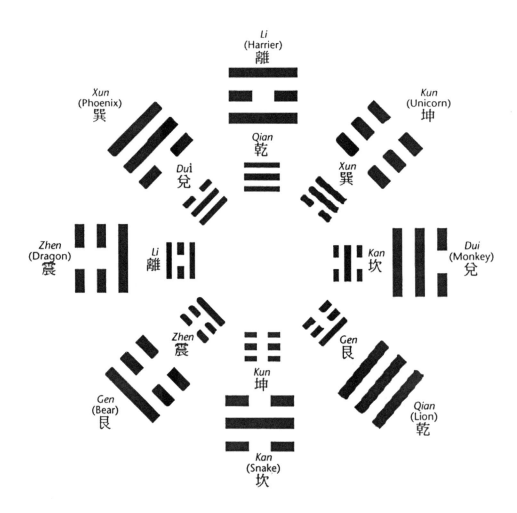

Figure 1-8. The Eight Trigrams and the Eight Palms

relates the "lion palm" to the *Qian* trigram, and represent this trigram with a lion (Figure 1-8). It also relates the "returning body palm" to the *Kun* trigram, and represents this trigram with a *Lin* (a fabulous deer); it relates the "smooth posture palm" with the *Kan* trigram, and represents this trigram with a snake; it relates the "lying palm" to the *Li* trigram, and represents it with a sparrow hawk; it relates the "single palm change" with the *Zhen* trigram, and represents it with a dragon; it represents the "back body palm" with the *Gen* trigram, and represents it with a bear; it relates the "wind-wheel palm" to the *Xun* trigram, and represents it with a phoenix; it relates the "embracing palm" with the *Dui* trigram, and represents it with a monkey.

In Baguazhang, other than the explanation by Sun Lu-Tang which we have discussed earlier, it was also said that the head is *Qian* (☰), because it is located on the top of Bagua, and this indicates that the head is upward and suspended (Figure 1-9). The legs are *Kun* (☷), which is on the bottom of the Bagua symbol. The symbol for *Kun* is made up of six dashes, since the two legs each have three sections: thigh, calf, and foot. In addition, it also implies that the two legs have more freedom to move around more easily (i.e., six broken lines are easier to move around than three straight lines). *Kun* (extreme Yin; legs) is said to follow *Qian* (extreme Yang; head), which results in the generation of thousands of lives (i.e., actions). The abdomen is *Kan* (☵), which symbolizes that the Qi in this center (i.e., Lower *Dan Tian*) is full and abundant, while the four limbs

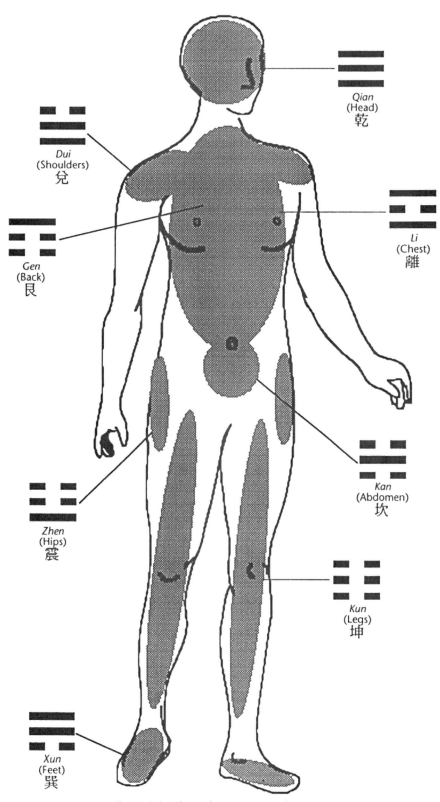

Figure 1-9. The Eight Trigrams in the Fist

can be insubstantial whenever necessary. The chest is *Li* (☲), which implies that the internal is insubstantial, and that the air in the chest should be unrestricted and free to move around. When the air energy (Qi created from air) is manifested, the external power is solid and strong.

The hip is *Zhen* (☳), which demonstrates that the top is insubstantial while the bottom is substantial. This means that the hips should be firm and rooted. When the foundation has a firm root, the upper body can move freely without disturbing the foundation. The back is *Gen* (☶), in which the top is firm and solid, while the bottom is insubstantial. This trigram is often called an upside-down bowl, indicating that the top is firm like the head, while the back is arced like a bowl (i.e., the elbows are sunken and the shoulders are arced in and dropped). The two feet are *Xun* (☴), representing the wind which can move around freely. In this symbol the bottom line is insubstantial, implying that the feet can move around freely like the wind, while the top of the body remains firm. Finally, the two shoulders are *Dui* (☱), in which the top is insubstantial while the bottom two lines are solid. This implies that the two shoulders should be relaxed and dropped.

Continuing on, Baguazhang has eight basic palms, and each palm contains another eight palms for a total of sixty-four, which matches the sixty-four diagrams in the Bagua. In addition, the strategy of Baguazhang's footwork *Jiu Gong Bu* (nine palace stepping) was derived from *Luo Shu* (The Book of Lou),[18] which was used in the Bagua discussion in the *Zhou Yi*.

The theory for explaining the meaning of the trigrams in Bagua is called *Yi Li* (Theory of Change). Baguazhang also uses the *Yi Li* to explain the movements, strategies, and techniques. Since the techniques were derived from the *Yi Li*, it is the root of Baguazhang.

According to the *Yi Li*, there are three types of "change": "simple change," "variable change," and "no change." Let us first discuss the "simple change." According to the *Yi Li*: "easy, then easy to understand; simple, then easy to follow."[18,40] This means that it can be understood easily, and you can execute it simply by following the rules. This is the basic concept of *Yi* (i.e., change). Therefore, the King Zhou Wen, who wrote the *Zhou Yi*, summarized the millions of natural variations and derivations into two simple opposite but mutually corresponding facets: Yin and Yang. Although Yin and Yang are simple and easy, the variations which come from them are countless, and include all phases of natural phenomena. This is why the *Zhou Yi* says: "one Yin and one Yang is called the 'Dao'."[18,41] This means that the Dao of nature is very simple and can be explained simply by Yin and Yang.

When we apply this "simple change" theory to Baguazhang, we can see that this simple and easy Yin and Yang rule has become the foundation of Baguazhang. For example, in Baguazhang fighting strategy, when you are circling to your left side, it is called "Yang Yi" which means "Yang pole." Naturally, if you circle to your right side, it is called "Yin Yi" (Yin pole). Continuing on from this basic definition, Bagua theory can be applied to the techniques. From refining of these most basic stepping movements, all of the Baguazhang techniques can be blended into stepping skillfully and naturally. In order to do this, the techniques and the strategic movements of the body are also divided into Yin and Yang categories. For example, attack is Yang while withdrawal is Yin, extending the arms is Yang while closing is Yin, moving forward is Yang while moving backward is Yin, raising upward is Yang while sinking downward is Yin, fast is Yang while slow is Yin, stiff *Jin* is Yang while soft *Jin* is Yin, exhalation is Yang while inhalation is Yin, etc. Every detail has been classified into Yin or Yang, which enables them to respond to and blend with the Bagua theory naturally and skillfully. Therefore, it is said: "one Yin and one Yang is called 'Fist'."[18,42]

Next, let us discuss "variable change." The *Yi Li* says: "generating birth is called *Yi*."[18,43] This means that everything in this universe is constantly changing, which is the basic concept of "variable change." In the *Zhou Yi*, the causes of the variations are divided into three categories: "hard and soft, the variations are generated," "one close one open are called 'variations'," and "what are variations, the phenomena of evolving (or advancing) and degenerating (or retreating)."[18,44] That implies that when there is a variation, then the situation is able to change and move around. This is the essential key to removing stagnation and resistance.

Baguazhang has also adopted this concept in its strategies and techniques, which are constantly changing according to the basic theory of "close and open," "hard and soft," and "advance and retreat." Because of this, when you are practicing Baguazhang, you are always moving and changing. Everything is alive inside every movement. After you have mastered the basic techniques which are based on Bagua theory, you vary them and make them alive according to the situation. Moving enables you to avoid the enemy's substantial and attack his insubstantial, moving enables you to place your opponent in a confusing situation. Therefore, the basic rule of Baguazhang is: "use movement against stillness," and "moving is the foundation and variation is the technique."

Finally, the *Yi Li* also utilizes the theory of "no change." The *Zhou Yi* says: "moving and stillness have their regular rules."[18,45] Regardless of how you change or move, you must follow definite natural rules. These rules make it possible for nature to repeat itself without destroying itself. It is these rules which have allowed this universe to survive for millions of years. These rules are the Dao of nature, and they cannot be disobeyed or betrayed. Night comes after sunset, and when the sun rises, the day arrives. This is as unvarying as the changes of the seasons and all other natural cycles.

In addition, the *Zhou Yi* says: "(When) the heavens are noble and the earth is humble, then *Qian* and *Kun* are firm."[18,46] This means that the rule that *Qian* represents the heavens and is on the top, while *Kun* represents the earth and is on the bottom, cannot be changed. Following the rule of "no change," the *Zhou Yi* points out that: "the positions of the heavens and the earth are firm, the Qi of the mountain and of the lake communicate with each other, the thunder and the wind mutually correspond, and finally water and fire do not interfere with each other."[18,47] It is from this concept that the Pre-Heaven Bagua diagram (*Xian Tian Gua*) was derived (Figure 1-10). The Post-Heaven Bagua was derived from this diagram and the seasonal changes caused by the angle of the sun's rays (Figure 1-11). Climate and changes in the weather can be calculated from the Post-Heaven Bagua, and the rules of these calculations also cannot be changed. If you are interested in further discussion of the Post-Heaven Bagua, please refer to the *Yi Jing*.

Naturally, the derivations of Baguazhang also follow the rules of "no change." For example, in the body, in order to maintain the fullness of Qi in the abdomen and in order to enable the air to circulate smoothly, the chest must be loose. Therefore, it is said: "the middle of *Li* (☲, representing the chest) is insubstantial and the middle of *Kan* (☵, representing the abdomen) is full."[18,48] In the techniques, the basic rules of moving, "twisting, spinning, walking, and turning," and the basic rules of manifesting *Jin*, "rolling, drilling, struggling, and wrapping" cannot be disobeyed. In addition, the basic principle of "using moving as the foundation, and using variation as the technique" also cannot be changed. The application of Yin and Yang theory in the techniques, and the way they correspond and mutually support each other, must also be followed. In fact, these principles are the essence of Baguazhang. If you stray from these rules, then what you are practicing cannot be called Baguazhang.

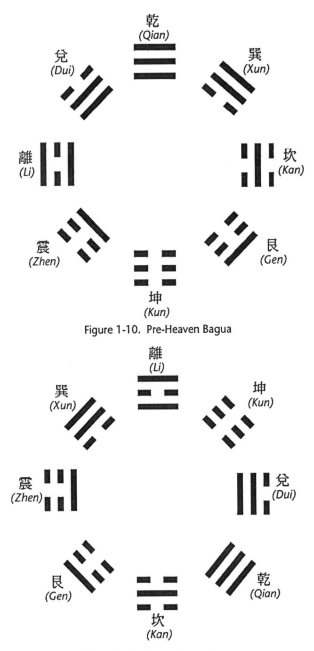

Figure 1-10. Pre-Heaven Bagua

Figure 1-11. Post-Heaven Bagua

1-6. The History of Baguazhang

The martial arts history which has been passed down to us is fairly vague. In fact, it was not until this century that an effort was made to trace back this lost history. It seems odd to us today that such a thing could happen. However, if we look at the historical background of the Chinese martial arts, we will see that it is, in fact, understandable that a martial art could remain so little known.

First, after so many thousands of years of development, there were countless numbers of martial arts styles in every period of Chinese history. This made it impossible for the government to keep a formal record of them, especially since martial artists and soldiers were never very highly regarded by the society.

Second, a majority of the most highly skilled martial artists avoided publicity and practiced in the mountains. More than two thirds of the Chinese martial arts originated within religions such as Buddhism, Daoism, and Islam. Many religious practitioners kept themselves in seclusion as they strived to cultivate themselves for enlightenment. Martial arts training was only a part of their training as they developed themselves both mentally and physically. For such people, political power, wealth, and reputation were as insubstantial as clouds. Because of this, there are many more records of priests who achieved Buddhahood or enlightenment than there are about important martial events.

Third, since most of the Chinese population was illiterate, even in the last century, it was very difficult to compile and record history. In fact, in order to preserve the essence of the arts, the secrets of each style were often composed into songs or poems which could be more easily remembered by illiterate people.

Because of these reasons, the history of each style was passed down orally from generation to generation, instead of being written down. After being passed down for many years, with new stories being added occasionally, the history eventually turned into a story. In many instances, a more accurate record can actually be obtained from martial novels written at that time, since they were based on the customs and actual events of the period. For example, the novels *Historical Drama of Shaolin (Shaolin Yen Yi)* by Shao Yu-Sheng [49], and *Qian Long Visits South of the River (Qian Long Xia Jiang Nan)* by an unknown author, were written during the Qing dynasty about two hundred years ago.[50] The characters and background in these novels are all based on real people and events of the time. Of course, some liberties were taken with the truth, but since the novels were meant to be read by the public of that time, they had to be based very strongly on fact. Because of these and other similar novels, most martial styles are able to trace back their histories with some degree of accuracy.

This is the case with the history of Baguazhang. Nobody actually knows exactly who created Baguazhang. In fact, it was only in the Qing dynasty (1644-1912 A.D.), that the first hand-written history of this style was composed.

Lan (blue) *Yi* (small house attached to a pavilion) *Wai Shi* (historical novel), *Jing Bian Ji* (Safeguard the Border Record): "In the second year of Jia Qing (1797 A.D.), there was a person from Shan Dong Ji Ning (named) Wang Xiang who taught Feng Ke-Shan the fist techniques; Ke-Shan learned his techniques completely. In the spring of the 15th year of Jia Qing (1811 A.D.), Niu Liang-Chen saw that the Eight Square Steps were contained in Ke-Shan's fist techniques. Liang-Chen said, 'Your stepping looks like marching Bagua.' Ke-Shan asked, 'How do you know it?' Liang-Chen replied, 'What I learned was *Kan Gua* (i.e., Water).' Ke-Shan said, 'What I learned was *Li Gua* (i.e., Fire).' Liang-Chen said, 'You are *Li* and I am *Kan*, both of us *Kan* and *Li* may interact and learn from each other."[51,52] This record confirms that Baguazhang has existed for at least two hundred years.

From the middle period of Qing Dao Guang (1821-1850 A.D.) to Guang Xu Sixth year (1881 A.D.), Baguazhang reached its peak, and was considered in its most popular and greatest period especially in northern China. According to the available documents, it seems likely that the popularity of Baguazhang during this period was due to the Baguazhang Master Dong Hai-Chuan (Figure 1-12). Since then, a more accurate and complete history of the art has been kept.

There are a few documents available to us which describe that Master Dong Hai-Chuan actually learned his Baguazhang arts from a *Daoist* named Dong Meng-Lin in Jiu Hua Mountain, *An* Hui

Province.[53] Dong Meng-Lin was called *Huang Guan Dao Ren* (The Yellow Cape Daoist) in the Daoist society and called *Bi Deng Xia* (Blue Lamp Chivalry) or *Bi Cheng Xia* (Blue Clear Chivalry) in the Chinese martial arts society. He taught Baguazhang to three disciples: Dong Hai-Chuan, Li Zhen-Qing, and Bi Yue-Xia (Table 1-1). Among these three, Dong Hai-Chuan has been the most well known and has passed down most of the students. Therefore, we have the more complete historical documentation of Dong Hai-Chuan.

Dong Hai-Chuan was born in Zhu village, Wen An County, Hebei Province on the 13th of October, 1797 (Qing Jia Qing 2nd year), and died on the 25th of October, 1882 (*Qing Guang Xu* 8th year).[54] Dong Hai-Chuan taught many students, the best known of whom were Cheng Ting-Hua (?-1900 A.D.), Yin Fu (1842-1911 A.D.) (Figure 1-13), Liu Feng-Chun (1855-1900 A.D.), Li Cun-Yi (1849-1921 A.D.) (Figure 1-14), Shi Li-Qing, Song Chang-Rong, Zhang Zhao-Dong (1858-1938 A.D.) (Figure 1-15), and Liu Bao-Zhen. From one of the sources, it is believed that Liu Bao-Zhen did not only learn Baguazhang from Dong Hai-Chuan but was also considered as the second disciple of Li Zhen-Qing, a classmate of Dong Hai-Chuan.[55] If this information is true, then it was not only Dong Hai-Chuan who had a close relationship with his other two classmates, but also his students. One of Master Liang Shou-Yu's Baguazhang masters, Wang Shu-Tian (1908-?) (Figure 1-16), was a student of Liu Bao-Zhen's student, Guo Meng-Shen.

Cheng Ting-Hua, who was the second disciple of Dong Hai-Chuan and was commonly regarded as Dong's best student, was born in Cheng village, Shen County, Hebei Province. Because he managed an eyeglass business, he was also known as "Glasses Cheng." Cheng Ting-Hua died in 1900 while resisting foreign troops during the Opium War. Among his students, the best known are his oldest son, Cheng You-Long (1875-1928 A.D.) (Figure 1-17), his youngest, son Cheng You-Xin (Figure 1-18), Zhou Xiang (1861-? A.D.), and Sun Lu-Tang (1860-1932 A.D.) (Figure 1-19). Sun Lu-Tang wrote two very valuable books in 1916 and 1925: *The Study of Bagua Fist* and *The Study of Bagua Sword*.[16,56] In fact, one of master Liang Shou-Yu's Baguazhang teachers was Zheng Huai-Xian (1896-1981 A.D.) (Figure 1-20), who was a student of Sun Lu-Tang. Yan De-Hua, a student of another one of Cheng Ting-Hua's students, Zhou Xiang, wrote a book: *The Practical Applications of Baguazhang Maneuvers* in 1939.[57] In addition, a student of Cheng You-Long, Sun Xi-Kun (Figure 1-21), who wrote a book, *The Genuine Baguazhang Maneuvers,* also contributed a great effort in promoting Baguazhang during that period.[58]

Yin Fu, who was the first disciple of Dong Hai-Chuan, modified what he had learned from Dong Hai-Chuan to originate what is now called the Yin style of Baguazhang; he also taught many stu-

Figure 1-12. Dong Hai-Chuan (1797-1882 A.D.) and his tomb.

Figure 1-13. Yin Fu
(1842-1911 A.D.)

Figure 1-14. Li Cun-Yi
(1849-1921 A.D.)

Figure 1-15. Zhang Zhao-Dong
(1858-1938 A.D.)

Figure 1-16. Wang Shu-Tian
(1908-)

Figure 1-17. Cheng You-Long
(1875-1928 A.D.)

Figure 1-18. Cheng You-Xin

Figure 1-19. Sun Lu-Tang
(1860-1932 A.D.)

Figure 1-20. Zheng Huai-Xian
(1896-1981 A.D.)

Figure 1-21. Sun Xi-Kun

dents. Two of his students, Yin Yu-Zhang (Figure 1-22) and Gong Bao-Tian, both wrote books entitled *Baguazhang*. These books, which were published in 1932, are valuable contributions to our understanding of the art.[59,60] One of Gong Bao-Tian's students, Liu Yun-Qiao (1909-1992 A.D.) (Figure 1-23), had taught Baguazhang in Taiwan until 1991. In addition, another student of Yin Yu-Zhang, Pei Xi-Rong (Figure 1-24), contributed great effort in developing Baguazhang in southern China. Yin Yu-Zhang has a student, Jiang Hao-Quan (Figure 1-25), currently teaching in the United States.

Fu Zhen-Song (1872-1953 A.D.) (Figure 1-26), a good friend of Sun Lu-Tang, also brought the Baguazhang art to southern China and became one of the pioneers in developing Baguazhang there. Fu's eldest son, Fu Yong-Hui (Figure 1-27), continued his father's steps and with great effort, contributed in spreading Baguazhang in southern China. Another student of Dong Hai-Chuan, Li Cun-Yi (1849-1911 A.D.), also passed down his art to many students. Among them, Shang Yun-Xiang (1863-1938 A.D.), Hao En-Guang, Zhu Guo-Fu (1891-1968 A.D.) (Figure 1-28), and Huang Bo-Nian (Figure 1-29) have contributed significantly to the popularity of Baguazhang. Huang Bo-Nian was one of the Baguazhang teachers in Nanking Central Guoshu Institute before World War II. Huang Bo-Nian wrote a well-known book called *Dragon Shape Baguazhang*.[61] In addition, a student of Shang Yun-Xiang, Jin Yun-Ting (Figure 1-30), had a student named Ling Gui-Qing (Figure 1-31) who also made a large contribution to the popularity of both Xingyi and Bagua in that period. Huang Bo-Nian has a student, Fu Shu-Yun (Figure 1-32), currently teaching in the United States.

Naturally , Zhang Zhao-Dong also had many students. Among them, Jiang Rong-Qiao (1890-? A.D.) (Figure 1-33), wrote a very valuable Baguazhang book: *The Expounding of Baguazhang Techniques*.[51] Another student, Han Mu-Xia, had a student named Wu Meng-Xia (Figure 1-34) who wrote the book: *The Essence of Baguazhang Maneuvers*.[62]

In addition, *Peng* Zhao-Kuang, whose teacher Yang Rong-Ben studied with Shi Li-Qing, passed down a valuable manuscript: *The Principles of Ba Palm Maneuvers* in 1955.[63] Also, Zhang Jun-Feng, whose teacher Gao Yi-Sheng (1866-1951 A.D.) (Figure 1-35) studied with Song Chang-Rong, passed his manuscript: *The Important Meaning of Baguazhang* on to his students, Wu Meng-Xia (also Han Mu-Xia's student) and Wu Zhao-Feng (Figure 1-36).[64]

In addition to these older publications, an author named Ren Zhi-Cheng wrote a book called: *Yin Yang Eight Coiling Palms,* in 1937 (Figure 1-37).[65] It is interesting to note that Ren Zhi-Cheng's teacher, Li Zhen-Qing was a classmate of Dong Hai-Chuan, and though both of them learned from Dong Meng-Lin, Dong did not learn Yin Yang Baguazhang. This tells us that in the time of Dong Hai-Chuan there were probably several versions of Baguazhang already in existence.

Currently, the best-known styles of Baguazhang are *Wudang, Emei, Yin Family,* and *Yin Yang*. Some of the representative old masters of Baguazhang well known today are Sha Guozheng (Figure 1-38), Li Ziming (1900-1993 A.D.) (a student of Liang Zheng-Pu) (Figure 1-39), Lu Zijian (Figure 1-40) (who learned from a Daoist, Li Chang-Ye on Emei Mountain), and Tian Hui (Yin Yang Baguazhang) (Figure 1-41).

Baguazhang has another branch which was developed in Korea. It was credited to Lu Shui-Tian (1894-1978 A.D.) (Figure 1-42), who brought Baguazhang to Korea when he moved his family there during the Sino-Japanese War. Mr. Lu's teacher was Li Qing-Wu and unfortunately, the origin of his Baguazhang is not clear.

Baguazhang has become so popular in China since the beginning of this century that it is impossible to discover all of its practitioners. The only ones who can be traced (and, in some cases, whose pictures can be found) are those who have written books, passed down documents, or who had been mentioned in any of the books. There are probably hundreds more who had mastered the styles, but we have no way of knowing their names. Furthermore, after so many

Figure 1-22. Yin Yu-Zhang

Figure 1-23. Liu Yun-Qiao (1909-1992 A.D.)

Figure 1-24. Pei Xi-Rong

Figure 1-25. Jiang Hao-Quan

Figure 1-26. Fu Zhen-Song (1872-1953 A.D.)

Figure 1-27. Fu Yong-Hui

Figure 1-28. Zhu Guo-Fu (1891-1968 A.D.)

Figure 1-29. Huang Bo-Nian

Figure 1-30. Jin Yun-Ting

Figure 1-31. Ling Gui-Qing

Figure 1-32. Fu Shu-Yun

Figure 1-33. Jiang Rang-Qiao (1890-? A.D.)

Figure 1-34. Wu Meng-Xia

Figure 1-35. Gao Yi-Sheng (1866-1951 A.D.)

Figure 1-36. Wu Zhao-Feng

Figure 1-37. Ren Zhi-Cheng

Figure 1-38. Sha Guozheng

Figure 1-39. Li Ziming (1900-1993 A.D.)

Figure 1-40. Lu Zijian

Figure 1-41. Tian Hui

Figure 1-42. Lu Shui-Tian
(1894-1978 A.D.)

The following tables represent generations as started by Dong Meng-Lin.

Table 1-1

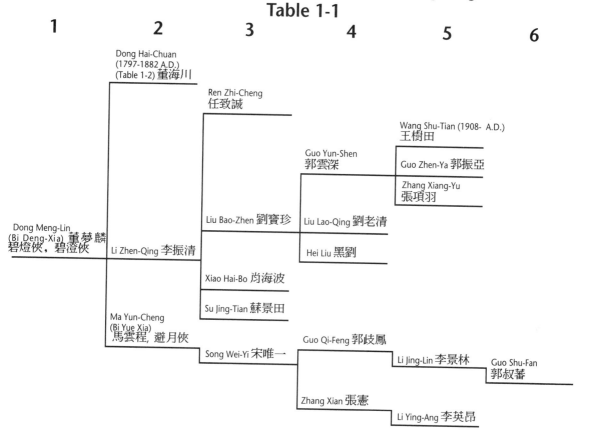

1	2	3	4	5	6

Dong Hai-Chuan
(1797-1882 A.D.)
(Table 1-2) 董海川

Ren Zhi-Cheng
任致誠

Wang Shu-Tian (1908- A.D.)
王樹田

Guo Yun-Shen
郭雲深

Guo Zhen-Ya 郭振亞

Zhang Xiang-Yu
張項羽

Dong Meng-Lin
(Bi Deng-Xia) 董夢麟
碧燈俠，碧澄俠

Li Zhen-Qing 李振清

Liu Bao-Zhen 劉寶珍

Liu Lao-Qing 劉老清

Hei Liu 黑劉

Xiao Hai-Bo 肖海波

Su Jing-Tian 蘇景田

Ma Yun-Cheng
(Bi Yue Xia)
馬雲程，避月俠

Song Wei-Yi 宋唯一

Guo Qi-Feng 郭歧鳳

Li Jing-Lin 李景林

Guo Shu-Fan
郭叔蕃

Zhang Xian 張憲

Li Ying-Ang 李英昂

Table 1-2

2   **3**   **4**   **5**

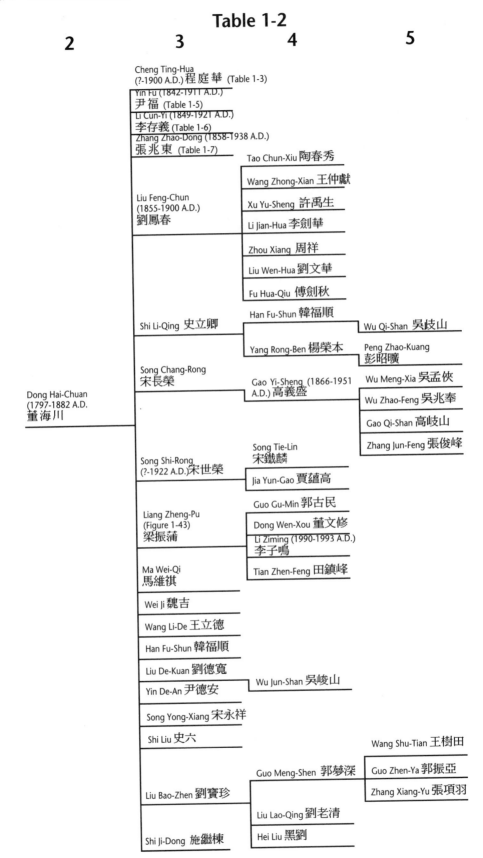

Cheng Ting-Hua
(?-1900 A.D.) 程庭華 (Table 1-3)

Yin Fu (1842-1911 A.D.)
尹福 (Table 1-5)

Li Cun-Yi (1849-1921 A.D.)
李存義 (Table 1-6)

Zhang Zhao-Dong (1858-1938 A.D.)
張兆東 (Table 1-7)

Tao Chun-Xiu 陶春秀

Wang Zhong-Xian 王仲獻

Liu Feng-Chun
(1855-1900 A.D.)
劉鳳春

Xu Yu-Sheng 許禹生

Li Jian-Hua 李劍華

Zhou Xiang 周祥

Liu Wen-Hua 劉文華

Fu Hua-Qiu 傅劍秋

Shi Li-Qing 史立卿

Han Fu-Shun 韓福順

Wu Qi-Shan 吳歧山

Yang Rong-Ben 楊榮本

Peng Zhao-Kuang
彭昭曠

Song Chang-Rong
宋長榮

Gao Yi-Sheng (1866-1951
A.D.) 高義盛

Wu Meng-Xia 吳孟俠

Wu Zhao-Feng 吳兆奉

Gao Qi-Shan 高岐山

Dong Hai-Chuan
(1797-1882 A.D.
董海川

Zhang Jun-Feng 張俊峰

Song Tie-Lin
宋鐵麟

Song Shi-Rong
(?-1922 A.D.)宋世榮

Jia Yun-Gao 賈蘊高

Guo Gu-Min 郭古民

Dong Wen-Xou 董文修

Liang Zheng-Pu
(Figure 1-43)
梁振蒲

Li Ziming (1990-1993 A.D.)
李子鳴

Ma Wei-Qi
馬維祺

Tian Zhen-Feng 田鎮峰

Wei Ji 魏吉

Wang Li-De 王立德

Han Fu-Shun 韓福順

Liu De-Kuan 劉德寬

Yin De-An 尹德安

Wu Jun-Shan 吳峻山

Song Yong-Xiang 宋永祥

Shi Liu 史六

Wang Shu-Tian 王樹田

Guo Meng-Shen 郭夢深

Guo Zhen-Ya 郭振亞

Liu Bao-Zhen 劉寶珍

Zhang Xiang-Yu 張項羽

Liu Lao-Qing 劉老清

Shi Ji-Dong 施繼棟

Hei Liu 黑劉

Table 1-3

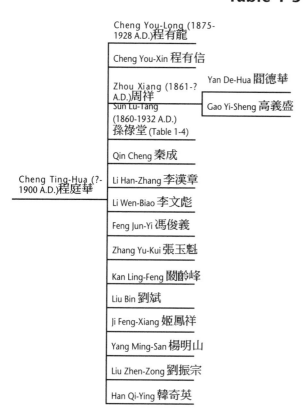

Cheng Ting-Hua (?-1900 A.D.) 程庭華
- Cheng You-Long (1875-1928 A.D.) 程有龍
- Cheng You-Xin 程有信
- Zhou Xiang (1861-? A.D.) 周祥
  - Yan De-Hua 閻德華
  - Gao Yi-Sheng 高義盛
- Sun Lu-Tang (1860-1932 A.D.) 孫祿堂 (Table 1-4)
- Qin Cheng 秦成
- Li Han-Zhang 李漢章
- Li Wen-Biao 李文彪
- Feng Jun-Yi 馮俊義
- Zhang Yu-Kui 張玉魁
- Kan Ling-Feng 闞齡峰
- Liu Bin 劉斌
- Ji Feng-Xiang 姬鳳祥
- Yang Ming-San 楊明山
- Liu Zhen-Zong 劉振宗
- Han Qi-Ying 韓奇英

Table 1-4

Sun Lu-Tang 1860-1932 A.D.) 孫祿堂
- Sun Cun-Zhou 孫存周
- Chen Wei-Ming 陳微明
- Jin Yun-Ting 靳雲亭
- Zheng Huai-Xian (1896-1981 A.D.) 鄭懷賢
  - Ling Gui-Qing 凌桂青

Fu Zhen-Song (1872-1953 A.D.) 傅振嵩
- Fu Yong-Hui 傅永輝

Zhou Xiang (1861 -? A.D.) 周祥
- Yan De-Hua 閻德華
- Gao Yi-Sheng 高義盛

Cheng You-Long (1875-1928 A.D.) 程有龍
- Sun Xi-Kun 孫錫坤

Table 1-5

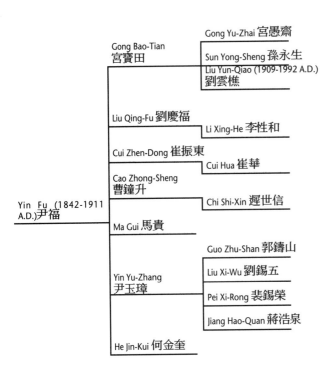

Yin Fu (1842-1911 A.D.) 尹福

- Gong Bao-Tian 宮寶田
  - Gong Yu-Zhai 宮愚齋
  - Sun Yong-Sheng 孫永生
  - Liu Yun-Qiao (1909-1992 A.D.) 劉雲樵
- Liu Qing-Fu 劉慶福
  - Li Xing-He 李性和
- Cui Zhen-Dong 崔振東
  - Cui Hua 崔華
- Cao Zhong-Sheng 曹鐘升
  - Chi Shi-Xin 遲世信
- Ma Gui 馬貴
- Yin Yu-Zhang 尹玉璋
  - Guo Zhu-Shan 郭鑄山
  - Liu Xi-Wu 劉錫五
  - Pei Xi-Rong 裴錫榮
  - Jiang Hao-Quan 蔣浩泉
- He Jin-Kui 何金奎

Table 1-6

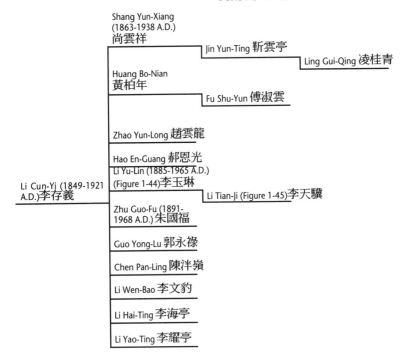

Li Cun-Yi (1849-1921 A.D.) 李存義

- Shang Yun-Xiang (1863-1938 A.D.) 尚雲祥
  - Jin Yun-Ting 靳雲亭
    - Ling Gui-Qing 凌桂青
- Huang Bo-Nian 黃柏年
  - Fu Shu-Yun 傅淑雲
- Zhao Yun-Long 趙雲龍
- Hao En-Guang 郝恩光
- Li Yu-Lin (1885-1965 A.D.) (Figure 1-44) 李玉琳
  - Li Tian-Ji (Figure 1-45) 李天驥
- Zhu Guo-Fu (1891-1968 A.D.) 朱國福
- Guo Yong-Lu 郭永祿
- Chen Pan-Ling 陳泮嶺
- Li Wen-Bao 李文豹
- Li Hai-Ting 李海亭
- Li Yao-Ting 李耀亭

Table 1-7

	Han Mu-Xia 韓慕俠	
	Jiang Rong-Qiao (1890-? A.D.) 姜容樵	Wu Meng-Xia 吳孟俠
Zhang Zhao-Dong 張兆東	Zhao Dao-Xin 趙道新	
	Liu Hu-Hai 劉湖海	
	Wang Jun-Chen 王俊臣	

Figure 1-43. Liang Zheng-Pu

Figure 1-44. Li Yu-Lin

Figure 1-45. Li Tian-Ji

years of being modified by different masters, there are now many different styles of Baguazhang. Naturally, the basic theory and foundation of all of these styles remain the same. It is very interesting today to see that each style has taken the same basic theory and principles and developed its own unique characteristics in both training and applications.

Currently, there are more than thirty different in-depth publications of Baguazhang in China. However, Baguazhang in the United States is still very new. The first English-language publication on Baguazhang, by Robert W. Smith, appeared in 1967.[66] A book by Lee Ying-Arng appeared in 1972,[53] and recently a couple of books by Jerry Alan Johnson, and one Johnson co-authored with Joseph Crandall, were published in the 1980s'.[67,68] It was not until the beginning of the 1980's that Baguazhang gradually became as well-known as Xingyiquan to martial artists in the West. It would be very beneficial during this developmental stage of the art if there were more publications available in English. We hope that people who are experienced in Baguazhang will do their part in popularizing this great art in the West.

1-7. The Contents of Baguazhang

We can see from the available documents that Baguazhang covers a very wide field of training. It includes not only barehand techniques, but also many weapons. Even for the Baguazhang developed only in Emei Mountain, there are more than fifteen different barehand routines and many different weapon training routines.

Excluding the barehand routines, and in addition to the four basic weapons: saber, sword, staff, and spear, Baguazhang also uses other weapons such as Spring Autumn Long Handle Saber, Hook-Sword, Deer Hook Sword, and crutch. Among them, Deer Hook Sword *(Lu Jiao Dao)* is a special and unique weapon to Baguazhang (Figure 1-46). Deer Hook Sword is named because they are shaped like deer's antlers. They are also called the *Zi Wu Yuan Yang Yue* (Zi Wu Mandarin Duck Axe). *Zi* and *Wu* are two of the twelve Celestial Stems which represent midnight (*Zi*) and noon (*Wu*). *Zi* also represents the extreme Yin of the day while *Wu* represents the extreme Yang. The two weapons are used together –l ike a pair of Mandarin ducks, they are inseparable. Another name for these weapons is *Ri Yue Qian Kun Jian* (Sun Moon Qian Kun Sword). The sun and *Qian* represent Yang, while the moon and *Kun* represent Yin.

In this section we will list the various versions of sequences or practice routines for both bare-hands and weapons which the authors could find in the available documents. Since it is impossible to include all of these in this volume, if you are interested in them you may refer to the original sources. Then, for information purposes, we will list some of the available Baguazhang bare-hand sequences or routines which have developed only at Emei Mountain. From this list, you will see how wide and great Baguazhang has become in China.

I. General Known Baguazhang Sequences:

Barehand:

1. 八卦八形掌 *Bagua Ba Xing Zhang* (Bagua Eight Shape Palms)[69]
2. 八形掌 *Ba Xing Zhang* (Eight Shape Palms)[16]
3. 龍形八卦掌 *Long Xing Baguazhang* (Dragon Shape Baguazhang)[61]
4. 九宮三盤掌 *Jiu Gong Sanpanzhang* (Nine Palace Three Coiling Palms)[70]
5. 五行三合掌 *Wu Xing San He Zhang* (Five Element Three Combined Palm)[71]
6. 游身八卦連環掌 *You Shen Bagua Lian Huan Zhang* (Sinuous Body Bagua Linking Sequence)[72]
7. 尹氏八卦掌－六十四式 *Yin Shi Baguazhang-Liu Shi Si Shi* (Yin Style Baguazhang-Sixty Four Postures)[73]
8. 三十六腿法 *San Shi Liu Tui Fa* (Thirty-Six Leg Techniques) No publication is available.
9. 七十二腿法 *Qi Shi Er Tui Fa* (Seventy-Two Leg Techniques) No publication is available.
10. 程氏八卦掌 *Cheng Shi BaguaZhang* (Cheng Style Baguazhang)[74]
11. 傅氏八卦掌 *Fu Shi Baquazhang* Fu Zhen-Song (Fu Style Baguazhang)[75]
12. 武當八卦掌 *Wudang Baguazhang*[76]
13. 姜氏八卦掌 *Jiang's Baguazhang*[51]

Matching:

1. 八卦掌對練 *Baguazhang Dui Lian* (Baguazhang Matching Training) *Please refer to this book.*

Figure 1-46. Deer Hook Sword

Weapons:

1. Deer Hook Sword:
    A. 子午鴛鴦鉞，日月乾坤劍，鹿角刀 *Zi Wu Yuan Yang Yue, Ri Yue Qian Kun Jian, or Lu Jiao Dao* (Deer Hook Sword) *Please refer to this book.*

2. Saber:
    A. 八卦刀 *Bagua Dao* (Bagua Saber)[77]

3. Sword:
    A. 連環劍 *Lian Huan Jian* (Linking Sword)[78]
    B. 連環純陽劍 *Lian Huan Chun Yang Jian* (Linking Pure Yang Sword)[79]
    C. 八卦劍 *Bagua Jian* (Bagua Sword) *No publications available.*

4. Staff:
    A. 連環盤龍棍 *Lian Huan Pan Long Gun* (Linking Coiling Dragon Staff)[80]
    B. 五行棒 *Wu Xing Bang* (Five Element Staff)[81]

5. Spear:
    A. 戰身槍 *Zhan Shen Qiang* (Battle Body Spear)[82]
    B. 八卦槍 *Bagua Qiang* (Bagua Spear) *No publication available.*

6. Other Weapons:
    A. 春秋刀 *Chun Qiu Dao* (Spring Autumn Long Handle Saber)[83]
    B. 八卦鉤 *Bagua Gau* (Bagua Hook-Sword) *No publications available.*
    C. 八卦枴 *Bagua Guai* (Bagua Crutch) *No publications available.*

Next, we would like to introduce some of the barehand Baguazhang sequences which are practiced in Emei Baguazhang styles.

Emei Barehand Baguazhang:[1]

1. 生門八卦掌 *Sheng Men Baguazhang* (Generation Door Baguazhang) – Follows the theory of *Yi Jing* which holds that "constant generation is called *Yi*."

2. 生門八卦打引 *Sheng Men Bagua Da Yin* (Generation Door Baguazhang Matching Set).

3. 僧門八卦掌 *Seng Men Baguazhang* (Monk Family Baguazhang) – Monk Family is a martia style from Emei Mountain. From Qing dynasties, Shaolin martial techniques have constant-ly been imported to Emei Mountain. Many Shaolin monks resided in Emei Mountain, and their combined techniques eventually merged to create this "Monk Family" style.

4. 峨嵋游身八卦連環掌 *Emei You Shen Bagua Lian Huan Zhang* (Emei Swimming Body Bagua Linking Palms).

5. 峨嵋游身八卦掌 *Emei You Shen Baguazhang* (Emei Swimming Body Baguazhang) - This sequence specializes in neutralizing, withdrawing, and dodging.

6. 峨嵋八卦連環掌 (1) *Emei Bagua Lian Huan Zhang* (1) (Emei Bagua Linking Palm)- Characteristics include circular "muddy walking," Qi sunk to the Lower *Dan Tian*, Calmness and Moving mutually adopted, ability to attack and defend, unification of mind and body, Yin-Yang and substantial-insubstantial, opening and closing, stepping lightly and agilely, and walking like a river stream.

7. 峨嵋龍形八卦掌 *Emei Long Xing Baguazhang* (Emei Dragon Shape Baguazhang) – Sudden walking, turning, and changing positions.

8. 峨嵋先天八卦掌 *Emei Xian Tian Baguazhang* (Emei Pre-Heaven Baguazhang).

9. 太乙火龍八卦掌 *Taiyi Huo Long Baguazhang* (Tai *Yi* Fire Dragon Baguazhang).

10. 峨嵋八卦掌 *Emei Baguazhang* (Emei Baguazhang).

11. 峨嵋形意八卦掌　*Emei Xingyi Baguazhang* (Emei Xingyi Baguazhang).

12. 峨嵋八卦梅花掌　*Emei Bagua Mei Hua Zhang* (Emei Bagua Plum Flower Palms).

13. 峨嵋八卦連環掌　(2) *Emei Bagua Lian Huan Zhang* (2) (Emei Bagua Linking Palms).

14. 龍形八卦掌　*Long Xing Baguazhang* (Dragon Shape Baguazhang).

15. 游身龍形八卦掌　*You Shen Long Xing Baguazhang* (Swimming Body Dragon Walking Baguazhang).

16. 峨嵋青城八卦掌　*Emei Qingcheng Baguazhang* (Emei Qingcheng Baguazhang).

17. 峨嵋陰陽八卦掌　*Emei Yin Yang Baguazhang* (Emei Yin Yang Baguazhang).

The above is only a partial list of the barehand Emei Baguazhang and it does not even include the sequences and training methods of all of the various weapons. Furthermore, there are many other sequences, techniques, and training methods which have not yet been discovered. Chinese "Yin-Yang Bagua" philosophy is very deep and profound. Baguazhang, as an internal martial art, originated from this philosophy and is equally deep and profound. Therefore, it is literally impossible for an individual to learn all forms or styles of Baguazhang in one lifetime, nor is it possible to introduce all of Baguazhang in a single book. What we do hope to contribute with this book (to the best of our ability) is an introduction to this philosophy, theory and practice.

References

1. *The Complete Book of Sichuan Wushu*, (1989). 四川武術大全。

2. Chen Yan-Lin, *Compilation of the Yang's Taijiquan, Saber, Sword, and Fighting Set*, (1943). 楊氏太極拳，刀，劍，桿，散手合編。陳炎林著。

3. Bensky, Dan, ed., *The Shanghai College of Traditional Medicine, Acupuncture, A Comprehensive History*, (Eastland Press,1981), 47.

4. *Id.* at 47.

5. *Id.* at 67-73.

6. 花拳繡腿。

7. 練拳不練功，到老一場空。

8. 外練筋骨皮，內練一口氣。

9. 滿招損，謙受益。

10. 子曰:"三人行，必有我師。"

11. 人外有人，天外有天。

12. 竹高愈躬。

13. 敬人者，人恆敬之。

14. Xu Qin-Ting, *The Research of Yin Jing*, (Hong Kong, The World Publication Company, 1976). 易經研究，徐芹庭博士。

15. 易有太極，是生兩儀，兩儀生四象，四象生八卦。

16. Sun Lu-Tang, *The Study of Bagua Fist*, (Peking, 1916). 八卦拳學。孫祿堂著。

17. 太極本混混沌沌，無形無意，而其中卻含有一氣，其氣流行宇內，無所不至，而生機萌焉。名曰"一氣。"亦曰"先天真一之氣。"由是氣而生兩儀，而天地始分，陰陽始判。

18. Kang Ge-Wu, *Zhongguo Wushu*, Peking, (Peking, Today's Chinese Publications, 1990). 中國武術實用大全，康戈武編。

19. 乾三連，坤六斷，震仰盂，艮覆碗，離中虛，坎中滿，兌上缺，巽下斷。

20. 十三勢者，棚、擺、擠、按、採、挒、肘、靠，此八卦也。進步、退步、左顧、右盼、中定，此五行也。棚、擺、擠、按，即乾、坤、坎、離，四正方也。採、挒、肘、靠，即巽、震、兌、艮，四斜角也。進、退、顧、盼、定，即金、木、水、火、土也。合之則為十三勢也。

21. 練後天補先天。

22. 練後天返先天。

23. 練先後天合一。

24. 借後天有形之身，以行有為變化之道，則能補先天之氣。

25. 見習拳術者，須當練精化氣，以氣化神，以運使內氣為功，以川流不息為旨用，求後天補先天之法。

26. 拳無拳，意無意，無意之中是真意。

27. 循著次序漸漸習去，自始至終無有乖戾之氣。久之，四體手足動作可以隨意指揮。故能上下相連，手足相顧，內外如一、渾然天理。

28. 天人相類。

29. 天人相通。

30. 天人感應。

31. 天道與人道統一。

32. 天為一大天，人為一小天。

33. 天人合一。

34. 得天氣之清者為之精，得地氣之靈者為之靈。二者皆得，方為神化之功。

35. 人法地，地法天，天法道，道法自然。

36. 外練筋、骨、皮，內練精、氣、神。

37. 形神相親，表裡俱濟。

38. Kang Ge-Wu, *Supra* note 18, at 61.
    中國武術實用大全，康戈武編。

39. 集成拳術，復按易理，定八卦，合五行。

40. 易則易知，簡則易行。

41. 一陰一陽謂之道。

42. 一陰一陽謂之拳。

43. 生生之謂易。

44. "剛柔相推而生變化。""一合一闢謂之拳。""變化者；進退之象也。"

45. 動靜有常。

46. 天尊地卑，乾坤定矣。

47. 天地定位，山澤通氣，雷風相薄，水火不相射。

48. 離中虛，坎中滿。

49. *少林演義*，作者不詳。

50. *乾隆下江南*，作者不詳。

51. Jiang Rong-Qiao, *The Expounding of Baguazhang Techniques*, (Reprinted by Five Continents Publishing Company, 1985). *八卦掌法闡宗*，姜容樵著。

52. 八卦掌法最早的來源，不知起於何時。在『籃簃外史』，「靖邊記」，有這樣的記載：「嘉慶丁巳（嘉慶二年），有山東濟寧人王祥教馮克善拳法，克善盡得其術。庚午春（嘉慶十五年），牛亮臣見克善拳法中有八方步，亮臣曰：爾步法似合八卦。克善曰：子何以知之？亮臣曰：我所習坎卦。克善曰：我為離卦。亮臣曰：爾為離，我為坎，我兩人離坎交宮，各習其所習可也。」

53. Lee Ying-Arng and Yen Te-Hwa, *Pa-Kua Chang for Self-Defense*, (1972).

54. Liu Xing-Han, *Swimming Body Bagua Linking Palm*, (1986). *遊身八卦連環掌*，劉興漢主編。

55. Personal family record of Master Wang Shu-Tian.

56. Sun Lu-Tang, *The Study of Bagua Sword*, (Peking, 1925). *八卦劍學*，孫祿堂著。

57. Yan De-Hua, *The Practical Applications of the Baguazhang Maneuvers*, (Tianjin, 1939). *八卦掌使用法*，閻德華著。

58. Sun Xi-Kun, Tianjin, *The Genuine Baguazhang Maneuvers*, (1943). *八卦掌真傳*，孫錫坤著。

59. Yin Yu-Zhang, *Baguazhang*, (Shandong, 1932). 八卦掌，尹玉璋著。

60. Gong Bao-Tian, *Baguazhang*. 八卦掌，宮寶田著。

61. Huang Bo-Nian, *Dragon Shape Baguazhang*, (Shanghai, 1936). 龍形八卦掌，黃柏年著。

62. Wu Meng-Xia, *The Essence of Baguazhang Maneuvers*. 八卦掌要義，吳孟俠著。

63. Peng Zhao-Kuang, *The Principles of Ba Palm Maneuvers*, (1955). 八掌綱要，彭昭曠著。

64. Zhang Jun-Feng, *The Important Meaning of Baguazhang*. 八卦掌要義，張俊峰著。

65. Ren Zhi-Cheng, *Yin Yang Eight Coiling Palms*, (Tianjin, 1937). 陰陽八盤掌，任致誠著。

66. Smith, Robert W, *Pa-Kua: Chinese Boxing for Fitness and Self-Defense*, (Tokyo, 1967).

67. Johnson, Jerry Alan, *The Master's Manual of Pa Kua Chang*, (Ching Lung Martial Arts Association, 1984).

68. Johnson, Jerry Alan and Joseph Crandall, *Classical Pa Kua Chang*, (1990).

69. Pei Xi-Rong and Pei Wu-Jun, *Bagua Eight Shape Palm*, (Hunan Scientific Technical Publishing Company, 1990) 14-23. 八卦八形掌，裴錫榮、裴武軍編著。

70. Liu Xing-Han, *Swimming Body Bagua Linking Palm*, , (1986) 93. 遊身八卦連環掌，劉興漢主編。

71. *Id.* at 96. 遊身八卦連環掌，劉興漢主編。

72. *Id.* at 107. 遊身八卦連環掌，劉興漢主編。

73. Zhang Lie, *Yin Style Baguazhang*, (Peking Agriculture Univerisity Publications, 1988). 尹氏八卦掌，張烈著，北京農業大學出版社。

74. Johnson, Alan and Crandall, *Supra* note 68, at 75.

75. Johnson, Alan and Crandall, *Supra* note 68, at 84.

76. Pei Xi-Rong and Li Chun-Sheng, *Wudang Wugong*, (Hunan Scientific Technical Publishing Company, 1984) 115. 武當武功，裴錫榮、李春生主編。

77. Johnson, Alan and Crandall, *Supra* note 68, at 140.

78. Liu Xing-Han, *Swimming Body Bagua Linking Palm*, (1986) 145. 遊身八卦連環掌，劉興漢主編。

79. *Id.* at 164. 遊身八卦連環掌，劉興漢主編。

80. *Id.* at 193. 遊身八卦連環掌，劉興漢主編。

81. *Id.* at 220. 遊身八卦連環掌，劉興漢主編。

82. *Id.* at 130. 遊身八卦連環掌，劉興漢主編。

83. *Id.* at 120. 遊身八卦連環掌，劉興漢主編。

Chapter 2

The Essence of Baguazhang
八卦掌之精華

2-1. Introduction

Many of the Baguazhang practitioners of the past were illiterate. When the masters wanted to pass on their wisdom, they would put their experiences into songs and poems, since these were easier to remember than prose. Such poems contained the key points of the art, and were secretly passed down to only the most trusted students. Only in the last century have most of these poems been revealed to the general public. In the next two chapters, we will translate and comment upon many of these secret songs and poems.

Although these songs and poems have played a major role in the preservation of the knowledge and wisdom of the masters, in many cases the identity of the authors and the dates of origin have been lost. These songs and poems, which contain the theory, training methods, key points, and above all the experiences accumulated over the past few centuries, provide Baguazhang practitioners with excellent guidelines for their training. They are the essence and root of the Baguazhang style. If your practice diverges from these guidelines, then it should not be classified as Baguazhang.

Because of cultural differences, it can be very difficult to translate these ancient Chinese writings. Many expressions would not make sense to the Westerner if translated literally. Often, knowledge of the historical background is necessary. Furthermore, since many sounds have several possible meanings, anyone trying to understand a poem or write it down has had to choose from among these meanings. For this reason, some of the poems have several variations. The same problem can occur when the poems are read. Many Chinese characters have several possible meanings, so reading involves interpretation of the text even for the Chinese. Also, the meaning of many words has changed over time. When you add to this the grammatical differences (generally no tenses, articles, singular or plural, or differentiation between parts of speech) you can find it almost impossible to translate Chinese literally into English. In addition to all of this, it helps if the translator has had much of the same experiences and understandings, as well as similar intuitive feelings, as the original author, in order to convey the same meaning.

Bearing these difficulties in mind, this book's authors have attempted to convey as much of the original meaning of the Chinese as possible, based on their own experience and understanding of the Chinese internal martial arts. Although it is impossible to totally translate the original meaning, the authors feel that they have managed to express the majority of the important points. These translations have been written as close to the original Chinese text as possible, including such things as double negatives and, sometimes, idiomatic sentence structure. Words which are understood but not actually written in the Chinese text have been included in parentheses. Also, some Chinese words are followed by the English in parentheses, e.g., *Shen* (Spirit). To further assist the reader, the authors have included commentary with each poem and song. For reference, the original Chinese of each song has been included with its translation.

To become proficient in Baguazhang, you must study these ancient documents carefully, ponder them deeply, and apply them to your practice. Through comprehension and constant practice, you will soon grasp the key essence of the art. Only when you have reached this stage will you be able to blend your own concepts into what you have learned. Without this foundation, you will only lead yourself down the wrong path, away from true Baguazhang. You should always remember: **Appreciate and value the past, study and practice intelligently now, and in the future learn humbly from other talented masters**.

2-2. Translation of Ancient Secrets

1. Total Song of Baguazhang [1,2,3]
八卦掌總歌

八卦掌，走為先，收即放，去即返，變換虛實步中參。走如風，站如釘，扣、擺、穿、翻、換法精。腰為纛，氣為旗，眼觀六路手足先。行如龍，坐如虎，行似江河靜如山。陰陽手，上下翻，沿肩墜肘氣歸丹。抱六合，勿散亂，氣血遍身得自然。

Baguzhang, walking is first, withdraw (and) immediately release, go (and) immediately return, change and vary the insubstantial and substantial in the stepping. Walk like the wind, stand as if nailed, the changes of techniques for arcing, swaying, boring and turning are clear. The waist is the (emperor's) banner, the Qi is the (general's) flag. The eyes look in the six directions, the hands and feet (move) first. Walk like a dragon, sit like a tiger, walk like a river, be still like a mountain. Yin and Yang hands, up and down turning, sink the shoulders and drop the elbows, Qi returns to the *Dan* (i.e., Lower *Dan Tian*). Embrace the six harmonies, do not be random and disordered, Qi and blood (circulate in) the entire body and gain its natural way (Dao).

In Baguazhang, walking is most important. You are always moving. When you withdraw, you immediately attack and when you advance, immediately return. The tricks of Baguazhang techniques are to keep changing while stepping. When you walk, you walk like wind and when you are still, you are rooted. The basic stepping, arcing, and swaying; basic hand techniques, boring, and turning, should be clear. In ancient times, the emperor's banner was the standard around which his troops would gather, and marked the center from which all commands originated. The waist directs your martial power and is therefore compared to a banner. During these ancient battles, generals would issue their orders by means of special flags. When a certain colored or shaped flag was raised, the soldiers would know to attack, withdraw, etc. The Qi is led by the mind, like soldier's being led by a general. When the intention is generated, the Qi moves first and the *Jin* follows. Therefore, Qi behaves like a flag. When you are in an alarming situation, the eyes pay attention to the six directions which include: front, rear, left, right, up, and down. Only when you can see clearly, are you able to step and move swiftly and quickly.

You must be firmly rooted both when you move and when you are still. Only with this rooted foundation can your hands turn and exchange easily from substantial to insubstantial and back again. When you move your hands, the shoulders and the elbows must be dropped and the Qi should be sunk to the Lower *Dan Tian*. The six harmonies include three internal harmonies and three external harmonies. The three internal harmonies are: *Xin* (emotional mind) and *Yi* (wisdom mind) harmonize, the *Yi* and the Qi harmonize, and the Qi and the *Li* (muscular power) harmonize. This implies that all of the *Xin*, *Yi*, Qi, and *Li* unify and coordinate with each other harmoniously The three external harmonies are: hands and feet harmonize, elbows and knees harmonize, and shoulders and hips harmonize. When these six important parts combine and coordinate with each other harmoniouslyyour mind will be firmed, Qi can be sunk, and the movements can be natural. Thus your entire body can act as one unit.

扣擺步，仔細盤，轉換進退在腰間，腳打七，手打三，手腳齊進莫遲緩。胯打走，肩打撞，委身擠靠暗頂肘。高不扼，低不攔，迎風接進最為先。數語妙訣拳中要，不用純功亦枉然。

Arcing and swaying stepping, carefully coiled (i.e., rooted). Turning, changing, advancing, and withdrawing are (controlled) by the waist. The feet strike seven and the hands strike three. The hands and feet advance together without delay. Thighs strike in walking, shoulders strike in bumping, lower the body, squeeze in near (the opponent) and elbow press (outward) clandestinely. High do not repress, low do not intercept, facing the wind to close (with the opponent) is the most important. Few words (describe) the important marvelous secret of the fist (i.e., Baguazhang). (If one) does not study intelligently, it will still be in vain.

Arcing and swaying stepping are the two major walking techniques in Baguazhang. When you walk, the legs must be rooted. Only then will you be able to use your waist to turn, change, advance, and withdraw skillfully. In Chinese martial arts, it is understood that the waist is like the steering wheel of a car, which not only controls the body's strategic movements but also directs the *Jin* manifested in the desired direction. In Baguazhang strategy, the legs compriise seven parts (70%) to the hands three (30%). When you execute your techniques at close range, you should use every part of the body to strike, such as the hips, shoulders, and elbows. When your opponent is standing high to charge with a high attack, do not repress; if he is low and strikes low, do not intercept. All of your efforts are to advance close to his body, which is the most advantageous position for the application of Baguazhang techniques.

Though there are only a few sentences in this poetry, the secret hidden within is marvellous. Only if you ponder humbly and intelligently, will you be able to grasp the keys of Baguazhang practice.

2. The Real Theory of Baguazhang[4]
八卦掌真理篇

順項提頂，溜臀收肛。

Soothe the neck and suspend the head, smooth the hips and withdraw the anus.

Soothe the neck means that the neck should be naturally and comfortably upright to support the head. This implies that the neck should not be tensed, which may be caused by continually looking upward or downward, or by tilting the head.

Suspend the head refers to holding your head up, so that it feels like you are being suspended from a wire attached to the top of your head. When the head is erect like this, the spirit of vitality can be raised.

Smooth the hips means from the back to the thighs should be a single plane, and that you should tuck your tailbone under your torso, expanding the joints in the lower back and relieving pressure on your sacrum. The pelvis should be like a bowl holding your organs, and neither tilt forward nor backward. When this is done correctly, the body will be upright and you will be able to find your center and obtain your balance. Only then can you be rooted. This is similar to the Taiji principle: "The tailbone should be upright" (*Weilu Zhong Zheng*).[5]

Withdraw the anus means to hold up your anus. It must be emphasized that holding up your anus is not the same thing as tensing and squeezing it. It is like you are holding up a bucket of water - though the mind is upward, the arm can still be relaxed. What you are looking for here is a light feeling of lifting up the anus, not squeezing it shut. This allows the spirit to be raised and the Qi to be condensed inward to the Lower *Dan Tian*, so that power can be stored. When you learn how to coordinate the expansion of your anus with the emitting of power, your *Jin* (martial power) can reach a high level.

鬆肩沉肘，實腹暢胸。

Loosen the shoulders and sink the elbows, solidify the abdomen and smooth the chest.

Loosen the shoulders means that the shoulders should not be tensed or raised, but should be loose and sunk. Sink the elbows means that the elbows should always be pointing downward.

Solidify the abdomen means to store Qi in the Lower *Dan Tian* so that your abdomen is full. This has the same meaning as the Taijiquan principle "*Qi Chen Dan Tian*" (the Qi is sunk to the *Dan Tian*)[6] and "*Nei Yi Gu Dang*" (internal should be full like rumbling)[7].

Smooth the chest means to make the chest loose and easy so that air can enter and exit through the lungs freely. This implies that when you practice, you should not tense your chest or hold your breath. The chest should feel natural and comfortable.

滾鑽爭裹，奇正相生。

Rolling, drilling, struggling (expanding), and encircling (wrapping), insubstantial and substantial mutually produce (each other).

This sentence is talking about the variations of *Jin*. Rolling (*Gun*) implies the circle rolling motion of the arms and shoulders. Drilling (*Zuan*) is a combination of a turning and forward motion, and therefore means the drill-like movement of the arms. Struggling (*Zheng*) means to use the force to expand. Encircling (*Guo*) implies to embrace in front of the chest. These are the four main Baguazhang arm movements which are used to manifest *Jin* to its maximum. When you combine rolling and drilling, the power can be strong and penetrating. When you combine expanding and embracing, your strategy can be alive. The insubstantial and the substantial can become exchangeable and mutually produce each other. When this is accomplished, not only can your power be strong, but your strategy can be mysterious.

龍形猴相，虎坐鷹翻。

Shaped (like a) dragon and looking (like a) monkey, sitting (like a) tiger and turning (and rolling like an) eagle.

This sentence implies the variations of your body's shape. The movements and the stepping should be swift and fast like a dragon, agile and alert like a monkey, rooted and solid like a sitting tiger, and turning and rolling like a flying eagle. Baguazhang's four unique characteristics are: "Walking" (*Zou*), "Watching" (*Shi*), "Sitting" (*Zuo*), and "Turning" (*Fan*). All of these characteristics can be manifested by imitating the four animals: dragon, monkey, tiger, and eagle.

擰旋走轉，蹬腳摩脛。

Twisting, spinning, stepping, and turning, rebounded stepping and frictional shin.

When you walk around a circle, your waist, elbows, palms, and neck must be turning toward the center of the circle. In this way will you create a strong spinning force towards the center. When you walk, the stepping must be light and walking power rebounding from the rear leg. Furthermore, when you walk your legs should cross each other closely, with your knees nearly touching. In this way will your walking be firm and rooted. If you walk with your two legs wide apart, then your walking foundation will be loose and you will float.

曲腿蹚泥，足心涵空。

Bent legs and muddy stepping, center of the feet hollow.

When you walk, you are bending your knees at a height that is most beneficial for you. The goal is to generate a firm root while you are walking. When you are stepping, it is like you are stepping on muddy ground. The feet should not be lifted too high from the surface of the ground as you move forward. In order to make the center of your feet hollow while you are walking, your heel and the ball should touch the ground simultaneously. In this case, your stepping will be firm.

起平落扣，連環縱橫。

Raise horizontal and fall buckled in, continuous both horizontal and vertical.

Your feet shoul be horizontal both when you raise them to step, or when you lower them to touch the ground. The feet are arced, so that the instep is turned inward slightly. When you are moving, your mind is continuous, your *Jin* is unbroken, and your movements are constant. Only then, through your mind, can you move up and down, left and right, forward and backward, continuous and smooth.

腰如軸立，手似輪行。

The waist firm like an axle and the hands move like wheels.

When you move, the waist is the center of your body, like the axle of a car. A car's axle must turn before its wheels can. When you want to change direction, you must change the angle of rotation relative to your direction of motion. Likewise, when your body is turning around, your hands should move like wheels rotating and turning. With good control of the waist and body movements, plus an agile circular motion of the arms and legs, your techniques will be powerful and skillful.

指分掌凹，擺肱平肩。

Fingers divided, the palms concave, unfold (i.e., smoothly extend) the forearms and horizontal shoulders.

This sentence talks about the positioning of the hands, arms and shoulders. The fingers should be opened and the center of the palms should be concave. The forearms should be extended comfortably toward the center of the walking circle. Finally, both shoulders should be sunk and kept at the same horizontal level.

椿如山岳，步似水中。

Stand like a mountain, move like flowing water.

When you stand still, you are like a mountain, firm and solid. When you move, you are like flowing water, smooth, swift, and fast.

火上水下，水重火輕。

Fire on the top and water on the bottom, the water is heavy and the fire is light.

According to the theory of the "Five Phases" in Chinese medicine (Table 2-1), the heart belongs to fire and the kidneys belong to water. The fire is light and the water is heavy. Therefore, the chest should be loose and light, while the Qi in the abdominal area should be full and solid.

意如飄旗，又似點燈。

The *Yi* is like a banner and also like a luminous lantern.

In ancient Chinese battles, banners and lanterns were commonly used to send signals to the soldiers, directing them; banners were used in the daytime and lanterns were used at night. This same analogy is used in all Chinese martial styles, the *Yi* is considered the banner or the lantern and represents the decision of the general. Once this decision has been sent out, the action begins.

腹乃氣跟，氣似雲行。

The abdomen is the root of Qi and the Qi moves like clouds.

Qi is stored in the Lower *Dan Tian*, which is located in the abdomen. Therefore, the abdomen is the residence of the Qi. In every action, the *Yi* (wisdom mind) is generated first, and the Qi naturally follows. This Qi (i.e., bioelectricity) energizes the physical body and manifests the *Jin*. In order to move the Qi smoothly, the Qi should move like a cloud, without any stagnation.

意動生慧，氣行百孔。

(When) the *Yi* moves, wisdom is generated and the Qi is able to be transported through hundreds of holes.

In Chinese Qigong practice, it is said: "Use your *Yi* to lead your Qi."[8] This means that when your *Yi* is generated, the wise decision is made. Under this intention, the Qi can be led to every tiny place of the body to unite the entire body as one fighting unit. In such instances, the entire body can be energized and the spirit of vitality can be raised.

展放收緊，動靜圓撐。

Develop to release or withdraw to tighten, moving or still (are all) supported with the round (energy).

This sentence implies that every action you make should be supported with a round feeling and round movements. For example, when you are still, your Qi is round and full. When you move, motions such as expanding, releasing, withdrawing, and tightening all carry with them rounded action. You should remember that **when your Qi and actions are round, your Qi can be full, your actions can be soft or hard, relaxed or taut, yielding or neitral, and your strategy can be alive**.

神氣意力，合一集中。

Shen (spirit), Qi, Yi, and Li, united and concentrated.

is the spirit of fighting. When this spirit is raised, the *Yi* is strong and the Qi can be full and abundant. When you have enough Qi to energize the physical body, your muscular power (*Li*) will naturally be strong. Therefore, when these four items unite and are activated to a high level, you will become a formidable combatant.

八掌真理，俱在此中。

The true principles of Bagua, are all inside.

All of the foregoing theories and their explanations make up the essence of Baguazhang. If you are truly interested in learning Baguazhang, you should ponder all of these theories.

3. Baguazhang Thirty-Six and Forty-Eight Secret Songs [9,10]
八卦掌三十六歌與四十八歌訣

In Baguazhang, there are two sets of secret songs which are said to have been passed down by Master Dong Hai-Chuan. The first set includes 36 songs for Baguazhang beginners, and the second set has 48 songs for advanced practitioners. It is widely believed and acknowledged that these songs are the essence of the Baguazhang. In this section, we will translate these two sets of songs and offer some commentary. First however, we would like to translate a short song which appraises these two sets of songs.

Song of Appraise
歌贊

三十六歌意真切，說說練練不為神。要得所傳真功到，凡人三年試驗深。

The meaning of the 36 songs is real and accurate. (If one) only talks and talks, practices and practices, (then he) will not be able to reach its spirit (essence). (If) wish to obtain these secrets and achieve the real Gongfu, one will have to spend (at least) three years to experience its depth.

The contents of the 36 songs are the real essence of the Baguazhang art. If you simply talk about it and practice without placing all your spiritual effort into it, you will never reach the essence of the art. If your goal is to reach the higher levels, you will need at least three years of hard practice to experience the real spirit of the art.

四十八法甚難求，見招使時不自由。十載純功研究到，單人武藝遨五州。

It is very difficult to reach (the final goals of) the 48 techniques. When these techniques are used, they cannot be applied freely (i.e., naturally and comfortably). (Only after spending) ten years of refined study and research, a single person's martial techniques can compete on the five continents.

From this song you can see that the 36 songs are mainly for beginners, and you will need about three years of serious study for successful training. However, in order to reach the higher levels of the Baguazhang skill, you must again spend at least ten years of refined study on the 48 songs.

A. 36 Secret Songs of Baguazhang
八卦掌三十六歌

1. 空胸拔項下含腰，拗胯拿膝抓地牢。沈肩垂肘伸前掌，二目須從虎口瞧。

   Empty the chest, pull (up) the head, and settle down the waist. Firm the thighs, control the knees, and grab the ground strongly. Sink the shoulders, drop the elbows, and extend the front palm. Both eyes must look out through the tiger's mouth.

   This first song is talking about the basic Baguazhang postures. The chest should cave in (i.e., be held in comfortably), the head should be suspended, and the waist should be relaxed and the body should be upright, with the back straight. In order to have a strong stance, the thighs should be squeezed slightly inward, the knees should be strongly locked, and the feet should "grab" the ground tightly. The shoulders and the elbows should be sunk. The front palm should extend forward and the four fingers (except the thumb) should point upward. All the fingers should be opened. The eyes look forward through the space between the thumb and the index finger (i.e., tiger's mouth).

   When you have accomplished this basic posture, then your stance and walking will be firm and rooted. Your chest will be loose for breathing, your abdomen will be relaxed, and the Qi can be full. When you focus your view through the tiger's mouth, you can focus your mind forward, and build up your sense of enemy.

2. 后肘先疊肘掩心，手再翻塌向前跟。跟到前肘合抱力，前后兩手一團神。

   The rear elbow first folds and it covers the heart. The hands then turn and collapse (i.e., settle the wrist) to follow the front. Follow to the front elbow with the embracing power. Both the front and the rear hands have a sole gathered *Shen* (spirit).

   This song is talking about the posture of the arms. The rear elbow should bend and protect the center of the body. The fingers of both hands should turn so that they point upward (except the thumbs), and the wrists should be collapsed and settled. The rear arm follows the front arm to its elbow area and extends forward. As you do this, both the arms and the chest should suggest an encircling, embracing energy pattern. Though the front and the rear arms are separated, the spirit that directs them is one. This means both arms coordinate with each other and with a single heart.

3. 步彎腳直向前伸，行如推磨一般直。曲膝隨胯腰拗足，眼到三面不搖身。

   Step with curve and extend forward with straight leg. (When) walking (the body) is erect like pushing a grindstone. Bend the knees and follow (i.e., coordinate and match with) the thighs, the waist must be sufficiently twisted. The eyes reach the three directions without swaying the body.

   This song is talking about stepping. While practicing Baguazhang, you walk in a circle. When you step, the feet should curve inward. In addition, when you walk your stepping leg should be straight and extended forward. Walking should be firm and rooted as if you were pushing a grindstone. Your knees must bend slightly, and should be completely coordinated with the thighs and waist. When you walk in this posture, even if your eyes watch the three directions (i.e., left, right, and front), you are stable, centered and balanced, without shaking.

4. 一式單鞭不是奇，左右循環乃為宜。左換右兮右換左，抽身倒步自合機。

   (Grabbing the secret of) the sole posture of "Single whip" is not marvelous. It is appropriate that (if you can apply it) left and right repeatedly. (If you can) change the left to right and right to left, (then you may) withdraw the body and step backward at the proper opportunity.

This song explains the importance of left and right technique exchanges. Even if you have grasped the secrets of movement and the applications of a single form, it is not marvelous. You should be able to exchange this technique, and skillfully apply it from the left side to the right, and vice versa. Then, when you advance or retreat you will feel natural, easy, and comfortable. This song means that in combat, you should be able to skillfully apply any technique.

5. 步既轉兮手也隨，后掌穿出前掌回。來去去來無二致，要像弩劍離弦飛。

The steps turn and the hands follow (i.e., coordinate with the steppings). The rear palm bores out and the front palm returns. To and fro, fro and to, without two goals. (It) must be like an arrow on a crossbow leaving the string.

This song is talking about the coordination of the hands and feet. When your stepping is turning, your hands follow and change back and forth. The rear palm bores forward and the front palm withdraws. When you exchange your palms, they both act the same, fast and accurate, just like an arrow fired from a crossbow.

6. 穿時直掌貼肘行，后肩改作前肩承。莫要距離莫猶豫，腳入膀兮是准繩。

When boring, the palm moves straight forward closely along the elbow. The rear shoulder will take the place of the front shoulder. Do not separate and do not hesitate. The foot enters the (opponent's) thighs is the correct rule (i.e., right way).

This song describes the keys of the boring palm. When your palm is boring forward, the fingers of the palm also point forward and closely follow the elbow of the other arm. Once the palms exchange their positions, the rear shoulder becomes the front shoulder, taking over the front shoulder's responsibilities. When you exchange arms, you should not hesitate and the movements of both palms should be closely coordinated. An important key to Baguazhang strategy is to gain an advantageous position by stepping your foot into the space between your opponent's legs. Doing this is called entering and occupying your opponent's empty door.

7. 胸期空兮氣領沈，背緊肩垂臂前伸。氣到丹田縮谷道，直拔顛頂貫精神。

The chest must be empty and the Qi is led to sink (to the *Dan Tian*). The back is tight, the shoulders are dropped, and the arms are extended forward. (When) Qi is led to *Dan Tian*, the "Grain path" is withdrawn. Pull the head straight upward to fill up the spirit of vitality.

This song is talking about how to transport the Qi. First, you should relax your chest area, which allows air to be taken in easily. When the front of your body is loose, the Qi can easily be led to the Lower *Dan Tian*. The back should be arced, the shoulders should be dropped, and the arms should extend forward. When you inhale to lead the Qi to Lower *Dan Tian*, the grain path (i.e., anus) should be withdrawn (i.e., you use reverse breathing). In Chinese martial arts, to store your *Jin*, first you must store your *Yi*. The coordination of reverse breathing enables you to lead the Qi to the Lower *Dan Tian* while inhaling. When you store your *Jin*, the anus is gently held upward; exhale and expand your anus as you emit your *Jin*. This allows the Qi to be led easily to the extremities to support your physical power. Whenever you store or emit your *Jin*, be sure to keep your head upright, and your spirit of vitality raised.

8. 走時周身莫動搖，全憑膝下兩相交。底盤雖講平腰胯，中盤也要下腿腰。

When (you) walk, the entire body should not sway. All (of this) relies on the two (calves) under the knees crossing each other (firmly). Though the (stability) of the lower section (of the body) concerns the balanced waist and thighs, the middle section (of the body) also needs the legs and waist.

This song refers to the means for keeping the body steady and firm while walking. When the body is discussed in Chinese martial society, it is normally divided into three sections. These three sections are called "*San Pan*" (three sections). *San Pan* includes the lower section (*Xia Pan*) from the knees down to the feet, the middle section (*Zhong Pan*) from the knees up to the solar plexus, and the upper section (*Shang Pan*) from the solar plexus up to the head.

This song says when you are walking, the middle and upper sections should be stable and not sway around. All motion depends on the lower section, which is below the knees. In order to have stable stepping, the waist and the thighs (i.e., middle section of the body) must be balanced. Even then, the balance of the middle section still depends on how the waist and legs coordinate with each other.

9. 吻唇閉口舌抵腭，呼吸全從鼻孔進。力用極時哼哈泄，混元一氣此為得。

Kiss (i.e., Lightly touch) the lips, close the mouth, the tongue touches the roof of the mouth. In the breathing, (the air is) all entered from the nose. When manifesting the *Li* to its maximum, use the *Hen* and *Ha* sounds to emit. Unite the whole Original Qi as one; it is called "Gaining."

This song talks about how to manifest the Qi from your physical body in order to maximize its power. Baguazhang uses reverse breathing. When you inhale, the Qi is sunk to the Lower *Dan Tian*, and the anus is withdrawn. When you exhale, the Qi is led to the muscles to energize them, and the anus is pushed out slightly. When you manifest your Qi into *Jin*, your tongue should always touch the roof of the mouth, connecting the Conceptional and Governing Vessels. When you inhale or exhale, the air enters and exits from the nose. In order to maximize your *Jin*, "*Hen*" and "*Ha*" sounds should be used. Only after you grasp this key - uniting the entire body's Original Qi and manifesting it into *Jin* - can you say you have gained the secret. If you are interested in knowing more about "*Hen*" and "*Ha*" sounds, please refer to *Advanced Yang Style Tai Chi Chuan - Vol. 1*, by YMAA.

10. 掌形虎口要撐圓，十指無名縫開展。先戳后打施腕骨，鬆膀長腰跟步鑽。

The shapes of the palms and the tiger mouth areas should be extended and round. The gaps between the ten fingers - (especially) the ring finger - must be opened and extended. First poke, then strike using the wrist bone. Loosen the shoulders and grow the waist, drill in following the stepping.

This song discusses the shape of the palm. The palms and the place between the thumb and the second finger (tiger mouth) should be round and extended like holding a ball. All ten fingers should be extended. When you use the hand to strike, the fingers point forward as if you are poking. Then settle the wrist, making the fingers point upward (*Zuo Wan*), in order to use the bottom of the palm to strike. When you use the palm to strike, the shoulders should be loose and the body extended (i.e., growing waist). Follow with a step, drilling into the opponent's body.

11. 上步合膝倒步拿，換掌換步矮身骸。進退退進隨機勢，只要腰胯巧安排。

Step forward with closed knees and step backward with controlled (root). (When) exchanging the palms and exchanging the stepping, the body skeleton should be low. Forward and retreat, retreat and forward according to the opportunity. This can be skillfully arranged merely with the waist and the thighs.

This song is talking about body movements. When you step forward and backward, the knees are closed, not wide open. Only then will your stepping be firm and rooted. When you exchange your palms while stepping, your body's posture should be low. The timing of advances and retreats depends on the situation and available opportunities. Success is decided only by how skillfully you can move your waist and thighs.

12. 此掌與人大不同，進步抬前乃有功。退步還先退后足，胯步盡外要離中。

This palm (i.e., Baguazhang) has a great difference from others. Stepping forward with moving front (leg first) is able to achieve success. Still, (when) stepping backward, the rear foot should retreat first. (When) stepping, try to keep on the outside (of the opponent) and away from the center (line).

This song talks about stepping. Baguazhang is very different from other martial styles for many reasons, but primarily for the stepping patterns it uses. For example, when you step forward in Baguazhang, you must move your front leg first, and when you retreat you must step with your rear foot first. Only then will your stepping be firm and rooted. In addition, when you step either forward or backward, you should keep away from the center line between you and your opponent. This center line is most dangerous while your are moving.

13. 此掌與人大不同，手未動兮胯先攻。未從前伸先后縮，吸足再吐力獨半。

This palm (i.e., Baguazhang) has a great difference from others. Before moving the hands, first the thighs attack. Before extending forward, first withdraw backward. (When) withdraw enough then emit, the effort is only half.

This song discusses the way *Jin* is stored. Before you attack with your hands, you first firm your root with your thighs. Only with this firm root can the power be strong. However, before you emit your *Jin*, you must first store it. When you can store and emit your *Jin* skillfully, you will be able to generate great power.

14. 此掌與人大不同，前掌后掌力相通。欲使梢兮先動根，招招如是不得鬆。

This palm (i.e., Baguazhang) has a great difference from others. The power (Li) of the front palm and the rear palm is connected. (If you) wish to use the endings, first move it's root. Every form like this do not treat lightly.

This song is talking about the way of emitting *Jin*. One of the most important keys of emitting *Jin* in Baguazhang is that all of the strikes start from their roots. For example, the shoulders are the root of the hands and the feet are the roots of the body. In addition, the front and rear hands must be coordinated and act as a single unit. When you practice according to these rules, all of your manifestations of *Jin* will be rooted and powerful.

15. 此掌與人大不同，未擊西兮先擊東。指上打下孰得知，卷珠倒流更神通。

This palm (i.e., Baguazhang) has a great difference from others. Before striking the west, first attack the east. Pointing upward and strike downward, nobody is able to know. Rolling the pearl and reversing the current are more supernatural ubiquitously.

This song talks about palm usage. When you use the palms to attack, your opponent does not know where you are going to strike. In Baguazhang, the palms can look like they are striking forward when they are actually withdrawing backward. It may seem like you are striking upward, but instead you are attacking downward. Substantial seems like insubstantial and insubstantial looks like substantial. Moreover, if you are able to move and turn your palms skillfully - like a rolling pearl - and move forward and backward, your palms like a flowing current, then your opponent will be unable to figure out your intention and strategy.

16. 天然精術怕三穿，不走外門是枉然。他走外兮我走內，伸手而得不費難。

(Even) the natural refined techniques (i.e., skillful martial techniques) are afraid (of the) three "Borings." If not walk from external door, it is still in vain. (If) the opponent walks from outside, I walk inside. (Then) it is not difficult to extend my hand and gain.

A good martial artist will practice his techniques until they are natural and refined. Even higher level martial artists still are afraid of the three "Boring" (*San Chuan*) techniques in Baguazhang. "*San Chuan*" is one of the key techniques in Baguazhang, and when it is used to attack continuously, it can defeat many good martial arts experts. However, even if you use "*San Chuan*" but do not know how to enter the opponent's defended area from the side (i.e., external door, *Wai Men*), then your techniques will still be useless.

If your opponent also uses the strategy of entering your external door, then you must use the internal door to attack (relative to him, you are still on his side door). Then you may still attack your opponent with the boring technique without opposition.

17. 掌使一面不為功，至少乃須二面攻。一橫一直三角手，使人如在我懷中。

(If) using only one side of the palm (i.e., one palm attacks one side), the goal cannot be achieved. At least, it will need two sides (i.e., two palms from two sides) to attack. One sideways one forward will become triangle hands. This will make the opponent being controlled just like held in my chest (i.e., a certainty).

In Baguazhang, you should use both of your palms skillfully. If you are able to skillfully attack the opponent with only one of your hands, then you will not attack as successfully. Even if you do not know how to attack your opponent from either the top or the bottom (i.e., kicking), at the very least you should know how to use both of your hands skillfully. In Baguazhang, both of your arms form a triangle, with one arm sideways in front of your chest and the other extended forward. When you do everything correctly and dexterously, then you are sure to control your opponent like an object held to your chest.

18. 高欲低兮矮欲揚，斜身繞步不須忙。斜翻倒翻腰著力，翻到極處力要剛。

(When) high, desire to be low and (when) low, wish to raise. Diagonal body, circle stepping, do not hurry. Diagonal turning or reversed turning, the waist should conduct the power. When turning to the ultimate, the power must be hard.

This song is talking about the strategy of the body's movement. The first sentence can have two meanings. The first is that, when you are high you will change into low, and when you are low then you will raise into high. This helps prevent the opponent from figuring out your strategy. The second meaning is that, when the opponent is standing high or when he is tall, you will focus on a low attack. However, if he is low, then you will concentrate an attack higher up, such as his upper body or head.

When you are walking the Bagua circle, the body twists to face the center. Your stepping should be firm and steady. Unless you have practiced for a long time, walking too fast will make your root shallow. When you are turning your palms, regardless of which turn you do, all of them must originate from and be directed by the waist, with a firm root. When all the turnings reach their final target, the *Jin* should become hard.

19. 人道掌法勝在剛，拳經曾言柔內藏。個中也有人知味，剛柔相濟是所長。

People say that the winning of the palm technique is decided by the hard (*Jin*). The Fist Classic has also said that the soft (*Jin*) should be hidden within. In martial arts society, someone has discovered its taste (i.e., essence or secret). The mutual assistance of the hard and the soft should be raised (i.e., emphasized, cultivated, or practiced).

This song is discussing the manifestation of *Jin*, which should be either hard or soft. Though there are many sayings about how the *Jin* should be manifested, in Baguazhang the soft and hard *Jins* should mutually assist and correspond to one another.

20. 剛在先兮柔內藏，柔在先兮剛后張。他人之柔腰與手，我則吸腰步穩揚。

(If) the hard is first, then the soft should be hidden behind. (If) the soft is first, then the hard is manifested later. (To defeat) other people's soft, from the waist and the hands. (If) I am able to receive (my) waist (i.e., control and direct my waist) with steady stepping, then (I) will be winning.

This song continues the discussion of how to manifest *Jin*. If the hard *Jin* is being manifested, there must be some soft *Jin* hidden behind. This is necessary to prevent your opponent from using your hard *Jin* against you. When you are expressing hard *Jin*, the soft *Jin* is already prepared to deal with any sudden disadvantageous changes. If you use the soft *Jin* first, then after you neutralize and channel the opponent into a disadvantageous position, you may use hard *Jin* to manifest your muscular power to its maximum. In theory, hard *Jin* is more appropriate for an attack and soft *Jin* is better used for yielding and neutralization.

If your opponent is soft, and if he is not in an urgent situation, you should not use hard *Jin*. You must use your waist and hands skillfully to yield, lead, and neutralize his power. Only then will you have a firm stepping root, allowing you to win the battle.

21. 用到極時須轉身，脫身化影不留痕。如何變化端在步，出入進退腰先伸。

When the application (of a technique) has reached its limit, the body must be turned. Escape the body, and change into shadow without leaving a trace. The key to change and variety is in the stepping. Exiting, entering, advancing, and retreating, the waist extends first.

This song is discussing the trick of the body's turning. When you are in an urgent position, you should turn your body to escape. When you escape, you are like a shadow and your opponent cannot figure out how you do it. The key to making this happen is in your stepping. All turning must begin with the waist, and the rest of the body follows.

22. 轉掌之神頸骨傳，轉項扭項手當先。變時縮頭發時伸，要如神龍首尾連。

The spirit of the turning palm (i.e., Baguazhang) is manifested from the neck bone. (When) turning and twisting the head, the hands should (move) first. When changing (the techniques), the head withdraws and when emitting, the head extends. (It) must be like a spiritual dragon connecting the head and the tail.

This song is talking about the spirit of Baguazhang. Baguazhang is also called "Turning palm." The spirit of Baguazhang is illustrated by the head, which is held as if suspended from above. The neck is upright and the spirit is raised. When you are turning your head to change direction, the hands should move first. When the *Yi* arrives, the Qi and the hands also arrive. When you are changing techniques, conserve your energy and store your *Jin*. During this time, your neck is withdrawn and relaxed. When you are emitting your *Jin*, the neck extends and the spirit is raised. The movement of the entire body, from the head to the limbs, is just like a swimming dragon.

23. 打人須憑膀為根，膀在肩端不全伸。故欲進時進前步，前進后步枉勞神。

When striking the opponent, the upper arms must be used as the root (of *Jin*). The upper arms on the shoulder area should not extend completely. That means if (you) desire to advance, step forward with front leg. If (you) step forward with the rear leg, then the spiritual effort is in vain.

This song is talking about the tactics of attack. When you attack, the root of the strike is the upper arms, which are connected to the shoulder joint area. The shoulders should be sunk and not completely extended. Follow these rules and your striking power will be firm, rooted, and strong. In order to strike your opponent with power, you must utilize the momentum of the body's advancing movement. While doing this, you should step forward with the front leg instead of the rear leg. Stepping with the front leg makes you more firm and rooted while strik-ing.

24. 力足發自筋與骨，骨中出硬筋須隨。足跟大筋通胸脊，發招跟步力能摧。

The abundant power (i.e., strong *Jin*) is emitted from tendons and bones. The hard (*Jin*) origi-nates from bones and must coordinate with tendons. The big tendon on the heel is connected with the chest and spine (i.e., the entire body is united into one unit). When emitting techniques with following stepping, the power is able to smash.

This song describes the emitting of *Jin*. Physical power must be generated from the bones and tendons instead of the muscles. If the power is emitted from the muscles, it will be stagnant and slow. When the Qi stored in the bone marrow is manifested in the action of tendons, its power can be very fast and penetrating. Because the tendons of the feet are connected to the upper body, the entire body should act as one unit. If you are able to use the advancing forward stepping power, it can smash your opponent easily.

25. 眼到手到腰腿到，心真神真力又真。三真四到合一處，防己有餘能制人。

The eyes arrive, the hands arrive, and the waist and the legs arrive. The *Xin* (i.e., emotional mind) is real, the spirit is real, and the power is also real. The three "Reals" and the four "Arrives" combined into one place. There is a surplus to defend yourself, and (it) is able to defeat the opponent.

This song is talking about the mind, the spirit, and the action. In order to make your Qi abun-dant for fighting, you must first raise up your emotional mind (*Xin*). Yet this emotion must be under the control of your wisdom mind (*Yi*). In this way can your spirit of vitality be raised to a high and real level. When your Qi is abundant and your spirit is high, you will be able to energize the mus-cles and tendons to their maximum efficiency. When you are in a highly alert and agile condition, your eyes, hands, waist, and legs will move as one unit. If you have reached this stage in your Baguazhang training, you can not only defend yourself, but can also control your opponent.

26. 力要剛兮更要柔，剛柔偏重力難收。過剛必折真物理，優柔太甚等與休。

The power should be hard, and even more, should also be soft. Too much of hard or soft, the power is hard to withdraw (i.e., control). (When it is) too hard, it is easy to break, (this is) the real object theory (i.e., natural theory). Too much of the elegant softness is equivalent to truce (i.e., useless).

This song is again talking about hard and soft *Jins*. *Jin* power should be hard as well as soft. If it is either too hard or too soft, it will be either too stagnant or too weak. In either case, the power is not alive and can be easily neutralized. When it is too hard, the power can be broken and bor-rowed, and when it is too soft, the power will not be strong enough to defeat an opponent.

27. 剛柔相濟是何言，剛柔相輔總無難。剛柔當用乾坤手，掀天揭地海波瀾。

What is the saying of the mutual supporting of the hard and the soft? It has never known diffi-culty if the hard and the soft mutually assist (each other). Hard and soft should use the *Qian* (i.e., Yang) and *Kun* (i.e., Yin) hands. This enables (one) to open the heaven, expose the earth, and cause the great wave in the ocean.

This is again talking about the hard and the soft *Jins*. Hard and soft *Jins* should mutually assist each other. When the hard and soft *Jins* combine with the Yin and Yang palms (i.e., insubstantial and substantial palms), its power can be very great and hard to defeat.

28. 人剛我柔是正方，我柔人剛法亦良。剛柔相宜腰求勝，解此糾紛步法強。

(When) the opponent is hard and I am soft, (this) is the right way. (However), if I am soft and the opponent is hard, the method is also good. The hard and the soft mutually coordinate and win (i.e., control) from the waist. The conflict (i.e., battle) is decided on whose stepping is better.

This song is talking about how to use the hard and the soft *Jins* skillfully. When the opponent is hard, you may use the soft *Jin* to yield, lead, and neutralize. In this case, your techniques will be varied and alive. However, if the opponent's power is soft and if the situation allows, the hard *Jin* can force the opponent into an defenseless situation. The most important factor in winning a battle is knowing the timing, and recognizing the right opportunity to apply the techniques. Only then can the power vary and exchange from hard to soft and from soft to hard according to the situation. In all of these situations, you must also know how to use the waist to direct the *Jin*, and how to use the stepping to create an advantageous situation.

29. 步法動時腰先提，收縮合宜顯神奇。足欲動兮腰不動，跟蹌邁步慢時機。

When stepping, the waist is raised first. (If) retreating and withdrawing are appropriate, the marvelous (result) can be demonstrated. (If) the feet desire to move but the waist does not move, the stepping will be slow and unsteady and the opportunity will be delayed (i.e., lost).

This song is talking about how the waist can affect the stepping. Your center of gravity is normally located in the waist area. If you raise up your waist slightly when you step, you will be able to walk more agilely. When the waist is kept loose, you are more able to retreat or advance with correct timing. When you desire to step you must keep the waist area relaxed and steady. This helps to maintain your center and when you step, you will be steady and rooted. If you are not able to stabilize, center, and balance yourself while you are walking, you will be unable to appreciate opportunities for attack or execute techniques with correct timing.

30. 轉身變法步莫長，擦地而行莫要慌。看准來勢方伸手，巧女穿針穩柔剛。

(When) turning the body and changing the techniques, the stepping should not be long. Wiping the ground while walking; do not lose self-possession. Accurately look at the coming postures (i.e., attacks) then extend your hands. (Like) a cute girl threading a needle, be steady, soft, and hard (i.e., firm).

This song discusses movement. The stepping should always be coordinated with the body and the techniques. When you step, do not reach too far. Step in short distances; this can increase your stepping speed and stability. In Baguazhang, the stepping is as if you are walking on muddy ground. Baguazhang stepping is commonly called "*Tang Ni Bu*" (walking muddy steps).

When you walk like this, your stepping will be firm. With coordinated stepping, and an understanding of the opponent's intention, the moment will come to attack. The entire action is just like threading a needle: accurate, firm, and steady.

31. 人持利器我不忙，飛劍遙遙到身旁。看他來路哼哈避，邪不勝正法頗良。

(When) the opponent carries a sharp weapon, I am not busy (i.e., alarmed). The flying sword reaches my side from distance. Watch its coming and use the *Hen* and *Ha* (i.e., the sounds of emitting and neutralizing *Jins*) to avoid. It is a good rule that evil cannot defeat the righteous.

This song is talking about the psychology of fighting barehanded against an armed opponent. When you encounter such a situation, you should remain alert but do not panic. You must learn to trust your training, and be confident that you will coolly handle the situation under the principles of attack and defense. You must believe that evil will always be defeated by the righteous.

32. 短兵相接似難防，那怕純利似魚腸。伸手來取囊中物，指山打磨妙中藏。

It seems hard to protect (yourself) when the short weapons are contacting (i.e., battle with short weapons). (I will) not be scared even (if the weapons are) as sharp as the Yu Chang sword. Extending (my) hands to seize it (i.e., to handle the situation) is just like picking up an object in a bag. Pointing (to) the mountain and striking the grind stone, the marvel is hidden within.

This song is talking about the strategy of fighting against an opponent with a short weapon. The Yu Chang (Fish Intestine) sword was a famous sword in Chinese history known for its sharpness. If I want to defeat the opponent who is using a sharp short weapon, the best way is by using faking techniques. The reference to the mountain and the grindstone is meant to symbolize a feint to one area, and an attack to another. In themselves, the mountain and the grind stone do not have any likeness or relationship. However, if you point your fingers to the mountain, your may draw your opponent's attention, distracting him while offering you a chance to attack the grindstone. In order to defeat an armed opponent, you must cheat him with both faking techniques and actual strikes.

33. 人眾我寡力難強，巧破千鈞莫要忘。一手不勞憑指力，犁牛猶怕反弓張。

The opponents are many, it is hard to fight against (them) with strength. Do not forget that the tricks (i.e., strategy) is able to break (i.e., defeat) a thousand pounds. One hand (i.e., a single person) cannot defeat (the opponent) depending solely on strength. Though the ox (is strong), yet it still fears the extension of the reverse bow.

This song talks about how to fight if there are many opponents. When you encounter this situation, you should avoid using force against force. You will not be able to compete with the combined forces of many opponents with your own force. You must instead use your wisdom and cunning. Often, wisdom is more powerful than a thousand pounds.

In ancient China, a whip was commonly used to urge oxen and horses. Normally, the whip was also used as a bow. When the bow was unstrung, it became a whip (reverse bow). The ox is a very strong animal, yet it is still afraid of the whip. The reason that a human is able to control an ox is simply because our wisdom is higher than theirs. When you fight against many opponents at the same time, you should use your wisdom and fake the opponents, avoiding the strong and attacking the weak. Conserve your energy and use strategy to confuse your opponents.

34. 伸手不見掌前人，又無油松照彼身。收縮眼皮努睛看，底盤掌使顯神奇。

(When) extending hands, (you) cannot see the opponent in front of (your) palms. Again, there is no oil lamp to illuminate the opponent's body. Withdraw the eyelids (i.e., relax) and strive to see. (Then, you can firm) the ground portion (i.e., of the body) and manifest your palms marvelously.

This song is talking about fighting in the dark. Since neither you nor your opponent can see each other, you should calm down your mind, relax your eyelids and search for any sign of movement. If you are tense and open your eyes too wide, then too much of your concentration will be focused on your eyes, and they will actually become a distraction. You should calmly, alertly and firmly pay attention to your surroundings. Only then will you move with a firm root, and the power of your palms can be demonstrated successfully.

35. 冰天雪地雨擰滑，前腳橫施且莫差。翻身切忌螺絲轉，高低謹防乃為佳。

Icy sky (i.e., cold weather), snowy ground (i.e., ground covered with snow), (again it is) raining, it is slippery. Do not hesitate to place the front foot sideways. When turning the body, must not

spin like a screw. It is good if aware of these carefully either high or low.

This song illustrates what you should be aware of when you fight on slippery ground. When you step or are even standing still, your front foot should be turned slightly sideways. Doing this will enable you to move or stand with more stability. When you turn your body, do not spin or you will loose your foundation. You should turn slowly and carefully. Under such weather conditions, it does not matter if your posture is high or low, you must be very cautions.

36. 用時最要是精神，精神煥發耳目真。任憑他人飛燕手，蟻鳴我聽龍虎吟。

When used (i.e., to fight), the most important (key) is the spirit of vitality. When spirit of vitality is brilliant and luminous (i.e., scintillating), the ears and the eyes are real (i.e., alert). (It) does not matter if the opponent's hands are (as fast as) a flying swallow, an ant's shouting to my listening is like a tiger's roaring.

This song is talking about fighting spirit. When your spirit of vitality is raised, you will be wholly alert to your situation. In this case, your ears and eyes will react fast and naturally. Even if your opponent's hands move as fast as a flying swallow, you will still be able to see them clearly. When you are in this highly alert condition, even the smallest sound or movement will seem as clear as a tiger's roar.

Ending Praise Song
歌贊

掌法拳法云師傳，傳出日久莫忘記。我歌我歌三十六，字字句句有深義。

The palm techniques, the fist techniques, gathered from teacher's pondering. Do not forget after long days of passage. Our songs, our secrets, there are thirty-six. Word, word, sentence, sentence, has deep meaning.

It is believed that these thirty-six songs were the secrets of Master Dong Hai-Chuan, which were the result of his ponderings and experiences. Every word and every sentence has a deep meaning. Those Baguazhang practitioners who take the time to study and comprehend them will surely find them an indispensable guide to the art.

B. 48 Secret Songs of Baguazhang
八卦掌四十八歌

1. Body Movement Method: (*Shen Fa*) 身法

手到步到要相隨，手到步落力必微。手腳俱到欠腰力，去時遲慢抽回難。

The hand arrives, the stepping must follow. The hand arrives and then the falling of stepping, the power must be weak. (Even if) the hand and feet arrive at the same time, but the waist lacks power, then when it goes (i.e., attacks), it will be late and slow and (when) withdrawing, it will also be difficult.

This song implies that, in order to have great manifestations of power, the hands, the stepping, and the waist should coordinate with each other perfectly, and synchronize as one unit. For example, if the hands arrive first, then afterward the stepping, the power will be weak. However, even if the hands and the stepping coordinate perfectly, without the coordination of the waist, both the attacking and the withdrawing will still be slow and stagnant.

2. Observing Method: (*Xiang Fa*) 相法

對御群敵相法先，未曾進步退當辨。退則審勢知變化，以逸待勞四兩牽。

Encountering the grouped enemies, first (you) observe (i.e., inspect) the situation. Before (your) advance, it is natural that (the first concern is) the withdrawing. (When) withdrawing, (you) should gauge the situation and know the (enemies') variations. Use the easiness to wait for the labor (i.e., use defense against offense) and use the four ounces to lead (i.e., neutralize)(the opponent's attack).

When you face many opponents at the same time, you must first calmly observe the situation. Since it is very difficult to defeat many opponents, it is prudent to first attempt to find a way to withdraw and escape from the surrounding enemies, so that you are not overwhelmed. Considering the situation in such a calm, detached manner will help to combat the fear you will naturally feel. When you fight against many opponents, you should also be concerned with conserving your energy. Don't be the aggressor when the odds are so against you. Take it easy and use defense as your offense. This situation will not resolve itself quickly. Try to last as long as possible, and look for an opportunity to escape.

3. Stepping Method: (*Bu Fa*) 步法

未曾動梢先動根，手快不如半步跟。進退出入只半步，制手避招而安神。

Before moving the ending, first move the root. (Even if) the hands are fast, still is not as speedy as moving with half stepping. (When) advancing for entering or withdrawing for retreating, use only half stepping. (This will allow you) to control the opponent and defend against the attacks with a peaceful spirit (i.e., mind).

When you are emitting or withdrawing your hands, you should first move their root. The shoulders are considered the root of the hands. Though the hands can move fast, they are still not as effective or speedy in a fight as is the half stepping strategy. When you step, the safest and fastest method is to use half steps instead of whole steps. The entire body can then act as one unit, and you will be able to advance and withdraw quickly and confidently. The half stepping technique is the key to advancing and withdrawing while maintaining root and stability.

4. Large Stepping Method: (*Mai Bu*) 邁法

功夫本從彎步來，兩手變化隨步開。高挑低摟橫掩避，推托帶領不離懷。

(Baguazhang) Gongfu originated from the bent stepping (i.e., stepping with bent knees). The variations of the two hands expands (i.e., extended) following the stepping. High, pick up; low, blush; and sideways, dodge to avoid. Pushing, lifting, carrying, and leading do not leave the chest.

All Baguazhang techniques are built on the foundation of stepping. The hand techniques are also varied and follow the stepping. Only when your hands techniques coordinate with skillful stepping are you capable of handling any possible conflict. When you apply the techniques in pushing, lifting, carrying, and leading, your hands should not come away from the chest area. You will then be able to keep your center and prevent your chest area from being exposed to the opponent's attack.

5. Continuous Stepping Method: (*Lian Bu Fa*) 連步法

連步必三費功夫，使手要簡自然無。搭手轉身是空手，機會恰巧是江湖。

(It takes) too much Gongfu if the continuous stepping must be three. The usage of hands should be simple, (then it) will be natural without being restricted. (Once) contact with the (opponent's) hand, (immediately) turn the body is insubstantial. (You will be) a real "River and Lake" (*Jiang Hu*, i.e., expert) if (you are able to) catch the right opportunity.

If all your stepping movements always involve three steps, then you are much too restricted and have wasted Gongfu (i.e., energy-time) in your training. How you step in a fight depends upon the situation, but it should always be simple and fast. In the same way, the applications of the hands' techniques should be simple. Only then will you be able to vary them naturally, skillfully, and freely. In a fight, once you make contact with the opponent's hands, immediately turn your body and become insubstantial. This will trick your opponent into advancing, and he will enter your trap. Naturally, you must utilize accurate timing for this opportunity. "*Jiang Hu*" means "River-Lake," and denotes those martial arts experts who have traveled around the river and lake many times.

6. Pause Stepping Method: (*Dun Bu Fa*) 頓步法

頓步不要兩相濟，前虛后實至參差。前要站齊前后仰，亦且腰短少靈機。

In pause stepping, both (legs) do not support each other mutually. The front (leg) is insubstantial and the rear (leg) is substantial; both are mutually exchangeable. (If) the front (leg) must also be the same (i.e., substantial as the rear leg), then the body will either lean forward or backward. In addition, the waist will also be lacking the capability of agility and mobility.

Before you change the form in Baguazhang walking, there is often a short pulse. This short pulse in stepping is called "*Dun Bu*." When you are in the pulse stepping, the front and the rear legs should be crossing and interchangeable. The front leg should be insubstantial, and the rear leg should be substantial. If you do not do this, your legs will be double weighted, and this could cause your body to easily lean forward or backwards. Not only that, this poor stepping posture can also affect your waist's agile movements.

7. Hand Method: (*Shou Fa*) 手法

偏沈則隨雙重滯，外硬裡軟抬槍式。橫推裡勾身有主，只有吸手腰腹隨。

Partial and sunk, then will follow (the opponent); double layering (i.e., mutual resistance), then stagnant. External is hard and internal is soft, like the posture of holding a spear. (When coming) sideways, (you) push, and (when) attacked from inside, (you) hook; (then your) body has a master. (You) only look for the sticking hands with the following of the the waist and the abdomen.

If your power is not centered and sunk, it can be easily led by your opponent. If your strength and your opponent's mutually resist each other, then your strength will be slow and stagnant. When you apply your power, even though it looks hard externally, it is actually soft internally. This is like the trick of handling a spear. The power can be varied, free, unrestricted and yet strong. If the opponent attacks you from the side, you use push to handle the problem; if the opponent attacks you from the center (i.e., internally), you use hook to neutralize him. It does not matter how you handle the attacks, you always keep yourself centered both mentally and physically. What you are looking for is how to stick and adhere to your opponent's hand, and how to use your waist and abdomen to dominate the encounter.

8. Techniques of *Li* (or *Jin*): (*Li Fa*) 力法

人說冷彈脆快硬，我說冷快是一般。脆硬細分無二致，發動全憑心力合。

People say there are cold, spring, breaking, speedy, and hard (*Jins*). I say the cold (*Jin*) and the speedy (*Jin*) are the same. (If we) distinguish brittleness and hardness in detail, there is no difference. The emitting (of *Jin*) all depends on the combination of the Heart (i.e., emotional mind) and the *Li* (muscular power).

In Chinese martial arts, *Jin* and *Li* are commonly used to categorize the strength of the power manifested. The main difference between them is that with *Jin*, the Qi is of more concern and with *Li*, muscular power is emphasized more. Though many people like to distinguish between different *Jins* or Lis in detail, the trick of manifesting them is actually the same. All of the manifestations of *Jin* and *Li* actually originate from the combination and the coordination of the mind and the physical body.

9. Techniques of Storing *Li*: (*Cun Li Fa*) 存力法

只會使力不會存，力過猶如箭出弦。不但無功卻有害，輕輸重折且失身。

Only know how to use the *Li* and do not know how to store it, then the *Li* can be over manifested, just like the arrow is released from the bow. (It) will fail to achieve the goal but will also bring harm. (If) the defeat is light, you lost the battle, if the defeat is heavy, then bend and lose the body (i.e., life).

When you manifest your power, you should not release it completely, like an arrow is released from a bow. Instead, you should keep and store some of the power to prepare for the next action. In this case, your power will be continuous and not broken. Even though your mind is focused on offense, you must not neglect defense. If you release your power completely, once you are neutralized and attacked, you will not be able to retreat to a defensive position. Consequently, you will lose the battle.

10. Techniques to Continue *Li*: (*Xu Li Fa*) 續力法

力著他人根已斷，若再續力彼難逃。此法隨時沖前步，長腰長膀一齊交。

(When your) power reaches the opponent, (his) root is broken. If (you) further continue (your) power, the opponent will be hard to escape. The method is to follow the timing and use the thrust forward stepping. (In addition,) extend (your) waist and extend arms and apply them together.

It does not matter if you are attacking your opponent or neutralizing his attack, once your power is emitted, you should have broken his root and destroyed his balance. If you catch this opportunity and attack continuously, it will be very difficult for your opponent to escape. The method of reaching this goal is that once you have caught the right timing, you thrust forward with all your body's power, extending your body and arms as much as possible in order to reach your opponent.

11. Subduing the Opponent's Method: (*Xiang Ren Fa*) 降人法

快打慢兮不足誇，強制弱兮不為佳。最好比人高一著，顧盼中定不為發。

It should not be proud if the fast defeats the slow. It should also not be pleased if the strong beats the weak. The best is (that you are) better than others in one step further. (The trick is) look to the left, beware of the right, and be steady in the center; (when) it is not appropriate, do not emit.

To use speed and strength to defeat an opponent is not strange and marvelous. The best way is to use the techniques and strategy to handle a situation skillfully. A true expert will not win a battle solely by strength and speed. He will also know the strategy of centering, and be aware of the entire situation. Then he will be able to catch the best opportunity to manifest his techniques most effectively.

12. Techniques to Decide Winning: (*Jue Sheng Fa*) 決勝法

彼力千鈞快如梭，避強用順快不挪。千人只有三五近，稍伸手腳不能遮。

The opponent's power is a thousand pounds and fast as the weaver's shuttle. (You should) avoid the strength and use the following strategy. (If he is) fast, (you can solve the problem) simply with movement. (If there are) thousands of opponents, only three to five are able to (get) close to you. Just extend your hands and legs; (they) cannot stop you (from escaping).

Jun was the unit of weight used in earlier times. One *Jun* equals 30 catties. A catty is an Asian unit of weight generally equivalent to 1 1/3 pounds. The shuttle was used to weave cloth in ancient China. A skillful weaver could move the shuttle so fast that you could not see his or her hands.

If your opponent is both powerful and fast, then you should use your moving strategy in order to avoid his strong power and to confuse his speedy attacks. Even though you are facing thousands of opponents, you should not be scared. Only three to five persons will be able to get near you at any one time. You should be confident in handling three to five attacks at once, and when you decide to escape, no one can stop you.

13. Application of Methods: (*Yong Fa*) 用法

高打矮兮矮打高，斜打胖兮不須搖。前遇瘦長憑將帶，年邁無功上下瞧。

(When the opponent is) tall, (you) strike low and (when the opponent is) short, (you) strike high. Use the side strike to attack the fat (opponent), which (he) is limited to move around. (If) encountered a skinny and tall (opponent), then plug and pull. There is no merit (fighting) against an old man, (simply) look at him up and down.

When your opponent is tall, you focus on a low attack, and if he is short, you will concentrate on attacking his upper body. If you encounter a fat person, you should move to his side and attack him from there. Due to the limitations in his ability to move quickly, you will be able to put your opponent in a defensive situation. If you meet a tall and skinny opponent, then it will be easy for you to grab and pull. However, if the opponent is an old man, then you will not feel proud, even if you can win over him easily. Therefore, you should avoid the fight and only look at him with a confused and puzzled expression.

14. Encounter and Seal Method: (*Feng Bi Fa*) 逢閉法

手講三關腳要屈，一手三關腳直迂。肩肘腕胯膝可用，縮頭空胸步帶軀。

Hands (should) talk about three gates and the legs should be bent. Single hand's three gates (depend on) the leg's straight or curved. Shoulders, elbows, wrists, internal hips, and knees are useful. Withdrawing the neck, empty the chest, and (use) the steppings carry the body.

Three gates on the arms are the shoulders, the elbows, and the wrists. Three gates on the legs are the internal hips/groin, the knees, and the waist. The three gates on the arms and legs must coordinate and support each other. Only then will the hands be able to move with the stepping, and the stepping be varied in order to coordinate with the hand movements.

Whenever you encounter a dangerous situation, you should immediately seal your upper and lower three gates. All the variations of the three gates depend on how you step, either in a straight line or in a curved one. In addition to the coordination of the three gates on the arms and legs, you should also withdraw your neck and hold in your chest. In this position, you have sealed all of your vital areas and your posture is firm.

15. Pressing Fist Method: (*An Quan Fa*) 按拳法

五花八門亂如麻，長拳短打渾相加。你越快兮我越慢，我若發時鬼神怕。

Five flowers and eight doors (i.e., many styles) are random like hemp. The long fists and short strikes all are added together. The faster you are, the slower I am. (But) if I emit (my power), the ghost and the divine are scared.

Five flowers implies many techniques, and eight doors means various styles. Hemp is a fibrous plant used to weave rope and clothes. The hemp fibers are cut and, after drying, lie random and confused. The first sentence means that it does not matter what techniques from any given style the opponent is using, the principles will be the same. The fighting techniques can be long range, short range or a combination of the two. The faster your opponent is, the slower you will be in dealing with him. But if you have practiced diligently, once you are ready and have caught the opportunity to emit your power, it will be so powerful that even the ghosts and the divine will be afraid.

16. Against Plug and Grab Method: (*Zhai Na Fa*)　摘拿法

多少拿法莫誇技，二手拿一力固奇。任他神拿怕過頂，穿鼻刺目勢難攻。

Do not brag how many grabbing techniques (that you have). It is marvellous that the strength of two hands are able to control one. (However), it does not matter how skillful his grabbing is, (he is) afraid (the hands) are over the head. (In addition), boring the nose and poke the eyes are able to make (his) attack very difficult.

Though Baguazhang does not emphasize too many Qin Na applications, it does have a good strategy against Qin Na grabbing. It does not matter if your opponent grabs with one hand or two. Once your arm is grabbed, immediately raise it above your head. In this position, your opponent's power will be difficult to apply. In addition, you should also use the other hand to punch his nose or poke his eyes. In order to save himself, your opponent will have to release you from the grab.

17. Connect Single and Remedy with Double Method: (*Jie Dan Bu Shuang Fa*)　接單補雙法

莫說二手仗堅兵，一來一往是其能。閉住右手左無用，雙手齊來更無功。

Let us talk not but about the two barehands fighting against the strong weapons. One to and one fro is its capability. Sealing the right hand the left hand is useless. (If) coming with both hands, it is even harder (for him) to achieve his goal.

This song talks about fighting barehanded against an armed opponent. It does not matter if the opponent uses a single weapon or double weapons in both hands. For an effective attack, in order to balance the extended arm holding the weapon, the other hand is usually placed behind. Then you merely take care of his front hand with the weapon, and his other hand will be of no concern. However, if your opponent attacks with double weapons forward in both of his hands at the same time, then you must dodge and avoid his attacks. When you find him withdrawing, you then have a good opportunity to counterattack.

18. Pointing to the Mountain and Striking the Grindstone Method: (*Zhi Shan Da Mo Fa*)　指山打磨法

他人來手我不然，側身還擊我自還。他前還時我入手，他前封時三手連。

(When) the opponent's hand comes (i.e., attacks), I do not think so (i.e., it is ignored). Slant (my) body to return with an attack, is my natural return (i.e., reaction). (When) his front hand is returning, I enter (my) hand. (If) he uses his front hand to seal my attack, (I) use three linking attacks.

When the opponent attacks you, the best technique is to ignore the attack without intercepting or blocking. Simply dodge to the side, or incline your body to avoid the attack. While your opponent's mind is still in the attacking mode, you attack him from his side. In this situation, he must withdraw his attacking hand to save himself. When he withdraws his front hand, you should use the opportunity to attack him. If he seals the first attack while withdrawing, then continue attacking three times. This will break through his sealing.

19. Escape the Body and Change into the Shadow Method: (*Tuo Shen Hua Ing Fa*) 脫身化影法

他不來時我叫來，他前來時我化開。不須身避憑身取，步步不離二胯哉。

(If) the opponent does not come (i.e., attack), I call him to come. (When) he comes, then I yield and neutralize his coming. Do not need the body's avoiding (i.e., intercepting or blocking), depending (only) on the body's taking (i.e., movements). Every step do not ignore the (keys) of the two hips.

When you and your opponent both balance each other and neither attacks, you must fake your attack in order to force a reaction. When he attacks, immediately yield and withdraw. When you find him withdrawing, attack again immediately. In this case, you will place your opponent on the defensive. The key to making this strategy successful is to move your body around skillfully, instead of using just a hand to block or intercept. In order to move your body fast and steadily, you must keep the hips and thighs firm and agile.

20. Turning the Body to the (Opponent's) Back Method: (*Bei Hou Zhuan Shen Fa*) 背后轉身法

伸手要小步要大，開步半跨貼身抓。跨步落地蹲身轉，他若轉時我鷹拿。

(When advancing), extending hands must be small and the stepping must be big. (When turning), open your stepping (with) half hips (i.e., step) sticking with the (opponent's) body to grab. (When) the steps touch the ground, squat down to turn the body. If he (also) turns, then I grab him like an eagle.

In Baguazhang, turning is commonly used to sneak up to the opponent's back. When doing the turning body technique, the distance between you and the opponent should be short, separated only by half a step. This will prevent you from overextending your arms, and you will have root and strength for grabbing. When you step to advance, the step should be big and fast and when you turn, the step should be small, and the body squatting. If your opponent also turns while you are turning, immediately use a grab to destroy his turning balance.

21. Against Striking, Smashing, Chopping, and Bumping Method: (*Ke Za Pi Zhuang Fa*) 磕砸劈撞法

磕來還磕我要先，砸右換步左手招。劈來迭肘桩橫之，撞來乾坤手搖圈。

When strike comes and I strike back, I must be first. (If) smashing to my right, (I) change my steps and (use) the left hand to handle (the attack). (When) the chopping is coming, (I) flatten my elbow and (press him) horizontally. (If) he bumps me, (then I use) *Qian Kung* hands (i.e., both hands) to move a circle.

The best fighting strategy is "When the opponent does not move, you do not move. When your opponent moves slightly, you move first." This means the timing of the strike is very important. When your opponent moves slightly, his mind is on attacking and not on defending. If you attack him suddenly at this instant, you will catch a good opportunity to reach your goal. If your right side is attacked, shift your left leg forward and use your left hand to neutralize the attack. If he is chopping you, use the elbow to stroke him horizontally. In this case, he will lose his balance and striking power. If the opponent uses the shoulder or the body to bump you, simply use both hands to grab and circle while either retreating or turning your body to the side. This will lead his bumping power into emptiness.

22. Half Circle Hand Method: (*Ban Quan Shou Fa*) 半圈手法

他人手法多直線，跨上半步如等閒。即或指直打斜線，再跨半步不相干。

(If) the opponent's hand techniques are in a straight line, (you) step forward half step like nothing happening. Even if aiming forward but strike diagonally, again (you) step half step and ignore its coming.

If your opponent attacks you with the straight forward techniques, you simply circle to the side with half a step, you will be able to avoid his attack easily. Even if the attack is diagonally, you will still be able to avoid the attack with the half circle stepping.

23. Full Circle Hand Method: (*Zheng Quan Shou Fa*) 整圈手法

四面敵人我在中，穿花打柳任西東。八方憑勢風雲變，不守呆式不守空。

Four sides (full) with enemies and I am in the center, (I) bore the flower and strike the willow, (move) the west and the east as I wish. (To dissolve) the forces from eight directions depends on the variations of the wind and the clouds. Do not keep the dull technique and do not keep the emptiness.

Four sides means the front, the rear, the left, and the right. If you are surrounded on all four directions by many enemies, you will move like a butterfly boring into the bushes. In this case, you can solve the surrounded problem, escaping from the midst of your opponents.

Eight directions means the four sides and the four corners. If you are surrounded even more tightly on all eight directions, you cannot bore around as easily as before. You must move like the wind and the clouds to confuse the opponents. You must not keep steady in the same posture or keep the defensive position all the time. If you maintain a dull posture and a defensive position, you will be unable to exploit any possible chance to escape. The best way to fight so many opponents is to circle around. Keep changing insubstantial and substantial strategy to confuse the opponent and prevent them from coordinating with each other. Then, you will be able to create a good opportunity for your escape.

24. Mind (Heart)-Eye Method: (*Xin Yan Fa*) 心眼法

心如大將眼如法，見景生情能制他。最戀心痴眼不准，手忙腳亂費周折。

The heart (i.e., mind) is like a great general and the eyes act methodically (i.e., accurate and controlled). (When) the eyes see the scene, (immediately) the (mind) generates the emotion (i.e., idea), (then it is) able to defeat the opponent. The worst is (when) the mind is obscure and the eyes are not accurate, (then) the hands are busy and the feet are confused and the effort is wasted.

When you fight, your mind and eyes must coordinate with each other. When the eyes see what is happening, the mind immediately decides how to respond. Only then will your fighting be alert, agile, and effective. However, if your mind is not clear and the eyes' response to an action is slow and confused, then you are wasting your effort in your fighting.

25. Steady Eyes Techniques: (*Ding Yan Fa*) 定眼法

四面刀槍亂如麻，又當昏夜目無華，矮身定睛招路廣，步法實行自行他。

The sabers and spears (i.e., weapons) on four sides are random as hemp (i.e., many). Again it is a

dim and dark night that the eyes are not bright (i.e., cannot see clearly). Shorten (your) body and steady (your) eyes, inspect the path (i.e., surroundings) widely. (Then you will be) able to execute (your) decision and do what (you) wish.

If you are facing multiple armed opponents at a time when you cannot see clearly, you should keep your posture as low as possible. Your opponents will not be able to spot you or see your movement easily. You should also calm your mind, and focus your eyes on inspecting the surroundings. Through low posture, focused eyes, and careful listening, you will be able to understand the opponents intention and movements clearly.

26. Receiving the Weapon Techniques: (*Jie Qi Fa*)　接器法

長短單雙器固精，算來不如二手靈。鐵掌練來兵一樣，肉手偏我肱腕行。

Though it is essential (i.e., important or critical) that (if I) have long or short, single or double weapons, still, they (the weapons) are not as agile as both barehands. (If I) train (my) iron palms, it is the same as (I) have weapons. (If I) have only barehands, (then) I will aiming the (opponent's) forearms and wrists.

In a fight, if you have a weapon, naturally you will have an advantage for the battle. However, if you do not have a weapon, you should not allow yourself to panic. Afterall, a weapon is not necessarily as agile as both barehands. Especially if you have trained "Iron Sand Palm," then it is the same as if you have weapons. In ancient Chinese martial society, in order to have an effective self-defense capability, "Iron Sand Palm" training was very common. When you fight barehanded against an armed opponent, you should always focus your defense on sticking to and controlling his forearms and wrists. He will then not be able to manage his weapon skillfully.

27. Protecting the Body Techniques: (*Bao Shen Fa*)　保身法

以強勝弱不足誇，弱能勝強方是法。任他離弦箭快硬，左右磨身保無差。

(You) should not brag of using the strong to defeat the weak. To use the weak to beat the strong is the techniques (of Baguazhang). It does not matter if the arrow leaving the bow's string is fast and strong, (you) rub the (opponent's) body (i.e., closely stick with the opponent body) left and right, (it) guarantees no mistake.

If you are strong and are able to defeat your weak opponent, then you should not brag or be proud of yourself. However, if you are a weak person and able to overcome a strong opponent, then your techniques must be good. This is the way of Baguazhang. It does not matter if your opponent's power and speed are just like an arrow leaving the string of a bow, as long as you know how to stick to him closely, then he will not be able to execute his powerful attack on you effectively.

28. Confuse the Opponent Techniques: (*Luan Ren Fa*)　亂人法

心亂先從眼上亂，千招不如掌一穿。對準鼻梁連環使，跨步制人左右還。

(If) the mind is confused, first the eyes are confused. A thousand techniques are not as (effective) as a boring of the palm. Aim accurately at the nose bridge and attack continuously. Large step in to control the opponent with (the boring of) the left (hand) and return with the right.

Before a person's mind is confused, the attention of his eyes must first be distracted. If you desire to confuse your opponent, you may simply use the boring palm to continuously attack the area between the eyes with left hand and right hand. This will confuse his eyes and therefore his mind. When this happens, you will have created an advantageous opportunity to attack .

29. Open and Close Techniques: (*Kai He Fa*)　開合法

欲合先開是一般，見開防合不二傳。詐敗佯輸知卷土，指東打西意中含。

It is natural that if (you) desire to close, you first should open. There is no alternative that (when you) see the (opponent's) opening, (you) should be aware of closing. (When your opponent is) faking defeat and pretending to have lost, (you) know that (he will) return like the whirling dust. Pointing to the east, (actually) striking the west, the meaning is contented.

We all know that in order to close, you must first open. Therefore, when you see the opponent is opening, be aware of his closing. Conversely, when he is closing, be aware of his opening. When an opponent is defeated too easily, you must avoid being tricked. It is common that when an opponent is pointing to the east, he may in fact be aiming to the west.

30. Firm the South Techniques (i.e., The Method of Gauging the Situation): (*Ding Nan Fa*) 定南法

任他千手千眼快，守中中身是枉然。不到要時不伸手，伸手即教發手還。

It does not matter if (your) opponents are as fast as a thousand hands and a thousand eyes. (As long as) you keep (your) center and protect (your) body, (the opponents' attacks) will still be in vain. (If) it is not the time, (you) do not extend (your) hand (i.e., attack). (Once you) extend (your) hand, (you will) immediately force (your opponent's to) return (their) attacking hands.

It does not matter if there are many opponents who are attacking, as long as you know how to keep and protect your center, then all of the opponents' attempts will be in vain. When you are in this situation, you will pay more attention to defending instead of attacking. However, if you see a good opportunity you should not hesitate to attack. When you attack, it is so powerful and efficient that the opponents must retreat their attacks to protect themselves.

31. Closing Techniques: (*Qiu Jin Fa*) 求近法

封躲固是擴身法，躲過他人自逍遙。切忌遠擊尺步外，開門繞道法不牢。

Surely sealing and dodging are the techniques for keeping distance. (After) avoiding the opponent('s attack), (you) naturally are free. (However) remember to not strike (when you) are farther than few steps away. (The way of) opening the (opponent's) door by circling the path is not secure.

It is good if you know the methods of sealing and dodging skillfully. These techniques enable you to free yourself and to keep a safe distance from your opponent. However, if you keep doing so, you will also lose the proper distance of your attack with Baguazhang techniques. The best distance for application of Baguazhang techniques is less than a half step. If you always keep yourself on the defense, without ever attacking, then you will always be defeated.

32. Six Paths Techniques: (*Liu Lu Fa*) 六路法

他人六路是空兮，我之掌式六路觀。動步既能八方顧，瞻前顧后自無難。

(It does not matter if) the opponent's six paths are all empty, the postures of my palms inspect (i.e., are aware of) six paths. Since the moving steppings are able to look after the eight directions, it will not be difficult to take care of the front and the rear (attacks).

The six paths are the forward, the backward, to the left, to the right, upward, and downward. Even if there is a chance for you to attack the opponent's empty door in the six paths, you must still be aware of the eight directions around your body, and keep your postures in a position which will permit you to react immediately if there is a confrontation.

The eight directions means the four sides and the four diagonals. Since Baguazhang specializes in constantly moving and changing directions, you should be able to easily take care of attacks from all eight directions.

33. Unique Techniques: (*Bu Er Fa*) 不二法

法不准兮不妄發，發不中兮第二發。任他鬼神多妙靈，不勾魂兮亦裂牙。

(If your) techniques cannot be accurate (i.e., working), (you) do not emit. (If) the attack misses the target, (you immediately) charge (emit) the second strike. It does not matter if (the opponent is) as marvellous and spiritual as a ghost or the divine, (you) will be able to break (his) teeth if not seize (his) soul (i.e., kill the opponent).

This song reminds you that when you attack, you must be sure that you can hit the target before you emit. However, if you miss your first attack, you should immediately execute your second attack without hesitation. If you can catch the right opportunity and attack powerfully and continuously, you will be able to scare and hopefully defeat your opponent.

34. Prevent From Slipping Techniques: (*Fang Hua Fa*) 防滑法

冰天雪地步難勞，前橫后直記心梢。轉動須用小開步，切忌挺身打法高。

Frozen heaven and snowy ground, the firm steppings are difficult. Remember in (your) heart that the front (foot) is sideways and the rear (foot) is straight forward. (When) turning (you) must use the small opening steppings. Remember not to thrust (your) chest and strike high in (your) techniques.

When you are fighting on slippery ground, you must be very careful not to fall down. You do this by having your front foot turned sideways while the rear foot is straight. When you step, do not use large steps. Instead, you should use small steps. Do not stand high and thrust your chest and attempt to strike high. When you intend to strike high, your root will float.

35. Steady Stepping Techniques: (*Wen Bu Fa*) 穩步法

步不穩兮身必搖，腳踏實地勝千招。進軀足趾退懸踵，不扣步兮莫回瞧。

(When) the steppings are not steady, the body will also be shaking. The feet stepping on solid ground (i.e., rooted) are better than (charging) thousand techniques (without rooted). Advancing forward with the toes and retreating backward with suspended heels (i.e., lift the heel first). (If you are) not arcing (your) steppings, do not look backward (i.e., turn around).

When you are rooted and balanced in your walking, your body will not be shaky. An attack with a firm root is much better than if you charge a thousand times without a steady root. The reason for this is because, if you do not have a firm root, your attack will be weak and useless. In order to be steady in your walking, when you advance touch down with the toes first and when you step backward, land with the heel first. When you turn, you should use the arcing stepping which is specially designed and trained for turning the body.

36. Small Stepping Techniques: (*Xiao Bu Fa*) 小步法

回身轉步必須小，步大全身不靈巧。欲要轉身邁半步，人難擒兮人不曉。

(When) turning the body, the turning steps must be small. (If) steps are big, the entire body will not be agile and nimble. If (you) desire to turn (your) body, move with half steps. (Then it will be) hard for (your) opponent to seize (you) and know (your) intention.

This song tells you that when you are turning your body, the turning steppings should be small. When they are small, the movements can be fast and agile. Also, if you move only half a step each time, you won't reveal your intention to your opponent.

37. Palm Techniques: (*Zhang Fa*) 掌法

掌法雖有上中下，上下不過是架勢。圓轉自如是中盤，高下全以此變化。

Though palm techniques are classified top, middle, and bottom sections, actually, the top and the bottom are only postures. (In fact,) the palm techniques which (can be) turned with round and naturally are on the middle section. (The techniques on) the top and the bottom sections all depend on the variations of this (middle section).

Though the palm techniques can be classified into the high, middle, and lower levels, in fact, only those techniques applicable to the middle section can easily be round, natural, and skillful. The high and the low level techniques are used to coordinate with the techniques used on the middle section.

38. Forbid Bowing Forward Techniques: (*Ji Fu Fa*) 忌俯法

低頭如同眼不開，亦且身易往前栽。低頭貓腰中樞死，全步全掌使不來。

Bowing (your) head is just like (your) eyes not opening. In addition, the body can lead forward and fall easily. Bowing the head with the cat's waist (i.e., extend the head forward), (your) center body will be dead (i.e., dull). (In this case, you) will not be able to use your entire step and whole palm (i.e., entire capability of the skills).

When you fight, your head should not bow and extend forward. If you do this, it is the same as if you are closing your eyes. Furthermore, since your body is leaning forward, you have lost your center and can easily fall. Worst of all, when you extend your head forward, you will lose your center, balance, and root. Consequently, you will not be able to execute your techniques efficiently.

39. Forbid Looking Upward Techniques: (*Ji Yang Fa*) 忌仰法

緊背空胸靜中求，挺胸坦腹悔難防。疊肚吸腰來不及，最怕轉身不自由。

Tighten (i.e., arc) the back and empty (i.e., hold in) the chest, find (the actions) in the calmness. (If) thrust the chest and expose the abdomen, (you) will regret how hard to defend. (When a situation occurs, then you) fold in your stomach and withdraw your waist, it will be too late. What should worry (you) the most is that (you) will lose the freedom of turning (your) body.

When you are in a fight, your back should be arced and the chest held inward. Then your chest will be loose and comfortable while breathing. This will make you feel easy, and the mind can be calm. However, if you thrust out your chest and stomach, the front side of the body will be tense. This will result your movements being stagnant. Do not wait until the last second, when the combat is already on, to withdraw your chest and abdomen. This will be too late. The worst part of poor posture is that it will hinder you from easily turning your body.

40. Upright Body Techniques: (*Zheng Shen Fa*) 正身法

全身力量在中懷，自身歪斜力不固。別看步歪身必正，發手如箭不停留。

The entire body's power is in the center chest. (If) self body is inclined, the power will not be strong. Though (sometimes) the steppings are tilted (i.e., curved), the body must remain upright. (Then you may) emit (your) hand as an arrow without stagnation.

When you fight, you must always remain centered. If your body is not centered, you will not have good balance or rooting, and the power you emit will be stagnant and weak. Although in Baguazhang your steppings are curved, your body should still remain upright. Only then can you emit your hands like arrows released from the bow.

41. Assist Body Techniques: (*Fu Shen Fa*) 輔身法

身如主宰腰腿隨，主正身強力能摧。進退閃躲憑身法，前無腰腿力必微。

The body is like a master in charge (the situation), the waist and the legs follow. (If) the body/master is upright and precise, the power (generated) will be able to smash (your opponent). Advance, retreat, dodge, and escape, all depend on the body movement. (If) all of these (are done) without waist and leg coordination, the (attacking) power must be weak.

The center body (i.e., the head and the torso) is like a master who takes charge of all actions. The waist and the legs are only used to coordinate the decisions and actions of the center body. If the body's decisions and actions are accurate and precise, with good coordination of the waist and legs, the power generated will be so great that it may crush any opponent.

42. Obstinate the Body Techniques: (*Yao Shen Fa*) 拗身法

人來制我已貼身，此時手腳不贏人。左右吸收回拗法，化險為夷把人擒。

(If) the opponent comes to attack me and (his) body has already adhered (to me), at this moment, (my) hands and the legs cannot win the opponent (i.e., not effective). (Then, I should move my body) left and right to yield (the attack) and return with the body's turning (to his back). (This) will vary the danger into safety and be able to seize the opponent.

If the opponent is very skillful in sticking and adhering techniques such as in Taijiquan, he will find an opportunity to get closer to you and adhere to you. When you are already in a situation like this, your hands and legs will not be effective in striking. The way to deal with this condition is to move your body to the left and right to yield and neutralize his attacks. When you grasp the opportunity, you can turn your body and move behind his back. In this case, you will be able to dissolve the dangerous situation which you have encountered.

43. Big Side-Stepping Techniques: (*Kua Bu Ce Shen Fa*) 跨步側身法

穿梭直入勢難停，先發制人顯他能。若遇此手接連退，不如跨步側身靈。

(If the opponent's attack is) straight forward with boring, his advance will be hard to stop. (In this case, he has) already charged (his) attacks and manifested his capability. If encountering this (capable) opponent, (you) should continue retreating. (However), it is still not as agile as (if you can) step to the side with the big steppings.

If you encounter an opponent who is very talented in using the boring palm to attack you in a straight line, you will probably be forced to retreat continuously. However, if you continue your retreating while he continues his boring attack, you will not be able to improve your situation. The best way of solving this problem is to take a big step to the side. This will force your opponent to change his forward direction and slow down his attack. This will offer you an opportunity to counter-attack.

44. Left and Right Swinging Body Techniques: (*Zuo You Shuai Shen Fa*) 左右摔身法

閃躲東方西又來，搖身一變摔身開。左右連環皆如此，前推后捋腰安排。

Dodge and escape to the east, the attack from the west is again coming. (You simply) swing and vary (your) body (posture) and (again) throw (your) body away with distance. All left and right are repeated continuously like this. Push forward and pluck backward, the waist is able to arrange skillfully.

If you dodge and escape from your opponent's attack from the east, and again he attacks from the west, then you should move your body skillfully and keep a good distance from your opponent. When you do this, continue to move your body to the left and then to the right with the coordination of your palms. Then you will be able to find a good opportunity to push him forward and pluck and pull him backward. The success of all of this depends on how skillfully you manage your waist.

45. Squat and Sunken Body Techniques: *(Dun Bu Chen Shen Fa)* 蹲步沉身法

身高架大路上三，舉手招封勢所難。蹲身沉身便就下，入我機關用法寬。

(If the opponent's) body is high and the frame is big (i.e., strong), (he will focus his attacks) on the top three paths. (If I) lift (my) hands to block and to seal (the attacks), it would be difficult. (In this case, I should) squat the body and sink the posture, forcing (my opponent to) follow (my) low posture. (Once the opponent) enters my trick, (my) applications will be wide (i.e., numerous).

If your opponent is tall, big and strong, he will have expertise in attacking your upper body. The three paths means forward, left, and right. If you encounter an opponent like this, it will be very difficult to block or seal his powerful attacks. In this case, you should squat down and sink your body into a very low posture. This will restrict the opponent's attack and offer you more chances to attack and defend yourself.

46. Forbidden Grabbing Techniques: *(Ji Na Fa)* 忌拿法

八卦之手不講拿，我拿人兮我亦差。設前人多不方便，直出直入已堪誇。

The Bagua's hands (i.e., techniques) do not talk about grabbing. (If) I grab the opponent, I am also clumsy (as my opponent). Assume there are many opponents in front (of me), (the grabbing) will cause many inconvenience. Straight out and straight in will be enough to brag (i.e., handle the problem).

Baguazhang does not emphasize Qin Na techniques. Instead the palm techniques receive more attention. If you use the Qin Na techniques to control, you will be as clumsy as your opponent. Assume there are many opponents who are attacking you, if you control only one of them with your Qin Na techniques, all others can still attack you. This will still place you in a poor position. However if you are an expert in using your palms for attacking, then you will be able to enter and withdraw from the crowd of opponents as you wish.

47. Forbid Standing Techniques: *(Ji Zhan Fa)* 忌站法

渾元一氣走天涯，八卦真理是我家。招招不離腳變化，站住即為落地花。

(I rely on) the Entire Original Sole Qi to travel the heavenly remote places. The Bagua true theory is in my home. Every technique does not separate from the variations of the stepping. (If) standing still, (then) it is like the fallen flowers.

If your Entire Original Sole Qi (Pre-Heaven Qi) is strong and abundant, you will be so strong and your techniques so powerful that you can travel between heaven and earth without any enemy. You have mastered the true Bagua theory as completely as if in your own home. Each technique executed is not separated from the variations of your stepping. If you stand still when you fight, then you will be just like a fallen flower that people can step on as they wish.

48. Great Ultimate Techniques: *(Tai Shang Fa)* 太上法

力要足活招要准，即或使空三不紊。招套招兮無窮極，精神法術在手純。

The power must be sufficient and the alive techniques must be accurate. Even (your) attacks are entering emptiness (i.e., useless) for three times, (you are) not flustered (i.e., remain calm). The technique against technique and there is no end to it. The spirit of the techniques depends on the mastery.

When you execute your Baguazhang techniques, the power is strong and the techniques are alive and accurate. When you attack, even if your techniques have failed three times, you still remain calm and centered. In every technique which your opponent attacks you, you always have a counter technique to neutralize the attack. All of the calm fighting spirit and skills depend on how much you have mastered the techniques. This means that if you have mastered all your techniques that can be executed naturally and automatically, then you will have built up your confidence and skill of fighting.

4. Three Harms for Beginners [11]
初學入門三害

三害者何？一曰努氣。二曰拙力。三曰填胸提腹。用努氣者，太剛則折。易生胸滿氣逆肺炸諸症。譬之心君不和，百官自失其位。

What are the three harms? The first says "forced Qi," the second says "clumsy Li," and the third says "Full chest and lifted abdomen." Using "forced Qi" is too stiff and can be broken easily, (it can) easily generate the sicknesses of a chest full of adverse Qi and fry the lungs. It is like the heart sovereign is not in harmony, and the hundreds of officials lose their stations.

There are three dangers when a beginner starts to practice Baguazhang. These are: "Rushing the Qi," "Using too much muscular strength," and "Holding the breath."

It is said: "Use the mind to 'lead' the Qi." Qi is like water which can easily be led but cannot be pushed. When Qi is pushed, the mind will be broken and the Qi will not be continuous. Consequently, the Qi will flow upward and cannot be sunk to the Lower *Dan Tian*. When this happens, the heart and the lungs will be on fire (i.e., too Yang). When the heart is on fire, the entire body's Qi will be agitated and will lose its harmony

用拙力者，四肢百骸，血脈不能流通，經絡不能舒暢。陰火上升，心為拙氣所滯。滯於何處，何處為病。輕者肉中發跳。重者攻之疼痛。甚之可以結成瘡毒諸害。

Using "clumsy Li," (in) the four limbs and hundreds of bones, (the blood in) the blood vessels cannot be circulated and (the Qi in) the *Jing* (primary Qi channels) and *Luo* (secondary Qi channels) cannot be (transported) smoothly and harmoniously. (Consequently,) the Yin fire rises. The heart is stagnant (i.e., mind is not clear) due to the clumsy Qi. Where this Qi is stagnant, there is sickness. When it is light, the muscles jump, when it is heavy, it is painful when touched. Furthermore, it can cause harms such as poisonous boils.

When you use too much muscular power, the muscles and tendons will be tense. This will result in poor Qi circulation. When the Qi circulation is not smooth and harmonious, the excess Qi will stagnate deep inside the body, manifesting itself on the surface of the skin (Yin fire). In less serious cases, the nervous system will not obtain proper Qi nourishment, producing a twitch or "jump" in the skin or muscles. If the case is very serious, muscle cramps and pain will result. If this is not treated properly, the Yin fire can cause skin problems, such as poisonous boils.

填胸提腹者，逆氣上行不歸丹田。兩足無根，輕如浮萍。拳體不得中和。即萬法亦不能處時中地步。故三害不明，練之可以傷身。明之自能引人入聖。必精心果力，剔除淨盡，始得拳學入門要道。故書云：樹德務滋，除惡務本。練習諸君，慎之，慎之。

"Full chest and lifted abdomen," the adverse Qi moves upward and does not return to the *Dan Tian*, the two feet do not have roots, light like duckweed, fists and body cannot gain central harmony. Then the ten thousand techniques cannot be situated on a proper foundation. Therefore, (if) the three harms are not understood, training can harm the body. Understanding them will

naturally lead a person into an ascendant place (i.e., a higher level). One must do his best both in mind and effort to get rid of them. Then (he) can grasp the important way of entering the door of learning the fist (i.e., Baguazhang). That is why the book (i.e., passed down documents) says: "(One) must build up and nourish morality, get rid of the badness from its foundation." Those practitioners must be cautious, cautious.

Full chest means to inhale deeply, to fill up the chest fully with air. As you do this, your abdomen will also lift up into your torso. At this point, you should understand that deep inhalation is different from heavy breathing. When you inhale deeply, you are calm, relaxed, natural, and the breathing is smooth. However, if you merely breathe heavily, though you have taken in a lot of air, your lungs are tensed, your mind is excited, and you feel you are floating and without root. Even if you know more than a thousand techniques, they will be useless unless properly rooted.

Therefore, Baguazhang beginners should diligently ponder and comprehend these three harms. If you do not pay attention to them, then you may bring yourself more harm than health. An ancient proverb says: "To establish and cultivate the goodness and eliminate and correct the evil influence from its root."

5. Four Taboos and Four Harms [12]
四忌與四病說

凡初學者，其姿勢之正確與否君，實為將來比較勝負之結果。故習時，必先忌四形：1‧不可前伏；2‧不可後仰；3‧不可左斜；4‧不可右歪。故曰前伏後仰，皆身之病。左斜右歪，其勢不勁。

For the beginner, whether their postures are accurate or not determines the result of future victory or defeat. Therefore, when practicing, first forbid four shapes: 1. cannot bow forward; 2. cannot lean backward; 3. cannot incline to the left; 4. cannot tilt to the right. It is said: "Bowing forward and leaning backward are the sicknesses of the body. Inclining to the left and tilting to the right, the postures cannot (produce strong) Jin (i.e., martial power)."

When you practice Baguazhang, the first step is to regulate your body. When you regulate your body, the first thing is learning to keep your body in the center line, both physically and mentally. Only when you are centered both physically and mentally will you be balanced. Only when you are balanced (both physically and mentally) will you be able to build a firm root. Therefore, if you are not centered, the Jin manifested will not be rooted, and your power will be weak.

再忌四病，揮拳高舉，劈頭直下，拳高而腋下必空，其病一也。長衝直入，臂伸無餘，收縮必緩，緩則不傷必折，其病二也。

Again forbid the four sicknesses. (If) waving the fist, lift high, chopping from the head down, the fist will be high, and under the armpit must be empty. This is the first sickness. (If) lengthening the arm and straightening forward, the arm will be extended without reserve, (then) the backward withdrawing must be slow. (When you are) slow, then (if) not injured, (the arms) will be broken. This is the second sickness.

When you are fighting, you should not lift your arms higher than your chest. This will offer your opponent an opportunity to attack the area under the armpit. Under the armpit, there is a vital cavity called "Jiquan," which belongs to the heart Qi channel (Figure 2-1). When this cavity is struck, a heart attack or shock can occur. For this reason, almost all of the Chinese martial arts emphasize the sinking of both shoulders and elbows in order to avoid exposing the Jiquan to the opponent.

In addition, when you attack, you should not extend your arms to their maximum length. This will slow down your withdrawing capability. The worst possible result of this is that, after overextending your arms, your vital cavities on the upper body will be exposed to your opponent. Furthermore, when your arms are fully extended, they are more easily broken by a skilled opponent.

再練習或與人肉鬥時，若不將單換掌之半馬步站定，如僵立之碑石，則敵方稍一進步，即欲傾跌，其病三也。怒氣騰張，進退甚猛，必心昏，氣升，腦筋亦亂。腦筋亂，則手足無主，動作即不知如何措置，其病四也。拳經曰：'空心暗練養精神，如蛇吸食，內要精神，外要安穩。見之似婦，奪之似虎。' 是言當細味之。

When practicing or sparring with someone, if not standing steady and firm in the "Half Horse Stance" (*Ban Ma Bu*) in the Single Change Palm, (the body) stands stiff (i.e., firmly) like a tomb-

Figure 2-1   *Jiquan* Cavity (H-1)

stone; (when) the enemy advances slightly, it immediately feels like tilting and falling. This is the third sickness. The angry Qi is raised and expanded, advancing and withdrawing are very fierce. The heart (i.e., the mind) is dizzy, the Qi is raised, and the brain is also confused. (When) the brain is confused, the hands and feet do not have a master, the movements cannot be controlled. This is the fourth sickness. The Fist Classic said: "empty the mind and cultivate the spirit of vitality secretly. Like a snake sucking in the food, must have spirit of vitality internally, and must be peaceful and firm externally. When seen, like a lady; when seized, like a tiger." These words should be pondered carefully.

"Half Horse Stance" is a stance which can help a beginner build up a firm foundation and root in his techniques. You should be able to move easily, but not be moved easily. In order to reach this goal, you must first learn to keep your mental and physical centers, balancing yourself. Your root will thus be built up gradually.

Finally, the fourth sickness is of the mind. When you encounter a fight, you should not be excited and show your temper. If you lose control, your breathing will be fast, and the mind will be excited, scattered, and confused. If your mind has lost its calmness, your judgement will not be accurate. Naturally, your fighting techniques will be out of your control.

It is said in the Fist Classic that you should learn how to calm down your mind without being excited (i.e., empty your mind), and raise up your spirit of vitality. It is just like a snake charging to attack its victim, calm and alert both internally and externally. When it is calm, it appears as gentle and kind as a fair lady; but when it attacks, it is as strong as a fierce tiger.

6. Four Virtues, Eight Talents, and Four Manifestations [13]
四德八能四情

四德者：順逆和化，四者即拳中合宜之理也。順者，手足順其自然，往前伸也。逆者，氣力往回縮也。和者，氣力中正無乖也。化者，化其後天之氣力，歸於丹田而返真陽也。

What are the four virtues: follow, reverse, harmonize, and neutralize. These four are the theory of accordance and appropriateness. Follow (means) the hands and feet are extended naturally forward. Against (means) the Qi and the *Li* are withdrawing. Harmonizing (means) the Qi and *Li* are centered and correct, not weird. Neutralizing (means) neutralizing the Post-Heaven Qi and *Li* to return to the *Dan Tian* and then to return to the real Yang.

In Baguazhang, there are four important concepts which you should understand. When these four concepts are understood and applied to the postures and techniques, then both your internal Qi body and external physical body can be coordinated harmoniously. These four are: 1. Following the internal *Yi* and Qi, the physical hands and feet are extended for attack or defense naturally. 2. Reversing the natural feeling of expansion and extending, use the *Yi* to lead the Qi inward and downward to the Lower *Dan Tian*, and also condense it into the bone marrow. This is very important, since it is the Yin side of the action which can be used to withdraw or to neutralize. 3. Harmonize and smoothly manifest the Qi into muscular power (*Li*). From *Yi* to Qi to *Li*, the processes are harmonious and occur naturally. If the mind is not confused, the Qi can be led smoothly, and the *Li* can be manifested to its maximum. 4. Neutralizing and converting the Post-Birth Qi (i.e., the energy converted from air and food) into calm, clean, and pure Qi and store it in the Lower *Dan Tian*. The Pre-Birth (or Pre-Heaven) Qi converted from the Original Essence belongs to Yin while the Post-Birth (or Post-Heaven) Qi belongs to Yang. When the Post-Birth Yang Qi can be sunken and stored to the Lower *Dan Tian*, this Qi can be very beneficial for health and martial arts.

八能者：乃搬攔截扣，推托搙拎。八者，即拳中之性也。搬者，搬敵人之手足肩胯是也。攔者，攔敵人之手足如研肘是也。截者，按住敵人之手足胳膊腿是也。扣者，扣敵人之兩手並胸小腹是也。推者，推敵人之兩手並身，其中有單手推者，有雙手推者是也。托者，托敵人之兩手，有平托者，有望高托者是也。搙者，敵人抓住吾手，極力往回搙，或掛敵人之手皆是也。拎者，拎敵人之身，或敵人之兩手。往左右拎去，或往上拎，或往下拎，即使敵人不得中正之勁也。

What are the eight talents: move, block, intercept, grab, push, lift, pull, and haul. These are the natural qualities of the fist. Move is to move the opponent's hands, feet, shoulders, and hips. Block is to block the opponent's hands and feet by circling the elbows. Intercept is to intercept the opponent's hands, feet, arms, and legs. Grab is to grab the opponent's two hands, chest, and abdomen. Push is to push the opponent's two hands and body. There is a single hand push and double hand push. Lift is to lift up the opponent's two hands. There is lift horizontally and also lift upward. Pull is when the opponent is grabbing my two hands, (I) pull back with great effort or lead the opponent's hands back with circle (*Gua*). Haul is to haul the opponent's body, or opponent's two hands. Haul to the left or right, haul upward or downward. This is to make the opponent unable to gain the centering *Jin*.

Next, you should understand and master the eight basic techniques: move, block, intercept, grab, push, lift, pull, and haul. Since these are the most basic techniques for almost all of the Chinese styles, you must be talented in them. Move is able to control the opponent's arms, legs, shoulders, and hips as you wish. Then you will be able to dominate the entire battle situation. Block is through the circling of the arms to obstruct and stop the opponent's intention in his attacking limbs. Intercept is to disrupt the opponent's attacks which have already been emitted.

Grab is the capability to grasp the opponent's arms or body. This will offer you an opportunity to either control him or destroy his center through pulling. Push is used either to the arms (to seal the expanding of the opponent's arms) or directly to the body for an attack. Lift applies when your opponent is attacking you or blocking your attack. You immediately raise up his arms, especially the elbows, and either push horizontally to destroy his balance or push upward to expose his vital areas for further attack. Pull is when the opponent grabs your two hands, you pull back with great effort or lead the opponent's hands back with a circular motion. Haul is the mixture of pulling, leading, and carrying. The main purpose of hauling is to destroy the opponent's center and balance. Therefore, you may direct your power either to the sides, upward, or downward.

八能者，內含六十四事，合六十四卦也。八者，正卦也。即上乾下乾之類。六十四者，變卦也。即上乾下坤否泰互卦之類。所謂八搬，八扣，各有八，合而為六十四者，則謂拳中之性也。順逆和化，為六十四卦之德也。六十四卦含之於順逆和化四者之中而為德，行之於身者而為道，用之於外者而為情。情者，即起鑽落翻也。

Within the eight talents, there contains sixty-four things which match the sixty-four diagrams. The Eight (Trigrams) are the formal diagrams. It is the kind of (trigrams which) the top is *Qian* or the bottom is *Qian*. Sixty-Four (Diagrams) are "changing diagrams." It is the kind that the top is *Qian*, the bottom is *Kun*, *Pi*, and *Tai* mutual (related) diagrams. What is called "The eight movements" and "The eight grabbings" etc., within each of them, there again has eight. Total has sixty-four diagrams. These are the natural qualities of the fist. Follow, against, harmonize, and neutralize are the virtues of the sixty-four diagrams. (That means) within sixty-four diagrams, those that contain follow, against, harmonize, and neutralize four items are the virtues, and when (these virtues are) applied in the body, it becomes "Dao" (i.e., the way of Baguazhang). When they are expressed externally, they become manifestations (i.e., actions). (That means) manifestations are (the applications of) rising up for drilling, and dropping for turn over.

The Eight Trigrams (Bagua) are considered to be fixed in the rules of nature. However, after they are further derived, they become sixty-four changeable diagrams and are related to many things such as emotions, luck, thinking, time of the day, seasons, etc. Since the eight talents are related to the Eight Trigrams, and each of these eight talents again contains eight techniques, there are in total sixty-four techniques which can be varied according to various situations.

If you apply the four virtues (follow, against, harmonize, and neutralize) smoothly into these sixty-four techniques, the sixty-four techniques will become "Virtues." When these sixty-four virtues are applied to the body, it is the "Dao" (i.e., way) of Baguazhang. When this "Dao" is manifested externally, it becomes the four manifestations, or the actions, of Baguazhang. These four actions are rising, drilling, falling, and turning over.

且八能用時，或明而用之，或暗而用之，或打破彼之身式而用之，或化開彼之法式而用之，或剛進而用之，或柔進而用之。或進而用之，或退而用之，或誘而用之。或指上而用之下，或指下而用之上。或指左而打右，或指前而打後，或指此而打彼，或彼剛而我柔，或彼柔而我剛。或彼矮而我高，或彼動而我靜，或彼靜而我動。或看地之形式，伸縮往來，分別而用之。

In addition, when the eight talents are applied, either used in obvious ways or used in hidden ways, either used to strike and destroy the opponent's posture or used to neutralize the opponent's techniques, either used to advance with hard methods or used to move in with the soft methods, either used to advance or used to withdraw, either used to induce (the opponent), or used to point upward and strike downward, or point downward and attack upward, or point left and charge right, or point forward and blow to the rear, or point here and strike there, or the opponent is hard and I am soft, or the opponent is soft and I am hard, or the opponent is low and I am high, or the opponent is moving while I am calm, or the opponent is calm while I am moving, or observe the shape of the ground, either extend or withdraw, to or fro, use them according (to the situations).

This long sentence stresses that there are many possible applications of the eight talents, but that you should apply them according to the actual situation. Only then may these eight talents be alive.

地形者，遠近險隘，廣狹死生之類也。且身式將動而未動時，務要週身一家，合外內一道。再觀彼之身式高矮，量彼之情形虛實，察彼之氣質薄厚，將彼奸詐虛實等等，得之於心。隨便酌量用之，而能時措之宜。至於拳內用法，名目雖廣，然無論如何動作變化，總以四情為表則也。四情用的合當，則能與性德合而為一道也。

What are the shapes of the ground (i.e., environmental conditions)? They are (relates to) the danger in far or close distance, wide or narrow, which could be dead or alive. In addition, when the body is going to move and yet is not moving, the entire body must act as one family (i.e., unified), the internal and external must be harmonized. Again observe the opponent's body either high or low, gauge the opponent's situation either insubstantial or substantial, inspect the opponent's Qi quality either thin or thick, then understand the opponent's craftiness, insubstantial and substantial, etc. in the heart (i.e., memorize). (Then I) will be able to control the situation as (I) wish and also be able to catch the right timing to handle (my techniques). As to the applications, though the names and categories are many, it does not matter how many variations of the movements, all according to the rules of the four manifestations. If these four manifestations are used properly, then (you are) able to unify the natural quality and virtues into one "Dao."

When you are in a fight, you should pay attention to the environment. Is the place long or short, wide or narrow? All of these can affect your strategy and may decide the outcome of the fight. Next, your internal *Yi* and Qi must unify with the external actions harmoniously and smoothly. You should regulate yourself both internally and externally before you fight. Then you are well prepared both mentally and physically. Finally, you should inspect your opponent closely. How tall is he, how fast can he react, how calm is his mind, or how sneaky he is, etc. Only after you know yourself and your opponent will you be able to set up an effective fighting strategy. However, it does not matter how you fight, you should always follow the rules and principles of the four manifestations, since they are the foundation of the Baguazhang. Only then have you accomplished "Dao" in Baguazhang.

7. Six Combinations and Four Extremities [14]
六合四梢解

人有血、肉、筋、骨。血、肉、筋、骨之末端曰梢。蓋毛髮為血梢，指甲為筋梢，牙為骨梢，舌為肉梢。四梢用力，變其常態，令人生畏焉。

Men have blood, muscles, tendons, and bones. The extremities of the blood, muscles, tendons, and bones are called "*Shao*." That is because the hairs are the extremities of the blood, the fingernails are the extremities of the tendons, the teeth are the extremities of the bones, and the tongue is the extremities of the muscle. When these four extremities have manifested their power, they can change their normal shapes and make people scared.

The human body is constructed out of blood, muscles, tendons, and bones. The extremities of these four things are called "*Shao*." It is believed in Chinese medicine that the hair is the extremity of the blood, and indicates the blood's condition. When the hair's condition is healthy, the condition of the blood is also healthy. The same theory holds that the fingernails are the extremities of the tendons, the teeth are the extremities of the bones, and the tongue is the extremity of the muscle. These four locations are frequently used for diagnosis in Chinese medicine.

It is also believed in Chinese Qigong and martial arts society that when the body's Qi is strong, these four extremities will be healthy. When strong Qi is manifested in these four extremities, its power can make the hair stand up, and the fingernails and teeth sharp and strong. This will make the opponent scared.

六合者，乃內外三合之總稱也。內三合，心與意合，意與氣合，氣與力合，乃為內三合。

What are the six harmonies (*Liu He*)? They are the total names of both the internal and external three harmonies. The internal three harmonies are the *Xin* (i.e., emotional mind) and the *Yi* (wisdom mind) harmonizes, *Yi* and Qi harmonizes, and Qi and *Li* (i.e., muscular strength) harmonizes. These are the internal three harmonies.

The word "*He*" can be translated as "Unify," "Harmonize," and "Coordinate." The six *He* include the three internal *He* and three external *He*. The three internal *He* include the unification of the emotional mind and the wisdom mind until they coordinate and harmonize with each other. In China, the mind generated from emotional disturbance is called "*Xin*." *Xin* means "Heart" simply because it is believed that the emotional mind is closely related to your heart. The mind generated from wise thinking and judgement is called "*Yi*" and means "Idea" or "Thought." When you are in battle, you should control your emotional anger and fear, and utilize your wise judgement. Then you will be calm and perceive the situation clearly.

It is understood that the *Yi* leads the Qi. Where your mind goes, the Qi follows. Therefore, if you are able to concentrate your mind to a higher level, your Qi will be stronger. Finally, the Qi and *Li* harmonize. *Li* is the physical strength generated from the muscles. When the Qi is led to the muscles, this muscular power can be greatly enhanced.

外者肩與胯合，肘與膝合，手與足合，內外統一，謂之六合。

The external three harmonies are the shoulders and the hips harmonize, the elbows and the knees harmonize, the hands and the feet harmonize. When the internal and the external unify, it is called "Six Harmonies."

The external three harmonies include the coordination of the shoulders and the hips, the elbows and the knees, and the hands and the feet. If you can coordinate these parts harmoniously, then you will be able to act as a one unit. Together with the internal three harmonies, your entire being - both physical and mental - will be augmented.

四梢用力於舌，蓋舌通心，心為一身之主，故舌捲則氣降，丹田愈壯耳。夫六合四梢為該拳練習運用，必不可陞之要訣也。

For the four extremities, should use the effort on the tongue. This is because the tongue is connected with the heart and the heart is the master of the entire body. Thus, when the tongue is curved (i.e., touching the roof of the mouth), the Qi will be sunken, and the (Qi in) *Dan Tian* will be stronger. Therefore, the six harmonies and the four extremities are the "must" in the training and the practice of this fist (i.e., Baguazhang). They are the important keys of promoting (the art).

Among the four extremities, you should concentrate most on the placement of your tongue. The tongue should be curved upward to touch the roof of your mouth. The reason for this is that the roof is the place where the last cavity of the Governing Vessel, *Yinjiao* (Gv-28), is located. The tip of the tongue connects with the last cavity of the Conceptional Vessel, *Chengjiang* (Co-24) (Figure 2-2). The Governing Vessel is a Yang vessel and the Conceptional Vessel is a Yin vessel. When the tongue is touching the roof of the mouth, these two Yin and Yang vessels will be connected. This connection helps to generate saliva in the mouth, and helps the body's Qi to sink to the Lower *Dan Tian*. If you are interested in more information about this, please refer to *The Root of Chinese Chi Kung* by YMAA.

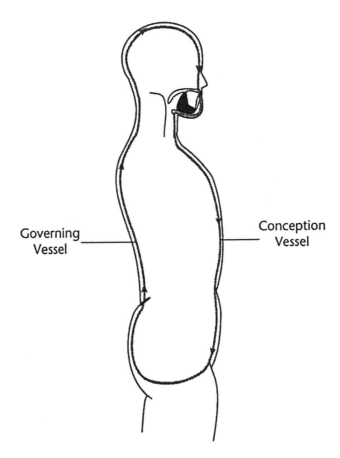

Governing Vessel

Conception Vessel

Figure 2-2.   Small Circulation

8. Fighting Songs of Baguazhang [15,16,17]
八卦掌戰手歌

A. Baguazhang Fighter's Secret Song
八卦掌戰手歌訣

八卦連環分五行，相生相克變無窮，六合歸一是根本，陰陽二字要分明。乾出巽入離與坎，艮往坤來震兌同，入門反正直斜走，橫沖直撞任縱橫。

Bagua linking is divided into "Five Phases." Mutual production and mutual conquest, (its) variations are unlimited. It is essential that the six combinations (or harmonies) are unified into one. Yin and Yang, the two words must be discriminated clearly. Exit with *Qian* and enter with *Xun*,

also *Li* and *Kan.* To with *Gen* and fro with *Kun,* also with *Jen* and *Dui.* **Enter the door and reverse the direction, walk forward and diagonally. Thrusting sideways and bumping in straight, forward, (I) move as (I) wish.**

Baguazhang is also called "*Bagua Lian Huan Zhang*" which means "Bagua Linking Palms." This is because when Baguazhang is performed, all the techniques are linked, one after another, continuously, without stopping. The basic movements of Baguazhang can be classified into five directions according to the theory of the "Five Phases" (*Wu Xing*). These five directions are: South belongs to Fire, North belongs to Water, East is Wood, West is Metal, and finally, the center is Earth (Figure 2-3). From the mutual production and conquest theory of the "Five Phases," the variations of the techniques can be limitless. The six combinations include internal three combinations (or harmonies) and external three combinations (harmonies). As explained earlier, the internal three combinations are: the combined heart (i.e., emotional mind) and *Yi* (i.e., wisdom mind), the combined *Yi* and *Qi*, and the combined *Qi* and *Li* (i.e., muscular power). The external three combinations are: the com-

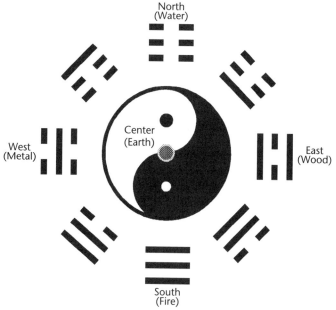

Figure 2-3.   Five Phases and Orientations

bined hands and feet, the combined elbows and knees, and the combined shoulders and hips. When the six combinations are unified into one and controlled by a sole spirit, the entire body can be an effective fighting unit.

When you execute Baguazhang techniques, you should also distinguish the differences between the Yin and Yang strategies and techniques. Insubstantial and substantial should be exchanged skillfully. When you move your body, you are following the moving strategy of the Bagua pattern. How you enter into or exit from the fighting field depends on the situation.

In order to provide training for proper strategic movement in Baguazhang, a specific walking pattern was developed. This pattern is called "*Jiu Gong Bu*" (Nine Palaces Stepping). This pattern is constructed according to the Eight Trigrams, together with the center point of the pattern. We will discuss this "Nine Palaces Stepping" in Chapter 4. After you have mastered the stepping, you will be able to enter and exit from any corner or any side, and in any manner that you choose. Only then, with the coordination of swift and skillful movements, can your Bagua techniques be executed efficiently and effectively

掌分九宮步法取，左右轉身變化精，出手順逆隨身起，落步開合四梢行。腿踢對面不見腿，掌出對手莫知情，翻轉身形勢無定，四門八腿變無窮。

The palms are applied with the coordination of the Nine Palace Stepping. Left and right turning the body, the variations are refined. Emitting hands either following or against (i.e., reversing) according to the body's movement. Falling stepping, open and close, four extremities are capable. (When) the legs kick, the opponent does not see the legs. (When) the palms attack, the opponent does not know (my) intention. (When I) turn my body, the postures are not defined. Four doors and eight legs, their variations have no limit.

When you execute your Baguazhang techniques, your palm and stepping techniques should coordinate with each other. When you turn your body, there are many variations, and each one of them is skillfully executed. Attacking with and withdrawing your palms should follow the body's movements. Only with proper coordination of the body's movements can the four extremities (i.e., arms and legs) be able to manifest to their full potential. The movement of your legs is so fast that your opponent cannot see them, and the variations of your palm techniques are so abundant that your opponent cannot perceive your intention. When you turn your body, your opponent cannot foresee this from your posture. The four doors means the four empty doors, which include the left, the the right, the top, and the bottom. The eight legs means the eight possible stepping directions, which include the four sides and the four corners. When you skillfully coordinate the movements of your legs and techniques, their variations can be unlimited.

遠攻長拳通短打，五行步法顯奇能，三十六招走為上，不招不架卻使空。打法須從身上起，手足齊到方為攻，身似強弓手比箭，消息只在后足蹬。

Far attacks with long fist and near with short strikes. The Five Phases stepping demonstrates its marvellous capability. The thirty-six strategies, walking (away) is the best, need not intercept and need not block, it could make (the opponent's attack) become void. The method of attacking must originate from the body. The hand and the foot arrive together is a (real) attack. The body is like a strong bow and the hands are like the arrows. The message (i.e., key) is only on the rear foot kicking.

When the opponent is at long range, attack with long range techniques. When he is close, you use short range strikes. In Chinese martial strategies, one of the most common and effective strategic infantry formations is called "Five Phases Tactical Deployment" (*Wu Xing Zhen*), in which troops are arranged according to the Five Phases - Metal (i.e., West), Wood (i.e., East), Water (i.e., North), Fire (i.e., South), and Earth (i.e., Center). Aside from techniques, you should also know the fighting strategy which will best allow you to defeat a given type of opponent. It was said that the 36 strategies in the Art of War were written by Sun Wu during Chinese Warring States period (453-221 B.C.). Among these 36 strategies, the last and best strategy is **Running Away**. In Bagua fighting strategy, "Walking away" is also considered to be best. Walking away from an attack could lead your opponent's attack into uselessness. Only when you are confident that you can reach your target do you execute a technique. When you attack, the movement is generated from the body; the hands and the legs must coordinate perfectly. Only then can the attack be effective, strong and fast, like an arrow shot from a bow. The success of this (i.e., escaping and attack) all depends on how skillfully you manage your rear leg.

起時無影落無形，去意好似捲地風，手起萬莫使空回，腕落不要枉落空。側身兩邊防左右，高低相隨巧妙生，往來橫豎依身變，腳打七分手三成。

There is no shadow when (I) arise and there is no shape when (I) fall. The intention of going (i.e., attacking) is just like the tornado wind. (When) the hand emits should not be back with nothing. The wrist fall should not be in vain. The body dodges to the two sides and beware of the left and right. High and low are following each other and the marvellous techniques can be generated. To or fro, sideways or straight, according to the variation of the body. The feet strike

seven, while the hands strike three.

In a fight, speed is one of the most important factors in winning. Therefore, when you raise or lower your body, you are so fast that your opponent cannot see how you do it. When you attack, your mind, fast as a tornado's wind, is sure that you have caught the best opportunity. Therefore, you will not attack in vain. When you fight, you are skillful in dodging, moving your body up and down, and you execute your techniques to the upper and lower body according to the situation. When fighting with Baguazhang, use 70% of the feet for striking and only 30% of the hands.

硬打硬進快招勝，左右橫進任意行，退若狸貓進似虎，腳打踩意不落空。上步對面人不見，拳出掌去不見形，手腳起落人莫覺，猶如幻影去無蹤。

Strike hard and advance hard, the fast techniques win. Left and right, advance from the side, executed as (my) wish. Withdraw like a fox and cat, and advance like a tiger. The feet strike with the stepping will not enter the emptiness (i.e., be in vain). (When I) step forward, the opponent cannot see (me). (When I) emit (my) fist and attack with (my) palm, (the opponent) cannot see the shape. The hand and foot's rising and falling, the opponent does not feel. It is just like a mirage disappearing without a trace.

When you advance and attack, you must be fast, the movements must be agile and skillful, and the power must be as strong as a tiger. When you withdraw, you act quickly like a fox or a cat. If you strike with good coordination in your stepping, your strike will not be in vain. Since you are moving so fast, your opponent cannot see or feel your intention or action.

二人比手無虛式，前進后退一寸爭，掌打須知出入步，去如流水進如風。竄縱跳躍無虛步，閃展騰挪手法精，寸步過快剪步穩，七歲打法要分明。

Two persons compete the hands (i.e., combat), there is no false posture (i.e., joking). Advance and withdraw, even one inch is contended. (When) the palms strike, (you) should be familiar with the stepping of entering and exiting. Going like flowing water and advancing like the wind. Escaping and jumping do not have void stepping. Dodging, extending, leaping, and moving, the hand's techniques are refined. The inch stepping is very fast and the scissors stepping is firm. Seven regions of striking must be discriminated clearly.

When you encounter a combat situation, you should not joke around and take it lightly. When you attack or withdraw, even one inch can make a great difference. Therefore, when you attack, coordinate with your stepping. Entering your opponent's empty door is a crucial key to successful attack. In addition to stepping, you must also possess speed in advancing and withdrawal, as well as skillful body movement and hand techniques. When you step forward or backward, do not step a large pace, step a small one instead. Then you will be stable, and your movement can be fast. As you step, both legs are close together like scissors. The seven regions include the head, the chest, the abdomen, the left and the right sides of the body, the arms, and the legs.

踏偏身探病在腿，前俯后仰亦是空，手腳齊到莫顯形，若見形影不為能。蟄龍未起雷先動，風吹大樹百枝傾，內要提防外要穩，虛實見景便生情。

(If) stepping in wrong place and too much extending of the body, its sickness (i.e., problem) is on the legs. Lean forward or incline backward, it is also void. The hands and legs arrive at the same time, and do not reveal your shape. If (the opponent) is able to see (my) shape and shadow, then (I) am unable. Before the hibernating dragon awakes, the thunder first roaring. The wind blows the big tree and a hundred branches break. Must pay attention internally and firm externally. When seeing substantial and insubstantial, the emotion is generated immediately.

If you do not train well, your stepping will not coordinate with your hand techniques smoothly. Consequently, you may step in and out incorrectly and your body will lose its firm root and expose your vital area to attack. Even if you have a firm root, your body should not lean forward or backward, and lose its centering. When you attack, your hands and legs arrive at the same time, with perfect coordination and great speed. If you can do this, your power will always be stored and ready for an attack. Once you execute your attack, raise up your spirit of vitality, coordinate with your breathing, and unify both internal Qi and external action. Then the power generated will be as strong as the gusting wind.

一手分為八手用，緊連不斷是真功，千招不如一招妙，萬招不如不落空。兩手變成多手用，用招多變方顯能，誰人解開無極法，保證到處得成功。

One hand is divided and used as the eight hands. Linking (the techniques) closely without broken is real Gongfu. Thousand (useless) techniques are not as marvellous as a single (useful) technique. Ten thousand techniques are not as effective as (a few) without falling emptiness. Vary the two hands and apply them as multiple hands. Apply the techniques with multiple variations, the talent can then be manifested. Whoever is able to comprehend the *Wiji* method, guaranteed be successful anywhere.

When you attack your opponent or defend against an attack, you are so fast it is as if you can multiply a single hand into eight hands. A good attacking strategy is to attack continuously, with great speed. This will force your opponent into a defensive and confused situation. When you attack, you do not have to use many complicated techniques. A good, simple, fast, effective and skillful technique is better than thousands of techniques that are not useful. When the techniques are simple, then you can be fast and fluid. Even though you have only two hands, you are fighting as though you have multiple hands. After you become familiar with the simple techniques, then the variations of the techniques can evolve automatically and naturally. Only when you are fighting and your mind is not in fighting, have you reached the stage of "*Wuji*" (i.e., no extremity state). This is the stage of "Fighting without fighting." Once you have mastered fighting skills and gained experience in fighting, all of your reactions will be natural and all of the techniques can be fast and effective. This is called *Wuji* state.

B. Baguazhang Secret Songs of Attacking Techniques
八卦掌技擊歌訣

1. Head: 頭

頭打之法進中央，靠山探穴兩肋旁。乳上乳下斜身取，此頭乃是掌中王。

The method of using the head to strike, entering the center. Lean against the mountain to explore the cavities is on the sides of two tendons. Above the nipple and under the nipple, pick up with incline body. This head is the king of the palms (i.e., Baguazhang).

In order to use your head to strike your opponent, you must first enter the opponent's center. To prevent him from using both of his hands to stop your attack, you must get close to his body (i.e., mountain) and push his arms to the sides. Then the cavities in the tendon area of the two shoulders as well as those located above and below the nipples will be exposed for striking with your head. In Chinese martial arts, the head strike is very common and effective at close range. The nose and the solar plexus are also commonly attacked with the head.

2. Shoulders: 肩

肩打一陰反一陽，大劈引手先去商。手換肩下要靠準，頭來肩打命必亡。

Shoulders strike with one Yin and reverse with one Yang. First (use) the big chop to lead the

(opponent's) hand out and gain his attention. The hands change by shoulder, and stroke accurately. (If) the head comes, (use) the shoulder to strike, (the opponent's) life would be ended.

When you use your shoulder to strike, strike with one side and again with the other. In order to use the shoulder to strike, you first use the big chop, catching your opponent's attention and forcing him to extend his hand to block your chopping. Once his arm is extended, immediately use your shoulder to accurately strike places such as the nipples, solar plexus, or under the armpit. However, if your opponent uses his head to strike you, you may immediately use your shoulder to strike his head. The shoulder strike can be enormously powerful, and a strike to your opponent's head can terminate his life.

3. Hands: 手

抓打擒拿雙手用，腳手齊到方為真。拳似炮形龍折身，手似劈山向前搶。

Grabbing, striking, seizing, and controlling, use both hands. It is real (Gongfu) when the feet and the hands both arrive together. The fist is like the cannon shape, the body bends like a dragon. The hand like chopping the mountain and rush forward.

When you apply hand techniques such as grabbing, striking, seizing and controlling, you should use both hands skillfully, and coordinate with the legs' stepping. When you attack with a fist, it emits as powerfully as a cannon, and arrives together with the legs' stepping. In order to generate this great power, the body must also move like a dragon, and store all the power in its posture. When you chop with your palm, it is like you are chopping a mountain with great forward rushing power.

4. Elbows: 肘

肘打三節不見形，直橫斜打用皆準。虎豹頭法意在肘，穿林交叉頂后心。

(When) the elbow strikes, (the opponent) cannot see the shape of the three sections. Strike straight forward, sideways, or diagonally, all accurate. The head acts like a tiger and a panther, the *Yi* (i.e., wisdom mind) is on the elbows. Boring the woods and crossing each other, the rear elbow is covering the heart.

The three sections are the hands, the forearms, and the upper-arms. When you use your elbow to strike an opponent, all the techniques are so accurate and fast that your opponent cannot see them coming. Though the external look of your head is alert and spiritual, like a tiger's or a panther's, your internal mind (i.e., intention) is focused on the elbows. When you use your two palms to bore toward your opponent's vital areas, the power is generated from the elbows. When you emit these boring palms, they are smooth and skillful, just like a butterfly boring through the woods. When one of the palms strike, the elbow of the other arm always protects the center of the body.

5. Inner Upper Thighs and Hips (*Kua*): 胯

胯打中節肩相連，陰陽相合力摧山。外胯去時里胯走，回身如鷹變式還。

The *Kua* strikes the middle section and is connecting (i.e., coordinating) with the shoulders. Yin and Yang combine, its power is able to crush a mountain. When the external *Kua* (i.e., hips) is going (i.e., striking), the internal *Kua* (i.e., inner sides of upper thighs) is ready to leave. Turning the body just like an eagle changes its (forward) posture and returns.

Kua is an area on the inner upper thighs, and also the external upper thighs (or hips). The internal sides of *Kua* are Yin, while the external sides are Yang.

In Baguazhang, the *Kua* is commonly used to strike the middle section of the opponent's body.

Normally, the external *Kua* can strike the opponent's abdomen, waist and hips - destroying his root and balance. The internal *Kua* is used to strike the opponent's own external or internal *Kua* for the same purpose. From the *Kua* up to the shoulder must all be connected and coordinated. In addition, you must also be rooted firmly in order to generate great power when using the *Kua* to strike an opponent,

In order to firm your root, the internal *Kua* (Yin) and the external *Kua* (Yang) must be unified as one. With this firm root, your power will be so strong that it can bounce your opponent off balance easily.

When you are using the *Kua* to strike your opponent, the distance between you and your opponent is very close. This means that you are in a most dangerous range. Therefore, right after your attack, you should immediately withdraw. This implies that when you are striking, you are already prepared to withdraw. When you withdraw, you are like an eagle turning its body in the air, fast, smooth and steady.

6. Knees: 膝

膝打幾處人不明，若用膝頂命必傾。斜打胯兮加肋力，形似猛虎出了籠。

When (my) knees strike, the opponent does not know how many places (I) will strike. If using the knee to strike upward, the life must be falling. Strike the *Kua* sideways with tendon's power. The shape is like a fierce tiger exiting a cage.

When you use your knees to strike your opponent, your opponent will not know where your knees are going to strike. If the knees are striking upward, they will be aiming at the groin, the solar plexus, or the chin, where the injuries can be fatal. In Baguazhang, the knees are also used to strike both internal *Kua* (inner upper thighs) and external *Kua* (hips) to immobilize the moving capability of the legs. When you use your knees to strike *Kua*, you must use the tendon's jerking power in order to generate a penetrating *Jin* (i.e., marital power), since the *Kua* muscles are very thick. The feeling of the strike is like a fierce tiger just released from a cage - fast and powerful.

7. Feet: 足

腳打去意刮地風，消息全憑後腳蹬。踩住敵人腳下落，功夫不到全是空。

(When) the foot strikes, the mind of going (i.e., attacking) is like the wind scraping the ground. The message (i.e., secret) is all relying on the kicking of the rear leg. Falling (my) feet to step on the enemy's (feet). (If) the Gongfu is not reached (i.e., good), then all is in vain.

When you use your feet to strike, the striking should not be high, but should be like the wind scraping the ground surface. When you use one foot to strike, the other should be firmly rooted. In order to generate a strong kick, the rear leg is used to balance the attack. Therefore, when you kick forward, the rear leg must bounce backward, and when your front foot kicks the left, the rear foot must bounce to the right. Then the power can be strong. Another trick of foot attacks is using the feet to step on the opponent's feet. This will temporarily stop your opponent from moving. However, in order to achieve this goal, your stepping Gongfu must be good. Otherwise, you will step on nothing and offer your opponent a chance to attack you. Furthermore, when you step on the opponent's foot, if your stepping is not firm, your opponent may still move around and destroy your balance.

8. Legs: 腿

腿法原有七二變，扣擺之中把敵算。下掃上擊各含意，點心點意手法先。

The legs' techniques had seventy-two variations originally (i.e., many). Plot against the enemy among the arcing and swaying (steppings). Sweep low and strike high, each has its own content (i.e., intention). When the *Xin* (i.e., emotional mind) and *Yi* (i.e., wisdom mind) are touched, the hands have already emitted.

Baguazhang uses 70% leg techniques, while using only 30% hand techniques. Therefore, there are many more techniques for the legs than there are for the hands. Arcing and swaying stepping are two of the main walkings in Baguazhang fighting. Your ability to put your opponent into a disadvantageous position depends on the quality of your arcing and swaying stepping. The leg techniques include attacks on the lower body, such as the lower limbs, or strike high, such as the abdomen or the chest. All of these must be applied with the right timing and opportunity. By coordinating the leg attacks with the steppings, the opportunity and the strike can occur in the same instant, without thinking.

C. Baguazhang Fighting Secret
八卦掌技擊要訣

出掌一伸手，氣把丹田沈。呼吸要自然，矯健如龍游。走則勁在足，換式腰是手。
前掌虛作伴，后手肘下守。正人先正己，轉身先轉步。進則前步進，退則後步退。
欲動我先靜，欲屈先伸手。

(When) extending (my) hand to strike with palm, the Qi must be sunken to the *Dan Tian*. The breathing must be natural, (the body movement should be) agile and strong, like a swimming dragon. (When) walking the *Jin* is on the feet, (when) changing postures, the waist (coordinates with) the hand. The front palm makes the false attack, the rear hand protects (the body) under the elbow. To correct (i.e., control) the opponent, first correct (i.e., stabilize) yourself. (When) turning the body, first turn the stepping. Advance, then the front leg advances (first). Retreat, then the rear leg retreats (first). Desire to move, first I should be calm. Desire to bend, first I extend my hand.

When you attack, the Qi is sunk to the Lower *Dan Tian*. This implies that when you attack, you use reverse breathing. When the power is emitted, the abdomen is expanded. When you move around, the breathing should be natural. The body moves bravely and strongly, like a swimming dragon. When you walk, the feet must be rooted, to give the *Jin* a place of origin. When you change the posture, the hands and the waist should coordinate with one another, acting as one unit. It is said: "The *Jin* is originated from the feet, directed by the waist, and manifested on the fingers."[18,19]

In Baguazhang, the front hand is used to fake the opponent. The rear hand should be kept under the elbow of the front arm, to protect the chest area and ready an attack. In order to defeat your opponent, you must regulate your mind, Qi, and postures. If you intend to turn your body, first turn your feet. When you advance, move your front foot first; when you retreat, move your rear foot first. When you intend to move, you must be calm; when you intend to bend your arm, you must first extend it. Yin and Yang should be mutually balanced.

人疾我先往，人來吾便走。動步窺左右，不忘顧前後。眼明觀六路，眼到意即有。
意有而氣重，氣至力在手。使梢先使根，勁在腳上走。掌隨步伐翻，步按掌動行。
腳練十年功，掌取強中手。

(When) opponent is retreating urgently, I move forward before him (i.e., attack faster than he can withdraw). (When) the opponent is coming (i.e., attacking), then I walk away. (When) moving (my) steps, (I) peek (my) left and right (i.e., beware of left and right). (I also) do not forget to watch the front and the rear. The eyes are bright, to watch the six paths. When the eyes arrive, the *Yi* (i.e., the mind) immediately generates. Once the *Yi* is generated, the Qi is heavy (i.e., abundant). When the Qi arrives, the *Li* is generated in hands. To move the ending, first move the root. *Jin* is (originated) from the walking feet. The palms turn, following the stepping. Step according to the palms' movements. Train the feet (i.e., legs) for ten years of Gongfu. The palms (i.e., battle) won by the strong hands (i.e., persons).

When your opponent is retreating very fast, you attack him even faster. When your opponent is advancing violently, you yield and avoid it. When you move, you are aware of the six paths - the left, the right, the front, the rear, the top, and the bottom. When the eyes see the opportunity, the mind is immediately generated, and reaction is instantaneous. With a strong and concentrated mind, the Qi can be strong and the muscles energized to their maximum efficiency. When you emit *Jin*, emit from its root. When you walk, the *Jin* is always on the bottom of your feet (i.e., rooted). The palm actions (i.e. techniques) coordinate with the stepping, and the stepping coordinates with the palm actions. In order to achieve such coordination, you will need at least ten years of study.

9. Baguazhang Turning Palm Secret Song [20]
八卦掌轉掌歌訣

八卦轉掌論陰陽，五行六合內中藏。七星八步九宮定，兩儀三才見柔剛。混元一氣培根本，四正四隅按八方。落步三盤掰扣步，發行四梢彎轉強。前掌虛實牛舌樣，后手埋伏肘下藏。進步有門退有法，變化反正掌陰陽。屈直橫豎斜正面，翻轉盤旋腰主張。內講五行分四梢，外有五行眼法強。

Bagua turning palms (i.e., Baguazhang) talks about Yin and Yang. The five phases and six harmonies are hidden within. The Seven Stars, the Eight Steppings, and the Nine Palaces are defined. (From) Two Poles and Three Powers, (we can) see the soft and the hard. Use the sole Original Qi to cultivate the foundation. Four sides and four corners to set the eight directions. Falling steps with three levels (of height) and walk with arcing steps. To emit four extremities, (use) bending and turning to enhance the strength. The front palm's insubstantial and substantial are like a cow's tongue. The rear hand is hidden under the elbow and ready for ambush. Advance the steps correctly and retreat with methods. In any cases of variation, the palms (demonstrate) Yin and Yang. Bend, straight, sideways, vertical, or diagonal; flipping, turning, or spinning, the waist is the control. Internally, (we) talk about the five phases and apply them in the four extremities. Externally, there are also five phases which can be strengthened from the eyes.

Baguazhang is also called "Turning Palms." Since Baguazhang was created based on Yin and Yang theory, all of its movements, strategies, and theories are classified into Yin and Yang. The Five Phases are Metal, Wood, Water, Fire, and Earth. The Five Phases relate to Yin and Yang, and therefore the relationships of the Five Phases are also used in Baguazhang. The Six Harmonies includes three internal harmonies and three external harmonies. The three internal harmonies are the *Xin* (i.e., emotional mind) and *Yi* (i.e., wisdom mind) harmonized, the *Yi* and the Qi harmonized, and the Qi and the *Li* (muscular power) harmonized. The three external harmonies are the hands and the feet harmonized, the elbows and the knees harmonized, and the shoulders and the *Kua* harmonized.

The seven stars are the seven principal stars which form the Big Dipper. In Chinese fighting strategy, the arrangement of the seven stars was commonly used as a model for strategic movement. The eight steps means the eight phases of the Eight Trigrams. The Nine Palace Stepping includes the eight corners of the Eight Trigrams, plus the center point (see Chapter 4). All of these three are common Baguazhang stepping patterns. Two Poles again means the Yin and Yang poles, and the Three Powers implies the powers of Heaven, Earth, and Man. When you know how to apply the Yin and Yang theory together with the manifestations of different powers, you will be able to channel your power into soft or hard, as you wish.

Regardless of your strength and agility, all physical manifestations of your power share the same foundation —s trong original Qi. Therefore, in order to improve your physical performance, you should always cultivate your Qi and build it to a more abundant level.

In Baguazhang or Taijiquan, your environment is divided into eight directions, the four formal directions (front, rear, left, and right) and the four diagonal directions (i.e., four corners). These form the Eight Trigrams. When you are fighting, once you move your feet to step, you have three potential heights to stand at, depending on your leg postures. At high level, you step like you are walking. In the middle level, you slightly squat down while walking. At the low level, you squat down very low in your stepping. No matter which height you use, the "Arcing Stepping" must be clearly executed. When you emit power through the four limbs, bending and twisting can make the power stronger. The front palm varies from substantial to insubstantial, and vice versa (like a cow extending and withdrawing its tongue). The rear hand remains hidden under the elbow of the front arm.

When you advance or withdraw, you know the techniques. All of the techniques have many variations, and yet still follow the theory of Yin and Yang. No matter how you move or execute the techniques, the waist is always the main control. Internally, the five internal organs correspond to the Five Phases and manifest themselves in the four limbs through the action of techniques. According to Chinese medicine, all internal organs are connected to the extremities through the Qi channels. The five internal organs are Lungs (metal), Liver (wood), Kidneys (water), Heart (fire), and Spleen (earth). These five internal organs are related to the emotions: the lungs relate to sadness, the liver relates to anger, the kidneys relate to fear, the heart relates to happiness, and the spleen relates to pensiveness. Furthermore, all these emotions are manifested in the eyes. Through the eyes, you can show your emotional agitation, raise up your fighting spirit, and turn emotions into power.

內講氣道分三節，外有手法分陰陽。步法走轉分八字，身法意氣仔細詳。柔身轉換不定勢，高低遠近無限量。腰法要合行四梢，眼法要合定八方。手法要合情變化，用法要合左右防。膀法要合陰陽變，身法要合扭轉強。胯法要合挨身使，膝法要合進身旁。步法要合進退快，閃展騰挪腰偏強。

Internally, (Baguazhang) talks about the Qi paths, and is divided into three sections. Externally, there are hand techniques, which are divided into Yin and Yang. Steppings in the walking and turning are classified into eight words. The body's movements, *Yi*, and Qi should be pondered carefully. Soft body, turning, and changing, do not have a definite posture. High or low, far or close, do not have limitation. The waist techniques must coordinate with the four extremities' movement. The eye techniques must combine (i.e., unify) with the eight directions. The hand techniques must vary according to the situations. When applying the techniques, be aware of the left and the right. The shoulders must coordinate with the variation of Yin and Yang. The body movements should match the strong power of twisting. The *Kua* techniques should be used when the body is closed. The knee techniques should be applied when the body is near. The stepping techniques must be fast in advancement and retreat. To dodge, expand, jump and move, the waist is specially emphasized.

The Qi stored in the Lower *Dan Tian* can follow three paths; one to the upper limbs, one to the lower limbs, and one upward through the center of the spinal column to nourish the brain and raise up the spirit of vitality. From the internal Qi, power is manifested externally, and the external forms are themselves divided according to Yin and Yang. When you walk in Baguazhang, you are following the eight corners of the Bagua pattern. These eight corners are represented by eight words: *Qian* (Heaven), *Kun* (Earth), Zhen (Thunder), *Xun* (Wind), *Kan* (Water), *Li* (Fire), Gen (Mountain), and *Dui* (Lake, Ocean) (Figure 2-4). When you walk and execute your techniques, the body movements, the *Yi*, and the Qi must be synchronized. In order to reach this goal, you must ponder and practice diligently.

When you change your position, there is no definite posture. How high or how low, how far or how close, depends on the situation. When you execute your techniques through the four limbs,

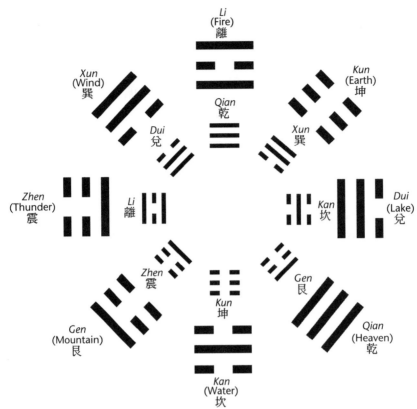

Figure 2-4. Bagua Diagrams

the waist is the center of control. As you move, the eyes should be aware of the eight directions. The hand techniques are emitted according to opportunity. Moreover, when you emit your techniques, you always beware of attacks from either your left or right.

When you use the shoulders to strike, Yin and Yang must be exchanged skillfully (i.e., left and right attacks interchangeably). The body should be twisted toward the center, where your opponent is standing. When the *Kua* techniques are applied, you must be very close to your opponent. When attacking with the elbow, you may be a little further away, but still in close. When you step, you should be able to advance and withdraw swiftly. When you dodge, expand, jump and move, the waist should always be the center of control.

頭打去意隨腰使，起落總須站中央。腳踏中門搶地位，掌行直穿上下忙。掌打起落頭手擋，肘打去意占胸膛。背緊胸空提谷道，肩打胯擊並陰陽。身法全靠丹蓄氣，兩手只在胸上藏。推托帶領隨身勁，搬扣劈進上下忙。八勢八母總由轉，以掌為母悟刀槍。文知八卦明道理，武曉易理亦生光。

The head has generated the attacking mind, the waist (movement) immediately follows. (Either) raise or fall, (you) must stand with center. The feet are stepping in the center door to occupy the important position. The palms move with straight boring, and busy in the top and bottom. (When) the palms strike either raising or falling, the hands are ahead for the job. (When) the elbow strikes, the going mind is aiming on the chest. The back is tight and the chest is hollow, the grain path is raised. The shoulder strikes and the hips bump, together with Yin and Yang. The (entire) body's techniques all depend on the storage of the Qi in the *Dan Tian*. Two hands are solely hidden above the chest. Push, lift, carry and lead, follow the body's *Jin*. Move, pluck, chop and forward, the top and the bottom are busy. The eight postures, the eight mothers, are all from turning. Use the palms as the mother (i.e., essential root) to comprehend (the theory) of the saber and spear. Scholarly, (I) know Bagua and understand the theory. Martially, (I) realize the theory of change, which is also able to enlighten (my understanding).

When your mind has generated the idea to attack, your waist immediately initiates the action. When you are using your palms, the best strategic position is to occupy the center door (i.e., the center line between you and your opponent). When you use your elbow, you should aim for your opponent's chest. When you store *Jin*, you are arcing your back, holding in your chest, and holding up your grain path (i.e., anus). When you are lifting up your anus, you are also holding in the *Huiyin* cavity (Figure 2-5). In Chinese martial arts, the secret of storing *Jin* is learning to coordinate your breathing while holding in the *Huiyin* cavity. When you do this, you lead the Qi inward and accumulate it in the Lower *Dan Tian*. This is the Yin side of *Jin* manifestation. Once you have accumulated your Qi to a high level, then you can manifest the Yang side of your *Jin* (i.e., emitting *Jin* or *Fa Jin*) through exhalation and the gentle expansion of the *Huiyin* cavity (i.e., also anus).

In ancient times, few martial artists knew how to read. Therefore, most of them did not know

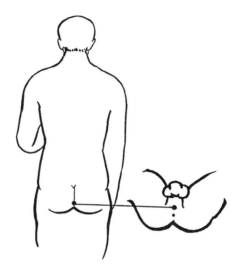

Figure 2-5. *Huiyin* Cavity (Co-1)

the *Huiyin* cavity. In order to make practice easier, and accomplish the same goal, the anus was commonly substituted for the *Huiyin* cavity. The reason for this is that, when the anus is lifted or expanded, the *Huiyin* cavity is also lifted or expanded.

When you are executing Baguazhang techniques, the mind, waist, hands, stepping (external side of technique) and Qi storage in the *Dan Tian* (internal side of technique) should all be considered. After you comprehend all of these secrets, you will be able to apply the same theories to the use of weapons. Therefore, the palm techniques in Baguazhang can be considered the mother (essence) of the entire art. All of these theories are built on the foundation of Bagua theory.

先師掌法傳至今，世人鮮有得其詳。莫說前人多保守，只怨己身功夫深。說明道理揆用意，樹茂枝繁根必藏。八卦先從轉掌起，精研其法乃得真。頭頂肩垂行氣下，直到丹田出入勻。臂間要分三節用，身法要停四梢均。步走圓圈分八卦，跟隨身手一團神。元氣須在肛門提，猿臂熊膀龍虎身。

The ancestral teacher's palm techniques have passed down till today. Very few of the world's people have obtained its detail. Let us not say the former people were more conservative, (we) should complain ourselves that (we) have not spent deep Gongfu for this. (Let me try) to explain the theory of Dao and ponder its meaning. The tree whose branches are luxuriant, its roots must be hidden deeply. Bagua first starts with the turning palm, (you should) study it painstakingly to obtain the real (essence). The head is up pressed, the shoulders are dropped, and the Qi is transporting downward until *Dan Tian*, and in and out uniformly. The arms should be used by dividing into three sections. (When) the body's (movement) stops, the four extremities should be balanced. The stepping is walking in a circle and is classified by Bagua (i.e., Eight Trigrams), which is following the body and the hands with sole spirit. The Original Qi must be raised from the anus. (You should have) the ape's arm, bear's shoulders, and the dragon's and tiger's bodies.

Many Baguazhang martial artists claim that the reason that their techniques are not high is because their teachers are conservative, and have hidden the secrets. In fact, what really happened was that the students did not practice enough, and did not ponder the theory deeply. Learning is like how a tree grows. The deeper the root, the more luxuriant the leaves and fruit.

The foundation of all theoretical practice should be the Turning Palm (i.e., Baguazhang). Ponder the theory and techniques painstakingly, and you will be able to grasp the real meaning of Baguazhang's secrets. These secrets are: the head should be upward, the shoulders are dropped, and the Qi is sunk. Furthermore, the Qi that enters and exits the Lower *Dan Tian* is uniform and smooth. The three sections of the limbs must be clearly discriminated. Once the body is steady, the four extremities coordinate with each other perfectly. When you walk in the Baguazhang circle, both the body movements and the steppings are all gathered in a sole spirit (i.e., the spirit of vitality is raised). Finally, the secret key to accumulating Original Qi in the Lower *Dan Tian* is holding up the anus.

二人對手腕中求，動手制勝步法分。上下前後左右使，肩肘膝胯里外輪。腿法出腿
不見腿，八卦起首腿為根。前後左右三十六，橫腿順提又切真。進退勾挂明暗腿，
連環陰陽並轉身。蹬踹蹁踩屈搓絆，習三熟純使無心。武術雖精教憑法，徒費心機
枉勞神。學習武藝功夫到，得了藝技不壓身。藝術出眾人尊敬，學問高強自超群。

(When) two persons are fighting, (the victory) can be seen from the wrists. In a battle, the winning is (also) decided from stepping. (When) moving upward, downward, forward, backward, left, and the right, the shoulders, elbows, knees, and hips - both internal and external - are (as round as) wheels. The leg's techniques are emitted without seeing the leg. The first important point of Bagua is that the legs are the roots. Forward, backward, left and right, total have thirty-six (techniques). The smooth side legs kick are also real. Forward, backward, hook, and repel, know the hidden legs. (You should) connect the Yin and Yang with the body's turning. Kicking, treading, limping, stepping, bending, twisting, and stumbling, practice repeatedly until it is so skilled and refined that the heart (i.e., mind) is no longer necessary. Though *Wushu* (i.e., Baguazhang) is refined (i.e., great), (its success) depends on the methods of teaching. (Without a correct way of teaching), (it is) wasting the mind and laboring the spirit without gain. (When) learning *Wuyi* (i.e., martial arts), the Gongfu must be there (i.e., energy and time must be spent). After gaining the art's techniques, the body will not be pressured (i.e., insulted). (If) the art techniques are splendid, everybody will respect (you). The knowledge will also be high and strong (i.e., abundant) and beyond the general public.

One way to predict victory between two combatants is by comparing the control over their wrists. When the wrist is alive, the techniques manifested through the palms and fingers will be agile and alert. In addition, you can also judge opponents' skill from their stepping. One whose stepping is swift, firm, and rooted, will have smooth and fast body movement, and his opponent will have great difficulty defeating him.

In order to make your techniques and stepping alive and fast, you must be able to move your elbows, shoulders, hips, and knees like a turning wheel. Only then will your opponent be unable to see your leg when you kick. The firmness of your root and the speed and skill of your kicking are the foundations of Baguazhang. There are sixty-six leg techniques in Baguazhang; all of them real and practical. These techniques can be categorized into forward, backward, hook, obvious, and the hidden legs. These legs techniques are connected with Yin and Yang, and turning the body is the key to executing them. Also included are kicking, treading, limping, stepping, bending, twisting, and stumbling. All of these techniques must be practiced repeatedly until they are all mastered.

Though *Wuyi* (i.e., martial arts) is a refined and high art, its success depends on teaching methods. A talented student can waste his natural gifts with an unqualified or inattentive master. The same holds true for a talented master with an untalented or unmotivated student.

10. Baguazhang Secret Songs of Application [21]
八卦掌用法歌訣

Song #1

掌分八勢轉為根，左旋右轉要縮身。二人相戰腕中求，動手取勝步法分。八卦奧妙
要學真，走穿撐翻人難進。任他巨力來打我，旋轉變化到彼身。八卦八形陰陽生，
六十四掌藏真情。練至筋骨通靈處，周身貫行縱橫行。

The palms (i.e., Baguazhang) are classified into eight postures, the "Turning" is the root (of the art). Left turn and right spin, the body should be shrunk (i.e., low). (When) two persons are fighting, the key to winning is in the wrist. (When) the fighting starts, the winning is decided by the stepping. The marvellous secrets of Bagua must be studied seriously. Walking, boring, twisting, and turning, the opponent is hard to enter. It does not matter how strong the power when he is striking me, (I) spin and turn (my) body close to his body. Bagua has eight shapes, and the Yin and Yang are generated. Sixty-four palms hide the real essence. Train the tendons and bones until reaching spiritual enlightenment, (the Qi could) circulate in the entire body, sideways or vertically (i.e., nowhere cannot be reached).

Baguazhang includes eight basic postures and is also called "Turning palm." The reason for this is because turning is the root of the entire art. When you turn any direction, in order to have a fast turning speed and a steady, firm foundation, your body posture must be low. When there is a fight, the winner is decided by the skill of his wrist movements, which are the root of the palms' techniques. An additional factor is the swiftness and smoothness of the combatants' stepping. In order to reach a high level of Baguazhang, Bagua theory must be thoroughly comprehended. Only then will you move and act as you wish, and make it hard for your opponent to execute his techniques.

No matter how great your opponent's attacking power, if you are skillful in your spinning and turning, you will be able to reach and get close to his body. In Baguazhang, there are eight animal shapes, and Yin and Yang theory is hidden behind all of them. From these eight shapes, the sixty-four palm techniques are generated. You should practice constantly, until all of your tendons and bones are relaxed as you move. Then you will be able to circulate your Qi to the entire body as you wish.

先天之氣要練習，剛柔相並細推尋。八卦掌法留意記，不怕猛漢力千斤。外重手眼
身法步，內修心神意氣根。升降開合練內功，丹田有寶妙無窮。哼哈意合吞吐妙，
霹靂一聲使人惊。乾坤艮巽分四隅，坎離震兌八卦成。

The Pre-Heaven Qi should be practiced. The hard and the soft mutually combine, study and ponder (it) diligently. The palm techniques of Bagua should be memorized carefully. Do not be afraid of even a fierce strong man who has thousand pounds of power. Externally, emphasize hands, eyes, body movements, techniques, and stepping. Internally, cultivate heart (i.e., emotional mind), spirit, *Yi* (i.e., wisdom mind), and Qi root. Ascending, descending, opening, and closing, train the internal Gong (i.e., Gongfu). There is treasure in the *Dan Tian*, and its marvel is unlimited. *Hen* and *Ha* minds combine with the marvellous secrets of swallow and spit (i.e., inhalation and exhalation), a sound of thunderclap could make the opponent scared. *Qian, Kun, Gen*, and *Xun* are classified at the four corners, (together with) *Kan, Li*, Zhen, and *Dui*, the Bagua

is completed.

The Pre-Heaven Qi (i.e., Original Qi) stored in the Lower *Dan Tian* must be cultivated. When this Qi is manifested, the soft and the hard powers can be skillfully demonstrated. The secret of the internal Gongfu of Baguazhang is in the Lower *Dan Tian*. Therefore, you must study and ponder this secret carefully. Internally, you must train your emotional mind, spirit, wisdom mind, and Qi until they are unified. Only then will you be able to move your Qi anywhere you wish. With the coordination of the *Hen* and *Ha* sounds with your breathing, you will be able to significantly manifest your internal Qi as external power.

Externally, you must master your Bagua techniques. With the strategic movements of the four directions (*Qian, Kun, Gen,* and *Xun*), and the four corners (*Kan, Li,* Zhen, and *Dui*), the Bagua techniques can be manifested to maximum efficiency. Once you can unify both internal and external training, you will not be afraid even if your opponent is a strong and violent person.

練功虛明三步妙，上下二氣不離中。八卦掌法貴三盤，三盤三節各分三。三盤功夫全在腿，趟泥步法意存丹。上下三丹水火濟，掌中力從涌泉行。練藝精心求其妙，証悟斯道得長生。

Training Gong (i.e., Gongfu) must comprehend the marvel of three steppings. The top and the bottom two Qi do not leave the center. The palm techniques of Bagua are precious (because of) the three (heights) of postures. Three postures and the three sections, again divided into three. The Gongfu of three postures are all on the legs. Muddy stepping techniques, the mind is on *Dan Tian*. The top and the bottom three *Dan Tians*, the water and fire mutually support. The power of the palms originate from the *Yongquan*. Train the arts with refined mind, and explore its marvels. This could verify and comprehend the Dao and gain longevity.

Three steppings are forward, backward, and sideways. If you are capable of using these three steppings skillfully, you will be able to execute your Baguazhang techniques effectively and powerfully. The Lower *Dan Tian* is the residence of the Original Qi. It does not matter if you are attacking or withdrawing, the Qi exits from the limbs or returns to the Lower *Dan Tian*. The Qi flow upward and downward must always be balanced, so that the Lower *Dan Tian* will always be the center of the Qi. It is said: "*Yi* is kept in Lower *Dan Tian*" (*Yi Shou Dan Tian*)[22]. This means that it doesn't matter if the Qi exits from or enters into the Lower *Dan Tian*, the mind is always kept on the Lower *Dan Tian*.

One of the main reasons that Baguazhang techniques can be so effective is because Baguazhang emphasizes three different heights of postures: upper, medium, and lower (*Shang Pan, Zhong Pan,* and *Xia Pan*). This enables you to move up and down with skillful coordination of the techniques. The three sections are the head, the trunk and the arms, and the legs. There is another saying that the three sections are the upper limbs, the trunk, and the legs. These sections are themselves divided into three subsections. The head includes the crown, the nose, and the chin. The trunk includes the chest, the waist, and the abdomen. The three sections of the legs are the thighs, the calves, and the feet. The three sections of the arms are the upper-arm, the forearm, and the hands.

The firmness of your three postures depends on the strength of your legs. When you walk, it is like you are walking on muddy ground. Your *Yi* (wisdom mind) is kept on the Lower *Dan Tian*. In all of your actions, the power originates from the *Yongquan* cavity on the bottom of your feet (Figure 2-6), is directed from your waist, and manifests through your palms.

In Chinese Qigong, the forehead (i.e., the third eye) is considered to be the Upper *Dan Tian*, the solar plexus is the Middle *Dan Tian*, and the abdomen is the Lower *Dan Tian*. The Lower *Dan Tian* is the residence of the Water Qi (also called Original Qi or Pre-Heaven Qi), which is converted from the Original Essence a person possesses from birth. The Middle *Dan Tian* is the resi-

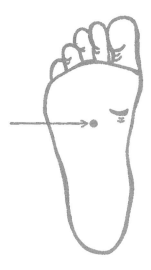

Figure 2-6. *Yongququn* Cavity (K-1)

dence of the Fire Qi, which is processed from the air inhaled and the food eaten. When both the Water Qi and the Fire Qi are intermixed and led upward to nourish the Upper *Dan Tian*, the spirit can be raised, and enlightenment reached. When you reach this stage, the Qi will be abundant and the spirit of vitality will be at its ultimate. One result of this is physical longevity.

Song #2

軟中求硬好，縮小綿軟巧。要講九節勁，言明得知曉。掌拳肘和腕，肩腰胯膝腳。
手眼身法步，慢慢往里找。左右變化廣，動肘賽猴貓。旋轉穩健步，站住泰山牢。
蠅虫不能落，輕時如鵝毛。學會八卦掌，比人招法高。

It is good to look for the hard within the soft. It is clever to shrink into small and be soft as cotton. (If we) want talk about the nine sections' *Jin*, (we) must say (i.e., specify) it clearly until it is understood. (These nine sections) are palms, fists, elbows, and wrists, also, shoulders, waist, hips, knees, and feet. (You) must look for it gradually (i.e., *Jin*) in the hands, eyes, body movement, techniques, and stepping. Left and right, the variations are wide. When moving, (it) is better (i.e., faster and more agile) than the monkey or cat. When spinning and turning, the steppings are steady and secure. When standing still, firmed like the Tai mountain. (You are so alert that) even a fly or an insect cannot land (on your body), and when (you are) light, (you are) like a goose feather. After (you) have learned Baguazhang, (your) techniques are better than other people's.

In internal Chinese martial arts styles, the soft is trained first. The reason for this is that it is harder to be soft than it is to be hard. If you can be soft, then you can also be hard. From the soft, you will be flexible, and your movements agile and swift. If you are hard, your power and movement will be dull and stagnant. It is only when you are soft that you can manifest your *Jin* (i.e., martial power) to all nine sections. Here, the nine sections are the palms, fists, elbows, wrists, shoulders, waist, hips, knees, and feet. In order to have strong *Jin*, you must have perfect coordination of these nine sections. To reach this perfect coordination, you must first develop it in the hands, eyes, body movements, techniques, and stepping. This will take time to practice and ponder until you grasp the trick for this coordination.

When you dodge to the sides, your variations can be numerous and the space you move can be wide. Then you can be agile and fast like a monkey or a cat. When you move, your steps are firm and steady. When you stand still, you are as solid as the Tai mountain. Tai mountain is located in Shandong province and is one of the five greatest mountains in China. You are so alert that even a fly cannot land on your body. When you are light, you are as light as a goose feather.

11. Nine Important Points of Practice [23]
入門練習九要

九要者何？一要塌，二要扣，三要提，四要頂，五要裹，六要鬆，七要垂，八要縮，九要起躦落翻分明。

What are the nine importances? First, there must be sinking; second, there must be arcing; third, there must be lifting; fourth, there must be pressing; fifth, there must be wrapping; sixth, there must be relaxing; seventh, there must be dropping; eighth, there must be contracting; ninth, there must be clearly distinguished rising up for drill, and dropping for turn over.

According to Master Sun Lu-Tang, there are nine vitally important points to which a Bagua practitioner should pay attention all the time. In this first paragraph, he lists these nine important points.

塌者，腰往下塌勁，尾閭上提督脈之理。扣者，開胸順氣，陰氣下降任脈之理也。提者，榖道內提也。頂者，舌頂上腭，頭頂手頂是也。裹者，兩肘往裡裹，勁如兩手心朝上托物，必得往裡裹勁也。

About "sinking," the waist (has) the downward sinking *Jin*, which is the principle of lifting the *Weilu* (i.e., tailbone) upward to (raise Qi in) the Governing Vessel (*Du Mai*). About "arcing," open the chest to soothe the air, which is the principle of sinking the Qi downward in the Conception Vessel (*Ren Mai*). About "lifting," lift the grain path (i.e., anus) internally. About "pressing," it means the tongue is pressing upward, the head is pressing (upward), and the hands are pressing (forward). About "wrapping," the two elbows have inward wrapping *Jin*, like the two palms facing upward to hold objects. (In this case,) they must have the inward wrapping *Jin*.

The waist is the location of your center of gravity. When the waist is sunk, the physical center will be firm, and you will be naturally balanced and rooted. In addition, the lower abdomen is the location of the Lower *Dan Tian*. When the Qi is sunk to this place, you will have your Qi energy center. Only when you are both physically and energetically centered can you lead the Qi to follow the spine upward and out to your arms (Figure 2-7).

When the chest is sunk naturally and easily, the lungs can take in and expel air smoothly. At this point, I would like to remind you that "Qi" in Chinese can mean both air (*Kong Qi*) or the inner energy (*Nei Qi*) circulating in the body. Although these two Qis are closely related, they are not the same thing. The Conception Vessel is located on the center line of the front of the body (Figure 2-8). When the front of the body is relaxed, air can be taken in smoothly, and the Qi can sink to the Lower *Dan Tian*.

In Chinese martial arts or Qigong, in order to lead the Qi inward and store it in the bone marrow, you must know how to coordinate your breathing and the anus (i.e., grain path). In fact, as explained previously lifting up the anus implies lifting up the *Huiyin* cavity (Figure 2-9). You should understand that in ancient times, most of Chinese were illiterate, and it was therefore very difficult to explain the *Huiyin* cavity. However, because when you lift up the anus you are also lifting the *Huiyin* cavity, the term "anus" was often used instead of "*Huiyin*" in the ancient poetry. A Taiji classic tells us: "Condense the Qi to bone marrow" (*Qi Ning Yu Sui*)[24,25]. This means to store the Qi to your bone marrow when you store your *Jin*.

"Pressing" includes three things. First, the tongue is pressed upward to the palate of the mouth. However, a light touch with the tongue to the roof of the mouth is better than pressing. If you press upward, the tongue muscles will become tense, making the Qi circulation stagnant. When the tongue is touching the roof of your month, you can connect the Conception Vessel (*Ren Mai, Yin Mai*) with the Governing Vessel (*Du Mai, Yang Mai*) and complete the small Qi circulation. For more information on this, please refer to *The Root of Chinese Chi Kung*, published by YMAA.

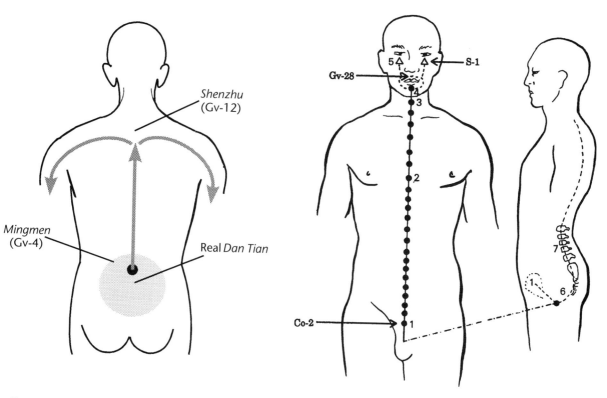

Figure 2-7.   Qi from Real *Dan Tian* to the Arms

Figure 2-8.   Conception Vessel (*Ren Mai*)

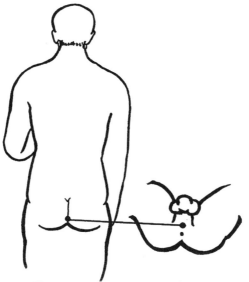

Figure 2-9.   *Huiyin* Cavity (Co-1)

Second, the head presses upward. When you are doing this, the head is suspended and upright. In this case, your spirit of vitality can be raised, and your mind will be alert. Finally, the base of your palm should also be pressing forward to strengthen the pushing Qi, manifesting the power there.

You must also have "Wrapping" *Jin*. This *Jin* is generated through the inward wrapping power of the two elbows. The two elbows should be positioned just as though you are holding two objects in your palms. The elbows must be sunk and the postures of the arms are firm.

鬆者，鬆開兩肩如拉弓然，不使膊尖外露也。垂者，兩手往外翻之時，兩肘極力往下垂勁也。縮者，兩肩與兩胯裡根，極力往回縮勁也。起躦落翻者，起為躦，落為翻，起為橫，落為順，起躦是穿，落翻是打，起亦打，落亦打，打起落，如機輪之循環無間也。

About "Relaxing," it is to comfortably open the two shoulders like pulling a bow, without exposing the shoulder tips (i.e., front of the shoulders) to the outside. About "Dropping," when the two hands are turning outward, the two elbows vigorously have dropping *Jin*. About "contracting," the internal foundations of the two shoulders and two thighs vigorously have contracting *Jin*. About "Raising up for drill and down for turn over," raising is for drill and down is for turning over. Raising is for sideways, down is for smoothness. Raising drill is boring and down to turn over is striking. Raising is for striking, down is also for striking. Strike up and down like the machine wheel's cycle without a gap.

"Relaxing" refers to the two shoulders. When the shoulder is extended, it is relaxed and comfortable like you are pulling a bow. If your shoulders are tensed when you pull a bow, they will shake and you won't be able to aim accurately. When you pull the bow, you should be firm but relaxed. It is the same for your shoulder's extension in Baguazhang.

In Baguazhang, not only should the shoulders be relaxed and sunk, but the elbows should also be "dropped." Only then will the manifestation of your palm techniques have a firm root. "Contracting" means that the two shoulders and the two upper thighs should press inward. When the two shoulders press inward (i.e., the chest is held in), you can store your *Jin* like a bow in your chest, ready for emitting. If you know how to do this right, the power emitted can be so strong and fast that your opponent will have great difficulty neutralizing it. In addition, when the upper thighs are pressing in, the legs can build a firm foundation for your root.

Finally, about "raising up for drill and down for turn over," "raising up" means the palms are raised for boring, or the legs are raised for kicking. The "down" implies the palms turning downward for striking, or the legs turning down for stepping or advancing. Raising can also be used to neutralize the opponent's attack to the sides, and down can also be convenient for leading the opponent's power into emptiness. It does not matter if you are raising or downing, both are effective in striking. If you can use raising and downing smoothly, your attacking will be like a spinning wheel, turning without interruption.

12. Important Keys of Techniques [26]
技法訣要

指前打后，指左打右。逢合必打，逢橫必打，逢直必斜。逢進必退，逢退必進。走打不定勢，八卦藝中是真形。

Point forward, strike backward. Point left, strike right. Encounter "closing," must strike. Encounter "sideways," must strike. Encounter "straight," must (strike) diagonally. Encounter

"retreating," must advance. (There is) no definite posture of walking or striking, (this) is the real shape of Bagua art.

In a real fight, even if your posture indicates forward movement, you may intend and plan to strike backward. If you look like your intention is on your left, you should instead attempt to strike your right. Whenever your opponent's arms are closing, his range must be short and his mind is not on striking. You should take this opportunity to attack. Similarly, when your opponent's force is leading to the sides, again strike. When you fight, there is no definite pattern of movement or postures which can allow your opponent to figure out your intention. Only then is it the real art of Baguazhang.

出手不見手，出手如鋼銼，回手如鉤杆。踢腿不見腿，踢腿如趟泥，走踢方為高。
腳打走去法，膝打不見形，肚打上身法，胯打挨身法。

Emitting hands without seeing hands. Emitting hands like a steel file. Withdrawing like a hooking stick. Kicking legs without seeing legs. When kicking, it is like you are walking on muddy ground. (Those who can) kick during walking are high (talents). The foot strikes in the technique of walking. (When the) knee strikes, the shape cannot be seen. The stomach is to strike the upper body and the thighs strike in closed body.

When you use your hand for striking, it is so fast that your opponent cannot see, and it is strong and powerful, as if a file is filing a piece of steel. When you withdraw your hands, your arm is like a barbed stick. When you kick, it is so fast that your opponent cannot see your leg. When you kick, it is like you are kicking on muddy ground, firm and rooted. The best and most effective technique for kicking is to kick while you are walking. When you are near your opponent and you use your knee to strike him, your opponent won't know how you did it. The upper body is used to strike your opponent's upper body, while your thighs are used to strike when your opponent is nearby. When you strike, your waist always directs the power.

高來則挑穿，低來則搬扣。手打三來腳打七。前腳走來全憑後腳蹬，腳踏中門不放
鬆。動如雷鳴似閃電，不動穩如泰山。

(If your opponent) coming high, then use "picking" and "boring" techniques. When coming low, then use "moving" and "grabbing" techniques. The hands strike three and the feet strike seven. The walking of the front leg relies on the bounce of the rear leg. The feet step into the center door (*Zhong Men*), do not take it easy. (When) moving, it is like thunder's roaring and lightning's flash. (When) still, it is steady like Tai mountain.

When your opponent attacks your upper body, the techniques of "Picking" and "Boring" can be used to counter. However, if your opponent attacks you low, then the techniques of "moving" and "grabbing" can be effective. In all the techniques, the hands should comprise only 30%, while the legs 70% of the motion. The power of moving forward originates from the rear leg. Whenever you can occupy the center door, you should do so immediately. "Occupy the center door" means to step in between his legs with either of your legs. This will put your opponent in a disadvantageous and urgent position. Your movement is powerful and fast, like thunder and lightning, and when you are still, you are steady like Tai mountain. Tai mountain is located in Sandong province and is one of five sacred mountains in China.

以靜制動，以逸待勞。你剛我柔，你柔我剛，要剛柔相濟。力求主動，放膽即成功
，猶疑不定必吃虧。力大者我走，力弱者我進。丹田一聲喊，要使對手惊。

Use the calmness to overcome moving, and evade to wait for exhaustion. You are hard, then I am soft. Your are soft, then I am hard. Must be hard and soft mutually supporting. Try vigorously to dominate the situation. Release the Gall Bladder (i.e., bravery) is the success. If hesitate and wonder, then will be disadvantaged (i.e., defeated). (Encountering) great power person, then I walk (i.e., yield). (Encountering) the weak, then I advance. (When) a shouting originates from *Dan Tian*, must be able to make the opponent scared.

When you fight, remain calm and wait for the right opportunity to execute your techniques. If you keep moving around, you will tire easily. Instead, take it easy, evade your opponent's attacks, and wait until he exhausts himself. When your opponent is hard, use soft to yield and neutralize, and when he is soft, emit your power strongly to overcome his softness. Hard and soft must be exchanged skillfully and naturally, then your opponent will not be able to figure out your intention and techniques. Then you can dominate the entire fighting situation. When you fight, you should not be scared and hesitant. According to Chinese medicine, the Gall Bladder is closely related to your courage. When the Qi in your Gall Bladder is strong and circulating smoothly, then you can be brave. Use your wisdom mind to judge the situation. When the opponent is strong, yield and avoid his strength, and if the opponent is weak, take the advantage and opportunity to advance. Qi is full and sunk to the Lower *Dian Tian*. When this abundant Qi is manifested with a shout, it can make your opponent scared.

13. The Important Keys of the Eight Techniques [27]
八法要訣

推托帶領須認清，搬扣刁黏用法精。見手莫慌隨機變，迎風接進不留情。

Pushing, lifting, carrying, and leading must be recognized clearly. The applications of moving, plucking, hooking, and sticking, must be refined. When seeing the hand (i.e., attack), do not be alarmed. (Instead should) vary according to the opportunity. (Once you have) faced the wind (i.e., encountered the combat) and near the opponent, (you) should not be merciful.

Pushing, lifting, carrying, leading, moving, plucking, hooking, and sticking, are the eight important key words in Baguazhang fighting. Therefore, you should understand them clearly and seek to refine the very essence out of them. When you encounter a fighting situation, you should not be alarmed. Instead, you should remain calm, and clearly use your mind to judge conditions. Only then can you vary your strategy and techniques according to the actual situation. Once the battle has begun, you should not show mercy or hesitate to execute your techniques. Remember **if you are merciful to your enemy, you are cruel to yourself**.

14. The Important Keys of the Five Shapes [28]
五形要訣

未曾出手觀虛實，剛柔相濟莫遲疑。龍行虎坐蛇猴燕，五形之妙要留意。

Before emitting hands, (first) observe the insubstantial and substantial. Do not hesitate and doubt that the hard and the soft should be mutually supportive of each other. Walk as a dragon, sit like a tiger, and also (move as) a snake, monkey, and swallow. Be aware of the marvel of the five shapes.

Before you attack, you should first understand the situation around you. Only if you clearly perceive both your opponent and yourself can you set up an effective strategy. When you apply your techniques, you should be neither too soft nor too hard. The best and the most effective techniques are done through coordination of the soft and the hard. You should walk as swiftly and smoothly as a dragon, and when you are still, you should be firm like a sitting tiger. Furthermore, in all of your movements you should act like the snake, monkey, and the swallow. Once you grasp the trick of these five animals' movements, you will have reached a deeper level of Baguazhang practice. Therefore, you should pay attention to these five shapes.

The Praise of the Dragon Shape: 龍形贊

雲龍探爪扑面掌，霧裡盤桓隱身形。搖頭擺尾穿雲過，探爪連環去又來。青龍探爪
如捉物，神龍鋪地起似風。

The dragon in the clouds extends its claws to manifest "attacking face palm." (It) is lingering around in the fog and hides its body. Swing its head, sway its tail and bore through the clouds. Its extended claws attack continuously to and fro. When the green dragon extends its claws (to attack), it is as easy as catching an object. When the reclining spiritual dragon is aroused, it is like the (blowing) wind.

This song emphasizes two things which you should do to imitate the dragon. First, your movements should be as swift, smooth, fast, and sneaky as a dragon. Then your opponent will never anticipate your actions. Second, when you extend your arms to attack, the attacks should be continuous and firm.

The Praise of the Tiger Shape: 虎形贊

惡虎扑食猛又凶，竄山跳洞顯奇能。猛虎當道人難過，穩坐石崖等鹿來。入洞回
身憑坐力，虎掌連環退步拍。

When a fierce tiger charges for its pray, it is violent and ferocious, jumping among mountains and leaping in and out of its cave to demonstrate its talent. When a fierce tiger is blocking on the way, nobody can pass easily. Firmly sitting on the rock cliff and waiting for the deer's arrival. When entering the cave and turning around the body, it depends on the sitting strength (i.e., the hip power). The tiger's palms strike forward continuously while stepping backward.

When you are attacking, you must be brave and strong like a charging tiger. Move around to set up a good strategy and manifest your talent. When you are still and waiting for your opponent's attack, you are like a sitting tiger, firm and rooted. When you step in for your attack, or when you are turning around your body for yielding, the power of the movement originates from the hips. When you are retreating, you are moving backward firmly, and your palms still attack continuously.

The Praise of the Monkey Shape: 猴形贊

猿猴出洞四面觀，通背護法急三拳。猴兒爬繩倒拉索，爬竿攀樹扯衣衫。白猿獻果
高舉手，偷桃墮枝把身翻。

When an ape or a monkey exits its cave, it observes the four directions (first). When a long armed monkey (*Tong Bei*) defends itself, it starts with three fast fist strikes. When a monkey is climbing a rope, it also pulls the rope backward. When climbing the bamboo pole and grabbing the tree branches, it pulls the (opponent's) clothes. When a white ape is offering fruit, it raises up both its hands. (It) steals peaches and falls from the branches with body's turning.

When you emit your hands to attack, first you should observe your four directions. If you are in an urgent situation, you may use three fast fist strikes to the opponent. This will bring your opponent's attention to himself and allow you an opportunity to retreat. When you fight, you should also be like a monkey, grabbing and pulling whatever you can of your opponent's body. This will destroy your opponent's balance and root, and offer you a chance to attack. When a white ape is raising up its hands to offer fruit (i.e., a fake technique), its mind is actually on the attack to the peaches (i.e., testicles) under the branches (i.e., limbs) of the lower body.

The Praise of the Snake Shape: 蛇形贊

白蛇吐信不留情，惡蟒纏腰似捆繩。怪蛇弄風連擺尾，坦途蛇過亦斜行。蛇走草梢
如飛箭，只見影來不見蹤。

A white snake spits its poison and shows no mercy. When a fierce python is wrapping around the waist, it is like a tightening rope. A strange snake excites the wind and waves its tail continuously. (Even) when the road is flat, the snake still moves diagonally. (When) the snake is creeping, the tips of grass (move) like flying arrows. (You can) only see the shadow and cannot see a trace.

When you emit your techniques, you must not show mercy to your enemy. It is said in Chinese martial arts society: "Mercy to your enemy is cruelty to yourself." The reason for this is that you can never know what your opponent is thinking during a fight. The best strategy to save yourself is to put your opponent in an indefensible condition. In Baguazhang, you turn your body and move around his body. If you are skillful, you will be just like a big python around your opponent, putting him in an urgent situation all the time. The strategy of Baguazhang is to use the round to defeat the straight. Therefore, move your body diagonally into the empty doors on your opponent's sides. When you move, you are blindingly fast, and your limbs act like flying arrows. You are so fast that no trace can be found.

The Praise of the Swallow Shape: 燕形贊

穿雲燕子快逍遙，玉燕抄食水上漂。紫燕斜飛輕又快，翻身展翅軟藏刀。穿雲入戶束身過，乳燕學飛起不高。

The swallow boring through clouds is fast and free. The jade swallow seizes its food on the water surface. The purple swallow flies diagonally, light and speedy. Turning its body and spreading its wings, a knife is hidden among the soft. Boring through clouds and enter the house, (it) tightens its body and passes. The baby swallow is just learning how to fly, it cannot be too high.

When you emit your "boring palm," it is just like a swallow passing through the clouds - fast, swift, and free. The attacks are precise and accurate like a swallow picking up its food on the water's surface. When the "boring palm" is used, since the front side of your opponent is well protected, it is often easier for you to enter from his sides. When your "boring palm" enters the opponent's defensive zone, it is light and speedy. With the palm's turning and repelling, a vital technique can sometimes be obscured from your opponent's view. When your palms are boring through, the palms are restrained and enter carefully. When you learn how to use the "boring palm," you should be like a baby swallow learning how to fly, and start with the basics.

2-3. Baguazhang and Bagua

In Chapter 1, we introduced some of the general and basic concepts of how Baguazhang is related to the Bagua and *Yi Jing*. In this section, we would like to translate and make some comments on a few important documents describing this relationship. While the previous discussion served you as a guideline, this chapter will lead you to the essence of this relationship.

Most of the material discussed in this section originated from Master Sun Lu-Tang's book *The Study of Bagua Fist*, published in 1916.[29] Master Sun's book was the first, and to our knowledge the only, book available which provides an in-depth study of the relationship of the Baguazhang and Bagua.

1. The Unification of Pre-Heaven and Post-Heaven in Bagua Fist Theory 八卦拳先天後天合一式說

周易闡真曰：‘先天八卦，一氣循環。’渾然天理從太極中流出，乃真體未破之事。後天八卦，分陰分陽，有善有惡，在造化中變動，乃真體已虧之事。真體未破，是未生出者，須當無為。無為之妙，在乎逆中行順，逆藏先天之陽，順化後天之陰，歸於未生以前面目，不使陰氣有傷真體也。真體有傷，是已生出者，須當有為。

有為之竅，在乎順中用逆，順退後天之陰，逆返先天之陽，歸於既生以後之面目，務使陽氣還成真體也。先天逆中行順者，即逆藏先天陰陽五行，而歸於胚胎一氣之中，順化後天之陰，而保此一氣也。

The Real Elucidation of Zhou said: "The Pre-Heaven Bagua is a theory of sole Qi's circulation." (It is) an entire heaven theory and was originated from Taiji. (It is) the events before the real body (i.e., physical body) is exposed (to heaven)(i.e., born). The Post-Heaven Bagua is divided into Yin and Yang, (which) carries goodness and evil, and keeps changing in its creation and derivation. (This is) the real (human) body's event which has already been defected. Before the real body is exposed means before birth. (It is) the state of "no action." The marvel of "no action" is that which can be smooth, even in the inverse situation. The Pre-Heaven's smoothness is hidden within the converse, which is able to smoothly naturalize the Post-Heaven's Yin and return it to the face (i.e., condition) before birth. (This) will prevent the real body's injury from the Yin Qi. (When) the real body is already injured, it is already born. (Therefore, we) should conduct the secret trick which could be helpful (to us). (This secret trick) is (knowing how) to use the inverse within the smoothness. Smoothly retreat the Post-Heaven Yin and inversely return it to the Pre-Heaven Yang. (In order to) return the face (i.e., physical condition) of the Post-Birth, (we) must enable (our) Yang Qi to be back to its real body. Conducting the smoothness within the Pre-Heaven inverse means, in the inverse there is a hidden (relation) of Pre-Heaven Yin and Yang Five Phases which could return (our condition) back to the sole Qi of embryo. (We must) smoothly neutralize the Post-Heaven Yin and protect this sole Qi."

In the book of *The Real Elucidation of Zhou*, it explains that when we talk about the Pre-Heaven Bagua, we are talking about the sole Qi. This Qi originates from the theory of Taiji. This Qi existed even before our birth. At this time, it is in the *Wuji* state (i.e., the state of no extremity). When you are in this state, the Qi can circulate smoothly and naturally without stagnation. However, after birth, everything in the world is divided into Yin and Yang. When you were born, you started to absorb food and air around you, and your mind was immediately affected by events happening around you. Your physical body and nonphysical mind are already damaged from the these impure subjects and events. This is very different from the "no action" state before you were born. When there is no action, then the Qi can move and circulate naturally and smoothly as it wishes. After birth, even though we exist in the inverse environment, the Pre-Heaven smooth circulation of Qi still exists in our body. Because of this, we can use this Pre-Heaven Qi to return our Post-Heaven Qi to the state before our birth. In order to reach this goal, we must know the secrets of how and why. Only then can we retreat from the Post-Heaven Yin (i.e., Qi), and return to the Pre-Heaven state. The method of doing this is hidden in the theory of the "Five Phases." The Five Phases include: metal, wood, water, fire, earth. After you comprehend the theory of the Five Phases, you should learn how to return the Post-Heaven Qi to the origin of your Qi, located where the embryo is carried, at the Lower *Dan Tian*.

後天順中用逆者，即順退已發之陰，歸於初生未發之處，返出先天之陽，以還此初生也。陽健陰順，復見本來面目。仍是先天後天，兩而合一之原物，從此別立乾坤，再造爐鼎。

What is the Post-Heaven using the inverse within the smooth? It is smoothly retreating the Yin which has been emitted, and leading it to return to the place where was just born and not yet emitted. Therefore, return the Post-Heaven's Yang to the just born state. When Yang is healthy and Yin is smooth, then again see the original face (i.e., state). This is the original object (i.e., goal) of unifying the Pre-Heaven and Post-Heaven. From then on, establish *Qian* and *Kun* separately, again build up the furnace (i.e., foundation).

After a person is born, he follows the natural course of growing, aging, and finally dying. To reverse this course, you must learn how to retreat (i.e., condense) the Yin (i.e., Pre-Heaven Qi), which has been manifested at its place of origin, the Lower *Dan Tian*. Then you may return to the

Pre-Heaven Yang (i.e., Pre-Birthnatural and uncontaminated physical body). This means that the goal of training Baguazhang, and in fact all of the Chinese internal arts, is to be as soft, natural, and pure as a baby. In order to achieve this, you must first learn how to condense or store the Qi in the Lower *Dan Tian*. Only then can you rebuild the firm Yin state of before your were born. It is also then that your Yang physical body can return to its natural condition - pure, clean, and healthy. When you have reached this goal, you will have unified the Pre-Heaven and Post-Heaven. From this state, again you can distinguish the Yin and Yang (i.e., *Qian* and *Kun*). That means that in order to reach a high stage of cultivation, at the beginning you must return your Yin Qi body and Yang physical body to their original states. From this beginning, they will again be distinguished and cultivated along the correct paths.

行先天逆中行順之道，則為九還七返大還丹矣。今以先天圖移於後天圖內者，使知真體未破者，行無為自然之道，以道全形，逆中行順，以化後天之陰。真體已虧者，行有為變化之道，以術延命，順中用逆，以復先天之陽。先後合一，有無兼用，九還七返，歸於大覺金丹之事了了。

What is the Pre-Heaven conducting the smoothness within the inverse? It is the Dao of the nine returns and seven returns. Now (let us) move the illustration of the Pre-Heaven drawing in the Post-Heaven drawing. This is to acknowledge that when the real body (i.e., physical body) was not yet exposed (i.e., born), the natural Dao of "no action" was executed. (From this, we) can express the entire shape (i.e., picture). Conduct the smoothness within the inverse and neutralize the Post-Heaven Yin. Those the real body has been defected is able to conduct the Dao of variation, therefore, to extend the life with method. Conduct the inverse within the smooth to recover the Pre-Heaven's Yang. The Pre-Heaven and Post-Heaven are unified and can be used either way. Those of the nine returns and the seven returns are the theory of the "great awakenings," and is the affair of the "golden elixir."

Not only should you know how to return your Qi and physical bodies to their original Pre-Heaven state, you should also know how to cultivate the Pre-Heaven Qi (i.e., the natural Dao) in the body which is already on the reverse path from health and longevity (i.e., mortality). In order to reach this goal, you must learn the methods "Nine Returns" and "Seven Returns." This means that after you return your body to the Pre-Heaven state, you should then learn how to cultivate your Original Qi. When this Qi reaches a more abundant level, you will learn to lead the Qi to the brain, nourishing and purifying it until finally establishing a spirit body which can have an eternal life.

Remember that Baguazhang was created and developed in the Daoist society of ancient China. Usually, in order to reach the final goal of enlightenment in the Dao, a Daoist would follow the procedures of: 1. Refine the Essence (*Jing*) and convert it into Qi; 2. Cultivate Qi and convert it into spirit (*Shen*); and 3. Train the spirit and return it to emptiness. On the path of this training, you will experience the "Nine Returns" and the "Seven Returns" of enlightenment during the process of spirit nourishment. Naturally, this is a very deep subject of Qi cultivation, and usually trained only in a monastery. It is beyond the scope of this book to explain these techniques, and nearly impossible to explain them in sufficient detail in any book at all. For more information, interested readers may refer to *Muscle/Tendon and Marrow/Brain Washing Chi Kung* by YMAA.

In order to express the unification of the Pre-Heaven and the Post-Heaven, the Pre-Heaven trigram is placed in the Post-Heaven trigram. This means the Pre-Heaven is within and is the root of the Post-Heaven. Those people whose Qi and physical bodies are healthy can train by following the natural path to cultivate the Pre-Heaven Qi and reach the goal of enlightenment. Those people whose Qi and physical bodies have already been damaged can change their condition, and thereby extend their lives. In order to reach this goal, they must learn how to return their Yin (i.e., Original Qi) to its original place (i.e., Lower *Dan Tian*), and also learn how to return their physical body to its Pre-Birth state. Afterwards, they can unify the Pre-Heaven and Post-Heaven. Only under these circumstances can they train the Dao of the "golden elixir," and finally reach the goal of enlightenment.

再以金丹分而言之，金者氣質堅固之意，丹者週身之氣圓滿無虧之形。總而言之，拳中氣力上下內外如一也，此為易筋之事也。今借悟元子，先後八卦合一圖，以明拳中拙勁歸於真勁也。

(Let us) talk about the "golden elixir." The gold (or metal) has the meaning of strong Qi and solid characteristic. The elixir, which is the Qi and manifested with round and without defect in the shape of the entire body. In all, the Qi and *Li* (i.e., *Jin*) in the fists, top and bottom, internal and external, are just one (unit). This is the training of the "muscle/tendon change." Now, (let us) borrow Wu Yuan Zhi's diagram of the unification of the Pre-Heaven and Post-Heaven Bagua so to understand how the dull *Jin* can be returned to the real *Jin* in the fist.

"Elixir" here means the Qi. The gold or metal is solid and strong. Therefore, the "golden elixir" means to train your Qi until it is full, abundant, and strong in your body. When you reach this stage, the physical body can manifest the Qi efficiently, and change from weak to strong. Under this sole Qi, your entire body, both internal and external, the top and the bottom, will unify and become one unit. This is the theory of the "real *Jin*" (martial power). If you would like to know more about *Jin*, please refer to *Advanced Yang Style Tai Chi Chuan, Vol. 1* by YMAA.

2. The Unification of Pre-Heaven and Post-Heaven in Baguazhang - Illustration
八卦拳先天後天八卦合一圖解

起點練法，仍照前者法則習之。但預知先後天合一之理，內外卦歸一之式，二者判別，且能使先天為後天之體，後天為先天之用。無先天則後天無根本，無後天則先天不成全。其理雖有先天為之本，然無外式之形，只能行無為自然之道，不能習之以全其體也。若使之先天健全，即借後天有形式之身，以行有為變化之道，則能補全先天之氣也。

At the beginning of training, follow the previous method to practice. However, (you) should early understand the theory of the unification of the Pre-Heaven and Post-Heaven. (That is) the manner of how internal and external trigrams unify into one, and (how) these two are distinguished. This will enable (you) to apply the Pre-Heaven condition into the Post-Heaven's body and the Post-Heaven becomes the application of the Pre-Heaven. Without Pre-Heaven, then the Post-Heaven will not have a root. Without the Post-Heaven, then the Pre-Heaven will not be completed (i.e., be manifested). The theory is, though the Pre-Heaven is a root, however, without the external shape, it can only fulfill the natural Dao of "no action." Therefore, it cannot be practiced and completed as a whole. If the Pre-Heaven is healthy, then it can borrow the Post-Heaven's formed body and conduct the useful Dao of variations. This is able to remedy the Pre-Heaven's Qi.

If you are a beginner, the first step of training is "regulating your body," which includes learning the correct posture and movement. During this learning period you must also study the theory of the Unification of the Pre-Heaven and the Post-Heaven (to understand how internal and external can be combined into one) and also be able to distinguish them clearly. Later, you can apply them and make the Pre-Heaven become the root of the Post-Heaven, and the Post-Heaven become the manifestation of the Pre-Heaven.

If you do not know how to apply the Pre-Heaven Qi in the Post-Heaven physical body, then there is no energy source of the physical body, and the manifestation for the physical body will be weak. Conversely, if you do not have a healthy physical body, the Qi will not flow efficiently, and its manifestation will not be complete. Therefore, in order to unify the Pre-Heaven and Post-Heaven, you must know the method of cultivating and training both the Qi and physical bodies.

但拳術未習熟時，似乎有分順伸逆縮，判而為二之意。其實是先天後天氣力不符，故有分而為二之理。且以拳術之理，分而言之，則為先後天。合而言之，則為渾然一氣。今以先天而言，則為拳中無形之勁，謂之性。性即身中無形之八卦也，亦為之先天。以後天而言，自有身形陰陽開闔伸縮，生出四象。四象者，各有陰陽謂之情。情者，手足身體旋轉動作，即成有形之八卦也，謂之後天。此是先後天分言，謂之開也。

Before you have mastered the fist techniques, it seems there is a distinction which divides the "follow to extend" and "inverse to withdraw" into two things. In fact, it is because the Qi and *Li* of the Pre-Heaven and the Post-Heaven are not in accord with each other. This is the reason why it is divided into two. (If we) discuss the theory of the fist techniques with the division, then it is divided into Pre-Heaven and Post-Heaven. (If) unified, then it is the abundant sole Qi. Now, (if we) talk about the Pre-Heaven, it is the *Jin* of no shape in the fist. This is called "natural virtue." This "natural virtue" is the Bagua of no shape within (our) body. This is what is called "Pre-Heaven." If (we) talk about the Post-Heaven, there are the body shape, Yin and Yang (distinctions), opening and closing, extending and withdrawing. This begets the four phases. Among these four phases, there also is Yin and Yang, and called "natural virtue." What is this "natural virtue," the hands, the feet, the body's rotation and movements which result in the Bagua with shape. This is called "Post-Heaven." This is discussed with dividing the Pre-Heaven and the Post-Heaven, and is therefore called "dividing."

Even if you understand the theory of the unification, if you are not familiar with the postures and techniques, you are still in the stage of "regulating your body." In this stage, you will feel that extension and the withdrawal seem to be two different actions. This is because you have not yet applied the theory of the Pre-Heaven and Post-Heaven unification in the fists.

If we discuss this according to martial arts theory, when dividing, Qi is distinguished into Pre-Heaven and Post-Heaven. When unified, it is the sole Qi. If the Pre-Heaven and Post-Heaven are distinguished, the internal *Jin* which cannot be seen will be the Pre-Heaven. The *Jin* or the martial power can be distinguished into the "internal *Jin*" and "external *Jin*." The "internal *Jin*" (*Yin Jin*) is the storage of the *Yi*, the Qi, and "the external *Jin*" (*Yang Jin*) is the manifestation of this *Yi* and Qi into the forms of power through the physical body. When the *Jin* manifests, the actions can be again distinguished into Yin and Yang, and become Four Phases: "opening" (Yang), "closing" (Yin), "extending" (Yang), and "withdrawing" (Yin). Again, each of these Four Phases includes Yin and Yang, and become Bagua (the Eight trigrams). This is the manifestation of the Pre-Heaven *Jin* (or internal *Jin*) into the actions of the body and the limbs, and the Post-Heaven *Jin* (or external *Jin*).

合而言之，人心即天理，天理即人心。意者心之所發，身體四梢是意之所指揮也。則拳中之氣，身體手足聽其指揮，循著次序漸漸習去。自始至終無乖戾之氣，則能盡其性矣。盡其性，則能復其未發意之初心。

(If we) talk about their unification, human *Xin* (i.e., heart, emotional mind) is the natural theory of heaven. The natural theory of heaven is (also) the human *Xin*. The *Yi* (i.e., wisdom mind) originates from *Xin*. The body's four extremities are directed by the *Yi*. Then, the Qi in the fist, the body, the hands, and the feet listen to its governing. Practice (the fist) following the order gradually. From the beginning until the end, there is no weird Qi, then the "natural virtue" can be manifested. This will make you recover the beginning *Xin* before the *Yi* is generated.

Now let us talk about the unification of the Pre-Heaven and the Post-Heaven. The *Xin* (i.e., emotional mind) originates from natural instincts and human emotion, which is touched and agitated by the surrounding environment. Therefore, emotional reaction is the natural Dao. After

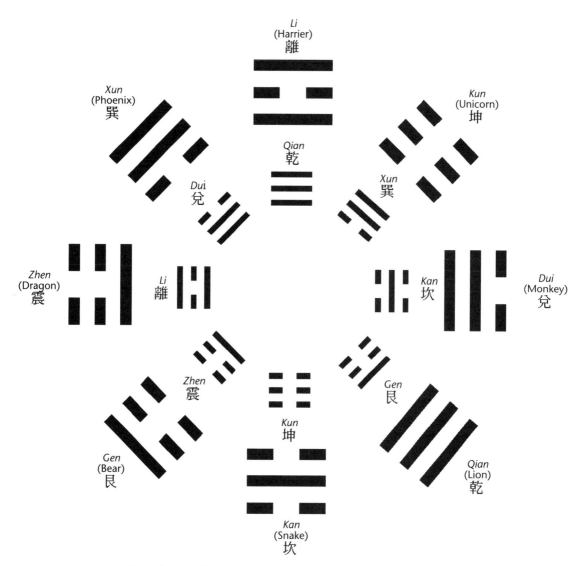

Figure 2-10.   The Unification of the Pre-Heaven and Post-heaven.

your emotional mind is agitated, then your wisdom mind (*Yi*) will be generated to judge the situation. From this *Yi*, the Qi can be led, and the body and limbs directed or governed. If you practice gradually, following the procedures of the *Xin* to *Yi*, from *Yi* to Qi, and from Qi to action, smoothly from the beginning to the end, you can manifest the decision of the *Yi* (which is generated from *Xin*) efficiently. Your entire body will then act as one unit. This is the unification of the Pre-Heaven and the Post-Heaven.

但拳術初練時，四體之作用，不能盡合於力，力不能盡合於氣，氣不能盡合於意，
似乎拳中伸縮有二式之別。若得其所以然，練習先後合一之理，惟其三害且莫犯，
謹守九要而不失，則四體身形隨著意，照法實力作去。久之四體手足動作，可以隨
意指揮，故能上下相連，手足相顧，內外如一，渾然天理。此時是先後天八卦合一
之體也。

However, when the fist is being trained, the four bodies' (i.e., four extremities') functioning cannot be in accord with the *Li* (i.e., muscular strength) and the *Li* cannot be in accord with the Qi, and Qi cannot be in accord with the *Yi*. It seems that there is a difference to extending and with-

drawing in the fist. If (you are) able to obtain (i.e., understand) the (above) reasons, and practice the theory of unification of Pre-Heaven and Post-Heaven, do not commit the mistakes of "three harms." Carefully keep the "nine importances" in mind without losing them, then the four bodies and the body shape can follow the *Yi* and perform the (correct) techniques. After a long time, the four bodies' hands and feet can be governed by the *Yi's* wishes, then the top and bottom can be connected, the hands and feet can look after each other, and both internal and external can unify as one. This is the great heavenly theory, and is the body of unification of the Pre-Heaven and Post-Heaven Baguas.

However, when you first learn Baguazhang, your *Yi*, *Qi*, and *Li* cannot yet coordinate. At this time, it seems that all the movements can be distinguished clearly as either Yin or Yang. In this stage you still do not understand the secret of the unification. It is just like you are learning how to drive. At first, you have to ascertain the locations of the brake, the accelerator, the steering wheel, etc. However, after you have driven for a long time, your mind will no longer be on driving. The distinctions all disappear, and you are driving without driving. When this happens, your internal and external are unified. Therefore, when you train Baguazhang, you have to keep practicing until all the postures and techniques can be applied automatically and without thinking. Then you will have unified the internal *Yi* and Qi with the external action. When you practice, you must always follow the correct techniques. Otherwise, you will build up bad habits, which could bring you more harm than health.

3. The Pattern of Yang Fire and Yin Amulet in Baguazhang
八卦拳陽火陰符形式

陽火陰符之理，始終兩段工夫。一進陽火，一運陰符。進陽火者，陰中返陽，進其剛健之德，所以復先天也。運陰符者，陽中用陰，運其柔順之德，所以養先天也。進陽火，必進至於六陽純全，剛健之至，方是陽火之功盡。運陰符，必運至於六陰純全，柔順之至，方是陰符之功畢。陽火陰符，功力俱到，剛柔相當，建順兼全，陽中有陰，陰中有陽，陰陽一氣，渾然天理。

The theory of the "Yang Fire" and the "Yin Amulet," from the beginning to the end, includes two sections of Gongfu. One is to advance the "Yang Fire," and the other is to manipulate the "Yin Amulet." The "Advance the Yang Fire" is to return to Yang from Yin, and so to approach the virtues of the solid and strength. Therefore, it is to recover the Pre-Heaven. To "Manipulate the Yin Amulet" is to apply Yin within Yang, and to manifest its virtues of softness and smoothness. Therefore, it is to nourish (i.e., cultivate) the Pre-Heaven. When advancing "Yang Fire," (you) must advance to the stage that all six Yangs are refined and complete. Then it is the final accomplishment of the "Yang Fire." When utilizing the "Yin Amulet," (you) must manipulate until all of six Yins are refined and complete, and reach the most soft and smooth stage. This is the final accomplishment of the "Yin Amulet." When the efficacies of the "Yang Fire" and the "Yin Amulet" are reached, the hardness and the softness are properly and mutually balanced, the strength and the smoothness are both complete. Within the Yang, there is a Yin, and within the Yin, there is a Yang. Both Yin and Yang have sole Qi. This is the great natural heavenly theory.

According to Chinese Yin and Yang philosophy, Yin represents negative, water, soft, weak or anything hidden within, while Yang expresses the positive, fire, hard, strong or anything manifested on the surface which can be seen. Only if you develop and train both Yin and Yang, will you have a firm root (Yin) and a strong body (Yang) to manifest the Yin. Therefore, in Baguazhang, there are two Gongfus which you must learn. One is learning how to manifest the Yang, which is called to "advance the fire." The other is learning how to store the Qi in the Lower *Dan Tian* and how to build the Qi up to an abundant level. This process is hidden within and cannot be seen from the external. When you advance the fire, you are leading the Qi (Yin) from the Lower *Dan Tian* and manifesting it as an action pattern. Therefore, you apply the Yin and recover the Pre-Heaven. When you store your Qi, you are soft and lead the Qi smoothly to the Lower *Dan*

Tian to nourish the Pre-Heaven.

According to Chinese medicine, there are twelve Qi channels in which the Qi circulates in our bodies. Six of these twelve channels belong to Yang, while the other six belong to Yin. The Yang channels lead the Qi to the Yang organs and to the muscular body, to energize them and manifest the Qi strength. The Yin channels lead the Qi to the Yin internal organs and nourish them. According to Chinese medicine, those Yin organs store the essence (*Jing*) and convert it into Qi. Later, this Qi can be either manifested or stored in the Lower *Dan Tian* for further use.

When you manifest your Qi into Yang form, you must learn how to maximally demonstrate its capability. Consequently, the power demonstrated can be strong. When you convert your essence into Qi and store it in the body, your body must be very soft so the Qi can be led naturally and smoothly to the deep places in the body. If you can reach this stage, then you can be soft as well as hard, and Yin and Yang can support each other mutually. All of this is done with the sole Qi, and this accomplishment is done according to the natural Dao.

圓陀陀，光灼灼，淨裸裸，赤洒洒，聖胎完成。一粒金丹寶珠懸於太虛空中，寂然不動，感而遂通，感而遂通。寂然不動，常應常靜，常靜常應。本良知良能面目，復還先天。一粒金丹吞入腹，始知我命不由天也。再加上工夫，煉神還虛，打破虛空，脫出真身，永久不壞，所謂聖而不可知之之謂神。進於形神俱妙，與道合真之境矣。

Round and complete, bright and shinning, clean as naked, and free as wished, the holy embryo will be completed. (Consequently), a grain of "golden elixir," as a precious pearl, will be suspended in the space of the great emptiness, still without moving. When it is touched, then it is comprehended. (When) it is still without moving, (it will) always correspond and then calm, (also) will always calm to correspond. The original face of the innate knowledge and ability will return to the Pre-Heaven. A grain of "golden elixir" is swallowed to the abdomen. Then (I) begin to realize that my life is not controlled by Heaven. Again, advance your Gongfu further, to refine your spirit and return to the emptiness. Break the voided emptiness (i.e., physical body), and cast the real body (i.e., physical body), (consequently) will never be destroyed (i.e., die). This is the spirit of what is sacred, which is beyond (our) knowledge. From this, it is able to enter the stage from which both the shape and spirit are marvellous, and truly combine with the Dao.

According to Chinese Qigong society, especially Daoist, when you condense the Qi in the Lower *Dan Tian*. Through a long period of cultivation, you can form a "Holy Baby" in the *Dan Tian* area. This "Holy Baby," after ten months of nourishment, will be mature and can be led to the spirit center (i.e., Upper *Dan Tian* or the third eye) to break through the blockage of the skeleton and contact the outside world. This is the stage where the "Spiritual Baby" is born. After this baby is born, it will take three years to nurse and ten years to train (i.e., by facing the wall). Then this "spiritual baby" can be independent. When this stage is reached, even after the physical body is dead, the fully mature spirit child can survive eternally. This is the stage of enlightenment (Daoism) or Buddhahood (Buddhism). If you are interested in this subject, please refer to *Muscle/Tendon Changing and Marrow/Brain Washing Chi Kung* by YMAA. Since Baguazhang was created in Daoist society, the ancient Baguazhang practitioners were also aiming for the establishment of this "Holy Spiritual Embryo." Once you reach this stage, through further cultivation you may gain eternal spiritual life, and reach the goal of enlightenment contrary even to our natural destiny of aging and death.

4. The Method of Refining the Spirit and Returning It to the Emptiness in Baguazhang
八卦拳練神還虛形式

拳術之道，有功用之理，有神化之理。上言陽火陰符是為功用，此言煉神還虛是為妙用。妙用之功，其法何在？仍不外乎八卦拳之式求之。故開闔動靜，起落進退，生克變化，以致無窮之妙，亦不離八卦。八卦不離四象，四象不離兩儀，兩儀不離一氣，一氣自虛無兆質矣。惟手足身體，外形不要著力，俱隨意而行之。然身體亦並非全不用力，其勁不過極力往回縮去，意在蓄神耳。

The Dao of fist techniques includes the theory of functions and the theory of spiritual derivation. What is mentioned previously about "Yang Fire" and "Yin Amulet" is the function. In this section, the discussion of "Refining the Spirit and Return It to the Emptiness" is the marvellous application. Where is method of reaching the Gong (i.e., Gongfu) of the marvellous application? There is nothing but looking for it in the Bagua postures. Therefore, opening and closing, moving and stillness, raising and falling, advancing and retreating, and the variation of the mutual generation and conquest, until the marvels of the no limitation, all cannot leave (the theory) of Bagua. Bagua does not separate from the Four Phases, the Four Phases do not leave the Two Poles, and the Two Poles cannot be apart from the sole Qi. (Once there is) sole Qi, then naturally empty without the slightest impurities. Only that the hands, feet, and the body should not be on *Li* (i.e., stiff muscular power), all should be conducted followed the *Yi*. However, it does not mean that the body should lack *Li* completely. Its *Jin* (i.e., martial power) is done with the great effort of withdrawing. The *Yi* is on storing the *Shen* (spirit).

The methods of advancing the Fire to strengthen the physical Yang body, and of condensing the Qi to the Lower *Dan Tian*, are aiming for applications of the forms and techniques. However, if you continue your training and reach the stage of refining your spirit and entering the level of fighting without fighting, then the marvelous applications of Baguazhang are unlimited.

This is similar to when you are learning to play a musical instrument, such as the piano. At the beginning, you are learning how to press keys in the right sequence, mechanically playing music composed by other people. However, after you have practiced for many many years, you may reach a stage where you can place your own emotions and spirit into the music naturally. Your mind will no longer be on playing, but on the spiritual feeling of the art. In this stage, the music has become a tool for expressing your spiritual self. Then you can create music from your feelings, naturally. In Baguazhang, when you reach this stage, you are a master.

The method of reaching this goal starts from the basic, simple forms which were constructed based on the Bagua theory. Even after you have mastered the forms, still your forms and the spirit spring from Bagua theory. From the Bagua, you can comprehend and apply the theory of the Four Phases. From the Four Phases, you can understand the Two Poles (i.e., Yin and Yang). Finally, from the Two Poles, you gradually reach the goal of unifying the internal and external with a Sole Qi.

外形身體手足，俱以意運用之。行之已久，身體氣力，化之似覺有若無，實若虛之意。每逢靜中動時，身子移出而不知己之動，則不知有己也。每與他人比較時，伸縮往來飛騰變化，如入無人之境。而身體氣力自覺無動，是不知己之動而靜，則不知有彼也。夫若是，則能不見而章，不動而變，無為而成，至拳無拳，意無意，無形無象，無我無他。練神還虛，神化不測之妙道得矣。

The external body, hands, and feet are all governed by the *Yi*. After practicing for a long time, (you feel that) when (you) derive (your) body's Qi and *Li*, it seems there but not there. This is the feeling of being in substantial and as if still insubstantial. Whenever encountering the movement in the stillness, the body has already moved and (you) do not know the moving. In this case, you have forgotten the existence of yourself. When (you) compete with others (i.e., fight), extending, withdrawing, forward and backward, jumping and raising, and varying and alternating, just like entering the place without opponent. Without feeling the moving of the Qi and *Li* by yourself, is because (you) do not recognize (your) moving and (the *Yi*) keep still (i.e., calm). Then, you do not know you have an opponent existing. If (you) can do so, then (you) can clarify without seeing, to vary without movement, to accomplish without action, to use the fist without

the fist, to execute *Yi* without *Yi*, without the shape and without the figure, without me and without him (i.e., opponent), the spirit has been refined into the emptiness. (This will enable you) reach the unexpected marvel of the spiritual derivation and gain the Dao.

When you practice Baguazhang, the most important factor for success is your *Yi*. Use your *Yi* to lead the Qi, and use your Qi to energize your physical body. Keep practicing until this process is so natural as to be automatic. Then, when you encounter a situation, all your reactions will be natural, and it will seem you are fighting without fighting. Then your Baguazhang will have entered into the stage of "Spiritual Emptiness." This is the stage of "the *Yi* of no *Yi*," "the fist of no fist," "the technique of no technique," "the shape of no shape," and "the enemy of no enemy."

5. Theory of No Extremity (Wuji Xue)
無極學

無極形式者，當人未學之先，心中混混沌沌，一氣渾淪舉動之間，但由天然之性也。而旋轉無度，起落無節，外失諸修，內失諸養，知順之所往，不知逆之所來。以至體質虛弱，陽極必陰，陰極必死，往往歸於無可如何之地。是攝生之術，講求無方，良可慨也。

The shape of *Wuji* is before a person learns (Baguazhang), (his) mind is confused and disordered. The sole Qi is entirely following the (natural) pattern, and all movements are initiated from the natural property (i.e., natural feeling). (Therefore,) there is no defined degree of turning, no control of the rising and falling, externally lost the cultivation and internally without nourishment. Knowing where the smooth is going, yet not knowing where the inverse coming from. It results in the body's quality being void and weak. The extremity of Yang must be Yin, and when Yin reaches its limit, must die. It always ends in the stage of not knowing how to handle the problem. Therefore, it is known that there is no medicine which could extend the life.

In Baguazhang, the *Wuji* state is the state before you start learning. At this time, your mind is confused and the Qi flow in your body is accomplished unconsciously. Your turning, rising and falling, or any other movements, are clumsy and inefficient, and do nothing to nourish your Qi internally. You know only the natural path of growing, aging, and death, yet do not know how to reverse the path to cultivate the Qi and the physical body. This results in the body's weakness. When the Yang (i.e., physical body) reaches its end, Yin must arrive and with it death. As this fate approaches, all means for prolonging an unhealthy life will be in vain.

惟聖人知逆運之機，修身之本，還元之道。總之不外形意太極八卦諸拳之理，一氣伸縮之道，明善復出之功，求立於至善之極點。以復先天之元氣，和而不流，中立而不倚，可與後世作法，亦可為萬物立命，此之謂無極而生太極之式也。

Only a saint is able to know the opportunity of changing destiny and to cultivate the root of the body. The Dao of returning to (our) origin, there is nothing but (what is constructed) on the theory of the Xingyi, Taiji, and Bagua fists (i.e., martial styles), on the Dao of the extending and withdrawing of the sole Qi, and on the understanding the benefit of returning to the beginning, then build (the foundation) on the ultimate point of extreme goodness. This will enable (you) to recover the Pre-Heaven Original Qi, harmonious and not turbulent, stand in the center without leaning, and become the example to later generations. This could also comprehend the meaning of the ten million lives. This is what is called the way of generating Taiji from *Wuji*.

The way to rule destiny is by cultivating your Qi, and training your body through Xingyi, Bagua, or Taiji. These arts were created by the saints or wise ancestors, who could see through problems and knew the way and the theory of preventing them. The method is nothing but comprehending the theory of the Qi's extending and withdrawing, and also learning how to apply the Qi to the physical body. Qi's extending means to expand the Qi to the skin surface and beyond, and is the theory used in skin/body breathing technique discussed in muscle/tendon changing Qigong. Qi's withdrawing means to condense the Qi to the bone marrow, and lead it to the Lower

Dan Tian, which is the theory of marrow/brain washing Qigong. If you can comprehend this theory, your Qi will be harmonious, peaceful, and neutral. Consequently, you Qi, mind, and physical body can be calm and centered. This is the way of *Wuji* in Baguazhang. Therefore, before you start your Baguazhang movements, you are in the *Wuji* state. The mind is calm and clear, the Qi circulating within is smooth and natural, and both the mental and physical bodies are centered.

6. Theory of Extremity (Taiji Xue)
太極學

太極形式者，無極而生，陰陽之母也。左旋之而為陽，右轉之而為陰。旋轉乃一氣之流行，太極即一氣，一氣即太極也。以體言則為太極，以用言則為一氣。時陽則陽，時陰則陰，時上則上，時下則下，陽而陰，陰而陽。一氣活活潑潑，有無不立，開闔自然，皆在當中一點子運用也。這一點子即是拳中左旋右轉開闔動靜，陰陽相交之中樞也。中樞者為人性命之本造化之原，丹田之氣，八卦拳之根蒂也。此氣是天地之根，陰陽之母，即太極是也，故兩儀由此而生焉。

The formation of Taiji is generated from *Wuji* and is the mother of Yin and Yang. Turning to the left is Yang and turning to the right is Yin. Turning is the way which the Qi circulates. Taiji is the sole Qi and the sole Qi is Taiji. If talking about the body it is Taiji, and if talking about the usage then it is the sole Qi. When the time should be Yang, it is Yang and when the time should be Yin, it is Yin. When it should be upward, it is upward and when it should be downward, then it is downward. Yang is derived into Yin and Yin derived into Yang. The sole Qi is alive and vivacious, nothing cannot be cultivated (i.e., established), opening and closing are natural. All of these depends on how (you) apply the central point within (your body)(i.e., Lower *Dan Tian*). This point is also the central control of the Yin and Yang, left turning or right turning, opening or closing, and moving or still of the fist. This central control is the origin of humanity and the root of life and derivation. The Qi in *Dan Tian* is the root of Bagua Fist. This Qi is the root of Heaven and Earth, the mother of Yin and Yang, and is also Taiji. Therefore, the two poles are generated from here.

This article mentions that Taiji (i.e., Great Ultimate) is generated from *Wuji* (i.e., No extremity) and is the mother of the two poles, Yin and Yang. From this, you can see that the origin of Taiji is from nothingness. It is just like life is generated from nothing within this universe. Once you have life, then thought and action begin, and Yin and Yang are divided.

In Baguazhang, to turn left while walking in the circle, or merely the left turning of the body while standing, is considered Yang, while turning right is considered Yin. When you turn, the Qi moves; this is the basic theory of Qi circulation. From the Qi's circulation, Yin and Yang are distinguished. Also, the Qi moves from the different states of the Yin and Yang. From this, you can see that the Qi and the Yin and Yang actually cannot be separated. The Taiji and the Qi are in fact just two faces of the same concept. Due to the distinction between Yin and Yang, the Qi will flow naturally as it should, upward or downward, left or right, etc. Furthermore, Yang - the extremity of Yin, is generated, and Yin - the extremity of Yang, is begotten. Once you understand this concept, the Qi can be established naturally and abundantly.

The trick to reaching this goal is in your Lower *Dan Tian*, which is located at the central point of your body. According to some sources, the *Dan Tian* is also named *Qihai* in acupuncture, but this really refers to the "false *Dan Tian*." Though this *Dan Tian* is able to generate Qi it cannot store it. The "real *Dan Tian*" is located at the center of the body, near the physical center of gravity (Figure 2-11). While this real *Dan Tian*, can store Qi, without proper training it is unable to generate Qi. Therefore, to be a proficient Qigong or internal arts practitioner, you must learn how to build up the Qi to an abundant level, and store it in the real *Dan Tian*. If you are interested in this

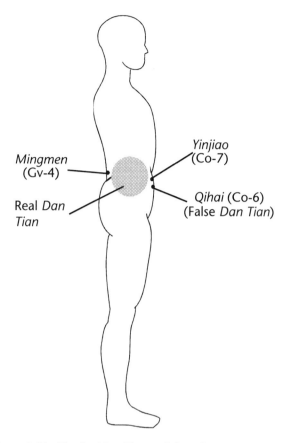

Figure 2-11. The *Real Dan* Tian and the False *Dan Tian*

subject, please refer to *The Root of Chinese Chi Kung*, by YMAA.

The Qi in the *Dan Tian* is the root and the essential force of Baguazhang. Therefore, Taiji is located in the Lower *Dan Tian*, where Qi resides. The two poles, Yin and Yang, are generated from this place.

7. Theory of Two Poles (Lian Yi Xue)
兩儀學

兩儀者，是一氣伸縮之理。左旋之則為陽儀，右轉之則為陰儀也。故前太極之式，一氣走去，如圖流行不息者為太極陽儀，是為氣之伸也。陽極必生陰，陰極必生陽也。譬如圓圖八卦，陽左升為日，陰右降為月，日來則月往，月往則日來。日月相推，而四時生焉。

The two poles is the theory of the sole Qi's extension and withdrawing. Left turn is the Yang pole, while right turn is the Yin pole. When the sole Qi moves, like in the picture which (the Qi) circulates without stop is called the Taiji Yang pole. It is the extension of the Qi. When Yang reaches its extremity, the Yin will be generated and when Yin reaches its extremity, the Yang will be generated. It is just like the round picture of Bagua (Figure 2-12), Yang ascends on the left and becomes the sun (i.e., extreme Yang) and Yin descends on the right and becomes the moon (i.e., extreme Yin). When the sun comes, the moon goes, and when the moon comes, the sun goes. The sun and the moon mutually keep their relations, then the four seasons are derived.

From the last article, we understand that the sole Qi is the origin of the two poles. From the

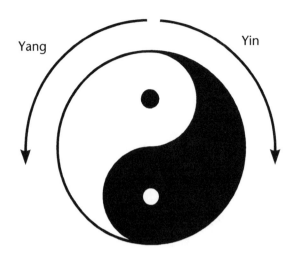

Figure 2-12. Yin Yang Taiji Diagram

manifestation of this sole Qi, the various actions are generated. In Baguazhang, the left turn (i.e., counterclockwise) is the Yang pole, while the right turn (clockwise) is the Yin pole. As shown in the Taiji symbol, Yin and Yang mutually evolve into each other. The left hand side moves upward to become Yang, and the right hand side moves downward to become Yin. As these two poles keep changing, the Qi will continue to flow, and the four seasons (i.e., Four Phases) are produced.

換身右轉流行不已，如圖則為太極陰儀，是氣之縮也。聖人云，鬼神之為德，日月之升降，皆屬天地自然之變化。而拳中兩儀右轉，左右有序，何莫非一氣之往來曲伸乎。故兩儀再生，而四象出焉。

When you change the body to turn to the right and move without stop, then is the Taiji Yin pole. It is the condensation of Qi. The ancient saint said:"The natural virtue of the ghost and the divine, the ascent and the descent of the sun and the moon, all belong to the natural variations of the heaven and the earth." However, the right turning of the two poles in the fist, left and right have their orders. Aren't the forward or backward and withdrawal or extension also the production of the sole Qi? Therefore, the two poles again generate and the Four Phases are yielded.

In Baguazhang, when you turn to your right, you are entering the Yin side of the Taiji symbol. In this Yin side, the Qi is condensed inward into the bone marrow and builds up the future root of the Yang manifestation. It is known that when the Yin and Yang keep their natural relations, the Four Phases will be derived. It is the same theory in the Bagua. If you know how to apply the Yin and Yang theory in the Baguazhang, then the Four Phases will be generated.

8. Theory of Four Phases (Si Xian Xue)
四象學

四象者，兩儀各生一陰陽也。太極生兩儀者，八卦拳之奇耦也。復於兩儀之中，各加一奇一耦，以象太陰太陽少陰少陽，而名為四象。四象即本拳之奇耦，各加一陰一陽，而分為金木水火也。在腹內則為心肝肺腎，在拳中則為前後左右，俗稱名為雙換掌也。言四象不及土者，太極即土也。拳中起躦落翻，動而未發謂之橫，橫者亦土也。因其生生不息謂之土，因其一氣運用謂之太極。太極也，土也。一而已，故不及土，僅言四象者，而土已在其中矣。

What is the Four Phases, is each of the Two Poles bears Yin and Yang independently. What is the "Taiji generates the Two Poles", is the "odd" and the "even" in Bagua fist. Again, in the Two Poles

add an odd and an even, which are to distinguish the "Ultimate Yin," "Ultimate Yang," "Lesser Yin," and "Lesser Yang," and named as "Four Phases." (Therefore), the Four Phases are on the "odd" and the "even" of the fist (i.e., Baguazhang) again add a Yin and Yang and therefore divide into metal, wood, water, and fire. In the body, they represent the heart (fire), liver (wood), lungs (metal), and kidneys (water). In the fist, they represent the front, the rear, the left, and the right and is customarily called the "double change palm." Why the Four Phases do not include the earth? Taiji is the earth. In the fist, that the *Hen* (i.e., sideways) action of just start to move but not yet to emit (the *Jin*) of the "raising to drill" and the "falling to turn" is the earth. That is, the *Hen* is the earth. It is because it has (the capability of) keeping generating (new) without stopping. It is because it is the applications of the sole Qi, and therefore it is Taiji. Taiji is the earth and since the earth is the self (foundation or root) of itself, therefore, when (we) talk about Four Phases. (In fact), the earth has already be included within.

As mentioned earlier, the Four Phases are derived from the Two Poles, and the Two Poles are generated from Taiji. The Two Poles are the odd and the even (i.e., Yin and Yang), or the Baguazhang. Again, the Yin and Yang are divided themselves into Yin and Yang. Therefore, the Four Phases can be distinguished. These Four Phases are named the "Ultimate Yin," "Ultimate Yang," "Lesser Yin," and "Lesser Yang." These four are generally expressed with the four elements, metal (Lesser Yin), wood (Lesser Yang), water (Ultimate Yin), and fire (Ultimate Yang). In our body they represent the four internal organs, the heart (fire), the liver (wood), the lungs (metal), and the kidneys (water). In the strategic expression in the fist, they represent the front (Ultimate Yang), the rear (Ultimate Yin), the left (Lesser Yang), and the right (Lesser Yin). The "Double Changing Palm" in the fist includes these four phases.

The final element, the earth, which has not yet been discussed, belongs to Taiji, which is in the center. Baguazhang includes two main fighting actions, "raise to drill" and "fall to turn." When you just generate your motivation for the action, and the *Jin* has not yet been manifested, this is the state of Taiji (i.e., *Hen* or earth). The earth is the center, and it can be changed to any direction wished. It also represents the *Yi* before any action, and therefore the action can be varied. This is also because the Taiji is the Qi in the Lower *Dan Tian*, not yet led for the energization of the physical body. Therefore, its variations are unlimited, and the generation can be ceaseless. The reason that the Taiji or the earth is not included in the Four Phases is because the Four Phases are derived from the Taiji, and therefore Taiji has already been included - since it is the root of the Four Phases.

夫四象既有陰陽，則八卦相交，彼此相盪，一卦可盪於八卦之上。八卦相盪，更可重為六十四卦，按易一卦六畫，下三畫象天地人三才也。上三畫相盪，因而重之，象天地人三才各有陰陽也。以明拳中各法左旋右轉，皆有陰陽之式也。故左旋象下三畫，頭手足象天地人三才也。右轉象上三畫，因天地人三才各有陰陽也。

Because there are Yin and Yang in each of the Four Phases, then the Eight Trigrams mutually interact and correspond with each other. Each of the Eight Trigrams can again correspond with the Eight Trigrams, and therefore are becoming Sixty-four Trigrams. According to the *Yi Jing* (i.e., Book of Changes), there are six lines to represent a trigram. The bottom three lines represent the "Heaven," the "Earth," and the "Human" - the "Three Powers." The top three lines are resonant (to Three Powers), and therefore overlap on the top. This symbolizes that the "Heaven," the "Earth," and the "Human," each have Yin and Yang. It is also used to clarify that the techniques in the left spinning and the right turn all have the pattern of Yin and Yang. Therefore, the left spinning symbolizes the bottom three lines and (implies that) the head, the hands, and the feet, correspond with the Heaven, the Earth, and the Human - the three powers. The right turning symbolizes the top three lines, it is because there is Yin and Yang in each of the Heaven, the Earth, and the Human.

From the Four Phases, again the Yin and Yang are generated in each phase, and therefore become the Eight Trigrams. Again, in each of the Eight Trigrams, there are another Eight Trigrams, totalling Sixty-four Trigrams in all. According to the *Yi Jing* (Book of Changes), each of the sixty-four trigrams can be represented by six lines. In these six lines, the bottom three lines represent the Heaven, the Earth, and the Human. In Baguazhang, they represent the head, the hands, and the feet. Each of the top three lines can again be divided into Yin (dash line) and Yang (solid line), which correspond to the bottom three lines, the head, the hands, and the feet. From these expressions, the movements of the techniques - such as the left turn and the right turn - can be clearly expressed.

八卦即四象之陰陽，六十四卦即陰陽配合之生氣。八卦成列，因而重之。則陰陽相交，自可生生無已，豈第六十四卦哉。雖至千卦萬卦，總不出乎六十四卦。六十四卦總是八卦，八卦總是四象，四象總是兩儀，兩儀總是一氣之流行也。紫陽讀參同契云：'一自虛無兆質，兩儀因一開根。四象不離二體，八卦互為子孫，六十四卦於此而生，萬象變動於此而出。'成哉斯言，可為此拳之鑒矣。

Bagua (i.e., The Eight Trigrams) is the Yin and Yang of the Four Phases, and the Sixty-four Trigrams are the life force from the interaction of the Yin and Yang. The Eight Trigrams can line up and therefore mutually layer. Then the Yin and the Yang mutually interact and (the derivations are) naturally produced without cease. (From this), how can it be only Six-four trigrams. It does not matter if there can be one thousand trigrams or ten thousand trigrams, they are all based on the Sixty-four Trigrams. The Sixty-four Trigrams are all from the Eight Trigrams. The Eight Trigrams are all founded on the Four Phases. The Four Phases are derived from the Two Poles. The Two Poles are finally initiated from the circulation of the sole Qi. (Zhao) Zi-Yang, after reading *Chan Ton Ci* (A Comparative study of the *Zhou Book of Change*) said:"The one (i.e., the sole Qi) started from the no ten million qualities (i.e., no impurities), the 'Two Poles' therefore generate its root. The Four Phases cannot be separated from these two bodies (i.e., Two Poles). The Eight Trigrams are mutually each others' sons or grandsons. The Sixty-four Trigrams are therefore produced from this, and the variations of the million phenomena are generated from this." Surely these words are sincere and true, and can be used as guidelines of the fist.

This paragraph concludes that, from the Eight Trigrams, even millions of trigrams could be derived or generated through mutual interaction. However, the original root for this production remain the sole Qi. This sole Qi is Taiji.

9. Heaven Trigram (Qian Gua; ☰) - Lion Shape
乾卦獅形學

乾卦者，天之象也。獅子掌者，拳之式也。乾者健也，陽之性也，三畫卦之名也。乾以形體言謂之天，以性情言謂之乾。其於物也，則為獅形。其物最嚴烈，其性最勇猛，能食虎豹之獸，有抖毛之威。以拳式之用言，則有金龍合口之式，有獅子張嘴之形，有白猿拖刀之法。在腹內則為氣，能資始萬物。在拳中，則為獅子掌，能萬法開端。此式以兩手極力伸出，內外上下一氣，有乾三連之象，又有起首三點之式。故取象為乾卦，其拳順，則週身血脈舒暢，氣力倍增。其拳謬，則乾遇震，而拳中不能無妄。乾臨坤，而心竅亦不能開通矣。學者於此，尤加謹焉。

The *Qian* Trigram is the phenomena of heaven. The lion palm is the pattern in the fist. The *Qian* represents the strength and is the natural virtue of the Yang. It is the name of the three line trigram. When specified as the shape and the body, it is heaven. When discussed as the natural virtue, it is *Qian*. When it applies to the object, it is the lion shape. This object is the most fierce, and its nature is the most brave and violent. It is able to eat animals, such as the tiger and panther. It has the awe of shaking fur. When discussed in the fist, then there is the posture of the golden dragon closing its orifice, the shape of the lion opening its mouth, and the technique of the white ape drawing its saber. In the body, it is Qi which is able to originate and nourish millions of objects. In the fist, it is the lion palm which is able to introduce millions of techniques. In this posture, the two hands are extended with great effort. The internal, external, up, and down

with sole Qi, and has the appearance of the three line linkage of the *Qian*. Again, there is a posture three points at the beginning. Therefore, it is adopted from its appearance as the *Qian* trigram. When its fist is smooth, then the entire body's blood vessels are comfortable and free. The Qi and *Li* can be enhanced twofold. If the fist is ridiculous, then the *Qian* is encountering the Zhen and the fist cannot move freely as wished. When the *Qian* is encountering the *Kun*, then the door of the heart (i.e., mind) will not be opened. (Therefore) the practitioner should be cautions about this.

In the *Yi Jing*, *Qian* represents Heaven, and means powerful, strong, and the greatest. In Baguazhang, according to Master Sun Lu-Tang, *Qian* symbolizes the lion palm simply because the lion palm is strong and its shape is like a lion. When this palm is smooth, the entire body's Qi and blood can circulate smoothly and comfortably. When this palm is not smooth, if encountering the dragon palm (Zhen Trigram), the movements and technical applications will be hindered. Moreover, when it meets the unicorn palm (*Kun* Trigram), which is the most Yin (i.e., soft, yield, and neutralized), the techniques can be neutralized and the mind can be confused.

10. Earth Trigram (Kun Gua; ☷) - Lin Shape
坤卦麟形學

坤卦者，地之象也。返身掌者，拳之式也。坤者順也，陰之性也，六畫卦之名也。坤以形體言，謂之地。以性情言，謂之坤。其於物也，則為麟形，其物為仁獸也，則有飛身變化不測之功。以拳式之用言，則有麒麟吐書之式，大鵬展翅之法，有白鶴獨立之能，有順勢返身旋轉之靈。以拳之形式言，謂之返身掌。此拳以兩手含住，返身轉去，內外上下和順，有坤六斷之形。故取象為坤卦，其拳順，則身體輕便快利，轉去如旋風。其拳謬，則腹內不能空虛，而身體亦不能靈通矣。學者加意研究，靈巧妙用由此而出焉。

The *Kun* trigram, is the phenomena of the Earth. It is the Returning Body Palm in the pattern of the fist (i.e., Baguazhang). *Kun* means to follow, and is the characteristic of the Yin which is the name of the six dash lines of trigrams. When discussing the body and the shape of the *Kun*, it is the Earth. When discussing the natural virtues, it is *Kun*. When it is applied to the object, it is the shape of the *Lin* (i.e., female of a wondrous, fabled animal resembling the deer). This object is a benevolent animal. It also has the capability of flying and unpredictable variations. When applied into the fist, then it has the posture of the *Qi Lin* splitting the book, the method of the roc spreading its wings, the capability of the white crane standing with a single leg, the spiritual agility of following the posture and returning the spinning body. In the Fist, it is "Returning Body Palm." This fist uses both hands to hold in and turn the body with spinning. The internal, external, the top, and the bottom, are all smooth. It has the shape of the *Kun*, with six broken lines. Therefore, it is adopted as *Kun* trigram. When fists are smooth, then the body is light, free, fast, agile and turning like a tornado. If the fists are incorrect, then the internal abdomen cannot be empty. Consequently, the body also cannot be agile and move easily. The learner should pay attention and research; nimbleness and marvellous tricks originate from this.

In the *Yi Jing*, *Kun* represents the Earth, and means peaceful, calm, kind, and gentle. In Baguazhang, according to Master Sun Lu-Tang, *Kun* symbolizes the unicorn palm simply because the unicorn palm is soft, yielding, and neutralizing. The *Qi Lin* is a legendary animal resembling a deer with a horn, in some ways similar to the western unicorn. This animal is tame, kind, calm, and peaceful. When this palm is smooth, the entire body can be agile, swift, light, and turn like the wind. When this palm is incorrect, the Qi cannot be led freely, and the body will not be agile.

11. Water Trigram (Kan Gua; ☵) - Snake Shape
坎卦蛇形學

坎卦者，水之象也。順勢掌者，拳之式也。坎者陷也。坎得乾之中陽，陽陷陰中，陽入而生潮，有坎中滿之象。故居正北水旺之方，其於物也，則為蛇形。其物最毒，其性最玲瓏，最活潑者也，有撥草之能。以拳式之用言，則有白蛇吐信之法，有雙頭蛇纏身之巧。以拳之形式言，謂之順勢掌。此拳外柔順而內剛健，有丹田氣足之形，內外如水，曲曲順流，無隙而不入。故取象為坎卦，其拳順，則丹田之氣足。丹田氣足，則道心生。道心生，則心中陰火消滅，而無頭眩目暈之患矣。其拳謬，則腎水虛弱，心火不能下降，頭暈眼黑必不免矣。

The *Kan* trigram is the phenomena of Water. It is the Smooth Posture Palm in the patten of the fist (i.e., Baguazhang). *Kan* means to submerge. *Kan* gains the middle Yang, and the Yang is submerged in the Yins, When Yang is within, the tide will be generated. Therefore, it has the phenomena of fullness in the *Kan* and is located in the North, where water is abundant. When it is applied to the object, it is the shape of the snake. This object is the most poisonous. Its nature is the most cunning, shrewd, and malicious. It has the capability of repelling the grass. When applied into the fist, it has the shape of the snake spitting poison, the skill of a double-headed snake's winding. In the Fist, it is "Smooth Posture Palm." In this fist, the external is soft and smooth, while the internal is solid and strong. It has the shape of the full Qi in *Dan Tian*. (The Qi flows in) both internal and external like water, curved and following the stream, no gap cannot be reached. Therefore, it is adopted as *Kan* trigram. When fists are smooth, the Qi in the *Dan Tian* is abundant. When the Qi is abundant and full, then the Dao of the mind will be generated. When the Dao of the mind is generated, then the Yin fire in the mind disappears. Therefore, there is no sickness of dizziness. If the fists are incorrect, then the kidneys' water is insubstantial and weak. The heart fire cannot be descended. Consequently, the head's dizziness and the eye's darkness cannot be avoided.

In the *Yi Jing*, *Kan* represents Water, and means sinking and full. According to Master Sun Lu-Tang, *Kan* symbolizes the snake, which of all animals is the most sneaky, poisonous, active, and alive. When it moves, it is smooth and natural. In the Baguazhang, it is the "Smooth Posture Palm." The reason for this is that this palm manifests its softness and smoothness externally, but is full, abundant, and strong internally. This implies that the Qi in the Lower *Dan Tian* is full and abundant. This Qi is able to circulate and flow freely like water. If this palm is performed smoothly, then the Qi is full, and is able to cool down the hidden fire Qi (i.e., heart fire) in the Middle *Dan Tian*. When this palm is executed incorrectly, then the water in the kidneys will be void, and the heart fire cannot be subdued. This could result in dizziness and heavy head problems, or even fainting.

12. Fire Trigram (Li Gua; ☲) - Harrier (Hawk) Shape
離卦鷂形學

離卦者，火之象也。臥掌者，拳之式也。離者麗也。離得坤之中陰，陰麗陽中，陰借陽而生明。故居正南火旺之方，其於物也則為鷂形。其物有入林之速，有翻身之巧。以拳式之用言，則有按點斫之法。此拳亦為大蟒翻身之式，亦有入洞之能。以拳之形式言，謂之臥掌。此拳則外剛健而內柔順，心中有空虛之象。故取象為離卦，其拳順，則心中虛靈而人心化。人心化則玄妙生矣。其拳謬，則心中愚昧不明，而拳中之神化不能得矣。故學者勉力格致誠意作去，以開心中愚滯，自得神化之妙道矣。

The *Li* trigram is the phenomena of Fire. It is the Lying Palm in the patten of the fist (i.e., Baguazhang). *Li* means to ornament. *Li* gains the middle Yin in *Kun*. Yin decorates within Yang. Yin borrows Yang and generates Yin, and therefore resides in the south, where fire is abundant. When it is applied to the object, it is the shape of the hawk. This object has the speed of entering the woods, the skill is of turning the body. When applied into the fist, then it has the method of pressing and pointing. This fist also has the posture of the python turning its body, and also has the capability of entering the cave. In the Fist, it is "Lying Palm." In this fist, the external is hard and strong while the internal is soft and smooth. It has the shape of the insubstantial in the mind, therefore it is adopted as *Li* trigram. When fists are smooth, then the mind is insubstantial and agile, and the mind is able to vary. If the mind is able to vary, then marvellous tricks can be generated. If the fists are incorrect, then the mind is stupid, confused, and not clear. Consequently, the spiritual variations of the fist cannot be obtained. Therefore, the learner should try hard to ponder and study intelligently, so to overcome the mind's stupidity and stagnation. This will obtain the marvellous Dao of the spiritual variations automatically.

In the *Yi Jing*, *Li* represents Fire, which is bright, with Yin hidden within. According to Master Sun Lu-Tang, the "Lying Palm" belongs to *Li* in Baguazhang, and represents the Harrier shape. The Harrier is a bird which is able to enter the woods speedily, and is able to turn its body in the air skillfully. This implies that the Lying Palm has the capability of attacking accurately, and with great speed. This palm also resembles a python turning its body strongly and smoothly. Therefore, it is powerful and solid externally and yet soft and smooth internally. Because it is soft and insubstantial internally, it belongs to *Li* trigram. When it is performed accurately, the mind can be insubstantial and agile. When the mind is insubstantial and agile, then the marvelous variations of the techniques can be generated. However, if this palm is executed incorrectly, then the mind will be confused, and reactions will be dull. The manifestation of the fist will not reach the high level of the spirit.

13. Thunder Trigram (Zhen Gua; ☳) - Dragon Shape
震卦龍形學

震卦者，雷之象也。平托掌者，拳之式也。震者動也。震得乾之初陽，初陽主生長。居正東木旺之方，其於物也，則為龍形。其物為鱗虫之長，有搜骨之法，有變化不測之功，有飛騰之象。以拳式之用言，則有烏龍盤柱之法，有青龍戲珠之能。以拳之形式言，為之平托掌。此拳外靜而內動，丹書云：‘靜中求動之象。’又一陽初動之意。故取象為震卦，其拳順，則肝氣舒和，其拳謬，則肝旺氣努，而身體不能入於卦爻九二之中和矣。學者於此勉力求和，而無肝氣沖目之患矣。

The Zhen trigram is the phenomena of thunder. It is the Horizontal Lifting Palm in the patten of the fist (i.e., Baguazhang). Zhen means to move. Zhen gains the beginning Yang of *Qian*. Beginning Yang dominates the growth, and belongs to the East, where the woods are abundant. When it is applied to the object, it is the shape of the dragon. This object is the leader of the animals, with scales, and has a method of searching the bones, the capability of variations, and the phenomena of flying. In the Fist, it has the methods of black dragon wrapping around the post, the capability of the dragon playing with pearls. When applied in the fist, it is "Horizontal Lifting Palm." In this fist, the external is calm and the internal is active. *The Elixir Book* said "the phenomena of the action in the calmness." It also has the meaning of beginning, which is just starting to move. Therefore, it is adopted as Zhen trigram. When fists are smooth, then the liver's Qi is comfortable and peaceful. If the fists are incorrect, then the liver's Qi is abundant but stagnant. Consequently, the body cannot enter into the nine/two harmonies in the trigrams. The learner should try hard to make the (liver's Qi) harmonious and without the sickness of the liver's Qi invading the eyes.

In the *Yi Jing*, Zhen represents Thunder. Thunder during cloudy or rainy days often appears in the early spring, when the weather is starting to change gradually into Yang (i.e., summer). The Spring implies the growing of nature. Zhen also symbolizes the dragon. The dragon is king of the scaled animals. According to Chinese legend, the dragon is able to change the weather, to fly, or even to vary its form. In Baguazhang, it is the Horizontal Lifting Palm. This palm is calm externally and active internally. It is the strategic technique in looking for the variation in the calmness. Because it implies the beginning action of a technique, it is like the early spring thunder, and therefore it belongs to Zhen. When this palm is performed correctly, the Qi in the liver will be smooth and harmonious. However, if this palm is trained incorrectly, the Qi in the liver will be too sufficient (i.e., Yang) and stagnant. According to the *Yi Jing*, the numbers nine and two are for peace and harmony. That is why when the liver's Qi is stagnant, the Zhen trigram cannot be manifested naturally.

14. Mountain Trigram (Gen Gua; ☶) - Bear Shape
艮卦熊形學

艮卦者，山之象也。背身掌者，拳之式也。艮者止也。艮得乾之末陽，末陽主靜。
故居東北陽弱之方，其於物也，則為熊形。其性最鈍，其物最威嚴，有豎項之力。
以拳式之用言，則有靠身之勇，有拔樹之能，有抖搜之法。以拳之形式言，謂之背
身掌。此拳上剛健而中下柔順，有靜止之形。故取象為艮卦，其拳順，則有氣根心
生色，睟然現於面，盎於背，施於四體之意也。其拳謬，則丹田之陽，不能升於脊
背，而胸內不能含合，心火亦不能下降矣。學者要知之。

The *Gen* trigram is the phenomena of the mountain. It is the Back Body Palm in the pattern of the fist (i.e., Baguazhang). *Gen* means to stop. *Gen* takes the position on the ending Yang of Qian (trigram). The ending Yang likes calmness, and therefore is located in the East-North, where the sun is weak. Applied to the animal, it is the bear shape. Its (i.e., the bear's) personality is the most dull, its appearance is the most awed, and it has the capability of straightening the neck (i.e., the head is upright and therefore the spirit is high). If talking about its applications in the fist, then it has the bravery of nearing the opponent, the capability of pulling a tree, and the method of shaking the body. If talking about its shape in the fist, then it is the "Back Body Palm." This fist is solid and strong on the top, and soft and smooth in the middle and the bottom. It is the appearance of calmness, and therefore is adopted as the *Gen* trigram (i.e., mountain). When the fist is smooth, then the root and the center of the Qi (i.e., the Lower *Dan Tian*) will generate color (i.e., noticeable), (the Qi) can be manifested on the face, strong on the back, and distributed to the four limbs. If the fist is (performed) inaccurately, then the Yang (i.e., Qi) on the *Dan Tian* cannot ascent on the back and chest, and cannot be hollowed (i.e., relaxed) Consequently, the heart fire cannot descend. The learner should know about this.

According to the *Yi Jing*, *Gen* represents the Mountain. *Gen* means near the end or stop. It expresses the ending of the Yang, and likes to be calm. Therefore, though it is strong, it is quiet and powerful. Because of this, this trigram symbolizes the bear. In the fist, it represents the Back Body Palm. This palm has the bravery of being near the opponent, the power of pulling the tree, and the techniques of jerking and shaking. Therefore, the power can be manifested in the upper body, while the lower body stays firmly rooted, soft, and still (i.e., firm like a mountain). If this palm is performed correctly, the root of Qi (i.e., Lower *Dan Tian*) will be firm, and its strength can be seen on the face. The Qi can also be led to the back upward and finally manifested from the limbs. However, if the palm is practiced incorrectly, the strong Qi in the Lower *Dan Tian* cannot be led along the spine, and the chest area cannot be relaxed and hollow. Consequently, the heart fire cannot be subdued, due to the tension of the chest area.

15. Wind Trigram (Xun Gua; ☴) - Phoenix Shape
巽卦鳳形學

巽卦者，風之象也。風輪掌者，拳之式也。巽者入也。巽得坤之初陰，初陰主潛進
。故居東南陽盛之方，其於物也，則為鳳形。其物為羽蟲之長，有展翅之功。以拳
式之用言，則有點頭之式，有挾人之法，此拳亦為獅子滾球之形。以拳之形式言，
謂之風輪掌。此拳上剛健而下柔順，有風輪之形，故取為巽卦。其拳順，則內中真
氣散於四肢百骸，無微不至，而身式行之如風輪，循環無間之形矣。其拳謬，則元
氣不能散布於週身，譬之方軸圓輪，氣機不靈，身式不順，而先後天之氣不能化一
矣。故學者於此拳中，務加意勤習焉。

The *Xun* trigram is the phenomena of the wind. It is the Wind Wheel Palm in the pattern of the fist. *Xun* means to enter. *Xun* gains the beginning Yin of the *Kun*. The beginning Yin likes to advance aggressively, and therefore is located on the East-South, where the sun is abundant. When it is applied to the object, it is the shape of the phoenix. This object (i.e., phoenix) has the expertise of the feather (i.e., birds) and insects, and has the talent of spreading its wings. If talking about its applications in the fist, then it has the appearance of nodding the head, and the methods of enforcing the opponent. This fist also has the shape of the lion rolling the ball. If talking about its shape in the fist, then it is the "Wind Wheel Palm." In this palm, the top is hard and strong, and the bottom is soft and smooth, which has the shape of the wind wheel. Therefore, it is adopted as the *Xun* trigram. When this fist is performed smoothly, then the internal real Qi is able to spread to the four limbs and hundred skeletons, no place cannot be reached. Consequently, there is an appearance that the body's action can be executed like the wind, and circling without gap. When this fist is incorrect, then the Original Qi cannot be distributed around the entire body. It is like the square axle and the round wheel (i.e., all kinds of machines), when Qi supply (i.e., power supply) is not functioning well and its manifestation is not smooth. This will cause the Pre-Heaven and the Post-Heaven's Qi's discord. Therefore, the practitioner should pay more attention in practicing this fist.

According to the *Yi Jing*, *Xun* represents the Wind. *Xun* means to enter like the wind, which can enter any gap. It possesses the beginning Yin of *Kun* (winter), when the wind starts to blow. Because it represents the wind, it can advance without being noticed. Normally, this phenomena can be seen in the South-East of China. The phoenix in China is considered a lucky bird, and is the leader of all birds. When the phoenix spreads its wings, it is powerful. In the fist, it represents the Wind Wheel Palm. This palm has the shape of round and rolling, like a lion rolling a ball, and the feeling of a wheel's turning. If this palm is performed correctly, the Qi can spread to the four extremities and everywhere can be reached. Furthermore, you will have a feeling like a windmill's turning. However, if the palm is practiced incorrectly, the Qi will be stagnant, the body's postures uncomfortable and the Pre-Heaven and the Post-Heaven cannot unify.

16. Lake Trigram (Dui Gua; ☱) - Monkey Shape
兌卦猴形學

兌卦者，澤之象也。抱掌者，拳之式也。兌者說也。兌得坤之末陰，末陰主消化。故居正西金旺之方，其於物也，則為猴形。其物最靈巧者也，有縮力之法，有蹤山之靈。以拳式之用言，則有白猿獻果之形，有猴兒啃桃之法，有龍蹲虎踞之式。以拳之形式言，謂之抱掌。此拳上柔順而中下剛健，有縮短之形，故取象為兌卦。其拳順，則肺氣清潤。其泉謬，則肺氣不和。至於氣喘咳嗽諸症，而不能免矣。學者深思悟會，而求肺氣清順焉。

The *Dui* trigram is the phenomena of the lake. It is the Embrace Palm in the pattern of the fist. *Dui* means to make happy. *Dui* gains the ending Yin of the *Kun*. The ending Yin is mainly responsible in assimilating (i.e., make event ended), and therefore is located in the West, where metal is abundant. When it is applied to the object, it is the shape of the monkey. This object (i.e., monkey) is the most agile and witty, and has the method of withdrawing power and the agility of jumping the mountains. In the application of the fist, it has the shape of the white ape offering the fruits, has the method of a monkey chewing the peach, and has the appearance of the dragon's squatting and the tiger's crouching. From the appearance of the fist, it is "Embrace Palm." This fist is soft and smooth on the top, hard and strong in the middle and the bottom, has the shape of shortening, and is therefore adopted as *Dui* trigram. When this fist is (performed) smoothly, the lungs' Qi will be clean and moisturized. When this fist is (performed) incorrectly, then the lungs' Qi is not harmonious, which could result in eventual sicknesses, such as asthma and coughing. The learner should ponder deeply and comprehend (its meaning), and aim for the lungs' Qi clean and smooth.

According to the *Yi Jing*, *Dui* represents the Lake. *Dui* means to cheer. It possesses the ending of the Yin. Ending Yin means to end an event and then begin again. Therefore, it is cheerful. According to the Chinese Theory of the Five Phases, metal is the end product of the dust which is hidden deeply under the ground. Metal is able to form a knife, and thereby to end a life. Most of the mountains are located on the west of China, where the metal is produced.

When *Dui* is applied to the animals, it is the monkey form. The monkey is agile and the most clever animal other than the human. It has the capability of jumping, hanging, and moving from one mountain to another. When applied to the fist, it is the Embracing Palm. When this fist is performed accurately, the lungs' Qi (i.e., metal in Five Phases) will be clear and clean. However, if this palm is practiced incorrectly, the lungs' Qi will not be harmonious. This may cause sickness related to the lungs.

References

1. Pei Xi-Rong and Pei Wu-Jun, *Bagua Eight Shape Palm*, (Hunan Scientific Technical Publishing Company, 1990) 13-14. 八卦八形掌，裴錫榮、裴武軍編著。

2. Pei Xi-Rong and Li Chun-Sheng, *Wudang Wugong*, (Hunan Scientific Technical Publishing Company, 1984) 115. 武當武功，裴錫榮、李春生主編。

3. Li Tian-Ji, *The Feats of Wudang*,, (Jilin Publishing Company, 1988) 630. 武當絕技匯編，李天驥主編。

4. Jiang Rang-Qiao, *The Expounding of Baguazhang Techniques*,, (Reprinted by Five Continents Publishing Company, 1985) 3-8. 八卦掌法闡宗，姜容樵著。

5. 尾閭中正。

6. 氣沈丹田。

7. 內宜鼓盪。

8. 以意引氣。

9. Pei Xi-Rong and Li Chun-Sheng, *Wudang Wugong*, (Hunan Scientific Technical Publishing Company, 1984) 116-117. 武當武功，裴錫榮、李春生主編。

10. Pei Xi-Rong and Pei Wu-Jun, *Supra* note 1, at 14-23. 八卦八形掌，裴錫榮、裴武軍編著。

11. Sun Lu-Tang, *The Study of Bagua Fist*, (Peking, 1916) 3-4. 八卦拳學，孫祿堂著。

12. Huang Bo-Nian, *Dragon Shape Baguazhang*, (1929) 6-7. 龍形八卦掌，黃柏年著。

13. Sun Lu-Tang, *Supra* note 10, at 7. 八卦拳學，孫祿堂著。

14. Huang Bo-Nian, *Supra* note 12, at 6. 龍形八卦掌，黃柏年著。

15. Liu Xing-Han, *Swimming Body Bagua Linking Palm*, (1986) 28. 遊身八卦連環掌，劉興漢主編。

16. Pei Xi-Rong and Pei Wu-Jun, *Supra* note 1, at 12-13. 八卦八形掌，裴錫榮、裴武軍編著。

17. Pei Xi-Rong and Li Chun-Sheng, *Supra* note 2, at 116. 武當武功，裴錫榮、李春生主編。

18. 勁發於腳，主宰於腰，形於手指。

19. Dr. Yang Jwing-Ming, *Advanced Yang Style Tai Chi Chuan - Tai Chi Theory and Tai Chi Jing, Vol 1*, (YMAA Publications, 1989) 213.

20. Pei Xi-Rong and Pei Wu-Jun, *Supra* note 2, at 13-14. 八卦八形掌，裴錫榮、裴武軍編著。

21. *Id.* at 11-12. 八卦八形掌，裴錫榮、裴武軍編著。

22. 意守丹田。

23. Sun Lu-Tang, *Supra* note 11, at 4-6. 八卦拳學，孫祿堂著。

24. 氣凝於髓。

25. Dr. Yang Jwing-Ming, *Supra* note 19, at 223.

26. Li Tian-Ji, *The Feats of Wudang*,, (Jilin Publishing Company, 1988) 632. 武當絕技匯編，李天驥主編。

27. *Id.* at 630. 武當絕技匯編，李天驥主編。

28. *Id.* at 630. 武當絕技匯編，李天驥主編。

29. Sun Lu-Tang, *Supra* note 19. 八卦拳學，孫祿堂著。

Chapter 3
Baguazhang Qigong
八卦掌氣功

3-1. Introduction

In Chinese martial arts society, virtually every style has its own Qigong training. Qigong practice enables a practitioner to manifest his techniques with more power and efficiency. Most Qigong practices that have evolved focus on their progenitive style's nature and characteristics. For example, for the Eagle Claw style, Qigong that can strengthen finger power (i.e., claw strength) is stressed. White Crane Style Qigong emphasizes the whipping power of the arms (i.e., wings). This principal also holds true in Baguazhang. Baguazhang Qigong specializes in training the body's turning, limb rotation and spinning, and the circular movements of stepping. In this section, we will introduce the well known Baguazhang Qigong set, Bagua Turning-Spinning Gong (*Bagua Zhuan Xuan Gong*)[1].

The Bagua Turning-Spinning Gong set consists of eight patterns of movements, including both stationary and stepping. It integrates the internal *Yi*, Qi, and *Jin* (martial power) with the external tendons, bones, and muscles. The movements utilize the entire body, which is a very important training to build up a solid foundation for your Baguazhang training. Because of this, this Qigong set especially stimulates the joints and muscles with turning and spinning movements. It also exercises the areas of the body that are not normally exercised, so that the entire body is exercised. In addition, the turning and spinning movements stimulate the acupuncture cavities by compressing and relaxing the muscles around the cavities. This stimulation loosens stagnant energy and allows the Qi circulating in the channels to flow smoothly throughout the body.

As you learn this set of Qigong exercises, practice one posture at a time until your movements are smooth. Then go on to the next posture and practice it until it is also smooth. Only after you are able to perform each posture smoothly should you combine them and train them as a complete set of Qigong exercises.

3-2. Bagua Turning-Spinning Qigong

Bagua Turning-Spinning Qigong
(Bagua Zhuan Xuan Gong)
八卦轉旋功

1. Preparation Posture (*Yu Bei Shi*)預備式

Oral Secrets:

心平氣和鎖心猿

Calm down (your) emotional mind (*Xin*) and harmonize your Qi to lock (i.e, control) the monkey heart (emotional mind).

The first step of Baguazhang Qigong, like many other Qigong practices, is to calm down your emotional mind. When your emotional mind is calm, your Qi can be peaceful and harmonized. The purpose of this training is to learn how to use your wisdom mind (*Yi*) to control or govern the emotional mind (*Xin*). In Chinese Qigong society, the emotional mind (*Xin*) is commonly compared to a monkey, since it is always jumping around and hard to calm down. Conversely, the wisdom mind (*Yi*) is compared to a horse, since the horse can be calm and its power can be strong and enduring.

Movements:

Stand upright with your feet together, and place the arms naturally at your sides (Figure 3-1). Next, shift your weight to your right leg, and step your left leg to your left about a shoulder's width apart.

Key Notes:

Relax your entire body. Breathe naturally. Concentrate your mind on training and avoid scattering thoughts.

2. Nourish Elixir Posture (*Yang Dan Shi*)養丹式

Oral Secrets:

頂沉內聚息綿綿

Sink the top and gather the internal (Qi), breathe slenderly and smoothly.

After you calm down your mind, you should then coordinate it with your breathing, and lead the Qi from the top of your head down to the Lower *Dan Tian*. You should breathe naturally, slenderly, and smoothly. Only when your entire body is be relaxed and natural can the Qi sink easily to the Lower *Dan Tian*. Once you lead your Qi to the Lower *Dan Tian*, you can condense it in your center

Movements:

Move your left foot to your left, a shoulder's width apart from your right. Raise both hands up to waist level, fingers pointing down at an angle and palms facing each other. Relax your shoulders, drop your elbows, settle your wrists, and hold your hands in an embrace, fingertips about one foot apart. At the same time, arc your chest in slightly to relax it further. Hold this posture and do 16 deep abdominal breathing cycles. (Figure 3-2).

Figure 3-1

Figure 3-2

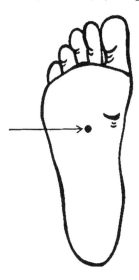

Figure 3-3

Key Notes:

Your head should have a slightly suspended feeling. When "embracing" with your hands, shift your weight back slightly. Position your knees directly over your Bubbling Well (*Yongquan*) cavity on the bottom of your feet, and grip the floor with your toes (Figure 3-3). Breathe slowly, evenly, and deeply. During inhalation, bring your attention to your Lower *Dan Tian*, and lead all the Qi from your extremities to your center of gravity - the Lower *Dan Tian* area. During exhalation, lead your Qi out to the extremities, loosen and expand each joint in your arm and shoulder, and use your mind to lead the Qi from the Lower *Dan Tian* upward, following the spine to the shoulders, elbows, and finally your fingers. Simultaneously perform a similar expansion through your legs. When you exhale, loosen and expand each joint, leading your Qi from your hips to your knees, ankles, and toes.

3. Push Mill Posture (*Tui Mo Shi*) 推磨式

Oral Secrets:

吐推吞拉圓轉磨

Exhale to push, inhale to pull; turn the mill with round motion.

In Chinese martial arts, in order to efficiently manifest the Qi into physical *Jin*, a practitioner must learn how to use reverse breathing (or Daoist Breathing). In reverse breathing, when you inhale, you withdraw your abdomen, and when you exhale, you expand your abdomen. Reverse breathing is part of our natural breathing cycle. Usually, we use normal abdominal breathing (or Buddhist Breathing). Normal abdominal breathing expands the abdomen on the inhale, and contracts it on the exhale. However, when you are emotionally aroused, your breathing can change automatically into reverse breathing. For example, when you are happy and laugh, the laughter itself is accompanied by abdominal expansion. Conversely, when you are sad and cry, inhalation is accompanied by abdominal contraction. Other than emotional disturbance, you will also change to reverse breathing automatically whenever you intend to manifest physical power. For example, when you are blowing a balloon, or when you are lifting a weight, your abdomen will expand as you exhale.

From this premise, we can infer that, since exhalation in reverse breathing facilitates the manifestation of physical power, then inhalation in reverse breathing can allow the storage of energy for later manifestation as such physical power. It is extremely important in such practice to maintain breathing in a natural, comfortable, continuous and easy manner. You must never force either your breath or energy in any way.

Movements:

Left Push Mill:

Bring your left foot next to the right foot, turning your palms down; inhale (Figure 3-4). Step to your front left corner with your left foot. Shift your weight forward into Bow stance while circling your palms horizontally and counterclockwise in an arc; exhale (Figure 3-5). Shift about 60% of your weight back to your rear leg, while circling your palms back next to your abdomen; inhale (Figure 3-6). Continue shifting your weight forward and back, coordinating your movements with exhalations and inhalations. Do eight complete revolutions. To complete the Left Push Mill, shift all your weight back to your right leg, bring your left foot next to your right foot and stand up; inhale (Figure 3-7).

Right Push Mill:

From Figure 3-7, step to your front right corner with your right foot. Shift your weight forward into Bow stance while circling your palm horizontally and clockwise arc; exhale (Figure 3-8). Shift about 60% of your weight back to your rear leg, while circling your palms back next to your abdomen; inhale (Figure 3-9). Continue shifting your weight forward and back, coordinating the movements with exhalations and inhalations. Do eight complete revolutions. To complete the Right Push Mill, shift all your weight back to your left leg, bring your right foot next to your left foot and stand up; inhale (Figure 3-10).

Key Notes:

Imagine that you are holding the handle of a mill, rotating it around and around. You can also imagine that your palms are connected to the ground by a column of Qi, leading it around in circles. As you circle your palms, shift your weight slowly and evenly. Exhale and inhale as your complete each circle. Be careful not to extend your knees over your toes as you shift your weight forward, and not to extend your lower back past your heel as you shift your weight backward.

Figure 3-4

Figure 3-5

Figure 3-6

| Figure 3-7 | Figure 3-8 | Figure 3-9 |

4. Rotate Palm Posture (*Zhuan Zhang Shi*) 轉掌式

Oral Secrets:

滾鑽爭裹撐八面

Roll, drill, struggle (i.e., expand and wrench), and wrap supporting eight directions.

Rolling, drilling, struggling, and wrapping are the four most basic technical movements in Baguazhang training. Struggling (*Zheng*) here means to struggle against someone, or to expand and wrench forcefully. If you can master these four basic techniques, you can fight against the eight directions easily. The eight directions include the four sides and four diagonal corners.

Movements:

Left Rotate Palm:

From Figure 3-10, start to exhale and step about 15 degrees to your front left with your left foot. Put about 70% of your weight on your right leg and 30% on your left leg. Extend both palms forward and to your left (Figure 3-11). Turn your upper body to your left while rotating your palms out. Your palms and back heel should be almost aligned in one vertical plane. Point both index fingers up, while squeezing the other fingers in slightly, to create a bow in each palm. Focus your eyes in the direction of the index finger of your upper hand; complete exhale (Figure 3-12). Hold this posture and do eight abdominal breathing cycles. To complete Left Rotate Palm, turn your waist back until you are facing forward, while straightening your arms in front of you; begin inhale (Figure 3-13). Then bring your left foot back next to your right foot, lower your palms next to your abdomen, and stand up; complete your inhalation (Figure 3-14).

Right Rotate Palm:

From Figure 3-14, step about 15 degrees to your front right with your right foot, begin to exhale. Put about 70% of your weight on your left leg and 30% on your right leg. Extend both palms forward and to your right (Figure 3-15). Turn your upper body to your right while rotating your palms out. Your palms and back heel should be almost aligned in one vertical plane. Point both index fingers up, while squeezing the other fingers in slightly, to create a bow in each palm. Focus your eyes in the direction of the index finger of your upper hand; complete exhale (Figure 3-16). Hold this posture and do eight abdominal breathing cycles. To complete Right Rotate Palm, turn your waist back until you are facing forward, while straightening your arms in front of

Figure 3-10

Figure 3-11

Figure 3-12

Figure 3-13

Figure 3-14

Figure 3-15

you; begin to inhale (Figure 3-17). Then bring your right foot back next to your left foot, lower your palms next to your abdomen, and stand up; complete your inhalation (Figure 3-18).

Key Notes:

As your palms rotate out and back, they should have rolling, drilling, wrenching, and wrapping *Jin*. Rolling *Jin* refers to the rotation of your arm. Drilling *Jin* refers to the drilling and the extending of your arm. Wrenching *Jin* refers to the torquing and settling of your palms. Wrapping *Jin* refers to the wrapping action accomplished by squeezing in your pinky, the crest of your palm, and the base of your thumb.

When holding this posture, pay attention to the Qi flow and the energization of your muscles. Every time you exhale, the Qi from your Lower *Dan Tian* should be lead out to your limbs, and should loosen up your limbs, one joint at a time. Your back should be rounded from the extensions of your arms; your hands should have the feeling of squeezing; and the center of your palms should have an expanded feeling. Your feet should feel like they are gripping the floor.

| Figure 3-16 | Figure 3-17 | Figure 3-18 |

Breathing should be slow and regular. Don't breathe forcefully, or in a way that makes your body move excessively. Keep your head upright and your chest relaxed at all times.

5. Spiral and Rotate Posture (*Pan Xuan Shi*)盤旋式

Oral Secrets:
腰如軸轉臂旋繞

Waist like an axle turning, arm swings around.

In Chinese martial arts, it is said that *Jin* originates from the legs, is directed by the waist, and manifested by the fingers. In a sense, the waist is like a steering wheel which directs the *Jin* generated from the legs to the extremities. When this steering wheel is controlled skillfully, you will be centered, balanced, and naturally rooted. From the waist's turning, the arms' swinging movements are generated. For each movement - from the legs, to the waist, and to the arms - the body is acting as one unit.

Movements:

Left Spiral and Rotate:

Shift your weight to your right leg and step to your left with your left foot, one shoulder width apart; begin to inhale. Next, shift your weight to your left leg, while extending your arms up to your left; palms face up; inhale (Figure 3-19). Shift your weight to your right leg and swing both arms horizontally to your right. The edge of your left palm strikes the Girdle Vessel (Waist). Your eyes focus in the direction of your right hand; complete exhale (Figure 3-20).

Grip the floor with your feet, distribute your weight evenly between both feet, and turn your body to your left as far as possible. At the same time, your left palm moves along the Girdle Vessel to your back, while maintaining the palm face up. The right palm moves down next to the left side of your waist. Your eyes look in the direction of your left hand; inhale (Figure 3-21). Shift your weight to your left leg and turn your waist to your left, while extending your arms up to your left. The right palm touches your left elbow; exhale (Figure 3-22).

Figure 3-19   Figure 3-20   Figure 3-21

Figure 3-22   Figure 3-23   Figure 3-24

Right spiral and Rotate:

Shift your weight to your right leg and swing both arms horizontally to your right; inhale (Figure 3-23). Shift your weight to your left leg and swing both arms horizontally to your left. The edge of your right palm strikes the Girdle Vessel (Waist). Your eyes focus in the direction of your right hand; exhale (Figure 3-24).

Grip the floor with your feet, distribute your weight evenly between both feet, and turn your body to your right as far as possible. At the same time, your right palm moves along the Girdle Vessel to your back, while maintaining the palm face up. The left palm moves down next to the right side of your waist. Your eyes look to your right; inhale (Figure 3-25). Shift your weight to your right leg and turn your waist to your right, while extending your arms up to your right. The left palm touches your right elbow; exhale (Figure 3-26).

Alternate between the Left and Right Spiral and Rotate Postures, a total of eight times each side. To finish this posture, turn your body until you are facing forward and your weight is evenly distributed on both feet, and extend both arms straight in front of you; inhale (Figure 3-27).

| Figure 3-25 | Figure 3-26 | Figure 3-27 |

Then bring your left foot next to your right foot and bring both palms down next to your abdomen; exhale (Figure 3-28).

Key Notes:

When you do the posture, keep the movements continuous. Use your waist to swing the arms around. When striking your waist with the edge of your palm, speed up your exhalation, increasing the amount of air exchange in your lungs. During the other movements, breathe evenly and smoothly.

6. Twist Turning Posture (*Ning Zhuan Shi*) 擰轉式

Oral Secrets:
身似繩擰頭頂懸

Body is twisted like a rope and the head is suspended from above.

In Baguazhang, you walk in a circular pattern. Your face, body, and arms are all twisted toward the center of the circle. It is therefore said that your body should be twisted like a rope. However, even though your body is twisted, your head should remain upright, as though suspended from above.

Movements:

Left Wrench and Turn:

Move your left foot to your left, about 12 inches from your right foot and hold your arms as though you were holding a ball in front of your chest, right arm on top; inhale (Figure 3-29). Then turn your right foot in about 45 degrees as you turn your body to your left (Figure 3-30). Next turn your left foot out until it is pointing to your rear, and turn your body as far to your left as possible. At the same time, extend and rotate your left palm up over your head, and push your right palm back next to your left armpit; exhale (Figure 3-31 and 3-31R). Keep this posture and do eight abdominal breathing cycles.

Right Wrench and Turn:

Turn your body back until you are facing forward, and hold your arms as though you were holding a ball in front of your chest, left arm on top, inhale (Figure 3-32). Then turn your left foot

Figure 3-28

Figure 3-29

Figure 3-30

Figure 3-31

Figure 3-31R

Figure 3-32

in until it is pointing inward at about 45 degrees as you turn your body to your right (Figure 3-33). Next turn your right foot out until it is pointing to your rear, and turn your body to your right. At the same time, extend and rotate your right arm up over your head, and push your left palm back next to your left armpit; exhale (Figure 3-34). Keep this posture and do eight abdominal breathing cycles. To complete this posture, turn your feet back until pointing forward. As you turn your body forward, lower both palms next to your abdomen. Then bring your left foot next to your right foot; inhale (Figure 3-35).

Key Notes:

Keep your head upright and don't raise your shoulders. While turning your body, rotate your torso muscles gradually. When holding the posture, your body should feel like a piece of rope with its strands intertwined. During exhalation, push your lower palm back, and continue rotating your extended arm slightly - creating a stronger wrenching feeling of your torso. Eyes look past your shoulders.

Figure 3-33

Figure 3-34

Figure 3-34R

Figure 3-35

7. Bore and Turn Posture (*Chuan Zhuan Shi*) 穿轉式

Oral Secrets:
沿圈擺扣蹚泥行

Arcing and swinging walking in the mud along the edge of a circle.

Arcing and swaying steppings (*Kou Bai Bu*) are two of the most basic walking methods in Baguazhang. In order to walk firmly and smoothly along the edge of a circle, in addition to using the arcing and swaying steppings, you must also image that you are walking on muddy ground. Refer to Figure 3-36 for the stepping pattern.

Movements:

From Figure 3-35, inhale; then step forward with your left foot and rotate your palms to your left as in the Rotate Palm Posture; exhale (Figures 3-37 and 3-38).

With your palms fixed in place, turn your left foot out slightly and step in an arc with your

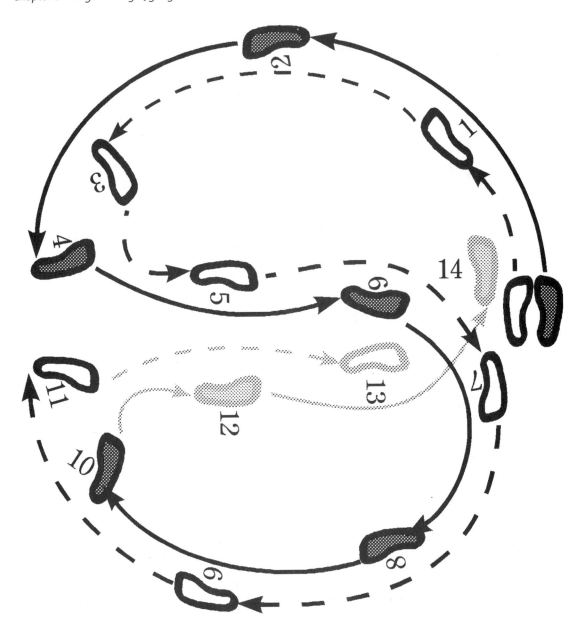

1=Figures 3-37 and 3-38   8=Figure 3-46
2=Figure 3-39   9=Figure 3-47
3=Figure 3-40   10=Figure 3-48
4=Figures 3-41 and 3-42   11=Figures 3-49 and 3-50
5=Figure 3-43   12=Figure 3-51
6=Figure 3-44   13=Figure 3-52
7=Figure 3-45   14=Figure 3-53

Figure 3-36   Bore and Turn Posture Stepping Pattern

Figure 3-37

Figure 3-38

Figure 3-39

Figure 3-40

Figure 3-41

Figure 3-42

right foot, foot turned in, (Figure 3-39). Step with your left foot in an arc, foot turned out (Figure 3-40). Next bring your right foot next to your left, foot turned in. Both feet are pigeon toed (Figure 3-41).

Right Overhand Boring:

Turn your body until your arms are in front of your chest and begin to lowering your left palm (Figure 3-42). Lower your left palm and execute a an overhand *Chuan* with your right palm. At the same time step forward with your left foot (Figure 3-43). Step in an arc with your right foot while extending and rotating your palms to your right (Figure 3-44). With your arms fixed in place, walk in a circular path for 5 more steps. On the fifth step bring your feet next to each other, both feet turned in (Figures 3-45 to 3-49).

Left Overhand Boring:

Figure 3-43 Figure 3-44 Figure 3-45

Figure 3-46 Figure 3-47 Figure 3-48

Turn your body until your arms are in front of your chest, and begin to lower your right palm (Figure 3-50). Continue to lower your right palm and execute an overhand *Chuan* with your left palm. At the same time step forward with your right foot (Figure 3-51). Step in an arc with your left foot while extending and rotating your palms to your left (Figure 3-52). With your arms fixed in place walk two steps in an arc (Figures 3-53 and 3-54).

At this point, you should be almost back to the starting location as in Figure 3-38. Next walk three steps in an arc as in Figures 3-39, 3-40, and 3-41. This will bring you to a ready position to do another right overhand *Chuan*. Repeat the right and the left overhand boring 7 more times.

To end this posture, after completing your last left overhand boring, follow the movements described in the next posture.

Key Notes:

When boring and turning, the movements must be smooth and continuous, without any pauses. Once the movements are smooth, you may wish to add a few more "sliding" steps in between boring and turning (changing directions). The size of your circle dictates the angle at which you

Figure 3-49

Figure 3-50

Figure 3-51

Figure 3-52

Figure 3-53

Figure 3-54

place your feet while stepping. Initially, you may wish to step in a large circle because the gentle angle makes it is easier to step. Then, as your leg joints become more flexible, gradually make the circles smaller and smaller. Before lifting your back foot up to step, you should feel as though you are pushing off the ground. During your steps, you should have the feeling of kicking forward, and as your stepping foot passes the stationary foot, you should have a feeling of splitting something with your feet. After your foot touches down, slide your foot forward a few inches more, like you slipped on mud. Your foot should slide forward carefully, as if you are searching for something.

8. Closing Gong Posture (*Shou Gong Shi*) 收功式

Oral Secrets:
轉旋八卦返先天

(Practice) turning-spinning Bagua to return to Pre-Heaven (condition).

One of the main purposes of Baguazhang practice is to transmute your body's Qi pattern from the Post-Heaven to the Pre-Heaven state. It is believed in Chinese Qigong society that the Pre-Heaven Qi which is converted from the Original Essence is pure, clean, and healthy - bringing the practitioner inner peace and longevity. Post-Heaven Qi, which is converted from air and food, is potentially more contaminated and harmful to health. Therefore, as do many other Chinese Qigong practices, Baguazhang Qigong emphasizes methods for returning the body to a Pre-Heaven state.

Movements:

From Figure 3-54, bring your right foot next to your left, both feet turned in (Figure 3-55). Lower and extend your right hand to your right, and turn both palms up (Figure 3-56). Raise both palms over your head, inhale, and lower them in front of your while straightening your legs, exhale (Figure 3-57). Continue lowering your palms until they are at your sides. Then turn your right foot until it is pointing forward, and bring your left foot beside your right foot; complete your inhalation (Figure 3-58).

Figure 3-55

Figure 3-56

Figure 3-57

Figure 3-58

Key Notes:

Pause slightly when you are in the Turn Palm Posture (Figure 3-54). Then continue, and finish the posture. Stand still for a few minutes, allowing your Qi to sink back to your Lower *Dan Tian*.

References

1. Kang Ge-Wu, *Zhongguo Wushu*, pp. 323-333, Today's Chinese Publishing Company, 1990. 中國武術實用大全，康戈武編。

Chapter 4

Basic Training Concepts
基本訓練概念

4-1. Introduction

In all Chinese martial arts, before starting any real training, a student must first learn and understand the important concepts and theories of his or her style. Only after understanding has been achieved will basic physical training begin. In this way a solid foundation is provided for later study. Without this foundation, a student's comprehension will be shallow, and he will never unfold the deeper aspects of the style.

In this chapter, we will discuss some basic concepts in Baguazhang, and introduce some key words of its training.

4-2. General Concepts

There are many concepts which are of crucial importance to the Baguazhang practitioner, especially for beginners. In this section we summarize these concepts, as developed by well known Baguazhang masters.

1. Three Training Procedures [1, 2] 三個練習步驟

There are three training procedures in Baguazhang practice. They are: a). defined postures; b). living postures; and c). varied postures. For the beginner, practicing the defined postures (and its associated movements) is the most important. The defined postures and movements are the aforementioned foundation of Baguazhang. When you are in this stage of training, you are learning the forms of Baguazhang which have been defined by past masters. In this stage, you must follow the rules and patterns set down by those who have gone before you, who created them according to the basic Baguazhang theory. You are like an artist learning for the first time to paint with a brush. You should learn the patterns slowly, step by step, until you feel natural and comfortable in every posture and movement. In this stage, you must regulate your body, and learn to accurately manifest the mind conveyed in the postures.

After you can perform the forms accurately and smoothly, then you must enter the stage of living postures. In this stage, your postures are natural and comfortable, and your movements become fast, swift, and smooth. You are now bringing the patterns you have learned to life. But even though you have reached this stage, you are still following patterns which have been created by others, like a painter copying easily the great works of others.

Finally, after practicing long and hard, you can master the postures and movements taught to you. With correct practice, they have become part of your natural movements and actions, and you have reached the stage where you may mix the patterns and movements skillfully, randomly, and energetically. When you reach this stage, not only can you apply the techniques in the applications skillfully and naturally, but you can also create new patterns according to your own understanding, without losing the essence of the art. In this stage, you are really a master of Baguazhang.

2. Three Heights of Postures (San *Pan*)[3] 三盤

"*Pan*" means sections of the body which includes "*Shang Pan*,""*Zhong Pan*," and "*Xia Pan*." "*Shang Pan*" means the "upper section" of the body, which includes the portion from the solar plexus to the top of the head. "*Zhong Pan*" (Middle section) covers the section from the knees up until the solar plexus. Finally, "*Xia Pan*" includes the portion from the knees down to the bottom of the feet. *Pan* is also commonly used to express the height of the postures. Again, they are classified into three levels of height: high posture (*Gao Pan*), middle posture (*Zhong Pan*), and low posture (*Di Pan*). When *Pan* is used to express the height of the postures, it has the meaning of "coiling" and "creeping." It therefore also involves the concepts of rooting, attaching, adhering, and sticking. The high posture is the same as your normal walking height. It has the weakest root of the three heights, but allows you to step quickly. This height is normally used when you are at long range from your opponent, and the situation is not dangerous.

The middle height posture is used when you enter into the middle and short ranges, where your opponent can reach you with simple kicks and punches, or with only a short hop. At this range you need a firm root, so you squat slightly. At this height you can keep a good root yet move with good speed. This is the most common height used in Baguazhang practice today.

The low posture is generally used to develop strength and endurance in the legs. In this posture, the knees are bent very low. This is the best way to train leg Qigong. This low posture training is very important in the traditional Chinese martial arts, because if you have strong legs you can move quickly and still maintain a strong root. Please read Chapter 5 for the three *Pan* training.

3. The Eight Basic Palms[4] 基本八掌

There are eight basic patterns or methods of using the palm in Baguazhang. As a Baguazhang practitioner, you should distinguish them clearly.

a. Upward Palm (*Yang Zhang*): (Figure 4-1) 仰掌

The palm faces upward, with all the fingers open and extended, and the thumb raised slightly. When done correctly, the center of your palm will be slightly concave.

b. Downward Palm (*Fu Zhang*): (Figure 4-2) 俯掌

The palm faces downward, with all the fingers open and extended, and the thumb lowered slightly. When done correctly, the center of your palm will be slightly concave.

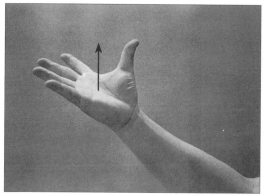

Figure 4-1

Figure 4-2

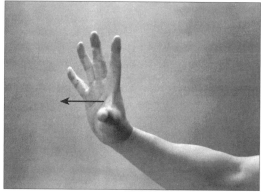

Figure 4-3

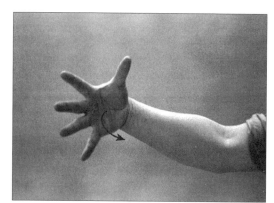

Figure 4-4

c. Upright Palm (*Shu Zhang*): (Figure 4-3) 豎掌

The open palm faces either forward, sideways or inward. The four fingers are all extended upward, and the thumb is fully extended, so that the skin between the thumb and index finger is stretched taught The wrist is settled.

d. Embracing Palm (*Bao Zhang*): (Figure 4-4) 抱掌

The palm faces toward the body and all five fingers are extended. The thumb extends upward and the elbow is bent inward as if you were embracing someone.

e. Chopping Palm (*Pi Zhang*): (Figure 4-5) 劈掌

The palm faces sideways, the fingers are pointing forward, and the thumb is pointing slightly upward. The edge of the palm is down as if you were using it to chop. This palm has also been called "*Ce Zhang*" (Sideways Palm).

f. Scooping Palm (*Liao Zhang*): (Figure 4-6) 撩掌

The palm faces inward, the thumb points upward while the other four fingers are downward as if you were using your palm to scoop up something. In Baguazhang, this palm scoops inward and then turns forward.

g. Picking Palm (*Tiao Zhang*): (Figure 4-7) 挑掌

The palm face sideways. The fingers are first open and pointing forward. They then turn to point upward, as if you were picking up something.

Figure 4-5

Figure 4-6

Figure 4-7

Figure 4-8

h. Screwing Palm (*Luo Xuan Zhang*)**:** (Figure 4-8) 螺旋掌

All five fingers are open; they first point forward and then turn upward. Rotate the arm as you raise it in a screwing motion.

4. Six Basic Leg Postures[5] 基本步型

One of the most important characteristics of Baguazhang is its firm leg postures, either in stationary position or while "walking" or "stepping." Learning the correct leg postures is an essential part of the training. Here, we will introduce the six basic leg postures in Baguazhang.

a. Arc Stepping (*Kou Bu*)**:** (Figure 4-9) 扣步

In Arc Stepping, both of your feet are arced inward. It is usually used together with Swing Stepping.

b. Swing Stepping (*Bai Bu*)**:** (Figures 4-10 and 4-11) 擺步

In Swing Stepping, you turn one of your feet outward to prepare for walking. It is usually used together with Arc Stepping and called "*Kou Bai Bu*" 扣擺步

Figure 4-9

Figure 4-10

Figure 4-11

Figure 4-12

Figure 4-13

Figure 4-14

c. Bow Stance (*Gong Bu*): (Figure 4-12) 弓步

Bow Stance is one of the most common stances in the Chinese martial arts. In this stance, your rear leg is straight while the front leg is bent. The toes of the front leg are turned in slightly. The body should be upright, and facing in the same direction as the front leg.

d. High False Stance (*Gao Xu Bu*): (Figure 4-13) 高虚步

This stance is very common, especially in the northern styles. In this stance, all of your weight is on your rear leg, and only the toes of the front foot touch the ground, so that you can easily kick or step with it.

e. Half Horse Stance (*Ban Ma Bu*): (Figure 4-14) 半馬步

The Half Horse Stance is similar to the regular Horse Stance. The difference is that one of the leg bears about 60% of the weight, and the other about 40%, and the body is turned toward the leg which bears the lighter weight.

f. Single Squat Down Stance (*Pu Bu*):
(Figure 4-15) 仆步

This stance is also called "Tame the Tiger Stance" (*Fu Hu Bu*), and is also very common. Squat down on one leg while keeping the other one out straight. Both feet should be parallel, and the bent knee should be pointing forward.

Figure 4-15

5. Basic Postures of Baguazhang[5, 6]

After you have familiarized yourself with the basic leg postures, then you should apply them to the general body postures. Next, we will translate and comment on a secret song describing the key points of the general postures of Baguazhang. From this song, you will have a clearer picture of how the postures should look in Baguazhang.

The Oral Secrets of the Basic Postures

基本庄勢口訣

兩手互捧如抱嬰，含胸拔背似捆繩。抽身長手千斤墜，宛若猿猴摘果形。

The two arms are embracing each other as if holding a baby. Hold in the chest and stretch the back like a stretched rope. Free the body and extend the arms with a thousand pound drop (i.e., firm root). The shape is like an ape picking up fruit.

When you extend your arms out in front of you, it should feel like you are holding a baby at your chest. Therefore, your chest is arced inward and your back is stretched. When your arms and body are formed like this, you will have a greater strength in both arms. When you move your body or extend your arms for any purpose, your root must always be firm and solid, like you are carrying a thousand pound weight. The image is of an ape standing on a branch, picking fruit. The ape must maintain his balance on the tree limb, even as he reaches up and out for the fruit.

由靜而動周身運，氣導血隨龍虎奔。腰乃坐纛心為令，扣膝坐步不八丁。

From calmness to action, the entire body moves. Qi is led and the blood follows, (like) the running of the dragon and tiger. The waist is the settled banner and the heart (i.e., mind) is the commander. Arc the knees with the squat stance, with the posture of neither the (Chinese) word of *Ba* nor *Ding*.

Once you decide to move, your entire body moves as a single unit. Use your wisdom mind (*Yi*) to lead the Qi. When the Qi moves, the blood will naturally follow. You are so energized that the blood circulating in your body flows as smoothly as a dragon's swimming, and as strong as a tiger's running. When the heart (i.e., emotional mind) is agitated and decides to act, the waist will direct the power. The banner in an army is used to pass the orders of the commander, and directs the movements of the soldiers. While standing stationary, you squat down in a posture not like the Chinese words either *Ba* (八) or *Ding* (丁). This means that the position of the two feet should be neither like *Ba* nor *Ding*.

定勢半魚步七星，氣沈丹田神貫頂。兩臀下垂提谷道，二目注視虎口中。

Form the (advantageous) situation with Half Fish (*Ban Yu*) and step with Seven Stars (Qi Xing). Qi is sunk to the *Dan Tian* and the spirit (*Shen*) reaches the top (i.e., head). The two hips settle downward and lift the grain path (*Gu Dao*). The two eyes concentrate on looking through the center of the Tiger Mouth (*Hu Kou*).

Fish Stepping (*Yu Bu*), which is also called Yin Yang Fish Stepping (*Yin Yang Yu Bu*), is commonly used in Baguazhang. Circle around your opponent, and when you see an opportunity to attack, you enter the center of the circle, continue out the other side in the reverse direction, and continue your circling (Figure 4-16). Since you pass through the center of the circle, this kind of stepping is sometimes also called "*Ban Yu Bu*" (Half Fish Stepping).[7]

The Seven Stars are the seven principal stars which form the Big Dipper in the constellation Ursa Major. Since ancient times this pattern has been used as a model for both strategic maneuvers in battle as well as an individual's movements in a fight. If you are skillful in using the Half Fish and Seven Star strategies, you can create an advantageous situation.

When you are in a hostile situation, your Qi should be sunk to the Lower *Dan Tian*. When you store *Jin* (i.e., martial power) for an attack, your hips should be firmed and settled while holding up your anus. "*Gu Dao*" (grain path) refers to the anus.

When you are ready for a fight, not only should you raise up your spirit of vitality, but you must also pay close attention to your opponent. *Hu Kou* (Tiger Mouth) is the area between the thumb and the index finger. Since your front palm is raised as high as your eyes, if you look through the *Hu Kou* area, your eyes should focus forward on your opponent.

心虛腹實舌上卷，扣齒呼吸換液津。沈肩墜肘向內合，前手食指與眉平。

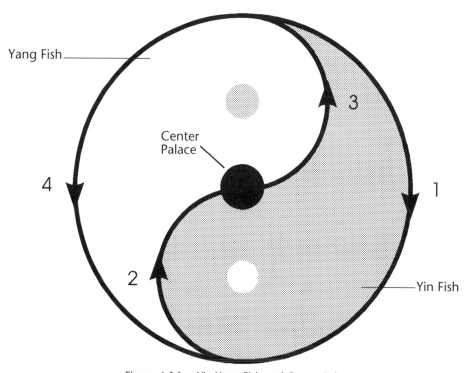

Figure 4-16   Yin Yang Fish and Center Palace

The heart is insubstantial and the abdomen is solid, the tongue is curled upward. Breathe with closed teeth (i.e., closed mouth) and exchange the saliva. Sink the shoulders, and the elbows are dropped and closed inward. The index finger of the front hand is as high as the eyebrow.

When you are in a fight, your mind should be tricky (i.e., insubstantial), so that your opponent will not know your intentions. The Qi stored in the Lower *Dan Tian* should be full and abundant and the tongue should be curled upward to touch the roof of the mouth, connecting the Yin Conception and Yang Governing Qi Vessels (Figure 4-17). The shoulders are sunk and the elbows are dropped. The two arms embrace inward. The position of the front hand should be as high as your eyebrow.

6. Six Training Keys[8]

In one of the ancient documents, there is a song which includes six parts of small songs; each part discusses different key points of Baguazhang postures. Following are the translations of and commentary on these six songs.

A. The Song of Beginning Posture 起勢歌訣

竪形立勢掌如拳，陰陽掌法內外間。審勢分明知閃躲，防身斜側識端偏。

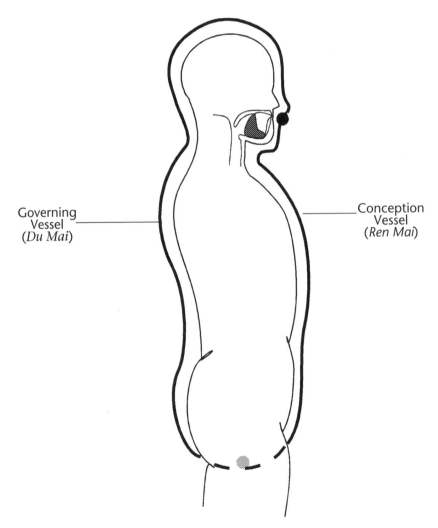

Governing
Vessel
(*Du Mai*)

Conception
Vessel
(*Ren Mai*)

Figure 4-17   Small Circulation

進功推托步偷半，插打劈穿學貴全。欲免臨場心手亂，閒居發憤讀斯篇。

Upright shape to form the posture and the palms are like the fists. The techniques of Yin and Yang palms are between the internal and external. Investigate the (different) situations and distinguish them clearly, (you will) know (the way of) dodging and avoiding. To protect the body with diagonal or sideways (movement), (you should) recognize (even) a small difference. (When you) attack with pushing or lifting, (use) the stealing half step. (It is precious if) learning poking, striking, chopping, or boring completely. When a situation occurs, in order to avoid the confusion and disorder of the emotional mind and the hands, (you) should ponder these few articles intelligently while (you) have time.

The correct body posture of Baguazhang has the head suspended and the torso upright. Even though Baguazhang specializes in using the palms to strike, its fighting theories are the same as those in which the fists are used to attack. The palms are distinguished into Yin and Yang palms, which can apply and correspond to each other both internally and externally. Before combat, you should first investigate and familiarize yourself with the entire situation. Then you will know how to avoid or even escape from the danger. In order to effectively protect yourself, you must distinguish even the slightest difference between each technique. The key to advancing uses half-stepping techniques. When you use half-stepping techniques, you will be fast and stable, and the power will be naturally strong. You should learn and master such basic techniques as poking, striking, chopping and boring, which will give you confidence when you encounter a situation. The way of reaching this goal is through continuous technical practice and theoretical study.

B. The Song of the Hand Techniques 手法歌訣

撐拳托掌若風煙，劈穿抓拿勢貴偏。挺去牽來腳管硬，勾搬裹挽削劈連。
三盤內外須純練，前後高低混打全。一日無間三歲滿，保能發手倒山巔。

The extending fist and the lifting palm are (as swift) as wind and smoke. The chopping, boring, grabbing, and controlling, their postures are important in (striking) from the sides. Thrust forward and pull backward, the legs are solid (i.e., firm). Hooking, shifting, wrapping, and holding, continued with paring and chopping. The three heights both internal and external must be trained diligently. Front, rear, high, and low (strikes) are mixed to complete the attack. Training without interruption everyday for full three years, guaranteed that when emitting (your) hands, (it is) able to turn over the mountain.

In a fight, speed is the most important factor. Therefore, when you emit your attack, it is as fast as wind and as swift as smoke, so that your opponent cannot figure out your intention. When you attack with chopping, boring, grabbing and controlling techniques, the most effective angle for attacking is from your opponent's side. This is because it is much easier for your opponent to defend if you attack from his front. When you charge an attack or pull to neutralize a strike, the most important factor in making the techniques effective is that you have a firm root. If you use hooking, shifting, wrapping, holding, paring and chopping techniques, the attacks must be continuous. All success depends on the firmness of your root. You must practice all three different heights ceaselessly. Furthermore, the internal and the external must be unified. Your strategies should include the high strike, the low strike, forward, and backward. Only after you are able to mix all of these moving strategies will your techniques be alive and effective.

C. The Song of the Eyes Techniques 眼法歌訣

兩眼凝神若朗星，頭端審勢更分明。瞻前顧後疾如電，展動周旋似轉輪。

戲定敵人身手腳，乘虛攻擊莫留情。臨場對敵人難進，全在雙眸一團神。

Two eyes' spirit is condensing like shimmering stars. Use the top of the head to investigate the situation even more clearly. Look to the forward and beware of the rear, acting as fast as lightening. (When) expand to move in cycle or rotation, it is like turning a wheel. Watch firmly the opponent's body, hands, and feet. Take the opportunity of (opponent's) void and attack without showing mercy. When encountering the situation, the enemy is hard to advance. All of these depend on the gathering spirit of the two eyes.

Your fighting spirit is expressed through your eyes. When you have a sharp, focused fighting spirit, your techniques and power can be potently manifested, and you may also make your opponent scared. When your spirit is raised, you will be highly alert, and therefore you can react very quickly against any action which is harmful to you. Baguazhang specializes in circular motion. This is the key aspect and the most basic fighting concept of the entire art. Therefore, you should practice the circular motions until they rotate smoothly. Always pay attention to your opponent's slight movements, which may offer you a clue to his next action. When you sense an opportunity, you should not hesitate to attack. If you are able to demonstrate all of the spirit and show it in your eyes, you will have won the battle.

D. The Song of the Body Movements 身法歌訣

身如游龍手平分，直豎身昂腿護陰。斜立足分丁八步，勢如跨馬彎弓行。
腳腿不浮身便穩，平起平落腳踩靈。足動腳跟同進退，肩投腰趁臀齊行。
翻身腹縮隨舒卷，偏閃騰挪勢勢承。練習如常寡敵眾，橫沖直撞莫停留。

The body (moves) like a swimming dragon and both hands are divided equally. The body is straight upward and the legs are protecting the groin. Stand diagonally with the feet positioned as the word *Ding* or *Ba*. The appearance is like riding the horse, which has the shape of a bow. (If) the legs are not floating, the body will be steady (i.e., firm). Raise and fall horizontally, and the feet's steppings are agile. When the feet move forward and backward, the heels are moved together. When the shoulder advances, the waist follows, and the hips are also moving together. (If) turning the body, withdraw the abdomen and curl comfortably. Dodge to the side and jump (for an action), every form should be responsible (i.e., sure). Practice as usual and few can defeat many. Thrust to the sides and bump straight forward, do not hesitate.

When you move your body, you are agile and swift like a swimming dragon. Even though you are moving fast, both your hands are equally balanced. The body should be kept straight upright and the front thighs should be locked inward to protect the groin. When you are standing or walking, your two feet should be positioned as Chinese words either *Ding* (丁) or *Ba* (八). The upper body should be curved inward in the bow shape, which allows you to store the *Jin*. When you stand or walk, the legs firmly adhere to the ground. This will keep you from "floating," and your postures will be steady. When you move forward, backward, upward, or downward, your entire body moves with balance. If you step forward, your entire foot adheres to the ground like you are walking on muddy ground. Once a part of the body moves, the entire body moves. If you have to turn your body, you should squat down to firm your root and curl in your abdomen area in order to stabilize your physical center. This increases your stability when moving swiftly. When you start any action, you should be sure of what you are doing. The technique without a firm and confident mind will be useless. Even if you are alone, if you practice intelligently, you can defeat many opponents. When you encounter many opponents, you should thrust and bump in any direction which is advantageous to you. This will help to misdirect your opponents' attention, and provide an opportunity to gain the advantage.

E. The Song of the Techniques 法的歌訣

個中奧妙在深玄，掌在師傳學在專。掌法千般學不盡，機關百種卒難言。

水到渠成三載力，鋼須精練始削間。總之熟練能生巧，處處相承節節連。

The marvellous trick of individual (technique) is hidden deeply and mysteriously. The palm techniques are learned from teacher, however, the expertise comes from (continued) learning. The palms techniques are more than thousands and they cannot be learned completely. The tricks (i.e., fighting strategies) are hundreds and hard to describe entirely. It takes three years of effort to complete a channel when water arrives. Every part (of the training) is mutually related and every section is connected.

In Chinese martial arts, although the outward look of each technique is easy and seems simple, the real essence and the application in each one are hidden deeply. Usually, with guidance from a teacher and individual practice, in time you will spontaneously comprehend these secrets. Therefore, though you may learn many palm techniques from a teacher, in order to be proficient in this art you must continue learning and practicing. There are an unlimited number of techniques and strategies; it would be impossible for one person to learn them all in one lifetime. Therefore, you should remain humble and study diligently. You must practice for at least three years, and when the situation arrives, you will be ready for action. When you practice, from the beginning till the end, every second and lesson is mutually related and contributes to a deeper understanding. You must treat the entire art as a whole unit; it cannot be separated into mere theory and practice.

F. The Song of the Steppings 步法歌訣

兩膝彎步力自然，屈前直後練成堅。之從順閃騰挪步，玄經斜擊反回圈。
翻覆旋風肩平硬，膝雄跟端帶勾鐮。

Two knees are bent when stepping and the strength is natural. The front is bent and the rear is straight, train them until firmed. Stepping with zigzag shape to follow, dodge and jump smoothly. Move stealthily with attack diagonally, could allow you to turn around. To turn over the tornado, the shoulders must be horizontal and strong. The knees are strong and the heels follow with a sickle's hooking.

When you step, both knees are bent and the legs are naturally strong. You should train your legs with the front one bent and the rear one straight, until they are both firmly strong. When your opponent is attacking you continuously, the best counter is either to step in a zigzag pattern, dodge skillfully, or jump away. If you can move stealthily and press your attack from the sides of your opponent, you can turn your body around easily. To escape your previously awkward situation, you must firm your shoulders so that you maintain your balance. Furthermore, you should use your knees to strike your opponent, and use your feet to hook your opponent's leg skillfully In this case, you can turn around the entire fighting situation.

7. Nine Palaces (*Jiu Gong*) and Nine Palaces Stepping (*Jiu Gong* Bu)[9] 九宮，九宮步

An important part of stepping training in Baguazhang uses the "Nine Palaces" (*Jiu Gong*). This is an arrangement of nine posts placed in a special pattern, and is used to develop stability and speed of stepping.

Eight of the Nine Palaces are related to the Eight Trigrams. The Center Palace (*Zhong Gong*) is also called "Yin Yang Fish" (*Yin Yang Yu*), since from this center your strategy, movements or techniques can vary from Yin to Yang or vice-versa (Figure 4-16). To use the Nine Palaces, you walk swiftly around the posts, changing directions and striking the posts with various techniques. This practice is called "Nine Palaces Stepping" (*Jiu Gong Bu*), "Flying in Nine Palaces" (*Fei Jiu Gong*), or "Yin Bagua."

This is a very valuable training exercise. In the beginning, the practitioner moves very quickly among the posts, which are viewed as nine opponents. At first, you should practice without touching the posts, moving in specific patterns with Baguazhang stepping methods. Imagine that you are fighting nine opponents, and keep changing your techniques so that you can attack these opponents efficiently without exposing yourself to their attacks. This training develops walking speed, stability, a sense of enemy, and the ability to quickly vary your techniques.

When you have practiced enough so that you can walk and move your body skillfully and quickly, you then learn how to attack. It is important not to rush into the next phase of the training too quickly, because if you start to use techniques before you have developed your root and stability, your attacks will be ineffective.

There are two patterns for walking around the posts which have proved to be the safest and most useful. The basic pattern is called "*Tai Yi Xing Jiu Gong Zhi Fa*" (The Sole Ultimate Technique of Walking Nine Palace), and the second pattern is its reverse (Figure 4-18). This pattern was described by Xu Yue: "Two and four are shoulders, left is three and right is seven, carry nine and stand on one, five is in the center."[10] This means that if you follow the pattern of the Post-Heaven Bagua Trigram (Figure 4-19), you start with *Kan*, and then move to *Kun, Zhen, Xun*, Center, *Qian, Dui, Gen*, and finally to *Li* to complete the cycle. When you follow this pattern, it is called "*Shun Chuan*" (Following Through), while following the reverse patten is called "*Ni Chuan*" (Reverse Through).

In your initial training, walk following the regular pattern. After you have reached number nine (*Li*), then follow the reverse pattern, and finally return to number one (*Kan*). Keep in mind all the requirements for correct posture and accurate stepping, which were discussed previously, and walk following the pattern slowly and steadily. After you are familiar with both of the patterns, then you should increase your walking speed. Don't lose your stability and rooting, even if

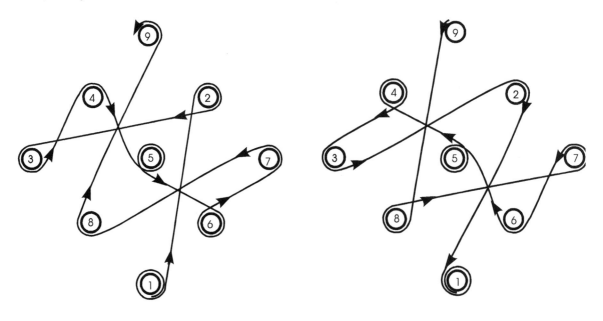

Smooth Boring Pattern   Reverse Boring Pattern

Figure 4-18: Nine Palaca Stepping Pattern

you are walking quickly. After you have trained for a while and can move around the posts quickly and without touching them, you should add the hand forms to strike, push, press, bump, pull, or hook. Once you reach this stage, you have built a firm foundation of Baguazhang walking.

4-3. Important Key Words in Baguazhang Training

1. Sixteen Key Words of Baguazhang[11]
十六字訣

Practitioners of Baguazhang should understand and practice the following 16 secret words. These 16 words include the essence of Baguazhang.

1. Boring (*Chuan*): 穿

In Chinese, *Chuan* means "boring" or "passing through." It is like a piece of thread passing through the eye of a needle. It is also like a butterfly boring through flowers. The implication is that of penetrating or boring through something. *Chuan* can be practiced by yourself or with a partner. There are many ways of executing *Chuan* technique in Baguazhang. Here we will only introduce some typical ones for your reference.

Underhand *Chuan*:

When practicing Underhand *Chuan*, stand upright. Extend one arm in front of you and place the other palm at the crease of your elbow. To change to the other side of Underhand *Chuan*, rotate and fold your front forearm in, palm down; while rotating and boring your other palm forward from under the withdrawing arm, palm up (Figure 4-20).

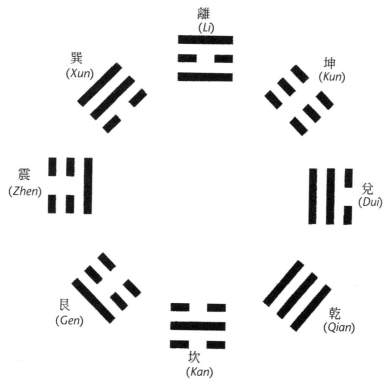

離
(Li)

巽
(Xun)

坤
(Kun)

震
(Zhen)

兌
(Dui)

艮
(Gen)

乾
(Qian)

坎
(Kan)

Figure 4-19: Post-Birth Bagua Symbol

| Figure 4-20 | Figure 4-21 | Figure 4-22 |

Overhand *Chuan*:

When practicing Overhand *Chuan*, stand upright. Extend one hand in front of you and place the other palm under the elbow, palm down. To change to the other side of Overhand *Chuan*, rotate and fold your extended forearm in and cover the palm down while rotating the other hand with palm facing upward and extending forward over the bending arm (Figure 4-21). You can change from a Underhand *Chuan* to a Overhand *Chuan* by extending your arm from either under or over the folding arm.

Backward *Chuan*:

To practice this *Chuan*, stand with your feet about two shoulder widths apart. Bring both palms next to your chest with your palms facing down. Then shift your weight to your right leg while rotating and boring your left palm backward and downward at an angle with the palm facing upward (Figure 4-22). To change to the other side, first shift your weight back to the center while moving both palms in front of your chest again. Shift your weight to your left leg while rotating and boring your right palm backward and downward at an angle.

Once you are smooth with the stationary *Chuan* drills, you can add the legs to make the movements more alive. You can have your right leg forward while executing a right hand *Chuan* or you can have your left foot forward depending on how your perceive your opponent's attack.

Two-Man *Chuan* Practice – 1:

This first two-man *Chuan* practice is a *Chuan* drill for toughening your arms and stabilizing your root. To practice this drill, you and your partner stand feet together and face each other with arms at your sides. Both of you then step to each other's right with your right legs, while extending your right arm forward and left arm back (Figure 4-23). You should contact each other's right forearm, then slide along each other's arm, and finish in a Bow Stance. As you slide your arms pass each other, you should attempt to push your opponent off balance while stabilizing your own stance. To do the drill on the other side, simply step back and then step forward with your left foot, and extend your left arm forward and right arm back.

| Figure 4-23 | Figure 4-24 | Figure 4-25 |

Two-Man *Chuan* Practice – 2:

This two-man *Chuan* practice is another example of a two person drill. First, Gray starts by executing a Right Overhand *Chuan*. Black intercepts and covers it down with his left forearm (Figure 4-24) while extending his right palm over his left palm toward Gray's face (Figure 4-25). Gray then intercepts with his left forearm. and covers Black's right arm down while extending his right palm over his left palm toward Black's face (Figure 4-24). This drill can also be done with moving stances to make the exercise more alive. Naturally, you may also mix in other *Chuan* techniques and make the drill more practical.

2. Moving, Shifting, or Rotating (*Ban*)搬

In Chinese, *Ban* means "to move," "to shift," or "to rotate." In Baguazhang, it means to move, to shift, or to rotate the root of the opponent's power away, so that his power cannot be manifested, or to put your opponent in a defensive position. For example, Gray intercepts Black's right punch with his left hand while grabbing Black's elbow with his right hand. Gray than rotates both hands counterclockwise, executing a *Ban* maneuver (Figure 4-26).

3. Intercepting (*Jie*)截

In Chinese, *Jie* means "to intercept." In Baguazhang, it is a maneuver for intercepting an opponent's attack. For example, Gray intercepts Black's right punch with both forearms and locks it in place (Figure 4-27).

4. Blocking (*Lan*)攔

Lan means to block the opponent's further movement or attack. For example, when Gray has noticed Black's intention to attack, he immediately uses both hands to push and block Black's right arm, preventing Black's further movement (Figure 4-28).

5. Walking (*Zou*)走

Walking is the most fundamental drill in Baguazhang. It trains your stability in motion, as well as extending your Qi to your the palms and legs. Before walking, stand with your feet shoulder width apart. Hold your arms up in an embracing posture, with palms facing you with fingers opened. Then rotate both palms out until facing forward and lower both palms to your abdomen level. You chest should be slightly arced and your back rounded. Put your attention on your arc-

Figure 4-26

Figure 4-27

Figure 4-28

ing chest, arms, and middle fingers of your palms. When you stand in this posture for just a few minutes, you will feel a strong flow of Qi expanding from the center of your body. You can also feel the Qi flow at the center of your palms. Next, learn how to walk with Bagua stepping in a straight line, firmly and steadily. Finally, walking in a Bagua circle (Figure 4-29).

6. Turning Over (*Fan*): 翻

Fan is to train the *Jin* of uprising, which can turn a poor defensive situation into an advantageous offensive one. *Fan* is commonly practiced with a partner. For example, when Black grabs Gray's wrist, Gray neutralizes the grab by circling his right hand up (Figure 4-30). Gray then initiates an attack by rotating his palm and pressing down on Black's forearm, setting up to grab Black's wrist (Figure 4-31). Black can now neutralize Gray's right hand by turning his right hand over Black's wrist.

7 Twisting (*Ning*): 擰

Ning is a Qin Na technique. For example, Gray may first attack with a right palm *Chuan* to Black's throat. When Black intercepts with his right forearm, Gray immediately grabs and hooks Black's wrist down, while initiating another attack with his left palm to Black's neck. Black intercepts with his free hand (his left arm). Gray then grabs hold of Black's left wrist with his left hand. Finally, Gray twists Black's arms counterclockwise to control Black. This is an ideal situation (Figure 4-32). This shows an example of maneuvering to set your opponent up into a totally defenseless situation.

8. Turning (*Zhuan*): 轉

Zhuan is a movement of the body used against a push or a press. For example, if Gray pushes Black's back (Figure 4-33), Black can turn his body around either to his right or left to neutralize Gray's push, while setting up an attack (Figure 4-34).

Figure 4-29

Figure 4-30

Figure 4-31

Figure 4-32

Figure 4-33

Figure 4-34

9. Pushing (*Tui*): 推

In Baguazhang, whenever you have a chance, you can push your opponent's body and throw him off balance. However, pushing is also commonly used to lock and seal the opponent's movements. For example. Gray can intercept Black's attack (Figure 4-35) and then stick and push down Black's arms to seal them (Figure 4-36).

10. Supporting Up (*Tuo*): 托

Tuo is a technique which can be used to lock the movement of the opponent's arm or to create an opening for an attack in the opponent's vital areas. For example, Gray uses his right hand to control Black's wrist, while also using his left hand to lift up Black's upper-arm (elbow), consequently locking Black's right arm (Figure 4-37). The leverage action locks Black's elbow and exposes Black's armpit.

| Figure 4-35 | Figure 4-36 | Figure 4-37 |

11. Carrying Away (*Dai*): 帶

Dai is a technique which neutralizes by "yielding" and "leading." For example, when Black's wrist has been grabbed by the Gray's right hand, Black yields and lifts his right hand upward to neutralize (Figure 4-38). Immediately, he steps his right leg backward, while using both hands to lock Gray's arm and carry away Gray's aggressive grabbing power (Figure 4-39).

12. Leading (*Ling*): 領

Ling leads the opponent's power into emptiness, which often also offers you an opportunity to attack. For example, when Black bores his right palm into Gray's throat, Gray intercepts with his right arm, grabs Black's wrist, and leads Black's arm back and up, while simultaneously attacking Black's armpit area with his left elbow (Figure 4-40).

13. Reeling (*Chan*): 纏

There are many reeling techniques in Baguazhang practice. Reeling has the connotation of creeping, coiling, and wrapping. For example, when Black's shoulder is being grabbed by Gray's left hand, he uses his left hand to control Gray's right hand, while reeling his right hand around Gray's left arm to lock it down (Figure 4-41).

14. Adhering (*Zhan*): 黏

Zhan means using your hands to attach or stick to an object. For example, if Gray adheres to Black's forearm, ready for further action (Figure 4-42).

15. Grabbing (*Kou*): 扣

Kou means grabbing, and is a common technique that is used in almost all styles of martial arts. When *Kou* is done, you should have a feeling like an eagle grabbing his prey with his talons. One of the most common grabbing techniques is to grab the opponent's wrist to immobilize his arm movement (Figure 4-43).

Figure 4-38

Figure 4-39

Figure 4-40

Figure 4-41

Figure 4-42

Figure 4-43

16. Hooking (*Diao*): 刁

Diao is similar to *Kou*, but not exactly the same. When you hook onto your opponent's arm or wrist, you are not grabbing tightly with your fingers around his arm, but simply executing a clamping maneuver that restricts your opponent's arm movement. This limits your opponent's mobility and still leaves your hooking arm alive and agile for attacking.

Hooking can be practiced with two persons. To practice this technique, stand in Horse Stance facing each other and extend your right arm forward, touching each other's forearm (Figure 4-44). Then hook onto each other's wrist and pull back slightly (Figure 4-45). Then release the hook, pull your arms back and repeat with the other arm.

2. Twenty-Four Key Words on Hand Techniques[12]
二十四字訣

| Figure 4-44 | Figure 4-45 | Figure 4-46 |

There is another document which explains the Baguazhang hand techniques by using a set of twenty-four words. Some of these words are the same as those discussed in the 16 secret words. Even though the words are the same, the implied meaning and application are not completely the same. By this point, you should understand that even though the word itself may contain only a single meaning, the manifest actions associated with this same word can be many. The examples used as explanation of the actions serve only as a highlight for each word. If you can study both of these documents and ponder them carefully, you can gain a better understanding of these words.

1. Reeling (*Chan*) and Wrapping (*Juan*): 纏，卷

These two words are often used in conjunction with one another. The difference with *Chan* and *Juan* is that *Chan* means coiling forward or backward, like a snake coiling on a branch; *Juan* means wrapping an object in place. For example, if Black is attacking with his right hand, Gray will intercept with his right hand and then reel his right hand down along the Black's arm (Figure 4-46). Right after his reeling, he immediately uses both hands to wrap around Black's right wrist and control it (Figure 4-47)

2. Rolling (*Gun*) and Turning Over (*Fan*): 滾，翻

Gun has the meaning of rolling forward and *Fan* is simply turning over. These two key words describe the maneuvers against a hook or a grab. For example, when Black's right wrist is hooked by Gray's right hand (Figure 4-48), he neutralizes Gray's hook by rolling his right elbow towards Gray's body, while using his left hand to grab Gray's right hand (Figure 4-49). Finally, Black circles his elbow down towards Gray's elbow while turning Gray's elbow counterclockwise (Figure 4-50). This will lock Gray's arm, making him immobile.

3. Hooking (*Gau*): 鉤

This key word is the same as *Diao* discussed earlier. It describes the technique of hooking your hand onto your opponent's arm. Another example of hooking is when Gray use his right hand to hook the Black's right hand attack (Figure 4-51).

4. Draw Back (*Gua*): 挂

Gua is a movement in which you use your hand to direct the opponent's power backward

Figure 4-47

Figure 4-48

Figure 4-49

Figure 4-50

Figure 4-51

Figure 4-52

either from the inner or outer part of his arm. For example, when Black punches Gray with his right hand, Gray uses his right hand to intercept and direct black's punching power backward and to the side (Figure 4-52).

5. Opening (*Huo*):豁

Huo is a technique in which you coil and drill your hand to the inner side of your opponent's elbow, exposing his body for an attack. For example, Black first intercepts Gray's left punch with his right forearm (Figure 4-53). Black then yields back slightly, while coiling his right hand towards the inside of Gray's elbow, exposing Gray's body (Figure 4-54).

6. Picking Up (*Tiao*):挑

Tiao is both an intercepting technique against a punch, or a neutralizing technique against a grab. For example, when Gray punches his left hand to Black's face, Black simply uses his right

| Figure 4-53 | Figure 4-54 | Figure 4-55 |

arm to intercept the punch (Figure 4-55). If Gray had been grabbing Black's wrist, Black may also have neutralized the grab by picking up his forearm.

7. Pushing (*Tui*):推

Pushing is a very common techniques in every style. Pushing has been explained earlier, therefore we will not repeat it here.

8. Supporting (*Tuo*):托

This was also explained earlier. It is a technique using a single hand or both hands to hold up the opponent's arm to expose his vital areas for an attack (Figure 4-56). Alternatively, you may use both hands to lock upward the opponent's arm for a Qin Na control.

9. Carrying Away (*Dai*) and Leading (*Ling*): 帶，領

To carry away the opponent's arm (or body) and to lead it backward (or to the side) is called *Dai* and *Ling*. These two key words were described earlier. Another example of *Dai* and *Ling* is when Gray uses his right hand to grab Black's wrist, while using his left upper-arm to carry and lead Black backward and to the side (Figure 4-57).

10. Rotating (*Ban*): 搬

Rotating is usually used to against the joints. For example, when Gray uses both hands to rotate Black's arm and lock it in place (Figure 4-58).

11. Half Grabbing (*Kou*): 扣

The explanation of *Kou* here is slightly different from the Kou explained earlier. Here, Kou uses the fingers to "half" grab the opponent's wrist or arm. For example, Gray uses his right fingers to "half" grab Black's forearm with fingers pressing on the cavity Neiguan (Figures 4-59 and 4-60).

12. Intercepting (*Jie*) and Blocking (*Lan*): 截，攔

Even though these two words were explained earlier, their meanings here are slightly different from the earlier explanation. *Jie* is a technique describing an interception, and *Lan* is a technique

Figure 4-56

Figure 4-57

Figure 4-58

Figure 4-59

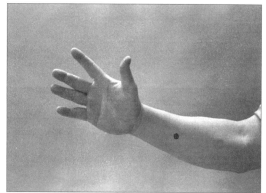

Figure 4-60

describing the stopping of your opponent from further attack or escape. For example, Black intercepts Gray's attack with his left hand, then locks Gray's arm by pressing his right palm on Gray's bicep (Figure 4-61).

13. Paring (*Xiao*) 削

Xiao is an action resembling the act of a saw cutting forward. For example, Gray intercepts Black's right punch and extends the edge of his right palm to pare Black's neck (Figure 4-62).

14. Chopping (*Pi*) 劈

Pi describes the action of chopping down. For example, Black uses his right hand to chop Gray's neck while grabbing his right wrist (Figure 4-63).

15. Smashing (*Za*) 砸

Za is the action of smashing with the back of your fist or forearm. For example, Gray uses his left forearm to smash downward to Black's elbow while grabbing his right wrist (Figure 4-64).

| Figure 4-61 | Figure 4-62 | Figure 4-63 |

16. Scooping (*Liao*): 撩

Liao is the action of scooping. It generally describes an upward scooping attack toward your opponent's groin. For example, Black uses his right hand to scoop forward and upward toward Gray's groin, while using the left hand to repel or grab Gray's right wrist (Figure 4-65).

17. Advancing (*Jin*): 進

Jin is the action of a forward attack, usually associated with stepping toward the space between the opponent's two legs. For example, Gray steps his left leg to the space between Black's two legs, while using both his hands to push Black's chin and chest (Figure 4-66).

18. Retreating (*Tui*): 退

Tui is the action of backward retreat. It is usually associated with a defensive maneuver. For example, to neutralize the advance force in the last example, Black simply steps his left leg backward while turning his body to retreat (Figure 4-67).

19. Dodging (*Shan*) and Evading (*Duo*): 閃，躲

Shan is the action of dodging an attack by stepping to the side instead of retreating backward. *Duo* is an action to avoid being attacked. The actions implied by these two key words allows the defender to avoid an attack while placing himself in a position to counterattack. In *Shan* and *Duo*, you are usually side stepping instead of retreating. This maintains the distance between you and your opponent, which allows you to simultaneously initiate an offensive maneuver as you avoid the attack. If you were to simply retreat backward to avoid the attack, you put yourself out of range for a counterattack. For example, when Gray initiates an attack, Black simply steps his right leg to the side, while using his right hand to block (Figure 4-68). In this case, Black has set up an opportunity to attack by kicking his right leg to Gray's right knee. The above explanations of the key words can only offer you a concept of the movements. Do not be restricted by the techniques in the examples. You should pick up the concepts of the techniques and apply them in a flexible and skillful manner.

Figure 4-64

Figure 4-65

Figure 4-66

Figure 4-67

Figure 4-68

References

1. Jiang Rang-Qiao, *The Expounding of Baguazhang Techniques,* p. 8, Reprinted by Five Continents Publishing Company, 1985. 八卦掌法闡宗，姜容樵著。

2. Li Tian-Ji, *The Feats of Wudang,* p. 633, Jilin Publishing Company, 1988. 武當絕技匯編，李天驥主編。

3. Jiang Rang-Qiao, *Supre* note 1, at 9. 八卦掌法闡宗，姜容樵著。

4. *Id.* at 10-12. 八卦掌法闡宗，姜容樵著。

5. Pei Xi-Rong and Li Chun-Sheng, *Wudang Wugong,* p. 108, Hunan Scientific Technical Publishing Company, 1984. 武當武功，裴錫榮、李春生主編。

6. Li Tian-Ji, *Supra* note 2, at 630. 武當絕技匯編，李天驥主編。

7. Kang Ge-Wu, *Zhongguo Wushu,* p. 478, Today's Chinese Publishing Company, 1990. 中國武術實用大全，康戈武編。

8. Pei Xi-Rong and Pei Wu-Jun, *Bagua Eight Shape Palm,* p. 8, Hunan Scientific Technical Publishing Company, 1990. 八卦八形掌，裴錫榮、裴武軍編著。

9. Kang Ge-Wu, *Supra* note 7, at 478. 中國武術實用大全，康戈武編。

10. 二四為肩，六八為足，左三右七，戴九履一，五居中央．

11. Pei Xi-Rong and Li Chun-Sheng, *Supra* note 5, at 110-15. 武當武功，裴錫榮、李春生主編．

12. Li Tian-Ji, *Supra* note 2, at 632-33. 武當絕技匯編，李天驥主編．

Chapter 5
Body Conditioning Training
強身訓練

5-1. Introduction

In Chinese martial arts society, it is said "Train fist (i.e., sequence or forms) and not *Gong*, when (you are) old, all in vain," (*Lian Quan Bu Lian Gong, Dao Lao Yi Chang Kong*)[1]. This means that if you practice only the forms and patterns of a style, without training the most basic Qigong and *Jin Gong*, then when you get old, all of your effort will have been in vain. In the last chapter, we introduced some basic Baguazhang Qigong training. From that training, you can build up strong Qi in your Lower *Dan Tian*, and also learn how lead this Qi to the extremities for *Jin* manifestation. Naturally, after you have mastered the Baguazhang and comprehended its essence, you can create some other Qigong trainings which can strengthen the inner side of Baguazhang training.

After you have strengthened your Qi, then you should learn how to apply it in your physical body, and manifest the techniques in a most effective manner. This is *Jin Gong*. *Jin Gong* is usually built upon the basic trainings. In this chapter, we will introduce these basic concepts and trainings. To become a proficient Baguazhang practitioner, you should pay close attention to the training in this chapter. Remember, this chapter will help you build a firm root and foundation for the entire practice of Baguazhang.

We also know that strength and endurance are often necessary for effective techniques. Because of this, almost all Chinese martial styles have exercises for developing them. In addition to conditioning the muscles, the exercises also train the practitioner in leading Qi to the muscles, so that they can be energized to their maximum, as well as teaching how to use the mind to control the the physical body in a more natural and coordinated way. In truth, body conditioning training is the foundation of successful martial technique. Without this foundation, you will not be able to last long in a fight, or execute your techniques powerfully.

Up until recently, a soldier's ability to survive on the battle field depended almost solely upon his conditioning, his techniques, and his power. Battles normally lasted for several hours without a break, so any soldier with poor techniques and low endurance were eliminated quickly.

| Figure 5-1 | Figure 5-2 | Figure 5-3 |

However, the most important by-product of body-conditioning training is not in the physical body, but rather in the mental body. To complete the training, you have to conquer yourself, which means that you have to gradually build up perseverance and a strong will. This is especially difficult today, since we do not face certain death on the battlefield if we fail. However, if you can convince yourself that it is worthwhile, the mental benefits are still valuable today.

In this chapter, we will summarize some of the body conditioning used in Baguazhang. If you are able to train yourself with these traditional methods, not only will you build up a healthy body, you will also make your Baguazhang techniques more powerful and effective.

In the next section, we will first introduce some of the training exercises for conditioning the body. Then we will review some of the Baguazhang training for striking a post. Finally, in the third section, we will introduce a two person matching set for body conditioning.

5-2. Body Conditioning

In this section, we will first introduce some of the traditional body conditioning exercises, both walking and stationary. Then we will discuss solo and two-person root development. Finally, we will discuss exercises involving striking a post or tree trunk.

I. Carrying Weight:

The most basic body conditioning is done by performing Baguazhang walking and the sequence while carrying weights. You may, for example, carry bricks in your hands while practicing. To avoid injury, build up your muscles gradually by initially carrying only one brick in each hand while walking the Bagua circle. Once you can do this for ten minutes, practice with two bricks in each hand (Figure 5-1). As your strength increases, you may gradually increase the number of bricks (Figure 5-2). To build up the stability of your shoulders, you may carry cement blocks on them as you walk the circle (Figure 5-3).

To build up the endurance and strength of your legs, you can stand for several minutes in a low Baguazhang posture while carrying bricks in your hands (Figure 5-4). A traditional method of helping you maintain the same height during this kind of training is to do it under a board or table. This can be done as you practice standing in a stance (Figure 5-5), or even while walking

Figure 5-4

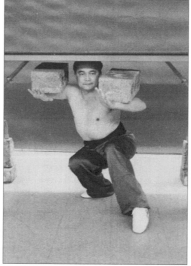

Figure 5-5

Figure 5-6

Figure 5-7

Figure 5-8

(Figure 5-6).

After you have trained this way for some time, and have built up your strength and conditioning, you can start training the Baguazhang sequences while holding bricks (Figures 5-7 and 5-8).

II. WALKING ON BRICKS OR POLES:

Many Chinese martial styles develop rooting by practicing standing or walking on bricks or poles. The bricks or poles are arranged in different patterns so that the fighting strategy of each style can be practiced.

You can do this kind of training by yourself or with a partner. The advantage of practicing with a partner is that it more closely resembles real fighting. When you practice by yourself, you have to imagine that you are fighting against someone.

When you train with a partner, first train without the bricks until both of you are moving at

Figure 5-9

Figure 5-10

Figure 5-11

Figure 5-12

Figure 5-13

the same speed and can coordinate your techniques (Figure 5-9). It is also advisable to practice walking on bricks by yourself before starting this with a partner (Figure 5-10). Then, once you are comfortable walking on bricks, and are also comfortable with a partner, training together will be enjoyable, safe, and profitable.

When you practice on bricks with a partner, first place the bricks flat on the ground (Figure 5-11). Once both of you can walk firmly with a good root, then stand the bricks on the long, narrow side (Figure 5-12). Finally, stand the bricks up on the small side (Figure 5-13). Once you are comfortable practicing barehand, you can then start to train with weapons (Figures 5-14 and 5-15).

Please remember that if you train unwisely, you can injure yourself. Be careful, and advance slowly. Remember that TRAINING SAFELY AND SLOWLY IS THE KEY TO PROGRESS.

III. Post Training:

Figure 5-14

Figure 5-15

Figure 5-16

We will now discuss training with a post or tree. The number of repetitions, force, and the duration of training should be built up gradually. The suggested repetitions and time in this section should only be used as a guide. You should start by hitting lightly, and gradually increase the force, number of hits, and the holding time.

We will first begin with some simple, basic routines. Once you are familiar with the training, you should practice free style and treat the post as your opponent. Your footwork and the position of your legs will vary according to how your imaginary opponent stands. To make the practice alive, you must adapt the techniques you have learned so that your strikes become powerful and natural.

Bagua Post Training

A. Examples of Training Routines
Example #1:

1. Beginning Position
Stand upright, about 3 feet from the post, with your palms in front of you at waist height, and the fingers pointing to each other (Figure 5-16).

2. Striking with the Inside of the Forearms
Step forward with your right leg next to the post. Swing your right arm diagonally up, hitting with the inside of your forearm (Figure 5-17). Pull your arm back and down, then swing it up clockwise, again hitting with the inside of the forearm (Figure 5-18). Repeat twelve times. While striking with your right arm, push against the post with your left hand.

When you finish hitting with your right arm, change your feet and repeat the training with your left arm.

3. Striking with the Palms
Switch your feet and pull your left arm back next to your chest, strike forward with your right palm, fingers up (Figure 5-19). Pull your right hand back and strike with your left hand (Figure 5-20). Pull your left hand back next to your chest, then strike with both palms together, your right hand on top, and the fingers pointing to the sides (Figure 5-21). Repeat this routine

Figure 5-17

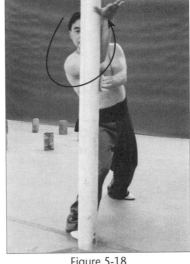

Figure 5-18

Figure 5-19

Figure 5-20

Figure 5-21

Figure 5-22

twelve times, then change your feet and repeat the same routine twelve times with the left palm striking first, then the right palm, and finally both palms, with the left palm on top.

Example #2:

1. **Beginning Position**

   Stand upright, about 3 feet from the post, hands in front of your waist, fingers pointing to each other (Figure 5-16).

2. **Striking with the Elbows**

   Step to the left side of the post with your right leg, and at the same time strike the post with your right elbow (Figure 5-22). Withdraw your right leg, and step in with your left leg and strike the post with your left elbow (Figure 5-23). Repeat twelve times.

   Next, draw your left leg back and step to the left of the post, then strike the post with the inside of your right forearm (Figure 5-24). Draw you left leg back and step to the right of the post with your right leg, and strike the post with your left forearm (Figure 5-25). Repeat

Figure 5-23

Figure 5-24

Figure 5-25

Figure 5-26

Figure 5-27

Figure 5-28

twelve times.

3. Striking with the Palms while Hooking with a Leg

Next, hook or strike the lower part of the post with your right leg while striking forward with both palms (Figure 5-26). Step back and hook or strike the post with your left leg while striking forward with both hands (Figure 5-27).

These are just examples of training routines. Use your imagination to create others. For example, you may use the back of a leg to hook while striking with a forearm (Figure 5-28). After you have practiced different routines for a while, are familiar with the footwork and understand how to generate power, you should start practicing free style. This is what brings the training to life.

B. An Example of Free Style Training

Figure 5-29

Figure 5-30

Figure 5-31

Figure 5-32

Figure 5-33

Figure 5-34

Vary your stances, footwork, and striking techniques to deal with how your imaginary opponent stands and moves. The following are only some of the possible variations.

You may start in the Horse Stance while striking with the outside of your forearm (Figure 5-29). Then step back with your left leg while striking with the outside of your left forearm (Figure 5-30). You may then step your right leg back and to your right while striking with the edge of your right palm (Figure 5-31).

Next, hook the lower section of the post with your right leg while striking high with your left hand and low with your right hand (Figure 5-32). Immediately follow with a strike with the outside of your right forearm (Figure 5-33).

Next, step your right leg to the other side of the post while striking with your right upper-arm (Figure 5-34). Continue by striking with the right side of your back (Figure 5-35), then with your upper back (Figure 5-36), and finally with your hip (Figure 5-37).

Draw back and face the post, and strike high with both hands (Figure 5-38). Put your head on

Figure 5-35

Figure 5-36

Figure 5-37

Figure 5-38

Figure 5-39

Figure 5-40

the post, raise your right leg, and push. This is used to toughen the forehead, which is often used to strike with (Figure 5-39). BE VERY CAREFUL NOT TO INJURE YOUR HEAD OR NECK IN THIS, OR ANY TRAINING.

5-3. Two-Person Body Conditioning Training

Two-person body conditioning is very popular in Chinese martial arts. Training with a partner, you find out what it really feels like to be struck and to strike another body. In addition, you can also train your "sense of enemy," and develop natural reactions to attacks.

In this section we will introduce a common example of this kind of training. Begin training with light power, and increase power gradually only as your bodies become tougher.

1. Blue and Gray stand facing each other about 3 feet apart (Figure 5-40). They raise their arms up to the sides as they inhale (Figure 5-41), finishing the inhale as their hands reach above their heads, and then press downward while exhaling until their hands reach stom-

Figure 5-41

Figure 5-42

Figure 5-43

Figure 5-44

Figure 5-45

Figure 5-46

ach level (Figure 5-42). As their arms descend, they squat down slightly.

2. Both take a step to their left and lower their bodies into Horse Stances, while swinging their right arms toward each other, contacting on the insides of the forearms (Figure 5-43). Both then swing their arms up clockwise, contacting again on the insides of their forearms (Figure 5-44). They then swing their right arms counterclockwise down, contacting on the outsides of the forearms (Figure 5-45).

3. Both shift all their weight to their left legs, and step forward with their right legs, touching only the ball of the foot to the ground. As they do this, they swing their right arms up, contacting on the outsides of the forearms (Figure 5-46).

4. They step forward with their left legs and pivot to the rear, with only the ball of the left foot touching the ground. As they do this, they swing their left arms up, contacting on the outside of the forearm (Figure 5-47). They swing their left arms down, contacting with the outsides of the forearms (Figure 5-48).

5. They step to their left with their left legs and swing their right arms down, contacting with

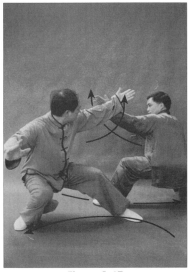

Figure 5-47

Figure 5-48

Figure 5-49

Figure 5-50

Figure 5-51

Figure 5-52

the insides of the forearms (Figure 5-49).

6. They stand up and bring both arms in front of their chests (Figure 5-50). They swing their right arms up and forward, and hook onto each other's wrist with their fingers, and pull down while stepping forward with their right legs (Figure 5-51).

7. They let go of each other, pull their right legs back and step to their right while lowering their left arms (Figure 5-52). They step forward with their left legs while swinging their left arms up, hooking onto each other's wrists, and pulling down (Figure 5-53).

8. They bring their left legs back into Horse Stances, while lifting their right elbows (Figure 5-54). They turn to their left and contact with the insides of their right forearms (Figure 5-55). They turn to their right and contact with the insides of their left forearms (Figure 5-56).

9. They lower their hands in front of their abdomens and stand up (Figure 5-57). They step

Figure 5-53

Figure 5-54

Figure 5-55

Figure 5-56

Figure 5-57

Figure 5-58

to each other's right with their right legs and extend their arms to the sides, hitting with their right shoulders (Figure 5-58).

10. They step back and lower their arms (Figure 5-59). They step to each other's left with their left legs and extend their arms to the sides, hitting with their left shoulders (Figure 5-60).

11. They step back and lower their arms (Figure 5-61). They step to each other's right with their right legs and extend their arms to front and rear, hitting with the right sides of their backs (Figure 5-62).

12. They step back and lower their arms (Figure 5-63). They step to each other's left with their left legs and extend their arms to front and rear, hitting with the left sides of their back (Figure 5-64).

13. They step back into the Horse Stance, leaving their arms extended to the sides (Figure 5-

Figure 5-59

Figure 5-60

Figure 5-61

Figure 5-62

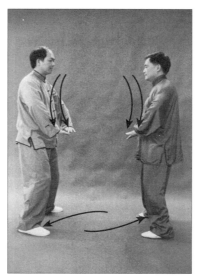

Figure 5-63

Figure 5-64

65). Gray stays in place. Blue kicks Gray's body with his right foot (Figure 5-66). Blue can hold Gray's arm as he kicks.

14. Blue sets his foot down. Gray turns slightly to his right (Figure 5-67). Gray kicks to Blue's body with his right foot (Figure 5-68).

15. Gray sets his foot down. Blue turns slightly to his left to get ready to kick (Figure 5-69). Blue kicks to the inside of Gray's right thigh with his right foot (Figure 5-70). Blue may hold Gray's arm as he kicks.

16. Blue sets his foot down (Figure 5-71). Blue kicks to the inside of Gray's left thigh with his left foot (Figure 5-72).

17. Blue sets his foot down. Gray kicks to the inside of Blue's right thigh with his right foot (Figure 5-73). Gray puts his foot down, then kicks to the inside of Blue's left thigh with his left foot (Figure 5-74).

18. Gray sets his foot down and punches to Blue's head with his right fist. Blue intercepts

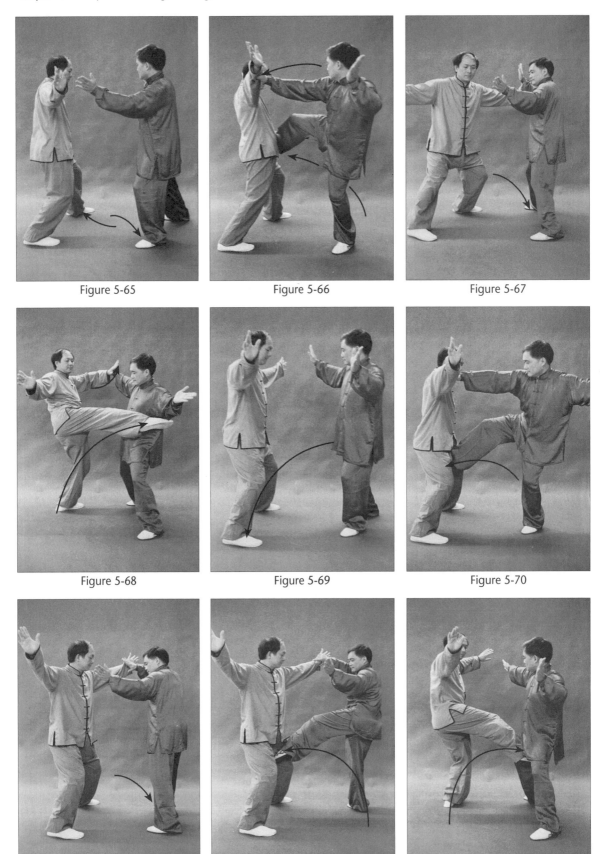

Figure 5-65

Figure 5-66

Figure 5-67

Figure 5-68

Figure 5-69

Figure 5-70

Figure 5-71

Figure 5-72

Figure 5-73

Figure 5-74

Figure 5-75

Figure 5-76

Figure 5-77

Figure 5-78

Figure 5-79

with his left arm, and steps forward with his left leg (Figure 5-75). Blue pulls Gray's arm to the left, and hits Gray's chest with his right forearm (Figure 5-76).

19. Blue steps back. Gray punches to Blue's head with his left fist. Blue intercepts with his right arm (Figure 5-77). Blue then steps forward with his right leg, pulls Gray's arm to his right, and hits Gray's chest with his left forearm (Figure 5-78).

20. Blue steps back and punches to Gray's head with his right fist. Gray intercepts with his left arm (Figure 5-79). Blue then steps forward with his left leg, pulls Gray's arm to his left, and hits Gray's chest with his right forearm (Figure 5-80).

21. Gray steps back. Blue punches to Gray's head with his left fist. Gray intercepts with his right arm (Figure 5-81). Gray then steps forward with his right leg, pulls Gray's arm to the right, and hits Gray's chest with his left forearm (Figure 5-82).

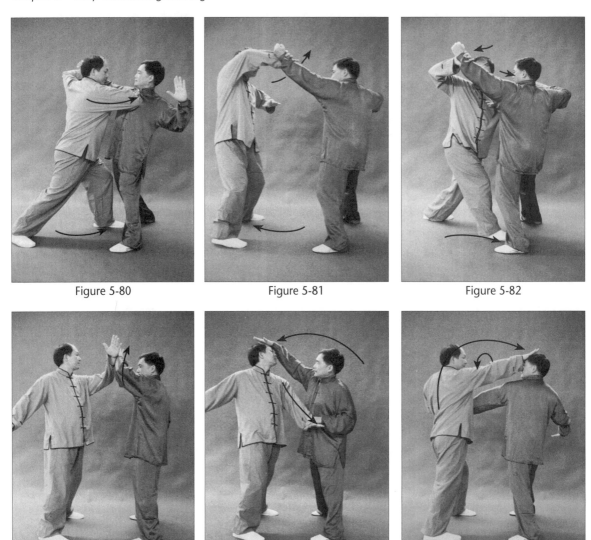

| Figure 5-80 | Figure 5-81 | Figure 5-82 |

| Figure 5-83 | Figure 5-84 | Figure 5-85 |

22. Gray steps back and chops to the left side of Blue's neck with his left hand. Blue intercepts with his left arm (Figure 5-83). Blue then pulls Gray's arm down while hitting Gray's forehead with his right palm (Figure 5-84).

23. Blue lowers his arms. Blue then chops to the left side of Gray's neck with his left hand. Gray intercepts with his left arm while using his right palm to strike Blue's forehead (Figure 5-85).

24. They bring their arms back to chest height (Figure 5-86). They steps forward to each other's right side while hitting with their right forearms (Figure 5-87). They turn their bodies away from each other, and lean back to hit with their upper backs (Figure 5-88). They then lean forward and hit with their buttocks (Figure 5-89).

Figure 5-86

Figure 5-87

Figure 5-88

Figure 5-89

After completing the last form, they both turn to face each other again and repeat the same routine from the low strikes with the inside of their right forearms (Figure 5-43). The routine can be repeated as many times as desired, but remember that consistently training a moderate number of repetitions is better than a large number of repetitions practiced only once in a while. To finish, simply stand up and face each other.

References

1. 練拳不練功，到老一場空．

Chapter 6
The Basic Eight Palms and Their Applications
基本八掌與應用

6-1. Introduction

Once you have completed some basic stances and drills, the first thing you should learn is the basic eight palms sequence or routine. Traditionally, each of the eight palms again includes eight fundamental movements; there are therefore a total of sixty-four strategic moving patterns in the sequence. After many years of development, even this basic eight palm set has deviated somewhat between styles. However, you should understand that no matter how it has been revised, the basic Baguazhang theory and principles remain the same. From practicing this eight palm sequence, a student will be led through the entrance of Baguazhang, and gradually internalize the core concepts of the art. Furthermore, from practicing this sequence, a student will also gain a basic knowledge of how Baguazhang fights. In this chapter, we would like to introduce these basic eight palms and also their martial applications. This basic sequence is also called "Dragon Shape Baguazhang," and was developed at Emei Mountain, China. This sequence is the root and the foundation of the Emei Baguazhang art. You should practice and master it until it is smooth and natural.

In order to help the Baguazhang practitioner understand the applications of each movement, in addition to the solo eight palm sequence, an eight palm fighting set was also created based on the techniques introduced in the sequence. We will introduce this fighting set in the third section of this chapter.

6-2. The Eight Palms

Baguazhang Eight Palms
(also called Dragon Shape Baguazhang)
基本八卦八掌（龍形八卦掌）

Commencing: (*Qi Shi*) 起勢

Stand upright, facing forward, with your feet together and your hands at your sides (Figure 6-1). Step your left foot to the side so that your feet are shoulder width apart (Figure 6-2). Raise

Figure 6-1

Figure 6-2

Figure 6-3

Figure 6-4

Figure 6-5

Figure 6-6

both hands up to the sides, with your eyes looking in the direction of your right palm (Figure 6-3). Continue raising your arms over your head then lower both palms down in front of you (Figure 6-4). Bend both knees slightly as you turn your body to your left and turn your head to the rear. As you turn, twist your right hand clockwise and cross both arms in front of your chest with the left arm on top. Your right palm should face up and your left palm faces to the side (Figure 6-5).

As you begin to turn your body to your right, raise your right arm to your chest and twist your left palm counterclockwise until the palm faces up (Figure 6-6). Continue to turn your body to your right while stepping forward with your right foot and circling your right arm clockwise in front of your body. Lower your left hand. Turn your body until your right hand, right elbow, and your face are all in the same plane as your left heel. You are now facing to your right rear corner (Figure 6-7).

Application:
Black attacks Gray's chest with his left fist and Gray intercepts with his left hand (Figure 6-

Figure 6-6A

Figure 6-7

Figure 6-7A

Figure 6-8

Figure 6-9

Figure 6-10

6A). Gray hooks Black's wrist with his left hand and locks Black's elbow with his right arm. Gray then steps forward and pushes his right hand toward Black's body to make him fall (Figure 6-7A).

I. SINGLE CHANGING PALM: (*DAN HUAN ZHANG*) 單換掌

1. Green Dragon Turns its Head: (*Qing Long Fan Shou*) 青龍返首

Movements:

Take a small step to your right with your right foot, the first of eight steps around a circle. Touch down to the floor lightly with the bottom of your foot. The foot should point slightly to the right. Your upper body posture does not change (Figure 6-8). Without changing your upper body posture, take a second step around the circle with your left foot. After your foot touches down, slide your foot forward a few more inches, like you are stepping in mud. Try to touch down with the entire foot, but beginners may start by touching down first with the ball of your foot (Figure 6-9). Continue walking until you take the seventh step (Figure 6-10). Pivot your right foot to the right, then bring your left foot up and set it down next to the right foot with the toes pointing inward so that both feet are somewhat pigeon-toed. Your knees should be bent. Ideally,

Figure 6-11

Figure 6-12

Figure 6-13

Figure 6-13A

Figure 6-14

Figure 6-14A

your body should now be facing in the same direction as when you started, but this is not crucial and you shouldn't try to force it (Figure 6-11).

Turn your body and swing your arms to the left (Figure 6-12). Swing them back as you raise your right leg (Figure 6-13). Set your right foot down with the toes pointing to the right, and turn your body 90 degrees to your right while continuing to wave your arms to the right (Figure 6-14).

2. Green Dragon Turns its Body: (*Qing Long Zhuan Shen*) 青龍轉身

Movements:

Step forward with your left foot and set the foot down next to your right foot. Both feet should point in slightly, and your knees should be bent. Turn your body to your right while crossing both hands in front of your body. Turn your head to the rear but do not move your feet. As you turn your body and head, twist your left hand counterclockwise. Cross both arms in front of your chest with your right arm on top. Your left palm should face up, and your right palm should face to the side (Figure 6-15).

Figure 6-15

Figure 6-15A

Figure 6-16

Figure 6-17

Figure 6-18

Figure 6-19

Twist your right hand counterclockwise, and circle your left arm from right to left while turning your body to the left and step forward with your left foot. Lower your right hand. Turn your body until your left hand, left elbow, and your face are in the same plane as your left heel (Figure 6-16).

Application:

Gray intercepts Black's left punch with his right arm (Figure 6-13A). Gray grasps Black's wrist, and steps forward with both his legs and use them to lock Black's left leg while extending his left hand to Black's chest (Figure 6-14A). Gray continues the previous movements and turns his body to his right to throw Black down (Figure 6-15A).

II. DOUBLE CHANGING PALM: (*SHUANG HUAN ZHANG*) 雙換掌

3. Green Dragon Turns its Head: (*Qing Long Fan Shou*) 青龍返首

Movements:

Without changing the posture of your upper body, walk eight steps around the circle, starting with your left foot. On your eighth step, step forward with your right foot, while pivoting on your

Figure 6-19A

Figure 6-20

Figure 6-20R

Figure 6-20A

left heel. Both feet should point in slightly, and your knees should be bent (Figure 6-17). Then wave your arm to your right in a circular motion (Figure 6-18).

4. Hawk Flies to Heaven: (*Yao Zi Zuan Tian*) 鷂子鑽天

Movements:

Reverse the direction of your arm movement, while turning your body to the left and lifting your left foot up and setting it down pointing to your left. As your arms swing back, your right hand descends to waist level (Figure 6-19). Step your right foot next to your left, both feet pointing in slightly, as your right hand rises to head level and your left hand drops down next to your knees (Figure 6-20) Figure 6-20R shows the front side of the posture. Push off with your left leg and begin spinning in a full circle on the ball of your right foot. When you push off, raise your left leg (Figure 6-21)

Figure 6-21   Figure 6-21A   Figure 6-22

Figure 6-22A   Figure 6-23   Figure 6-23A

5. White Snake Hiding in the Grass: (*Bai She Fu Cao*) 白蛇伏草

Movements:

Complete your spin and step down to your left with your left leg as you move your right hand next to your left shoulder (Figure 6-22). Lower your body as you push both hands to the sides and sink into Half Horse Stance (Figure 6-23)

Application:

Gray intercepts Black's left arm with his left arm (Figure 6-19A). Gray grabs Black's wrist and pulls it down while stepping forward with his right leg and boring to Black's neck with his right hand (Figure 6-20A). Gray then pushes off his left leg and spins counterclockwise to strike Black's back with his elbow (Figure 6-21A). Gray steps forward with his right leg, and hooks Black's neck with his right hand and places his left hand on Black's thigh (Figure 6-22A). Gray then lifts with his left hand and pulls with his right to make Black fall (Figure 6-23A).

Figure 6-24

Figure 6-25

Figure 6-26

Figure 6-27

Figure 6-28

Figure 6-28A

6. Green Dragon Turns its Body: (*Qing Long Zhuan Shen*)青龍轉身

Pivot on you left heel while turning your body to the left. Circle your left hand counterclockwise in front of your chest and move your right hand next to your waist (Figure 6-24). Step forward with your right foot and place it next to your left foot. The toes should point in slightly, and the knees should be bent. As you step your body turns, and your arms cross in front of your body with the left arm on top. The right palm should face up, and the left palm should face to the side (Figure 6-25).

Step forward with your right foot, toe in. As you step, turn your body to the right and swing your right arm in an arc to your right until it is pointing to your right rear corner. As you turn, rotate your left hand counterclockwise and lower it down (Figure 6-26).

Figure 6-29

Figure 6-29A

Figure 6-30

III. FOLLOWING THROUGH PALM: (*SHUN SHI ZHANG*)順勢掌

7. Turn and Spit Poison: (*Bei Shen Tu Xin*) 背身吐信

Movements:

Walk seven steps forward, starting with your right foot, without changing your upper body posture, until your right foot points slightly to the side (Figure 6-27). Pivot right on your right heel, and extend your left hand forward (Figure 6-28). Step forward with your left foot, circling your right hand over your head and bringing your left hand, palm up next to your body (Figure 6-29).

8. Dragon Tugs its Tail: (*Cang Long Suo Wei*)蒼龍縮尾

Movements:

Continuing from the previous movement, pivot on your left heel and begin to spin in a full circle to your left. Half way around, set your right foot down next to your left foot, and gradually bring your right hand down next to your left shoulder (Figure 6-30).

Application:

Gray intercepts Black's right arm with his left (Figure 6-28A). Gray coils his left hand forward and places it behind Black's lower back, steps forward with his right leg and strikes or pushes Black's chest or face with his right forearm or palm (Figure 6-29A). Gray turns his body to his left while pushing forward with his right hand and pulling with his left (Figure 6-30A). Gray continues turning his body to make Black fall (Figure 6-30B). The movements should be smooth and continuous.

9. White Snake Hiding in the Grass: (*Bai She Fu Cao*)白蛇伏草

Complete your spin and step forward with your left foot while sinking down and pushing both hands to the sides (Figure 6-31).

Figure 6-30A

Figure 6-30B

Figure 6-31

Figure 6-32

Figure 6-33

Figure 6-34

10. Green Dragon Turns its Body: (*Qing Long Zhuan Shen*) 青龍轉身

Movements:

Figures 6-32 to 6-34 repeat Figures 6-24 to 6-26.

IV. REVERSING BODY PALM: (*BEI SHEN ZHANG*) 背身掌

11. Green Dragon Turns its Head: (*Qing Long Fan Shou*) 青龍返首

Movements:

Figures 6-35 and 6-36 repeat Figures 6-11 and 6-12.

12. Swallow Enters the Forest: (*Yan Zi Ru Lin*) 燕子入林

Movements:

Swing your arms back to your right and step to your right with your right foot. Extend your right arm forward and lower your left hand to your waist (Figure 6-37). Take another step forward with your left leg while bringing your right hand back and boring forward with your left

Figure 6-35

Figure 6-36

Figure 6-37

Figure 6-37A

Figure 6-38

Figure 6-38A

palm, over your right. Your right hand should be palm down below your left elbow, and your left palm should face up (Figure 6-38).

13. Green Dragon Stretches its Claws: (*Qing Long Tan Zhua*) 青龍探爪

Movements:

Shift your weight to your right leg while raising your right arm and circling your left hand clockwise downward (Figure 6-39). Turn your body to your right while lowering your right elbow and straightening your left arm (Figure 6-40). Raise your right knee with the toe pointing down and extend your right arm forward. Both palms should face up (Figure 6-41).

Application:

Gray intercepts Black's right arm with his right hand (Figure 6-37A). Gray grabs Black's wrist and pulls down, while stepping forward with his left leg and boring into Black's neck with his left hand (Figure 6-38A). If Black avoids Gray's left hand, Gray brings his hand around Black's arm and strikes Black's groin (Figure 6-39A).

Figure 6-39

Figure 6-39A

Figure 6-40

Figure 6-40A

Figure 6-40B

Figure 6-41

14. Monkey Bends Tree Branches: (*Yuan Hou Ban Zhi*) 猿猴搬枝

Movements:

Step down and back with your right foot (Figure 6-42). Bring your hands next to each other (Figure 6-43). Then sink down as you strike forward with the side of your right hand and pull your left hand back. The right palm faces down, the left palm is facing up next to your waist (Figure 6-44).

Application:

Gray intercepts Black's left arm with his right hand and brings his left hand up next to his right (Figure 6-40A). Gray grabs Black's hand with both hands and twists clockwise down (Figure 6-40B). Gray lifts Black's arm as he hits him with his right knee (Figure 6-41A). Gray sets his right foot down and steps his left foot forward while pulling Black's arm back and striking him with his upper arm (Figure 6-44A).

Figure 6-41A

Figure 6-42

Figure 6-43

Figure 6-44

Figure 6-44A

Figure 6-45

15. Green Dragon Turns its Body: (*Qing Long Zhuan Shen*) 青龍轉身

Movements:

Stand up slightly and circle your right hand clockwise in front of your body (Figure 6-45). Figures 6-46 and 6-47 repeat Figures 6-15 and 6-16.

V. TURNING BODY PALM: (*ZHUAN SHEN ZHANG*) 轉身掌

16. Green Dragon Turns Its Head: (*Qing Long Fan Shou*) 青龍返首

Movements:

Walk three steps in a circular path, moving your left foot first. You should end with left foot forward (Figure 6-48). Turn your left heel to your left and lift your right foot up without bending your knee. At the same time, bring your hands up and cross in front of your body (Figure 6-49). Set your right foot down with the toes pointing to the right. Next, simultaneously turn your body to your right, extend your right arm, and lower your left hand (Figure 6-50). Without changing

Figure 6-46

Figure 6-47

Figure 6-48

Figure 6-48A

Figure 6-49

Figure 6-49A

your upper body posture, walk seven steps around in a circle, starting with your left foot. On your seventh step, step forward with your left leg next to your right (Figure 6-51). Swing both arms to your right (Figure 6-52).

Application:

Gray intercepts Black's left arm and hooks the wrist (Figure 6-48A). Gray holds Black's arm against his chest with his left hand, and moves his right arm under Black's arm and places his hand on Black's chest, and at the same time starts to hook Black's left foot with his right foot (Figure 6-49A). Gray pushes down with his right hand and lifts with his right leg and drops Black to the floor (Figure 6-50A).

17. Swallow Enters the Forest: (*Yan Zi Ru Lin*) 燕子入林

Movements:

Figures 6-53 and 6-54 are similar to Figures 6-37 and 6-38, the only difference being that the left palm bores out from under your right palm, instead of over your right palm.

Figure 6-50

Figure 6-50A

Figure 6-51

Figure 6-52

Figure 6-53

Figure 6-53A

18. Running Horse Turns its Head: (*Zou Ma Hui Tou*) 走馬回頭

Movements:

Bend your left arm in and rotate the palm outward as you turn 180 degrees to your right and step forward with your left foot (Figure 6-55). Look back as you lower your right arm and move your left hand next to your right shoulder (Figure 6-56). Lower your body and move your right hand next to your right foot (Figure 6-57).

Application:

Gray intercepts Black's right arm with his right hand (Figure 6-53A). Gray steps forward with his left leg and stabs to Black's armpit with his left hand while pulling Black's right arm with his right hand (Figure 6-54A). Gray pulls Black's arm down and locks the elbow from underneath with his left shoulder and grasps Black's wrist with both hands. Gray then steps to his right with his left foot, while pulling Black's arm down (Figure 6-55A). Continuing this motion, Gray drops Black to the floor (Figure 6-55B).

Figure 6-54   Figure 6-54A   Figure 6-55

Figure 6-55A   Figure 6-55B   Figure 6-56

19. White Ape Offers Fruit: (*Bai Yuan Xian Guo*) 白猿獻果

Movements:

Stand up slightly as you circle your right arm in front of you (Figure 6-58). Figure 6-59 repeats Figure 6-15. Extend both arms to your right with the wrists touching each other (Figure 6-60). Make a quarter turn with your body to your left and step forward around the circle with your left foot (Figure 6-61). Take a second step forward in a circular path with your right foot (Figure 6-62). Extend your right arm over your head, and your left arm in front of you, as you take another step forward (Figure 6-63). Continue stepping in a circular path five more steps. On your fifth step, bring your left foot next to your right foot. Both feet turn in with knees bent (Figure 6-64).

Application:

Black punches to Gray's chest with his right fist. Gray intercepts with his left forearm (Figure 6-59A). Gray then coils his left arm over Black's right and extends it to Black's back, while stepping forward with his left leg (Figure 6-60A). Gray continues by striking his right palm on Black's jaw and locking Black's head with his left hand (Figure 6-61A).

Figure 6-57

Figure 6-58

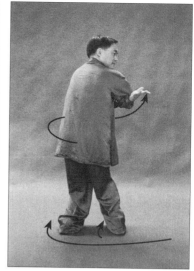

Figure 6-59

Figure 6-59A

Figure 6-60

Figure 6-60A

Figure 6-61

Figure 6-61A

Figure 6-62

Figure 6-63

Figure 6-64

Figure 6-65

Figure 6-66

Figure 6-66A

Figure 6-67

VI. Double Embracing Palm: (*Shuan Bao Zhang*) 雙抱掌

20. Lion Rolls the Ball: (*Shi Zi Gun Qiu*) 獅子滾球

Movements:

Circle your arms clockwise down (Figure 6-65). Step to your left with your left leg as you continue the movement of your arms (Figure 6-66). Step forward with your right leg and continue the circular motion of your arms over your head (Figure 6-67). Cross your left leg behind your right leg and continue to circle your arms (Figure 6-68). Pivot on your feet while sinking down and pushing both hands to the sides with the palms facing in (Figure 6-69).

Application:

Gray intercepts Black's right punch with his left arm (Figure 6-66A). Gray then grabs Black's wrist and pulls it over his head while stepping forward with his right leg and extending his right arm between Black's legs (Figure 6-67A). Gray continues by standing up and lifting with his right

Figure 6-67A

Figure 6-68

Figure 6-68A

Figure 6-69

Figure 6-69A

Figure 6-70

arm and pulling with his left to throw Black to his left (Figure 6-68A). Gray then steps back with his left leg and drops Black to the ground (Figure 6-69A).

21. White Ape Offers Fruit: (*Bai Yuan Xian Guo*) 白猿獻果

Movements:

Figures 6-70 and 6-71 repeat Figures 6-32 and 6-33. Extend both arms to your left with the wrists touching each other (Figure 6-71). Make a quarter turn to your right and step forward around the circle with your right foot (Figure 6-72). Take a second step around the circle by stepping forward with your right foot (Figure 6-73). Extend your left arm over your head and your right arm in front of you, as you take another circular step forward (Figure 6-74). Continue stepping in a circular path five more steps. At the fifth step, bring your left foot next to your right foot. Both feet turn in and the knees bend (Figure 6-75).

Figure 6-71

Figure 6-72

Figure 6-73

Figure 6-74

Figure 6-75

Figure 6-76

22. Green Dragon Rolls the Ball: (*Qing Long Gun Qiu*) 青龍滾球

Movements:

Circle your arms clockwise down and to your left (Figure 6-76). Continue circling your arms while stepping to your right with your right leg (Figure 6-77). Step forward with your left foot and continue the circular motion of your arms over your head (Figure 6-78). Cross your right leg behind your left foot and continue to circle your arms (Figure 6-79). Pivot on your feet while sinking down and pushing both hands to your sides, palms facing in (Figure 6-80).

23. Green Dragon Turns Its Body: (*Qing Long Zhuan Shen*) 青龍轉身

Figures 6-81 and 6-82 repeat Figures 6-45 to 6-47.

VII. GRINDING BODY PALM: (*MO SHEN ZHANG*) 磨身掌
24. Green Dragon Turns Its Head (*Qing Long Fan Shou*) 青龍返首

Figures 6-83 to 6-86 repeats Figures 6-48 to 6-51.

Figure 6-77

Figure 6-78

Figure 6-79

Figure 6-80

Figure 6-81

Figure 6-82

Figure 6-83

Figure 6-84

Figure 6-85

Figure 6-86

Figure 6-87

Figure 6-87A

Figure 6-88

Figure 6-88A

Figure 6-89

25. Wave the Fan in Front of the Gate: (*Ying Men Hui Shan*) 迎門揮扇

Movements:

Take a small step backward with your left foot and put all your weight on it while waving your right hand counterclockwise in front of your body (Figure 6-87). Continue the motion of your right arm to your left and lift your right foot off the floor (Figure 6-88). Take a step forward with your right leg and circle your right hand outward (Figure 6-89).

Application:

Gray intercepts Black's left punch and grabs it with both hands, while moving his right foot behind Gray's left foot (Figure 6-87A). Gray then hooks Black's foot up and drops Black to the floor (Figure 6-88A).

26. Phoenix Spreads Its Wings: (*Feng Huang Zhan Chi*) 鳳凰展翅

Raise your hands to chest height, with the heels of the palms touching each other, right palm

Figure 6-89A

Figure 6-90

Figure 6-90A

Figure 6-91

Figure 6-91A

Figure 6-92

on top, and raise your right foot (Figure 6-90). Step down with your right leg and turn your body a quarter turn to your right. Without loosing the palm connection, twist the palms so that the left palm is on top as you squat down (Figure 6-91). Step forward with your left leg. As you stand up, twist the palms so that the right palm is on top again (Figure 6-92). Extend both arms diagonally out to your sides with the palms up as you kick out with your right leg (Figure 6-93).

Application-A:

Gray intercepts Black's right arm with his right arm (Figure 6-89A). Gray grabs Black's wrist with his right hand, twists clockwise and pulls, while pressing his left forearm on Black's elbow and kicking to Black's shin with his right leg (Figure 6-90A). Gray continues his attack, stepping down on Black's leg and pressing and pulling with his arms (Figure 6-91A).

Application-B:

Gray intercepts Black's right arm with his left hand (Figure 6-92A). Gray then grabs Black's hand with both of his hands and twists counterclockwise to his left (Figure 6-92B). Gray continues to twist Black's arm as he pulls it past him and kicks Black's groin with his right leg (Figure 6-93A).

Figure 6-92A

Figure 6-92B

Figure 6-93

Figure 6-93A

Figure 6-94

Figure 6-95

27. Swallow Touches the Water: (*Yan Zi Chao Shui*)燕子抄水

Pull your right leg in toward your body, and draw your hands back in front of your right armpit. Both palms are facing outward, the right hand is on the outside (Figure 6-94). Step down and back with your right leg, and begin to lower your right hand (Figure 6-95). Squat down on your left leg and move your right hand down your right leg to your foot, with the palm facing to your rear (Figure 6-96).

Application:

Gray intercepts Black's left arm with his right arm and grabs Black's wrist with his left hand (Figure 6-95A). Gray then pulls Black's arm down, while coiling his right arm over Black's arm and extending it between Black's legs and placing his hand behind Black's right knee, as he lowers his body (Figure 6-96A). Gray shifts his weight to his front leg, thereby lifting Black's left leg with his right leg, and lifts Black's right knee with his right hand and drops Black to the floor (Figure 6-96B).

Figure 6-95A

Figure 6-96

Figure 6-96A

Figure 6-96B

Figure 6-97

Figure 6-97A

28. Reverse Windmill: (*Dao Ye Feng Che*) 倒拽風車

Movements:

Stand up slightly while circling your right hand clockwise in front of your body (Figure 6-97). Turn to your rear by pivoting on your right heel, and bring your left foot next to your right foot, while extending your left hand, palm upward and pulling your right hand back to the top of your left elbow (Figure 6-98). Step back with your right leg and turn to your right while striking out with your right elbow and bringing your left hand next to your body. Your palms face each other, right palm on top (Figure 6-99 and 6-99R). Sit back on your left leg and draw your right foot back part way with only the toes touching the floor, while striking out with your right fist (Figure 6-100).

Application:

Gray intercepts Black's right hand with his right hand (Figure 6-97A). Gray grasps Black's hand. He pivots on his right foot and turns his body to his right. As he does this, he rotates Black's arm clockwise and pulls it down and to his right, and pushes against Gray's elbow with

Figure 6-97B

Figure 6-98

Figure 6-98A

Figure 6-99

Figure 6-99R

Figure 6-100

his left forearm to keep it from bending (Figure 6-97B). Gray then brings his left leg up next to his right, and extends his left arm to lock Black's arm (Figure 6-98A).

VIII. ROTATING BODY PALM: (FAN SHEN ZHANG) 翻身掌

29. Green Dragon Flies into the Sky: (Qing Long Fei Sheng) 青龍飛升

Put your right heel down, pivot your right foot 90 degrees to the right, and bring your left foot next to your right foot while crossing both arms in front of you and turning your body to your right (Figure 6-101). Lower both elbows and bring your hands together with the wrist touching each other (Figure 6-102). Turn your body to face forward, while extending both arms out to your sides and stepping forward with your left leg (Figure 6-103) Take seven steps around the circle, starting with your left foot, until your left foot is forward (Figure 6-104).

Figure 6-101

Figure 6-102

Figure 6-103

Figure 6-104

Figure 6-104A

Figure 6-105

30. Fling your Sleeves in the Wind: (*Ying Feng Hui Xiou*) 迎風揮袖

Circle both arms clockwise, your right arm down and then up, and your left arm up and then down, while kicking with your right foot (Figure 6-105). Step down with your right leg and lower your body (Figure 6-106).

Application:

Gray intercepts Black's right arm with his left hand (Figure 6-104A). Gray then grabs Black's wrist with his right hand and pulls it down and to Black's left, at the same time stepping his right foot to the outside of Black's left foot and placing his left hand on Black's left knee (Figure 6-105A). Gray continues pulling Black's arm and pressing in and down on his knee, dropping Black to the floor (Figure 6-106A).

Figure 6-105A

Figure 6-106

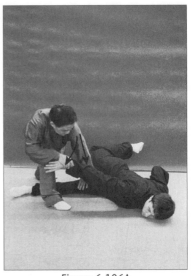

Figure 6-106A

Figure 6-107

Figure 6-107A

Figure 6-108

31. Monkey Kicks the Branches: (*Yuan Hou Deng Zhi*) 猿猴蹬枝

Step forward with your left foot (Figure 6-107). Kick with your right heel while chopping your right hand horizontally forward, palm up, and bringing your left hand next to your right forearm (Figure 6-108).

Application:

Black simultaneously kicks with his right foot and punches with his right fist. Gray steps forward with his right foot, toes pointing out, and intercepts Black's punch with his right hand and the kick with his left hand (Figure 6-107A). Black pulls his leg back and steps back, and withdraws his arm. Gray follows this motion by stepping forward, maintaining contact with Black's right arm with his left hand, and chops the side of Black's head with his right hand. This keeps both of Black's hands occupied, and opens Black's body (Figure 6-108A). Gray then kicks Black's chest with his right foot while keeping control of Black's arms (Figure 6-108B).

Figure 6-108A

Figure 6-108B

Figure 6-109

Figure 6-110

Figure 6-111

Figure 6-112

32. Swallow Touches the Water: (*Yan Zi Chao Shui*) 燕子抄水

Figures 6-109 to 6-111 repeat Figures 6-94 to 6-96.

33. Swallow Enters the Forest: (*Yan Zi Ru Lin*) 燕子入林

Stand up slightly while circling your right hand clockwise in front of your body (Figure 6-112). Step forward with your left leg while boring forward with your left hand over your right palm. Finish with your right palm over your left elbow (Figure 6-113).

34. Large Python Rolls Over: (*Da Mang Fan Shen*) 大蟒翻身

Begin turning 180 degrees to your right while circling both arms clockwise; with your right arm rising over your head, and your left arm folding in towards your body, palm down (Figure 6-114). Finish the turn and raise your right leg. Your arms continue circling until your right hand is extended in front of you and your left hand is extended behind you (Figure 6-115).

Figure 6-112A

Figure 6-113

Figure 6-113A

Figure 6-114

Figure 6-114A

Figure 6-115

Application:

Gray intercepts Black's right arm with both of his hands, and grabs Black's hand with his right hand (Figure 6-112A). Gray turns to his right, stepping forward with his left foot and placing it next to his right foot with the toes pointing sharply in, and immediately stepping his right foot to his rear. As he does this he also uses both hands to extend Black's arm outward and up, as well as rotate it clockwise (Figure 6-113A). Gray continues turning, rotating Black's arm clockwise, pushing the elbow upward with his left hand, and pulling the hand down with his right hand. He then kicks Black's ribs with his knee (Figure 6-114A). Gray continues to twist Black's arm and drops Black to the floor (Figure 6-115A).

35. Monkey Bends Tree Branches: (*Yuan Hou Ban Zhi*) 猿猴搬枝

Step down and back with your right leg while bringing your left hand forward and pulling your right hand in (Figure 6-116). Turn to your right and strike forward with the side of your right hand and pull your left hand back to your waist while sinking down (Figure 6-117).

Figure 6-115A

Figure 6-116

Figure 6-117

Figure 6-118

Figure 6-119

Figure 6-120

36. Fierce Tiger Catches its Prey: (*Meng Hu Pu Shi*) 猛虎扑食

Figures 6-118 and 6-119 repeat Figures 6-97 and 6-98. Step to your rear with your right leg, and touch the ball of your foot to the floor. Pivot 180 degrees to your right on your left heel as you extend both arms to your sides (Figure 6-120). Step forward with your right foot and bring both hands in front of your face, palms out (Figure 6-121). Bring your left leg next to your right while pushing forward with both palms (Figure 6-122).

Application:

Black punches with his left fist. Gray intercepts with his right forearm and locks Black's arm by pressing his left hand on Black's inner forearm (Figure 6-120A). Gray steps his right leg between Black's legs, and begins to press forward with both forearms (Figure 6-121A). Gray continues the movement by bringing his left leg up and locking Black's leg between his knees, while pushing forward with both forearms on Black's chest (Figure 6-122A).

Figure 6-120A

Figure 6-121

Figure 6-121A

Figure 6-122

Figure 6-122A

Figure 6-123

37. Green Dragon Turns its Body: (*Qing Long Zhuan Shen*) 青龍轉身

While turning your body to the right, cross your arms in front of you. The right arm is on top with the palm facing to the side, and left palm faces up (Figure 6-123). Turn to the left and step forward with your left leg, while circling your left arm from right to left, and lowering your right hand (Figure 6-124). Without changing your upper body posture, walk 3, 5, or 7 steps in a circle until your left foot is pointing in the same direction as you started (Figure 6-125).

38. Closing (*Shou Shi*):收式

Bring your right foot up a shoulder's width away from your left foot, and extend both arms to your sides (Figure 6-126). Raise both hands over your head, turn both palms down, and lower them to your waist level (Figure 6-127). Bring your left foot next to your right foot and lower both hands down to your sides (Figure 6-128).

Figure 6-124

Figure 6-125

Figure 6-126

Figure 6-127

Figure 6-128

Figure 6-129

6-3. The Eight Palms Fighting Set

Baguazhang Matching Set

八掌對練

1st Interchange:

1. Black and Gray stand facing each other about 6 feet apart (Figure 6-129). Black and Gray both begin raising their arms over their heads (Figure 6-130). They lower their arms, cross them in front of their chests, and turn their bodies to their left corners without turning their heads (Figure 6-131).

2. Both take a step to their left with their right legs, and extend their right arms out toward each other (Figure 6-132). They both take 8 steps around a circle. On the last step, each brings his left foot next to his right foot to face the other person (Figures 6-133 and 6-134).

Figure 6-130

Figure 6-131

Figure 6-132

Figure 6-133

Figure 6-134

Figure 6-135

3. Gray steps forward with his right leg and punches to Black's head with his right fist (Figure 6-135). Black responds by sidestepping to his right and circling both arms to his left to intercept the punch (Figure 6-136). Black coils his left hand from the inside of Gray's arm to the outside, and begins swinging both arms toward Gray's neck (Figure 6-137). Black continues his counterattack toward Gray's neck. Gray dodges Black's arms by sinking his weight to his left leg while bowing down to his left (Figure 6-138).

4. After avoiding Black's arms, Gray swings his body back and begins chopping to Black's knee with his right elbow and palm (Figure 6-139). Gray continues his swing while pivoting on his right heel a half circle. Black avoids Gray's attack by moving his right leg next to his left while pivoting on his left foot. At the same time Black chops to Gray's neck with his right hand (Figure 6-140). Gray and Black stand up, cross their arms in front of their chests, and look back (Figure 6-141).

5. They take a step to their left with their right legs while extending their right arms toward each other (Figure 6-142). They take 8 steps around a circle, and on the last step each one brings his left foot next to his right foot so that he faces the other person (Figure 6-143).

Figure 6-136

Figure 6-137

Figure 6-138

Figure 6-139

Figure 6-140

Figure 6-141

Figure 6-142

Figure 6-143

Figure 6-144

Figure 6-145

Figure 6-146

Figure 6-147

Figure 6-148

Figure 6-149

Figure 6-150

2nd Interchange:

6. Gray steps forward with his right leg and punches with his right fist to Black's head (Figure 6-144). Black responds by circling his right arm clockwise to intercept Gray's arm (Figure 6-145). Black continues by circling his left hand to Gray's elbow and beginning to step forward with his right leg (Figure 6-146). Black pushes Gray's arm down with his left hand and strikes to his neck with his right hand as he steps forward with his right leg (Figure 6-147).

7. Gray intercepts Black's right arm by raising his left arm (Figure 6-148). Black bends his right elbow and strikes to Gray's chest. Gray intercepts the attack by lowering his left arm and turning to his right (Figure 6-149). Black pivots to his rear on his right heel and attacks Gray's kidney with his left elbow. Gray senses Black's intent and steps forward with his left leg to avoid the attack (Figure 6-150).

8. Gray strikes to Black's head with his right elbow while bringing his left hand next to his exposed rib area. Black intercepts Gray's elbow with his right hand (Figure 6-151). Black

Figure 6-151

Figure 6-152

Figure 6-153

Figure 6-154

Figure 6-155

Figure 6-156

pivots on his left foot and steps in front of Gray with his right foot. As he does this, he grabs Gray's left wrist with his left hand, and slides his right hand down to Gray's right wrist, which he grabs and pulls (Figure 6-152).

9. Gray lowers his body, bends his right elbow and raises his right hand to break Black's grab and prevent his arms from being locked (Figure 6-153). Gray steps to his rear with his left foot and attacks Black's neck with his elbow. Black avoids the attack by lowering his body (Figure 6-154).

10. Black stands up immediately after avoiding Gray's arm, and circles his arms clockwise toward Gray's body while kicking/lifting Gray's left leg with his right leg, attempting to throw Gray to the ground. Gray simply lifts up his left leg to avoid the attack (Figures 6-155). Both step into a standard Green Dragon Turns Its Body Posture and follow by a standard Green Dragon Turns Its Head posture, until they are facing each other (Figure 6-156).

Figure 6-157

Figure 6-158

Figure 6-159

Figure 6-160

Figure 6-161

Figure 6-162

3rd Interchange:

11. Gray steps forward with his right leg and punches to Black's head with his right fist (Figure 6-157). Black intercepts the attack with his left hand and coils it over Gray's arm and down towards his body, while taking a step forward with his left leg (Figure 6-158). Black steps in with his right leg, slips his left hand around to the small of Gray's back, and moves his right hand toward Gray to press his chest. Gray intercepts Black's right hand by raising his left arm and stepping back with his right leg (Figure 6-159).

12. Gray continues his retreat by stepping back with his left leg. Black continues his attack by crossing his left leg behind his right leg and starting to turn to his rear. Black then completes his turn and takes a step forward with his left leg while lowering his body and attacking Gray's groin with his left palm. Gray then lowers his body and moves his right arm forward to intercept Black's attack (Figure 6-160).

13. Gray draws his right foot back next to his left, and crosses his arms in front of his chest. Black brings his left foot back next to his right, and crosses his arms in front of his chest

Figure 6-163

Figure 6-164

Figure 6-165

Figure 6-166

Figure 6-167

Figure 6-168

(Figure 6-161). Gray steps to his right with his right leg, and extends his right arm toward Black. Black steps to his left with his left leg, and extends his left arm toward Gray (Figure 6-162). Black and Gray both execute a Green Dragon Turns Its Head posture until they are facing each other (Figure 6-163).

4th Interchange:

14. Gray steps forward with his right leg and punches to Black's head with his right fist (Figure 6-164). Black circles his right arm clockwise to intercept Gray's arm, while crossing his right leg over his left (Figure 6-165). Black continues the motion by stepping forward with his left leg as he pulls Gray's right arm down and strikes to Gray's neck with his left hand. Gray intercepts Black's left arm by raising his left hand (Figure 6-166).

15. Gray grabs Black's hand and twists it counterclockwise as he turns his body to his left (Figure 6-167). Gray continues the motion by stepping his left leg behind his right and turning to face Black. As he does this, he keeps his grip on Black's hand and pushes Black's elbow with his right forearm (Figure 6-168).

Figure 6-169

Figure 6-170

Figure 6-171

Figure 6-172

Figure 6-173

Figure 6-174

16. Black neutralizes the lock on his elbow by lowering his left elbow, and he grabs Black's right hand with his right hand and twists it clockwise (Figure 6-169). Black continues to twist Gray's hand, and circles his left arm up over Gray's arm (Figure 6-170). Black continues the motion and raises his right knee while bending Black's wrist and pushing into him (Figure 6-171).

17. Gray circles his right arm clockwise and turns to his right to neutralize the lock on it, then attacks with his shoulder to Black's chest (Figure 6-172). Black yields to Gray's attack by turning to his rear on his left heel bringing his right leg back next to his left leg, and crossing his arms in front of his chest. Gray continues his previous motion, brings his right foot next to his left, and crosses his arms in front of his chest (Figure 6-173).

18. They each take a step to their right with their right legs, and extend their right arms toward each other (Figure 6-174). Black and Gray both execute Green Dragon Turns Its Head posture and finish facing each other (Figure 6-175).

Figure 6-175

Figure 6-176

Figure 6-177

Figure 6-178

Figure 6-179

Figure 6-180

5th Interchange:

19. Gray steps forward with his right leg and punches to Black's head with his right fist (Figure 6-176). Black intercepts Gray's arm by circling his right hand up and taking a small step to his left with his right leg (Figure 6-177). Black continues the motion and steps forward with his left leg to Gray's right side while striking with his left hand to Gray's throat. Gray raises his left hand to intercept Black's attack (Figure 6-178).

20. Black continues his attack by twisting his body to his right while grabbing and raising Gray's arm over his shoulder with both his hands (Figure 6-179). Black then steps back with his right leg and pulls Gray's arm down (Figure 6-180).

21. Gray steps forward with his left leg to neutralize Black's attack (Figure 6-181), then shifts his weight to his right and attacks Black's chest with his elbow (Figure 6-182).

22. Before Gray can complete his attack, Black shifts his weight to his right foot and swings his left arm towards the back of Gray's neck. Gray bows at his waist to avoid Black's arm

Figure 6-181

Figure 6-182

Figure 6-183

Figure 6-184

Figure 6-185

Figure 6-186

(Figure 6-183). Gray brings his right foot back next to his left foot and crosses his arms in front of his chest. Black brings his left foot back next to his right foot and crosses his arms in front of his chest (Figure 6-184).

6th Interchange:

23. Gray brings his hands together facing Black and takes a step to his left with his left foot. Black and Gray execute a White Ape Offers Fruit posture, ending with their arms extended towards each other (Figure 6-185). Gray steps forward with his right leg and punches to Black's head with his right fist (Figure 6-186). Black circles his left arm clockwise to intercept the attack, and coils it toward Gray's body (Figure 6-187). Black continues the motion and steps forward with his right leg while coiling his left hand behind Gray and beginning to strike to Gray's head with his right hand. Gray raises his left hand to intercept Black's right arm (Figure 6-188).

Figure 6-187

Figure 6-188

Figure 6-189

Figure 6-190

Figure 6-191

Figure 6-192

24. Gray swings his right arm toward Black's neck. Black avoids the attack by bowing at his waist (Figure 6-189). They each bring their right legs back next to their left legs and cross their arms in front of their chests (Figure 6-190). They turn to face each other, Gray extends his right arm toward Black, and Black extends his left arm toward Gray (Figure 6-191).

25. Gray steps forward with his left leg and punches to Black's head with his right fist. Black lowers his left arm and prepares to intercept the attack (Figure 6-192). Black circles his left arm up and intercepts Gray's arm (Figure 6-193). Gray kicks to Black's kidney with his right foot. Black intercepts the kick by lowering his left hand (Figure 6-194). Black continues the motion and steps forward with his right leg, and attacks Gray's groin with his right hand (Figure 6-195).

26. Gray lowers his right arm to intercept Black's right hand (Figure 6-196). Gray continues the motion and crosses his left leg behind his right, twists his body to his rear, and attacks Black's head with his left elbow. Black intercepts the elbow with his left hand (Figure 6-197).

Figure 6-193

Figure 6-194

Figure 6-195

Figure 6-196

Figure 6-197

Figure 6-198

27. Black then grabs both of Gray's elbows and rotates them counterclockwise (Figure 6-198). Gray pivots on his right heel and left toe (Figure 6-199). Gray continues the motion by stepping to his right with his right leg and then his left, and then brings his right next to his left while crossing his arms in front of his chest. Black simply brings his right foot next to his left foot and crosses his arms in front of his chest (Figure 6-200).

28. They both step forward with their right legs and extend their right arms toward each other (Figure 6-201). They both take seven more steps around a circle and finish facing each other (Figure 6-202).

7th Interchange:

29. Gray steps forward with his left leg and punches to Black's head with his left fist (Figure 6-203). Black takes a small step back with his left leg and circles his right arm up counterclockwise to intercept the attack (Figure 6-204). Black continues the motion by hooking Gray's left foot with his right leg. Gray simply lifts his leg up to avoid the attack (Figure 6-205).

Figure 6-199

Figure 6-200

Figure 6-201

Figure 6-202

Figure 6-203

Figure 6-204

30. Gray steps his left leg to the outside of Black's right leg while grabbing and pulling Black's right arm down with his left hand, and chopping to Black's neck with his right hand (Figure 6-206). Black circles his right arm clockwise to neutralize Gray's grab, and continue the motion upward to intercept Gray's right arm (Figure 6-207).

31. Black continues by grabbing Gray's hand with both of his hands, while lifting his right foot up to kick Gray's front knee (Figure 6-208). Gray avoids the kick by twisting his body to his left on his left heel and the ball of his right foot. Black continues his attack by locking Gray's right elbow (Figure 6-209).

32. Gray steps in front of his left foot with his right foot, pivots to his left to neutralize Black's lock on his elbow, and strikes upward to Black's chin with his left palm (Figure 6-210). Black lifts his left arm to intercept Gray's attack (Figure 6-211).

33. Black then kicks to Gray's mid-section with his right leg (Figure 6-212). Gray simply brings his right arm forward to intercept Black's kick, and attempts to lift Black's leg (Figure 6-213). Black steps down to prevent Gray from lifting his leg (Figure 6-214).

Figure 6-205

Figure 6-206

Figure 6-207

Figure 6-208

Figure 6-209

Figure 6-210

Figure 6-211

Figure 6-212

Figure 6-213

Figure 6-214

Figure 6-215

Figure 6-216

Figure 6-217

Figure 6-218

Figure 6-219

34. Gray swings his right arm up and chops to Black's neck while stepping forward with his right foot (Figure 6-215). Black intercepts Gray's right wrist with his left hand, grabs it and lifts it up, while extending his right arm up from under Gray's armpit (Figure 6-216). Black steps forward with his left leg and turns to his rear, slides his right hand up Gray's arm to grab his hand, and lowers his left hand to armpit height (Figure 6-217). Black continues the motion and hook kicks to Gray's front leg with his left leg. Gray avoids the kick by lifting his leg (Figure 6-218).

35. Black steps down and pulls Gray's arm down, while locking his left forearm under Gray's elbow. Gray follows Black by stepping down (Figure 6-219). Black steps to his right with his right leg. Gray takes a step forward with his left leg to release the lock on his elbow (Figure 6-220). Black steps to his right with his left leg, and Gray follows by stepping forward with his right leg (Figure 6-221).

36. Black twists his body to his right to try to break Gray's elbow. Gray bends his elbow and rotates his arm counterclockwise to neutralize Black's lock (Figure 6-222). Black lets go of

Figure 6-220

Figure 6-221

Figure 6-222

Figure 6-223

Figure 6-224

Figure 6-225

Gray's arm, and twists to his right to strike Gray's ribs with his left elbow (Figure 6-223). Gray turns to his left and stops Black's elbow with both hands (Figure 6-224) Black steps forward with his left leg, and turns back to attack Gray's head with his right fist. Gray shifts his weight back and steps his left leg to the outside of Black's right leg, and blocks Black's attack upward with both hands (Figure 6-225).

37. Black brings his right foot next to his left and crosses both arms in front of his chest. Gray bring his left foot next to his right and crosses both arms in front of his chest (Figure 6-226). Black and Gray both execute Green Dragon Flies Into The Sky posture, until their left arms are extended to their sides (Figure 6-227).

Figure 6-226

Figure 6-227

Figure 6-228

Figure 6-229

Figure 6-230

Figure 6-231

8th Interchange:

38. Gray steps forward with his left leg and punches to Black's head with his right fist. Black intercepts Gray's attack by circling his left arm clockwise (Figure 6-228). Black continues the motion by extending his right arm up from under his left arm and grabbing Gray's right wrist, and stepping forward with his right leg and pressing in on Gray's front knee with his left hand (Figure 6-229).

39. Gray steps back to avoid Black's attack to his knee. Black follows by stepping forward and clearing Gray's right arm to the left with his left hand, and begins to pull his right hand back to set up for a chop to Gray's neck (Figure 6-230). Black continues by chopping to Gray's neck with his right hand. Gray intercepts the attack by lifting his left arm (Figure 6-231). Black follows with another attack - a right heel kick to Gray's mid-section. Gray circles his left hand clockwise down to intercept the kick (Figure 6-232).

Figure 6-232

Figure 6-233

Figure 6-234

Figure 6-235

Figure 6-236

Figure 6-237

40. Gray then shifts his weight forward and chops to Black's neck with his right hand (Figure 6-233). Black circles his right arm up, palm in, to intercept the attack (Figure 6-234).

41. Black continues by sliding his left forearm under Gray's arm, grabbing Gray's wrist and twisting clockwise (Figure 6-235). Black continues to twist Gray's wrist as he steps forward with his left leg (Figure 6-236). Black steps forward with his left leg, turns back toward Gray, and raises his right knee (Figure 6-237). Black steps back with his right leg, and swings his left arm down to press Gray's front knee to the side with his hand, while locking Gray's elbow with his upper arm (Figure 6-238).

Figure 6-238

Figure 6-239

Figure 6-240

Figure 6-241

Figure 6-242

Figure 6-243

42. Gray pushes on Black's shoulder with his left palm to neutralize Black's lock on his right arm (Figure 6-239). Gray then brings his right foot back next to his left foot, and crosses his arms in front of his chest. Black brings his left foot back next to his right foot, and crosses his arms in front of his chest (Figure 6-240). Black and Gray both execute a Green Dragon Turns Its Head posture then extend both arms up (Figure 6-241).

43. Black and Gray lower their hands to their abdomens and straighten their legs (Figure 6-242). They both bring their left legs in next to their right legs, and lower their hands to their sides (Figure 6-243).

Black and Gray should now change sides and repeat the whole sequence from the beginning.

Chapter 7
Swimming Body Baguazhang
and Its Applications
游身八卦掌與應用

7-1. Introduction

After you have mastered the basic eight palms, then you can begin the higher levels of Emei Baguazhang training. In this chapter, we will introduce one of the best known sequences or practicing routines - Swimming Body Baguazhang. Naturally, since Baguazhang is a complex style with hundreds years of history, there are many intermediate and advanced level sequences which could lead a Baguazhang practitioner into proficiency. However, it is impossible to introduce all of them here. This chapter will serve best as a reference to assist your understanding. In order to help you understand the essence and the purpose of each movement, the martial applications are also included.

7-2 Swimming Body Baguazhang

Swimming Body Baguazhang is also known as Swimming Body Dragon Walking Baguazhang. Its movements are light and swift. It is externally soft and internally hard. Movements are continuously changing directions, with no interruption. Its movements are like a swimming dragon or serpent, swift and agile, and it is therefor aptly named Swimming Body Baguazhang. It is divided into Eight Left Palms and Eight Right Palms. That is, every palm may be practiced as in the figures or as mirror images of the figures. Each of the eight palms may be practiced as one sequence. Combining the eight palms becomes Swimming Body Baguazhang. Within each of the eight palms are eight primary palm techniques. The Swimming Body Baguazhang, therefore, contains eight times eight palms, or sixty-four palms.

Figure 7-1

Figure 7-1A

Figure 7-2

Figure 7-2A

Swimming Body Baguazhang
(also called Swimming Body Dragon Walking Baguazhang)
游身八卦掌（游身龍行八卦掌）

I. Swimming Body Palm (*You Shen Zhang*) 游身掌

1.1 Golden Needle Points Up to Heaven - Stabbing Upward Palm
金針指天上戳掌

Stand upright, facing forward with your hands by your sides (Figure 7-1). Extend and circle your left arm up and then down to the height of your solar plexus, palm facing down. Before your left arm completes its motion, extend your right arm in a circle up to chest height and extend it forward, palm facing to your left (Figure 7-2).

Figure 7-3

Figure 7-3A

Figure 7-3B

Figure 7-4

Application:

Gray intercepts White's right punch with his left forearm (Figure 7-1A). Gray then locks White's arm in place with his left arm while stepping forward and boring forward to White's throat with his right palm (Figure 7-2A).

1.2 Two Immortals Preach the Dao - Rear Plucking Palm

二仙傳道後採掌

Step forward, slightly to your left, with your left foot in a Bow stance; while extending both arms forward. Then shift your weight back and pull both palms back (Figure 7-3).

Application:

Gray intercepts White's double punch by extending both palms between Whites arms (Figure 7-3A). Gray then grabs a hold of White's wrists, separates them to the sides and pulls back and down. At the same time, Gray strikes to White's chest with his forehead (Figure 7-3B).

Figure 7-4A

Figure 7-5

Figure 7-5A

Figure 7-6

1.3 Turn the Head with Frictional Body - Press Leaning Palm

磨身回頭擠靠掌

Swing your left arm horizontally in front of you while stepping to your right corner with your right leg (Figure 7-4). Shift your weight forward while boring your right palm forward from under your left palm (Figure 7-5). Then shift your weight back to your left leg while pulling both palms back (Figure 7-6).

Application-A:

Gray simultaneously intercepts White's punch with his left palm and strikes to White's ribs with his right fingers (7-4A). Gray continues from the previous movement, hops forward and locks his right leg behind White's knee. He then drops Gray to the floor by striking to Grays chest with his right palm (Figure 7-5A).

Figure 7-6A

Figure 7-6B

Figure 7-6C

Figure 7-7

Figure 7-8

Figure 7-9

Application-B:

Gray intercepts White's right punch with his left hand (Figure 7-6A). White punches with his left hand, and Gray intercepts with his right hand (Figure 7-6B). Gray continues his movement by stepping behind White's right leg with his right leg and hooking his right arm around White's neck (Figure 7-6C).

1.4 Green Dragon Turns Its Body - Extending Sideways Palm

青龍轉身側探掌

Bring your right foot back next to your left foot while crossing both arms in front of your chest with your left arm on top. Both feet should point in slightly, both knees are bent, and both wrists bend so that the fingers of the left hand point up and the fingers of the right hand point down (Figure 7-7). Make a quarter turn with your body and step to your right with your right leg, while extending your right palm and lowering your left palm (Figure 7-8).

Figure 7-9A

Figure 7-10

Figure 7-10A

Figure 7-11

Figure 7-11A

Figure 7-12

1.5 Phoenix Takes Off Its Wings - Bump the Body Sideways

鳳凰拔翅側身撞

Walk in a circle for another seven steps until your left leg is forward. At this point you should be back at the starting location (Figure 7-9). Take another step forward with your right leg while striking out with your left elbow and pulling your right hand back (Figure 7-10).

Application:

Gray intercepts White's right arm with his right arm (Figure 7-9A). Gray turns his body to his right while pulling White's arm up and pressing his left arm forward and down (Figure 7-10A).

1.6 Immortal Twists His Waist - Locking the Throat Palm

仙子扭腰鎖喉掌

Draw your left elbow back to your waist while circling your right elbow up and then down in front of your face (Figure 7-11). Step your left leg to your right front, while continuing to lower

| Figure 7-12A | Figure 7-13 | Figure 7-14 |

your right elbow until your right hand is in front of your solar plexus, and at the same time bore your left hand forward, palm up (Figure 7-12).

Application:

White punches with his left fist to Gray's face. Gray turns his body to his left while intercepting and grabbing Black's wrist with his left hand, and at the same time presses White's elbow with his right forearm (Figure 7-11A). Gray then steps his right leg to his right and pushes White's arm down with his right arm while boring White in the throat with his left hand (Figure 7-12A).

1.7 Phoenix Spreads Its Wings - Walk with Swimming Body

鳳凰展翅游身走

Step forward with the right leg, toe out, and open the arms outward a little (Figure 7-13). Take another 4 steps in a circle until your right leg is forward (Figure 7-14).

1.8 Reverse to Tumble Heaven's Gate - Separating Knee Palm

倒跌天門別膝掌

Bring both hands in toward your chest as you begin to take another circular step with your left leg (Figure 7-15). Step down with your left leg while lowering your left hand and raising your right hand (Figure 7-16). Take another circular step forward with your right leg, toe out (Figure 7-17).

Application:

Gray intercepts White's left arm with his right arm and steps to his right with his left leg. At the same time, Gray pulls White's arm down and presses down on White's knee with his left hand until White drops to the floor (Figures 7-16A and 7-16B).

II. REVOLVING BODY PALM 旋身掌

2.1 Immortal Plucks Flower - Circling Feet with Boring Palm

仙子採花繞腳穿掌

Walk in a circle another 4 steps until your right leg is forward (Figure 7-18). Lower your right

Figure 7-15

Figure 7-16

Figure 7-16A

Figure 7-16B

Figure 7-17

Figure 7-18

hand to your waist and bring your left hand in front of your chest while turning your right toes slightly to your left (Figure 7-19). Bore your right hand upward with the palm up, and pull your left hand back to your waist while taking a circular step to your left with your left leg (Figure 7-20). Without moving your arms, take a circular step to your left with your right leg (Figure 7-21).

Application:

Gray intercepts White's right arm with his left forearm (Figure 7-20A). Gray then hooks White's arm down to his left, while hooking to White's front foot with his right foot and bores to White's neck with his right palm (Figure 7-21A).

2.2 Feudal Lord Turns His Body - Cover the Hand with Boring Palm

霸王轉身蓋手穿掌

Without moving your arms, step your left leg to your left (Figure 7-22). Step forward with your right leg while raising your right hand and turning your left palm up (Figure 7-23). Lower your

Figure 7-19

Figure 7-20

Figure 7-20A

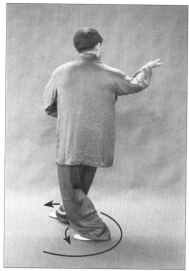

Figure 7-21

Figure 7-21A

Figure 7-22

Figure 7-23

Figure 7-24

Figure 7-25

Figure 7-26

Figure 7-26R

Figure 7-27

right palm while raising your left palm diagonally up to your left (Figure 7-24). Step your right foot to your right rear corner, while turning your body to that direction (Figure 7-25).

2.3 Cover the Heavens and Blanket the Earth - Sweep Sideways with a Thousand Pounds

鋪天蓋地橫掃千軍（鈞）

Raise your right hand until it is in front of your face, and shift your weight onto your right heel. Push off with your left foot and pivot on your right heel to make a full 360 degree turn (Figures 7-26, 7-26R, and 7-27).

2.4 Plant the Flower Under the Leaves - Pluck Pulling Palm

葉底插花採拔掌

Take a small step forward with your right foot, toe out, while lowering your left hand and turning the palm outward, and raising your right hand (Figure 7-28).

Figure 7-28

Figure 7-28A

Figure 7-28B

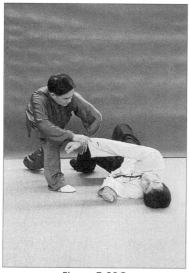

Figure 7-28C

Figure 7-29

Figure 7-30

Application:

Gray intercepts White's right punch with his right hand (Figure 7-28A). Gray then pulls Black's arm to his right while stepping to his right with his right leg and pressing White's knee with his left hand until he falls (Figures 7-28B and 7-28C).

2.5 Phoenix Flies to Heaven - Side Chopping Palm
鳳凰飛天橫切掌

Take another step forward with your left leg while raising your left hand in front of you (Figure 7-29). Snap kick with your right leg while chopping forward with your right palm and pulling your left hand palm down back toward your right shoulder (Figure 7-30).

2.6 Swallow Touches Water - Intercept Kicking Sealing Palm
燕子抄水截腿掌

As your right leg returns from the kick, step it to your rear while circling your right hand in front of your body (Figure 7-31). The right hand continues down to your right thigh, palm fac-

Figure 7-31

Figure 7-32

Figure 7-33

Figure 7-34

Figure 7-34A

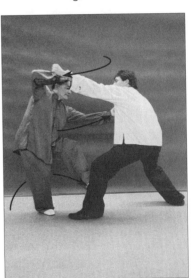

Figure 7-34B

ing to your rear (Figure 7-32). Continue until your palm is next to your right foot, palm facing the foot (Figure 7-33). Shift your weight to your right leg and stand up while blocking up with your right arm, striking with your left palm, and kicking with the sole of your left foot (Figure 7-34).

Application:

Gray intercepts White's left punch with his right hand (Figure 7-34A). He leads the attack upward while striking White's chest with his left palm and kicking White's knee with his left foot (Figure 7-34B).

2.7 Scoop, Carry, Press, and Chop - Turning Body Palm

撩挑壓劈翻身掌

Withdraw your left foot and step to the rear (Figure 7-35). Step to your left rear with your right foot while lowering your right palm and raising your left palm (Figure 7-36). Rotate your body and arms to your left as you spin on your right heel (Figure 7-37). Pivot on your left heel

Figure 7-35

Figure 7-36

Figure 7-37

Figure 7-37A

Figure 7-38

Figure 7-38A

to turn your foot to your left while chopping down with your right palm. Your left palm should simultaneously pull back to your right shoulder (Figure 7-38).

Application:

Gray intercepts and grabs White's right hand with his left hand (Figure 7-37A). Gray then turns his body to his left while pulling White's arm down and chopping to his biceps with his right palm (Figure 7-38A).

2.8 Chase and Advance Forward - Pluck Pressing Palm
追身進步採按掌

Step forward with your right leg and let the left leg follow up with a small step, and at the same time block upward with your right arm and strike forward with your left palm (Figure 7-39).

Figure 7-39

Figure 7-39A

Figure 7-39B

Figure 7-40

Figure 7-41

Figure 7-41A

Application:

White punches with his left fist (Figure 7-39A). Gray blocks up with his right forearm while stepping forward with his right foot and striking White's chest with his left palm (Figure 7-39B).

III. Swaying Body Palm 搖身掌

3.1 Swimming Body Spits Poison - Turning Body to Block Palm
游身吐信回身架掌

Step forward with your left leg while lowering your right hand and turning your left palm face down (Figure 7-40). Circle your right leg to your left, while boring forward with your right hand, palm up. At the same time, pull your left hand back to your right armpit (Figure 7-41). Circle to your left with your left foot to your rear, while lowering your palms to your chest (Figure 7-42).

Figure 7-41B

Figure 7-41C

Figure 7-42

Figure 7-43

Figure 7-43R

Figure 7-43A

Application:

As White punches with his left fist, Gray intercepts White's wrist with his right hand (Figure 7-41A). Gray steps his left foot forward and presses down on White's arm with his left hand (Figure 7-41B). Gray then steps forward with his right leg, pulls White's arm down with his left hand, and bores White's neck with his right hand (Figure 7-41C).

3.2. Step Forward to Control Foot - Right Splitting Palm

上步管腳右挒掌

Step sharply forward with your right leg and pull both hands to your right (Figures 7-43 and 7-43R).

Application:

White punches with his left hand (Figure 7-43A). Gray swings both arms clockwise to intercept the punch while sweeping White's ankle with his right foot (Figure 7-43B).

Figure 7-43B   Figure 7-44   Figure 7-44A

Figure 7-44B   Figure 7-45   Figure 7-46

3.3 Advance Step to Hook Foot - Left Cutting Palm
進步勾腳左切掌

Step sharply forward with your left leg and pull both hands to your left (Figure 7-44).

Application:

Gray intercepts White's punch with his left hand (Figure 7-44A). Gray then grabs and pulls White's wrist down and back. At the same time, Gray chops to White's neck with his right palm and hooks his left foot behind White's front leg (Figure 7-44B).

3.4 Step with Circle to Dodge the Body - Lower Poking Palm
繞步閃身下插掌

Shift your weight forward and pick up your right foot, and at the same time circle your right hand behind you and your left hand in front of you (Figure 7-45). Turn your body to your right and set your right foot down with the toes pointing to your right (Figure 7-46). Step your left foot next to your right foot, toe in (Figure 7-47).

Figure 7-47

Figure 7-48

Figure 7-49

Figure 7-50

Figure 7-51

Figure 7-51A

3.5 Drag Legs in Mud - Downward Rollback Palm

淌泥拖腳下攦掌

Take a small step with your right foot and turn your body to the rear (Figure 7-48). Bring your left foot next to your right foot while beginning to cross your arms in front of your chest (Figure 7-49). Complete the motion by crossing both arms in front of you, right arm on top (Figure 7-50).

3.6 Rotating Arm to Attach Hand - Diagonal Chopping Palm

掄臂搭手斜劈掌

Step to your left with your left leg while extending your left arm in front of you and your right arm behind you (Figure 7-51). Swing your right arm up and then down to chop down diagonally in front of you, while simultaneously pulling your left palm next to your right shoulder (Figure 7-52).

Figure 7-52

Figure 7-52A

Figure 7-53

Figure 7-53A

Figure 7-54

Figure 7-54A

3.7 Knee Strikes with Turning Body - Spread Wings Palm

膝撞回身展翅掌

Continue lowering your right hand while kicking with your knee (Figure 7-53). Step down to your left with your right leg (Figure 7-54). Stand up on your right leg and raise your left knee while opening your arms outward to strike with the back of the hands (Figure 7-55).

Application-1:

Gray intercepts White's left punch with his left hand (Figure 7-51A). He then grabs White's wrist and pulls it down while chopping to White's neck with his right hand (Figure 7-52A), and continues the movement by kicking with his knee to White's ribs (Figure 7-53A).

Application-2:

Continuing from the previous application, if White avoids Gray's knee, Gray then steps down while continuing to hold on to White's wrist with his left hand (Figure 7-54A). Gray continues the movement by standing up on his right leg while striking White's neck with the back of his right

Figure 7-55

Figure 7-55A

Figure 7-56

Figure 7-57

Figure 7-57A

Figure 7-58

hand. As the hand goes out, he also raises his left leg to balance the force of the right arm (Figure 7-55A).

3.8 Lion Swaying Its Body - Continuous Palm

獅子搖身連環掌

Move your left leg behind you and set it down to the right of your right leg. Pivot on your right heel and left toe to turn your body 180 degrees while swinging your right arm forward and your left arm palm down to your waist (Figure 7-56). Swing your left arm forward and bring your right hand palm up back to your waist (Figure 7-57). Strike forward with your right hand, palm down, while shifting your weight forward, and simultaneously bring your left hand next to your right shoulder (Figure 7-58).

Application:

Gray yields back while intercepting White's left punch with his left hand (Figure 7-57A). Gray then pulls White's arm down to his side with his left hand, while chopping to White's neck with his right hand (Figure 7-58A).

Figure 7-58A

Figure 7-59

Figure 7-60

Figure 7-61

Figure 7-62

Figure 7-62A

IV. DODGING BODY PALM 閃身掌

4.1 Circle Step to Dodge - Poking Downward Palm
繞步閃身下插掌

You now turn a full 360 degrees, as shown in Figures 59 through 62. Begin by lifting up your left foot and starting to turn your body, and at the same time bring both hands to your waist while twisting your arms so that the palms face the rear (Figure 7-59). Step down with your left leg, toes pointing to your left (Figure 7-60).

4.2 Lean Against the Mountain to Press and Stroke - Horizontal Circling Palm
依山擠靠平掄掌

Step forward with your right leg and pivot on both feet to turn to the rear (Figure 7-61). Shift your weight to your left leg and swing your right arm forward to complete the turn (Figure 7-62).

Figure 7-63

Figure 7-63R

Figure 7-63A

Figure 7-64

Figure 7-64A

Figure 7-65

4.3 Sparrow Hawk Pulls the Bow - Twisting Intercepting Palm
鷂子拉弓扭截掌

Pull your right hand next to your waist and strike forward with the side of your left hand while sinking your weight to the rear leg (Figures 7-63 and 7-63R).

Application:

Gray intercepts White's right arm with his left while chopping to White's neck with his right hand (Figure 7-62A). Gray continues his attack by grabbing and pulling White's elbow with his right hand while striking forward with his left hand (Figure 7-63A).

4.4 Secretly Seize to Break the Leg - Intercepting Elbow Palm
偷擒挫腿截肘掌

Move your right hand forward from under your left elbow while shifting your weight forward. Both palms are facing forward (Figure 7-64). Pull your right hand back with the palm to the side, and push your left hand forward while kicking with the sole of your right foot (Figures 7-65 and 7-65R).

Figure 7-65R

Figure 7-65A

Figure 7-66

Figure 7-67

Figure 7-68

Figure 7-69

Application:

White jabs in with his right fist, and Gray raises his right arm to intercept (Figure 7-64A). Gray then grabs and pulls White's arm back while pressing his left hand on White's elbow and kicking White's front knee with his right foot (Figure 7-65A).

4.5 Pluck the Helmet Behind Brain - Sealing Hand Shaking Palm

腦後摘盔擒手抖掌

Step down and back with your right leg while turning your right palm face up and placing your left hand on your right wrist (Figure 7-66). Swing your body to the rear and shift your weight to your right leg (Figure 7-67). Shift your weight back to your left leg and start to turn your body as you circle your arms counterclockwise over your head (Figure 7-68). As your arms descend and your body turns to your left, your right hand comes down to about throat level while your left hand moves down to your left side (Figure 7-69). Raise your left hand and

Figure 7-69A

Figure 7-70

Figure 7-70R

Figure 7-70A

Figure 7-71

Figure 7-72

lower your right hand slightly as your weight sinks into your rear foot and your body turns slightly to the right (Figures 7-70 and 7-70R).

Application:

Gray intercepts White's right punch with his right arm (Figure 7-69A). Gray then grabs and pulls White's arm back while pressing White's elbow with his left forearm and sinking his weight down (Figure 7-70A).

4.6 Tumble Heaven's Gate - Swimming Step to Separate Knee Palm
跌天門游步別膝掌

Shift your weight to your left leg and begin to raise your right hand from under your left elbow (Figure 7-71). Continue raising your right hand and lower your left hand while starting to walk in a circle (Figure 7-72). Take three more steps in a small circle until your right leg is forward (Figure 7-73).

Figure 7-73

Figure 7-73A

Figure 7-74

Figure 7-74A

Figure 7-75

Figure 7-75A

4.7 Heavenly King Attaches with Hand - Forward Pressing Palm

天王搭手前按掌

Pull your right hand back to your waist and bring your left hand up, and then down and forward, while lifting your right knee (Figure 7-74). Step down with your right foot and strike with your right palm, and simultaneously pull your left hand back to your abdomen (Figure 7-75).

Application:

White punches with his right fist and Gray intercepts with his right hand (Figure 7-73A). Gray grabs White's wrist and pulls the arm down as he kicks the elbow with his right knee and strikes White's shoulder with his left palm (Figure 7-74A). Gray then steps down on the outside of White's front foot and strikes White's face with his right palm (Figure 7-75A).

Figure 7-76

Figure 7-76A

Figure 7-77

Figure 7-77A

Figure 7-78

Figure 7-78A

4.8 Dodging Body Against the Wind - Continuous Palm

迎風閃身連環掌

Take a small step to your left with your left leg, then shift your weight onto it while pulling your right leg back and lowering your right arm (Figure 7-76). Continue the motion by circling your right arm clockwise up and to your right, bringing your left hand next to your right shoulder, and swinging your right leg to your left (Figure 7-77).

Pull your right hand in a semicircle down and to your left, and then back to your waist, and extend your left hand up to your right, and then forward. Each hand moves in a semicircle, together they make a full circle. At the same time, slide your right foot back and to your right (Figure 7-78). Again each hand moves in another semicircle, with the right hand circling out and to your left, and the left hand circling in to your abdomen. At the same time, step forward with your right leg (Figure 7-79).

Figure 7-79

Figure 7-79A

Figure 7-80

Figure 7-81

Figure 7-82

Figure 7-83

Application-1:

Gray intercepts White's punch with his left hand (Figure 7-76A). Gray then brings his right arm under White's arm and coils up to White's temple (Figure 7-77A).

Application-2:

Gray intercepts White's left punch with his left hand (Figure 7-78A). Gray continues by pulling White's arm down while stepping to the outside of White's front leg and chopping to his neck with his right hand (Figure 7-79A).

V. Boring and Chopping Palm 穿劈掌

5.1. Right Posture of Cartwheel - Thunder Palm

Swing your left hand back while lowering your right hand and shifting your weight to your left foot (Figure 7-80). Continue the motion of your right arm, circling up clockwise (Figure 7-81). Pivot on your right heel and turn the toes to your right (Figure 7-82).

Figure 7-84 Figure 7-85 Figure 7-86

5.2 Feudal Lord Covers Hand - Grabbing Throat Palm

霸王蓋手搶喉掌

Step forward with your left leg while lowering your right hand to your waist and circling your left hand up and then down in front of you (Figure 7-83). Continue lowering your left hand while boring your right hand over your left palm (Figure 7-84).

5.3 Fair Lady Brushes Hand - Skillfully Boring Palm

玉女拂手巧穿掌

Slide your left hand up from under your right elbow and bore forward, while pulling your right hand palm down next to your left elbow (Figure 7-85).

5.4 Swallow Touches Water - Boring Downward Palm

燕子抄水下穿掌

Lower your right hand down along your right leg to your right ankle, while sinking your weight to your left leg. As the hand passes under your right armpit, the palm is facing out. By the time it reaches the ankle, it is facing back toward the ankle (Figure 7-86).

5.5 Rotating Arm Continuously - Thunder Palm

掄臂連環劈靂掌

Shift your weight forward while standing up and lifting your right arm (Figure 7-87). Lower your right arm clockwise down and begin to circle upward (Figure 7-88). Continue circling your right arm clockwise up and to your right, and begin raising your left arm (Figure 7-89). Continue moving the arms in a circle and turning your body to the right until your left hand is forward (Figure 7-90).

5.6 Tumble Heaven's Gate - Swimming Step to Separate Knee Palm

跌天門游步別膝掌

Continue the motion, turning your body to your left as you swing your right arm up and forward, and then inward, while lowering your left arm (Figure 7-91). Your body continues to turn as your left hand swings up, and your right hand circles down and up (Figure 7-92). Your right arm circles up and to your right, your left hand sinks down to your waist, and your right

Figure 7-87

Figure 7-88

Figure 7-89

Figure 7-90

Figure 7-91

Figure 7-92

foot takes a step forward, moving in a circle in toward your left leg and then forward, with the toe now pointing out (Figure 7-93). Step down with your right leg (Figure 7-94). Step forward with your left leg (Figure 7-95).

5.7 Lean Against the Mountain to Press and Stroke - Elbow Linking Palm
依山擠靠肘連掌

Shift your weight to your left leg and step to your right while lowering your right arm (Figure 7-96). Step to the left with your left leg while circling your left arm counterclockwise forward (Figure 7-97).

5.8 Feudal Lord Forces His Way Up - Grabbing Throat Palm
霸王硬上搶喉掌

Bore forward with your right hand and pull your left hand back to under the right elbow, palm down, while stepping forward with your right leg (Figure 7-98).

Figure 7-93

Figure 7-94

Figure 7-95

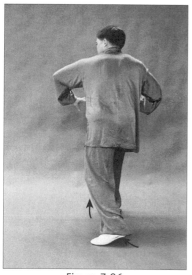

Figure 7-96

Figure 7-97

Figure 7-98

VI. TURNING BODY PALM 轉身掌

6.1 Randomly Rotate Heaven and Earth - Elbow Carrying Palm
亂轉乾坤肘帶掌

Swing both arms down clockwise while shifting your weight to your left leg (Figure 7-99). Continue the motion of your right arm while lifting and turning your right foot to your right (Figure 7-100). Lift up your left leg and spin to your right a full 360 degrees on the ball of your right foot. As you spin, the right arm comes down a little and then raises again (Figures 7-101 and 7-102). Cross your arms in front of your body, with your right arm on top, and your palms facing to the sides (Figure 7-103).

Application:

Gray lowers his right arm to intercept White's punch to his abdomen (Figure 7-99A). Gray then circles White's arm clockwise to his right and grabs the wrist while turning his body, striking to White's collar bone with his left hand, and kicking to White's groin with his left knee

277

Figure 7-99

Figure 7-99A

Figure 7-100

Figure 7-100A

Figure 7-101

Figure 7-101A

(Figure 7-100A). Gray lets go of White's wrist and continues to spin his body. He steps down while using his right elbow to strike White's collarbone (Figure 7-101A).

6.2 Green Dragon Turns Its Body - Left Swaying Palm

青龍轉身左擺掌

Turn to your left and take four steps around, almost a full circle. As you take your first step, extend your arms out and hold them in position (Figures 7-104, 7-105, and 7-106).

6.3 Brush Neck, Lead, and Carry - Rolling Back Arm Palm

抹脖牽帶攞臂掌

On the fourth step, circle both arms forward and begin to pull them in towards your left (Figures 7-107). Continue to pull both arms in while sinking to your left leg (Figure 7-108).

Figure 7-102

Figure 7-103

Figure 7-103R

Figure 7-104

Figure 7-105

Figure 7-106

6.4 Qi Rises to Ninth Heaven - Sealing Throat Palm

氣升九天閉喉掌

Push off your left leg and stand up, and bring your left leg next to your right leg while pressing to your right with your right forearm (Figure 7-109).

Application:

Gray intercepts White's left punch with his left hand (Figure 7-106A). Gray then grabs and pulls White's arm to his left side while stepping forward with his right leg and chopping to White's neck (Figure 7-107A). Gray continues by pulling White's arm down while pressing his forearm down on White's arm and shifting his weight back (Figure 7-108A). If White resists the pull and pulls back, Gray simply follows White's pull and strikes forward with his right forearm to White's neck (Figure 7-109A). Gray can then press down with his arm to make White fall (Figure 7-109B).

Figure 7-106A

Figure 7-107

Figure 7-107A

Figure 7-108

Figure 7-108A

Figure 7-109

6.5 Evade Body to Rotate Palm - Leaning the Body to Press
避身旋掌靠身按

Rotate your right forearm clockwise until your right palm is up (Figure 7-110). Continue rotating your forearm while stepping to your left with your left leg (Figure 7-111). Lower your forearm and turn your palm down (Figure 7-112). Push off your left leg and bring it next to your right leg while pressing to your right with your right forearm (Figure 7-113).

Application:

As White punches in with his right, Gray sets up to intercept his wrist by beginning to lift his right palm towards White's elbow (Figure 7-111A). Gray intercepts and grabs White's wrist with his left hand and pulls it down, while pressing White's elbow up with his right palm (Figure 7-112A). Gray continues his attack by sliding his right hand towards White's neck and pushing down, while continuing to twist White's wrist (Figure 7-113A).

Figure 7-109A

Figure 7-109B

Figure 7-110

Figure 7-111

Figure 7-111A

Figure 7-112

Figure 7-112A

Figure 7-113

Figure 7-113A

Figure 7-114

Figure 7-115

Figure 7-115A

Figure 7-116

Figure 7-116A

Figure 7-117

6.6 Side Sweep a Thousand Pounds - Brushing Eye Brow Palm

橫掃千鈞（軍）抹眉掌

Step to your left with your left leg and begin sinking into your left leg (Figure 7-114). Continue sinking as you swing both arms to your left (Figure 7-115).

6.7 Single Goose Leaves the Flock - Grabbing Throat Palm

孤雁出群搶喉掌

Bore forward with your left hand while simultaneously pulling your right hand back to the left elbow (Figure 7-116).

Application:

Gray intercepts White's right punch with both forearms (Figure 7-115A). Gray then pushes White's arm down with his right hand while turning his body and striking White's throat with his left hand (Figure 7-116A).

Figure 7-118

Figure 7-118A

Figure 7-119

Figure 7-119A

Figure 7-120

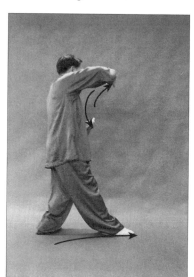

Figure 7-121

6.8 Avoid with a Diagonal Step - Brush Downward Palm
斜步閃身下抹掌

Begin lowering both arms (Figure 7-117). Continue lowering your right arm while drawing in your right leg (Figure 7-118).

VII. Leading and Carrying Palm 牽帶掌

7.1 Embrace Tiger and Return to the Mountain - Chasing Palm
抱虎歸山追身掌

Step out with your right foot to start walking in a circle and raise your hands in front of you (Figure 7-119). Step around with your left leg (Figure 7-120).

Application:

Gray yields back and intercepts White's right punch with his right hand (Figure 7-118A). Gray then steps to White's right side and pushes with both hands on White's back (Figure 7-119A).

| Figure 7-122 | Figure 7-122A | Figure 7-123 |

7.2 Feudal Lord Spins His Body - Supporting Beam Palm
霸王旋身托樑掌

Step to your right with your right leg as you circle your right hand counterclockwise and raise it slightly, and lower your left hand to waist level (Figure 7-121). Let the left hand continue upward and pull your right hand over your head as you twist your body a quarter turn to your right by pivoting on your right heel (Figure 7-122). Step forward with your left leg (Figure 7-123).

Application:

Gray intercepts White's right punch with his right hand (Figure 7-122A). Gray grabs White's hand and twists it down counterclockwise while lifting White's elbow and stepping forward (Figure 7-123A).

7.3 Hou-Yi Dodges His Body and Shoots the Sun
后羿閃身射太陽

Make a quarter turn to your left while lowering your left hand down behind you and pivoting your left foot to your left (Figure 7-124). Step forward with your right leg (Figure 7-125). Pivot on your heels and turn your body to the rear (Figures 7-126 and 7-127).

7.4 Cloud Above and Sweep Below to Cover the Heaven and the Earth
上雲下掃蓋天地

You are now going to spin 360 degrees in the opposite direction. Pivot your right foot and shift your weight onto it (Figure 7-128). Spin to your right on your right foot while beginning to raise your left hand (Figures 7-129 and 7-130).

7.5 Repel the Cloud to See the Sun - Seizing Arm Palm
撥雲見日擒臂掌

Take a small step down with your left leg and bring both hands up in front of you (Figure 7-131). Take a small step forward and strike forward with both palms (Figure 7-132).

Figure 7-123A

Figure 7-124

Figure 7-125

Figure 7-126

Figure 7-127

Figure 7-128

Figure 7-129

Figure 7-130

Figure 7-131

Figure 7-132

Figure 7-133

Figure 7-134

Figure 7-135

Figure 7-136

Figure 7-137

7.6   Rein the Horse at the Cliff - Knee to Heaven

懸崖勒馬膝頂天

Pull both hands back while lifting your right knee (Figure 7-133).

7.7   Horizontally Rotate Windmill - Close the Body to Smash

平轉風輪和身捶

Step down and back with your right leg while lowering your arms (Figure 7-134). Pivot on your heels to the rear and extend your right arm forward, palm up (Figure 7-135). Pivot back on your heels and shift your weight to your left foot as you bring your right hand over your head, palm still facing up (Figure 7-136).

7.8   Turn the Body to Wipe Arm - Leading and Carrying Palm

轉身抹臂牽帶掌

Continue the previous movement by lowering your right hand and extending your left arm to the side (Figure 7-137). Turn to the right to begin a 360 degree turn (Figure 7-138). Shift your

Figure 7-138	Figure 7-139	Figure 7-140

weight to your right foot and jump slightly off the ground, spinning 180 degrees in the air so that you come down facing the other direction (Figure 7-139). Maintaining the momentum, immediately turn another 180 degrees by stepping your right leg behind you (Figure 7-140).

VIII. DRAGO MOVING PALM 龍行掌

8.1 Jade Dragon Twists Its Waist and Bores to the Throat Skillfully
玉龍撐腰巧穿喉

Bore forward with your right hand as you pull your left hand back under the elbow, palm down (Figure 7-141).

8.2 Rebel Dragon Wraps the Neck and is Hard to Escape
逆龍纏頸難脫逃

Pull your right hand back and strike forward with the back of your left palm while shifting your weight to your back leg (Figure 7-142). Pull your left hand back and strike forward with the back of your right palm while lowering your body (Figure 7-143).

8.3 Flood Dragon Wraps the Post - Follow Up with a Step
蛟龍纏柱跟步上

Stand up and shift all your weight to your right leg while lowering your arms (Figure 7-144). Circle your left arm up and out in front of you while stepping to your right front (Figure 7-145). Step forward with your right leg as you pull you left hand down and strike forward with your right hand (Figure 7-146).

8.4 Sway Willow Against the Wind - Black Dragon Tail
迎風擺柳烏龍尾

Cross your left leg behind you while lowering your right arm to your side and swinging your left arm up in front of you (Figure 7-147). Pull your left hand back to your chest and swing your right hand forward while sweeping your right leg back and outward (Figure 7-148). Take a small step forward with the right foot and lower you body while extending your left arm to your side and making a small counterclockwise circle with your right arm (Figure 7-149).

Figure 7-141

Figure 7-142

Figure 7-143

Figure 7-144

Figure 7-145

Figure 7-146

Application:

Gray intercepts White's right punch with his right hand (Figure 7-148A). Gray slides his left foot behind his right while clearing White's arm to his left with his left hand. Gray then pulls White's arm back while swinging his right hand towards White's neck and swinging his right leg back to hit White's knee (Figure 7-148B). Gray steps his foot down to make White fall (Figure 7-149A).

8.5 Black Dragon Withdraws Its Body - Side Cutting Palm

蒼龍縮身橫切掌

Turn your body slightly to your left and begin to cross your arms in front of your body (Figure 7-150). Reverse the rotation of your body and continue to bring your arms closer to your body (Figure 7-151). Complete crossing your arms in front of your body, with your right arm on top, while moving your left foot next to your right foot (Figure 7-152).

Figure 7-147

Figure 7-148

Figure 7-148A

Figure 7-148B

Figure 7-149

Figure 7-149A

Figure 7-150

Figure 7-151

Figure 7-152

| Figure 7-153 | Figure 7-154 | Figure 7-155 |

8.6 Green Dragon Turns Its Body - Side Swaying Palm
青龍轉身側擺掌

Turn to your left and extend your arm to your left while stepping forward with your left foot (Figure 7-153).

8.7 White Dragon Swims and Turns - Return to the Immortal Mountain
白龍游轉返仙山

Walk as many steps as necessary around in a circular path until your body is facing the same direction as when you started the sequence (Figures 7-154 and 7-155). Turn your head forward and step up with your right foot as you begin raising both arms over your head (Figure 7-156). Lower your hands to waist height (Figure 7-157).

8.8 Black Dragon Worships Heaven and Offers a Bundle of Incense
(Golden Needle Points at Heaven-Stabbing Upward Palm)
玄龍拜天一注香（金針指天上戳掌）

Move your left foot next to your right foot. Circle your left arm out and up, then down to solar plexus height, palm down. Before your left arm completes its motion, extend your right arm and circle it up to chest height, palm facing to your left (Figure 7-158).

Closing: Eighty-Eight Palm Concludes - Close Qi Returns to Origin
八八掌畢氣歸元

Lower both hands to your sides (Figure 7-159).

Figure 7-156

Figure 7-157

Figure 7-158

Figure 7-159

Chapter 8

Bagua Deer Hook Sword
and Its Applications
八卦鴛鴦鉞與應用

8-1. Introduction

In order to survive and conquer in ancient battles, it was necessary to be proficient with weapons as well as with your bare hands. As in many other Chinese martial styles, Baguazhang techniques are also applicable to various different weapons. Ordinarily, the basic theories and principles of weapons use remain the same in all martial styles. But in Baguazhang, there is a weapon that is most unique, and historically has been trained only in Baguazhang styles. This weapon is called "Deer Hook Sword" (*Lu Jiao Dao*). The "Deer Hook Sword" is so named because the weapons themselves are shaped like a deer's antlers. They are also called the "Zi Wu Yuan Yang Yue" (*Zi Wu* Mandarin Duck Axe). *Zi* and *Wu* are two of the twelve Celestial Stems, and represent midnight *(Zi)* and noon *(Wu)* respectively. *Zi* also represents the extreme Yin of the day, while *Wu* represents the extreme Yang. The two weapons are used together - like a pair of Mandarin ducks, they are inseparable. Another name for these weapons is "*Ri Yue Qian Kun Jian*" (Sun Moon *Qian Kun* Sword). The sun and Qian represent Yang, while the moon and Kun represent Yin.

It is said that the "Deer Hook Sword" is specially designed to disarm the opponent. When one is used in each hand, they are characterized by continuous rotating and spinning, comfortable withdrawing and turning, agility in dodging, and skillful variation of techniques. Basic techniques are included in the sixteen words: hooking, sliding, seizing, controlling, pulling, cutting, picking, smashing, paring, drilling, chopping, mincing, brushing, smearing, leading, carrying, and neutralizing[1]. In this chapter, we will introduce a sequence of Bagua Deer Hook Sword with selected primary martial applications.

Figure 8-1

Figure 8-2

Figure 8-3

8-2. Bagua Deer Hook Sword

Emei Deer Hook Sword
(Emei Zi Wu Mandarin Duck Axe)
(Emei Sun Moon Qian Kun Sword)
峨嵋鹿角刀
峨嵋子午鴛鴦鉞
峨嵋日月乾坤劍

1. Commencing - Yin and Yang Unified 起勢 – 陰陽合一

Stand upright with both arms hanging naturally at your sides, holding the swords loosely (Figure 8-1). Move your left foot out to the side about the width of your shoulders, then raise the swords up slowly in front of you (Figure 8-2).

Figure 8-4

2. Equally Separate Two Poles 平分兩儀

Extend both swords to the sides and turn your body slightly to your right (Figure 8-3).

3. Green Dragon Turns Its Body 青龍轉身

Circle both swords over your head (Figure 8-4). While turning your body to the left, lower your arms and cross them in front of your chest with your right arm on the bottom (Figure 8-5).

4. Bagua Walking 八卦行步

Step forward with your right leg while swinging your right sword horizontally to your right (Figure 8-6). Take seven steps around a circle, and then bring your right foot up even with your left, so that you end up in the same spot you started in (Figure 8-7).

Figure 8-5

Figure 8-5A

Figure 8-6

Figure 8-6A

Application:

Gray blocks White's sword to his right with his left sword (Figure 8-5A). Gray then takes a small step forward and to his right and swings his right sword out to White's chest (Figure 8-6A).

5. Dispel the Grass to Search for the Snake 撥草尋蛇

Start circling both swords counterclockwise (Figure 8-8). As you circle the swords, rotate them 180 degrees. Lower your body and extend both swords to your right (Figure 8-9).

Application:

Gray intercepts White's sword and leads it to his left (Figure 8-8A). While sticking with and controlling White's sword with his left sword, Gray strikes White's abdomen with his right sword (Figure 8-9A).

6. Green Dragon Turns Its Body 青龍轉身

Shift your weight to your left leg while circling both swords horizontally clockwise, with the

Figure 8-7

Figure 8-8

Figure 8-8A

Figure 8-9

Figure 8-9A

Figure 8-10

Figure 8-11

Figure 8-12

Figure 8-13

Figure 8-14

Figure 8-15

left on top of the right (Figure 8-10). Step forward with your right foot and swing both swords to your right (Figure 8-11).

7. Bagua Walking 八卦行步

Take seven steps in a circle, and then bring up your right foot even with your left so that you are facing the opposite direction from your starting point (Figure 8-12).

8. Dispel the Grass to Search for the Snake 撥草尋蛇

Figures 8-13 and 8-14 repeat Figures 8-8 and 8-9.

9. Mandarin Ducks Leave the Water 鴛鴦出水

Bring your left sword up and back, then circle it downward as you shift all your weight to your right leg and raise your left heel (Figure 8-15). Step forward with your left leg and thrust your left sword up and out (Figure 8-16). Step forward with your right leg and thrust your right sword out while simultaneously pulling your left hand down to your side (Figure 8-17).

Figure 8-15A

Figure 8-16

Figure 8-16A

Figure 8-17

Application:

Gray blocks and seals White's sword down (Figure 8-15A). Gray uses his right sword to hold White's blade in place while stepping forward with his left leg and thrusting his left sword to White's neck (Figure 8-16A).

10. Autumn Wind Sweeps the Leaves 秋風掃葉

Cross your left leg behind your right and begin raising your left arm (Figure 8-18). Pivot on your left toe and right heel as your rotate your body to your left and swing your left sword out (Figure 8-19). Continue the swing of the arms as you step forward with your right leg. The right sword cuts downward in front of you as the left sword draws back toward your side (Figure 8-20).

Figure 8-18

Figure 8-19

Figure 8-20

Figure 8-20A

Figure 8-21

11. Large Roc Spreads Its Wings 大鵬展翅

Pull your right sword toward your chest as you shift your weight weight back slightly (Figure 8-21). Separate both swords (Figure 8-22).

Application:

Gray intercepts White's sword with his left sword and uses his right hook to attack White's neck (Figure 8-20A). If White uses his left hand to block Gray's right sword's attack, Gray sits back and use his right sword to slice White's waist. Gray then circles his sword towards White's waist (Figure 8-22A).

Figure 8-22

Figure 8-22A

Figure 8-23

Figure 8-24

Figure 8-25

12. Green Dragon Turns Its Body 青龍轉身

Bring your right foot in and step it to your left front. As you do this, circle both swords clockwise horizontally so that the left sword comes in toward your body and the right sword moves in and then out (Figure 8-23).

13. Dragon Swims Four Directions 龍游四方

Take three steps around a circle until you are facing forward again (Figures 8-24 to 8-26).

14. Mandarin Ducks Leave the Water 鴛鴦出水

Figures 8-27 to 8-30 repeat Figures 8-15 to 8-17

Figure 8-26

Figure 8-27

Figure 8-28

Figure 8-29

Figure 8-30

15. Autumn Wind Sweeps the Leaves　秋風掃葉

Figures 8-31 to 8-33 repeat Figures 8-19 to 8-20.

16. Large Roc Spreads Its Wings　大鵬展翅

Figures 8-34 and 8-35 Repeat Figures 8-21 and 8-22.

17. Remove the Cloud to See the Sun　撥雲見日

Step back with your right leg and shift all of your weight to it while beginning to swing your right sword and your left sword clockwise in front of you (Figure 8-36). Continue the motion of both arms so that the right sword cuts forward and the left one pulls back, as you raise your left leg (Figure 8-37).

Figure 8-31

Figure 8-32

Figure 8-33

Figure 8-34

Figure 8-35

Figure 8-36

Figure 8-36A

Figure 8-37

Figure 8-37A

Figure 8-38

Figure 8-39

Figure 8-40

Figure 8-41

Application:

Gray blocks White's blade with his right sword (Figure 8-36A). Gray clears White's blade to his left, and cuts forward to White's neck with his right sword while raising his left leg (Figure 8-37A).

18. Mandarin Ducks Play in Water 鴛鴦戲水

Step back with your left leg as you block or cut down with your left sword and pull your right sword back (Figure 8-38). Step back with your right leg as you block with your right sword and pull your left sword back (Figure 8-39). Step back with your left leg as you block with your left sword and pull your right sword back (Figure 8-40).

19. Male Attacks and Female Defends 雄攻雌守

Slide your right leg back while thrusting your right sword forward and pulling your left sword back (Figure 8-41).

Figure 8-41A

Figure 8-42

Figure 8-43

Figure 8-44

Figure 8-45

Application:

Gray steps back with his right leg, intercepts White's sword with his left sword and leads to his left while thrusting his right sword towards White's head (Figure 8-41A).

20. Split and Smash with Both Hooks 雙鉞劈砸

Shift all your weight to the right leg and lower both swords (Figure 8-42). Step forward with your left leg while swinging your left sword forward (Figure 8-43). Step forward with your right leg while swinging your right sword forward (Figure 8-44).

21. Lock the Throat with One Hook 單鉞鎖喉

Pull your right sword down while thrusting your left sword forward (Figure 8-45).

22. Angry Horse Parts Its Mane 怒馬分鬃

Pull your left sword diagonally down ansad your right sword diagonally up (Figure 8-46).

Figure 8-45A

Figure 8-46

Figure 8-46A

Figure 8-47

Application:

Gray intercepts White's sword with his right sword and leads it to his left, while thrusting to White's neck with his left sword (8-45A). He then draws his left sword back, and swings his right sword diagonally to White's neck (Figure 8-46A)

23. Split and Smash with Both Hooks 雙鉞劈砸

Draw your right foot back next to your left foot, with only the toes touching, and lower both swords (Figure 8-47). Step forward with your right leg while swinging your right sword forward (Figure 8-48). Step forward with your left leg while swinging your left sword forward (Figure 8-49).

24. Lock the Throat with One Hook 單鉞鎖喉

Pull your left sword down while thrusting your right sword forward (Figure 8-50).

Figure 8-48

Figure 8-49

Figure 8-49A

Figure 8-50

Application:

Gray blocks White's attack down and to his left with his left sword (Figure 8-49A). Gray continues by stepping forward with his left leg, and extending his left hand behind White's back. He then pulls White toward him while attacking his throat with his right sword (Figure 8-50A).

25. Angry Horse Parts Its Mane 怒馬分鬃

Swing the left sword up to your left and the right sword down to your right (Figure 8-51).

26. Split and Smash with Both Hooks 雙鉞劈砸

Draw your left leg back next to your right leg, with only the toes touching, and lower your left sword (Figure 8-52). Step forward with your left leg while circling your left sword up and

Figure 8-50A

Figure 8-51

Figure 8-52

Figure 8-53

Figure 8-54

down (Figure 8-53). Step forward with your right leg while swinging your right sword forward (Figure 8-54). Shift your weight back slightly while lowering your right arm over your left (Figure 8-55).

27. Er Lang Carries the Mountain 二郎擔山

Step your left leg behind your right leg, while raising the swords out to your sides (Figure 8-56).

Application:

Gray deflects White's sword to his left and attacks White's neck with his right sword. White raises his left arm to intercept the attack (Figure 8-55A). Gray hooks his right sword down, then towards White's groin, while crossing his left leg behind his right (Figure 8-56A).

Figure 8-55

Figure 8-55A

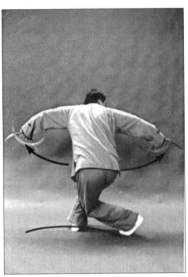

Figure 8-56

Figure 8-56A

28. Lift up the Knee and Hold up the Moon 提膝捧月

Pivot to your left on the ball of your left foot and the heel of your right foot, and swing your left sword over your head and down (Figure 8-57). Bring both swords in front of your chest, palms facing your body, while raising your right leg (Figure 8-58).

29. File with Sword to Scoop Up Groin 挫鉞撩陰

Thrust your right sword forward and pull the left sword back while kicking forward with your right foot (Figure 8-59).

Figure 8-57

Figure 8-58

Figure 8-58A

Figure 8-59

Application:

Gray locks White's blade with both swords while raising his leg (Figure 8-58A). Gray moves White's blade to the left, while thrusting his right sword toward White's chest and kicking to White's groin (Figure 8-59A).

30. Display the Hooks in Empty Stance虛步亮鉞

Lower your right leg, touching only the toe to the ground (Figure 8-60). Pivot your right foot and shift your weight onto it, while lowering your body, turning to the rear, and raising the heel of your left foot. Move the right sword in so that it is above the left sword (Figures 8-61 and 8-61R).

31. Four Door Stepping to File with Hooks Left and Right四門步左右挫鉞

Step your left leg to your left front corner, stand up, and swing your left sword down and to your left (Figure 8-62). Step forward with your right leg while circling both swords clockwise, with the left sword slightly leading the right (Figure 8-63). Step forward to your front right

Figure 8-59A   Figure 8-60

Figure 8-61   Figure 8-61R   Figure 8-62

corner with your right leg, and swing your right sword down and to the side (Figure 8-64). Step forward with your left leg while circling both swords counterclockwise, with the right sword slightly leading the left (Figure 8-65).

Application:

Gray deflects White's sword to the right with his left sword (Figure 8-62A). Sticking to White's sword, Gray circles his sword down and then out to his left, while stepping forward with his right leg, and swinging his right sword in a clockwise circle to attack the right side of White's chest (Figure 8-63A).

32. Yard Firmed Step to Hook and Lead 院庄步勾帶

Shift all your weight to your right leg, and draw your left leg part way back, with only the toe touching the ground, while rotating both swords 180 degrees clockwise (Figure 8-66). Step forward with your left leg to your front left corner, and begin to circle your left sword horizontally counterclockwise (Figure 8-67). Step to your left with your right leg while pulling your left sword in and swinging your right sword outward clockwise (Figure 8-68). Step to your left

Figure 8-62A

Figure 8-63

Figure 8-63A

Figure 8-64

Figure 8-65

Figure 8-66

Figure 8-67

| Figure 8-68 | Figure 8-69 | Figure 8-70 |

| Figure 8-70A | Figure 8-71 |

with your left leg, while continuing to circle both swords counterclockwise in front of you, so that the left sword moves out and the right sword moves in (Figure 8-69). Shift your weight back slightly, and continue to circle the swords so that the left sword moves in and the right sword moves out (Figure 8-70).

Shift all your weight onto your left leg while rotating both swords 180 degrees clockwise (Figure 8-71). Step forward with your right leg to your right front corner and begin to circle your right sword horizontally clockwise (Figure 8-72). Step to your right with your left leg while pulling your right sword in and swinging your left sword horizontally and clockwise forward (Figure 8-73). Step to your back right corner with your right leg while continuing to circle both swords clockwise, so that the right sword moves in and the left sword moves out (Figure 8-74). Shift your weight back slightly and continue to circle the swords, so that the left sword moves out and the right sword moves in (Figure 8-75).

Application:

Figure 8-72   Figure 8-73   Figure 8-74

Figure 8-75   Figure 8-76

Gray blocks White's sword to the left with his left sword and attacks White's neck by swinging his right sword counterclockwise (Figure 8-70A).

33. Swimming Dragon Shuttles Back and Forth 游龍穿梭

Rotate both swords 180 degrees clockwise and step forward with your right leg while circling your left sword down and back, and thrusting your right sword up and to your right (Figure 8-76). Take three steps in a small circle, starting with your left leg (Figure 8-77). Take three steps in a small circle, starting with your left leg (Figures 8-78 to 8-80).

Step forward with your right leg while circling your right sword down and back, and thrusting your left sword up and out (Figure 8-80). Pivot on your right foot, and step to the right with your left foot (Figure 8-81). Take two steps in a small circle, starting with your right leg (Figures 8-82 and 8-83). Step to your right with your right leg while lowering your left sword in front of you and bringing your right sword to your side (Figure 8-84). Continue lowering your left sword while thrusting your right sword up and out (Figure 8-85).

Figure 8-76A

Figure 8-77

Figure 8-78

Figure 8-79

Application:

Gray intercepts White's sword with his left sword, and thrusts his right sword toward White's neck. White intercepts Gray's right arm with his left arm (Figure 8-76A). Gray lowers his right sword to hold White's sword in place while crossing his left leg behind his right and turning his body to swing his left sword to White's groin (Figure 8-79A).

34. Circle Arms to Split and Cut 掄臂劈砍

Shift your weight back to your left leg while lowering both swords down to your left side (Figure 8-86). Shift your weight forward while swinging your right sword up and then down in front of you (Figure 8-87). Swing your right sword down to your right while swinging your left sword up and then down in front of you (Figure 8-88).

Figure 8-79A

Figure 8-80

Figure 8-81

Figure 8-82

Figure 8-83

Figure 8-84

Figure 8-85

Figure 8-86

315

Figure 8-87

Figure 8-88

Figure 8-89

Figure 8-89A

Figure 8-90

35. Beauty Looks in the Mirror 美女照鏡

Pivot your right foot, and sink your weight onto it as you turn to the rear, raise your left heel, and bring the two swords together. Your palms are facing your chest and the tips of the blades are pointing at each other (Figure 8-89).

36. Golden Chicken Lifts Its Wings 金雞挑翅

Turn to your right, then stand up on your right leg, raise your left leg, and swing both swords out and up to your sides (Figure 8-90).

Application:

Gray intercepts White's blade with both swords (Figure 8-89A). Gray seals White's blade

Figure 8-90A

Figure 8-91

Figure 8-92

Figure 8-93

down with his right sword while lifting his left sword up to cut White's arm (Figure 8-90A).

37. File Hooks with Attacking Steps 挫鈌擊步

Lower your left leg and bring both swords together, with the right sword on the outside (Figure 8-91). Shift your weight onto your left leg, turn part way to that side, and lower both swords (Figure 8-92). Stamp your right foot down next to your left foot and lift your left foot off the ground (Figure 8-93).

38. Rein the Horse to Ascend the Height 勒馬登高

Step forward with your left leg and kick with your right leg while swinging your right sword up and pulling your left sword in next to your chest (Figure 8-94).

Application:

Gray deflects White's sword down to his left with his left sword (Figure 8-93A). Gray then swings his right sword up towards White's face while kicking to White's groin with his right foot

Figure 8-93A

Figure 8-94

Figure 8-94A

Figure 8-95

(Figure 8-94A).

39. Goddess Waves Her Sleeves　仙女舞袖

Set your right foot down and pivot to your left, while extending both swords in front you (Figure 8-95). Turn to your right to swing the swords horizontally to your right (Figure 8-96).

40. Beauty Looks in the Mirror　美女照鏡

Shift your weight to your left leg, step your right leg to your left front corner, and turn to your rear (Figure 8-97). Slide your left leg back so that you are in a Cat Stance, and bring the two swords together. Your palms are facing in, and the sword tips are facing each other (Figure 8-98).

41. Split and Smash with Both Hooks　雙鉞劈砸

Turn to your right and lower both swords, then step forward with your left leg and swing the left sword over your head and down in front of you (Figure 8-99). Lower your left sword and swing your right sword up while stepping forward with your right leg (Figure 8-100). Draw

Figure 8-96

Figure 8-97

Figure 8-98

Figure 8-99

Figure 8-100

Figure 8-101

your right leg back next to your left leg as you swing your right sword down (Figure 8-101).

42. Stomp Foot and File with Hooks 震腳挫鉞

Begin to circle your right sword up as you get ready to lift your right knee up (Figure 8-102). Your right sword circles up, and then comes down as you lift and stomp down with your right foot. Your left sword follows the right sword; as it comes down in front of you, raise your left knee (Figure 8-103). Step forward with your left leg, thrust your right sword forward, and draw your left sword back under your right elbow (Figure 8-104). Pull your right sword back and thrust your left sword forward (Figure 8-105).

Application I:

Gray yields to White's attack, lowering his right sword to intercept White's blade (Figure 8-101A). Gray controls White's sword with his left sword, and swings his right sword up and then

Figure 8-101A

Figure 8-102

Figure 8-102A

Figure 8-103

down to White's head (Figure 8-102A).

Application II:

Gray blocks White's blade down and to his right with his right sword (Figure 8-103A). Gray cuts to White's wrist with his left sword while stepping forward with his left leg and circling his right sword to White's neck (Figure 8-104A). Gray pulls his right sword back to control White's sword, while circling his left sword to White's neck (Figure 8-105A).

43. Spin the Body to Lock with Hooks 旋身鎖鉞

Step forward with your right leg and bring both swords together. The palms are facing in and the tips of the swords are pointing toward each other (Figure 8-106). Cross your left leg behind your right leg and begin to turn your body (Figure 8-107). Pivot to your left on your left toe and right heel, and shift all of your weight onto your right leg (Figure 8-108).

Application:

Gray intercepts White's sword with his right sword and hooks on with his left sword (Figure 8-

Figure 8-103A

Figure 8-104

Figure 8-104A

Figure 8-105

Figure 8-105A

Figure 8-106

Figure 8-106A

Figure 8-107

Figure 8-107A

Figure 8-108

106A). Gray then crosses his left foot behind his right foot and breaks White's sword (Figure 8-107A)

44. Step Forward to File the Hook 上步挫勾

Step forward with your right leg while lowering and separating the swords to the sides (Figure 8-109).

Application:

Gray intercepts White's sword with his left sword, while holding his right sword in front of him (Figure 8-108A). Gray locks White's blade down with his left sword while cutting White's wrist with his right sword (Figure 8-109A).

45. Remove the Cloud and Play with the Moon 撥雲弄月

Shift your weight back slightly as you circle your right sword clockwise and your left sword counterclockwise (Figure 8-110). Step forward with your right leg and turn your body, so that your right sword circles down and then cuts across to your left, and your left sword draws up

Figure 8-108A

Figure 8-109

Figure 8-109A

Figure 8-110

Figure 8-110A

Figure 8-111

Figure 8-111A

Figure 8-112

Figure 8-113

Figure 8-114

Figure 8-115

and back (Figure 8-111). Circle your left sword to your right over your head (Figure 8-112). Step forward with your left leg and turn your body, so that your left sword circles down and then cuts across to your right, and your right sword draws up and back (Figure 8-113). Shift your weight back slightly as you circle your right sword clockwise and your left sword counterclockwise (Figure 8-114). Step back with your left leg and turn your body, so that your right sword circles down and then cuts across to your left, and your left sword draws up and back (Figure 8-115).

Application:

Gray blocks White's sword with his right sword (Figure 8-110A). Gray keeps White's sword in place with his left sword, while dropping down to cut to White's groin with his right sword

Figure 8-116

Figure 8-117

Figure 8-118

Figure 8-119

Figure 8-120

Figure 8-121

(Figure 8-111A).

46. Green Dragon Turns Its Body 青龍轉身

Turn your body a little further, and draw both swords in towards your body (Figure 8-116).

47. Bagua Walking 八卦行步

Step your right leg to your left front and swing your right sword horizontally out and to your right (Figure 8-117). Take three more steps around to complete a circle (Figure 8-118). Bring your left foot up parallel with your right (Figure 8-119).

48. Yin and Yang Unified into One 陰陽合一

Figure 8-122

Bring both swords together, with your palms facing in and the tips of the blades pointing toward each other (Figure 8-120).

49. Closing Posture to Return to the Origin 收勢歸元（源）

Lower both swords in front of you (Figure 8-121). Bring the swords to your sides and move your left leg next to your right (Figure 8-122).

References

1. 勾、掛、擒、拿，拉、割、挑、扎，削、攢、劈、剎，抹、撩、帶、化。

Chapter 9

Conclusion
結論

In conclusion, we would like to point out a few important things. First, after so many years of development, there are presently more than twenty different Baguazhang styles known to us. Even so, the fact remains that all of them developed out of the same Baguazhang theory and principles. The more you have an opportunity to learn from different sources, the more angles you will have toward viewing and understanding this profound Chinese internal martial art. Therefore, you must remain humble and ready to absorb ever more information and knowledge.

Second, even though space limitation does not allow us to introduce more sequences or routines in this book, nonetheless the theory and the principles in this volume are very complete. The theory and principles are the essence and root of the entire art; they can guide your training and lead you further into the profound depths of the art. Therefore, you should repeatedly read and ponder all of the treasured writings that have been passed down to us by the ancient masters. One day you will realize that you have grasped the key to the art and become a proficient Baguazhang practitioner.

Finally, we would like to encourage all qualified Baguazhang masters to share their knowledge through seminars, teachings, books, or even videotapes. Only through all of our efforts can we insure the proper preservation of this beautiful, refined art.

Appendix A

Translation of Baguazhang Qigong
*Bagua Turning-Spinning Qigong
(Bagua Zhuan Xuan Gong)*
八卦轉旋功

1. **Preparation Posture (*Yu Bei Shi*)** 預備式
心平氣和鎖心猿

Calm down (your) emotional mind (*Xin*) and harmonize your Qi to lock (i.e, control) the monkey heart (emotional mind).

2. **Nourish Elixir Posture (*Yang Dan Shi*)** 養丹式
頂沉內聚息綿綿

Sink the top and gather the internal (Qi), breathe slenderly and smoothly.

3. **Push Mill Posture (*Tui Mo Shi*)** 推磨式
吐推吞拉圓轉磨

Exhale to push, inhale to pull; turn the mill with a round motion.

4. **Rotate Palm Posture (*Zhuan Zhang Shi*)** 轉掌式
滾鑽爭裹撐八面

Roll, drill, struggle (i.e., expand and wrench), and wrap supporting eight directions.

5. **Spiral and Rotate Posture (*Pan Xuan Shi*)** 盤旋式
腰如軸轉臂旋繞

Waist like an axle turning, arm swings around.

6. **Twist Turning Posture (*Ning Zhuan Shi*)** 擰轉式
身似繩擰頭頂懸

Body is twisted like a rope and the head is suspended from above.

7. **Bore and Turn Posture (*Chuan Zhuan Shi*)** 穿轉式
沿圈擺扣蹚泥行

Arcing and swinging walking in the mud along the edge of a circle.

8. **Closing Gong Posture (*Shou Gong Shi*)** 收功式
轉旋八卦返先天

(Practice) turning-spinning Bagua to return to Pre-Heaven (condition).

Appendix B

Translation of Basic Eight Palms
Baguazhang Eight Palms
(also called Dragon Shape Baguazhang)
基本八卦八掌（龍形八卦掌）

COMMENCING: (*QI SHI*) 起勢

I. **Single Changing Palm: (*Dan Huan Zhang*) 單換掌**
   1. Green Dragon Turns its Head: (*Qing Long Fan Shou*) 青龍返首
   2. Green Dragon Turns its Body: (*Qing Long Zhuan Shen*) 青龍轉身

II. **Double Changing Palm: (*Shuang Huan Zhang*) 雙換掌**
   3. Green Dragon Turns its Head: (*Qing Long Fan Shou*) 青龍返首
   4. Hawk Flies to Heaven: (*Yao Zi Zuan Tian*) 鷂子鑽天
   5. White Snake Hiding in the Grass: (*Bai She Fu Cao*) 白蛇伏草
   6. Green Dragon Turns its Body: (*Qing Long Zhuan Shen*) 青龍轉身

III. **Following Through Palm: (*Shun Shi Zhang*) 順勢掌**
   7. Turn and Spit Poison: (*Bei Shen Tu Xin*) 背身吐信
   8. Dragon Tugs its Tail: (*Cang Long Suo Wei*) 蒼龍縮尾
   9. White Snake Hiding in the Grass: (*Bai She Fu Cao*) 白蛇伏草
   10. Green Dragon Turns its Body: (*Qing Long Zhuan Shen*) 青龍轉身

IV. **Reversing Body Palm: (*Bei Shen Zhang*) 背身掌**
   11. Green Dragon Turns its Head: (*Qing Long Fan Shou*) 青龍返首
   12. Swallow Enters the Forest: (*Yan Zi Ru Lin*) 燕子入林
   13. Green Dragon Stretches its Claws: (*Qing Long Tan Zhua*) 青龍探爪
   14. Monkey Bends Tree Branches: (*Yuan Hou Ban Zhi*) 猿猴搬枝
   15. Green Dragon Turns its Body: (*Qing Long Zhuan Shen*) 青龍轉身

V. **Turning Body Palm: (*Zhuan Shen Zhang*) 轉身掌**
   16. Green Dragon Turns Its Head: (*Qing Long Fan Shou*) 青龍返首
   17. Swallow Enters the Forest: (*Yan Zi Ru Lin*) 燕子入林
   18. Running Horse Turns its Head: (*Zou Ma Hui Tou*) 走馬回頭
   19. White Ape Offers Fruit: (*Bai Yuan Xian Guo*) 白猿獻果

VI. **Double Embracing Palm: (*Shuan Bao Zhang*) 雙抱掌**
   20. Lion Rolls the Ball: (*Shi Zi Gun Qiu*) 獅子滾球
   21. White Ape Offers Fruit: (*Bai Yuan Xian Guo*) 白猿獻果
   22. Green Dragon Rolls the Ball: (*Qing Long Gun Qiu*) 青龍滾球
   23. Green Dragon Turns Its Body: (*Qing Long Zhuan Shen*) 青龍轉身

VII. Grinding Body Palm: (*Mo Shen Zhang*) 磨身掌

24. Green Dragon Turns Its Head: (*Qing Long Fan Shou*)　青龍返首
25. Wave the Fan in Front of the Gate: (*Ying Men Hui Shan*)　迎門揮扇
26. Phoenix Spreads Its Wings: (*Feng Huang Zhan Chi*)　鳳凰展翅
27. Swallow Touches the Water: (*Yan Zi Chao Shui*)　燕子抄水
28. Reverse Windmill: (*Dao Ye Feng Che*)　倒拽風車

VIII. Rotating Body Palm: (*Fan Shen Zhang*) 翻身掌

29. Green Dragon Flies into the Sky: (*Qing Ling Fei Sheng*)　青龍飛升
30. Fling your Sleeves in the Wind: (*Ying Feng Hui Xiou*)　迎風揮袖
31. Monkey Kicks the Branches: (*Yuan Hou Deng Zhi*)　猿猴蹬枝
32. Swallow Touches the Water: (*Yan Zi Chao Shui*)　燕子抄水
33. Swallow Enters the Forest: (*Yan Zi Ru Lin*)　燕子入林
34. Large Python Rolls Over: (*Da Mang Fan Shen*)　大蟒翻身
35. Monkey Bends Tree Branches: (*Yuan Hou Ban Zhi*)　猿猴搬枝
36. Fierce Tiger Catches its Prey: (*Meng Hu Pu Shi*)　猛虎扑食
37. Green Dragon Turns its Body: (*Qing Long Zhuan Shen*)　青龍轉身
38. Closing (*Shou Shi*): 收式

Appendix C

Translation of Swimming Body Baguazhang
Swimming Body Baguazhang
(also called Swimming Body Dragon Walking Baguazhang)
游身八卦掌（游身龍行八卦掌）

I. Swimming Body Palm (*You Shen Zhang*) 游身掌

1.1. Golden Needle Points Up to Heaven - Stabbing Upward Palm
金針指天上戳掌

1.2. Two Immortals Preach the Dao - Rear Plucking Palm
二仙傳道後採掌

1.3. Turn the Head with Frictional Body - Press Leaning Palm
磨身回頭擠靠掌

1.4 Green Dragon Turns Its Body - Extending Sideways Palm
青龍轉身側探掌

1.5. Phoenix Takes Off Its Wings - Bump the Body Sideways
鳳凰拔翅側身撞

1.6. Immortal Twists his Waist - Locking the Throat Palm
仙子扭腰鎖喉掌

1.7. Phoenix Spreads Its Wings - Walk with Swimming Body
鳳凰展翅游身走

1.8. Reverse to Tumble Heaven's Gate - Separating Knee Palm
倒跌天門別膝掌

II. Revolving Body Palm 旋身掌

2.1. Immortal Plucks Flower - Circling Feet with Boring Palm
仙子採花繞腳穿掌

2.2. Feudal Lord Turns His Body - Cover the Hand with Boring Palm
霸王轉身蓋手穿掌

2.3. Cover the Heaven and Blanket the Earth - Sweep Sideways with a Thousand Pounds
鋪天蓋地橫掃千軍（鈞）

2.4. Plant the Flower Under the Leaves - Pluck Pulling Palm
葉底插花採拔掌

2.5. Phoenix Flies to Heaven - Side Chopping Palm
鳳凰飛天橫切掌

2.6. Swallow Touches Water - Intercept Kicking Sealing Palm
燕子抄水截腿掌

2.7. Scoop, Carry, Press, and Chop - Turning Body Palm
撩挑壓劈翻身掌

5.5. Rotating Arm Continuously - Thunder Palm
掄臂連環劈靂掌

5.6. Tumble Heaven's Gate - Swimming Step to Separate Knee Palm
跌天門游步別膝掌

5.7. Lean Against the Mountain to Press and Stroke - Elbow Linking Palm
依山擠靠肘連掌

5.8. Feudal Lord Forces His Way Up - Grabbing Throat Palm
霸王硬上搶喉掌

VI. Turning Body Palm 轉身掌

6.1. Randomly Rotate Heaven and Earth - Elbow Carrying Palm
亂轉乾坤肘帶掌

6.2. Green Dragon Turns Its Body - Left Swaying Palm
青龍轉身左擺掌

6.3. Brush Neck, Lead, and Carry - Rolling Back Arm Palm
抹脖牽帶攞臂掌

6.4. Qi Rises to Ninth Heaven - Sealing Throat Palm
氣升九天閉喉掌

6.5. Evade Body to Rotate Palm - Leaning the Body to Press
避身旋掌靠身按

6.6. Side Sweep a Thousand Pounds - Brushing Eye Brow Palm
橫掃千鈞（軍）抹眉掌

6.7. Single Goose Leaves the Flock - Grabbing Throat Palm
孤雁出群搶喉掌

6.8. Avoid with a Diagonal Step - Brush Downward Palm
斜步閃身下抹掌

VII. Leading and Carrying Palm 牽帶掌

7.1. Embrace Tiger and Return to the Mountain - Chasing Palm
抱虎歸山追身掌

7.2. Feudal Lord Spins His Body - Supporting Beam Palm
霸王旋身托樑掌

7.3. Hou-Yi Dodges His Body Shooting the Sun
后羿閃身射太陽

7.4. Cloud Above and Sweep Below to Cover the Heaven and the Earth
上雲下掃蓋天地

7.5. Repel the Cloud to See the Sun - Seizing Arm Palm
撥雲見日擒臂掌

7.6. Rein the Horse at the Cliff - Knee to Heaven
懸崖勒馬膝頂天

7.7. Horizontally Rotate Windmill - Close the Body to Smash
平轉風輪和身捶

7.8. Turn the Body to Wipe Arm - Leading and Carrying Palm
轉身抹臂牽帶掌

VIII. Dragon Moving Palm 龍行掌

8.1. Jade Dragon Twists Its Waist and Bores to the Throat Skillfully
玉龍撐腰巧穿喉

8.2. Rebel Dragon Wraps the Neck and is Hard to Escape
逆龍纏頸難脫逃

8.3. Flood Dragon Wraps the Post - Follow Up with a Step
蛟龍纏柱跟步上

8.4. Sway Willow Against the Wind - Black Dragon Tail
迎風擺柳烏龍尾

8.5. Black Dragon Withdraws Its Body - Side Cutting Palm
蒼龍縮身橫切掌

8.6. Green Dragon Turns Its Body - Side Swaying Palm
青龍轉身側擺掌

8.7. White Dragon Swims and Turns - Return to the Immortal Mountain
白龍游轉返仙山

8.8. Black Dragon Worships Heaven and Offers a Bundle of Incense
(Golden Needle Points at Heaven-Stabbing Upward Palm)
玄龍拜天一注香（金針指天上戳掌）

Closing: Eighty-Eight Palm Concludes - Close Qi Returns to Origin
八八掌畢氣歸元

Appendix D

Translation of Bagua Deer Hook Sword
Emei Deer Hook Sword
(Emei Zi Wu Mandarin Duck Axe)
(Emei Sun Moon Qian Kun Sword)

峨嵋鹿角刀
峨嵋子午鴛鴦鉞
峨嵋日月乾坤劍

1. Commencing-Yin and Yang Unified 起勢－陰陽合一
2. Equally Separate Two Poles 平分兩儀
3. Green Dragon Turns Its Body 青龍轉身
4. Bagua Walking 八卦行步
5. Dispel the Grass to Search for the Snake 撥草尋蛇
6. Green Dragon Turns Its Body 青龍轉身
7. Bagua Walking 八卦行步
8. Dispel the Grass to Search for the Snake 撥草尋蛇
9. Mandarin Ducks Leave the Water 鴛鴦出水
10. Autumn Wind Sweeps the Leaves 秋風掃葉
11. Large Roc Spreads Its Wings 大鵬展翅
12. Green Dragon Turns Its Body 青龍轉身
13. Dragon Swims Four Directions 龍游四方
14. Mandarin Ducks Leave the Water 鴛鴦出水
15. Autumn Wind Sweeps the Leaves 秋風掃葉
16. Large Roc Spreads Its Wings 大鵬展翅
17. Remove the Cloud to See the Sun 撥雲見日
18. Mandarin Ducks Play in Water 鴛鴦戲水
19. Male Attacks and Female Defends 雄攻雌守
20. Split and Smash with Both Hooks 雙鉞劈砸
21. Lock the Throat with One Hook 單鉞鎖喉
22. Angry Horse Parts Its Mane 怒馬分鬃
23. Split and Smash with Both Hooks 雙鉞劈砸
24. Lock the Throat with One Hook 單鉞鎖喉
25. Angry Horse Parts Its Mane 怒馬分鬃

26. Split and Smash with Both Hooks　雙鉞劈砸
27. Er Lang Carries the Mountain　二郎擔山
28. Lift up the Knee and Hold up the moon　提膝捧月
29. File with Sword to Scoop Up Groin　挫鉞撩陰
30. Display the Hooks in Empty Stance　虛步亮鉞
31. Four Door Stepping to File with Hooks Left and Right　四門步左右挫鉞
32. Yard Firmed Step to Hook and Lead　院庄步勾帶
33. Swimming Dragon Shuttles Back and Forth　游龍穿梭
34. Circle Arms to Split and Cut　掄臂劈砍
35. Beauty Looks into the Mirror　美女照鏡
36. Golden Chicken Lifts Its Wings　金雞挑翅
37. File Hooks with Attacking Steps　挫鉞擊步
38. Rein the Horse to Ascent the Height　勒馬登高
39. Goddess Waves Her Sleeves　仙女舞袖
40. Beauty Looks into the Mirror　美女照鏡
41. Split and Smash with Both Hooks　雙鉞劈砸
42. Stomp Foot and File with Hooks　震腳挫鉞
43. Spin the Body to Lock with Hooks　旋身鎖鉞
44. Step Forward to File the Hook　上步挫勾
45. Remove the Cloud and Play with the Moon　撥雲弄月
46. Green Dragon Turns Its Body　青龍轉身
47. Bagua Walking　八卦行步
48. Yin and Yang Unified into One　陰陽合一
49. Closing Posture to Return to the Origin　收勢歸元（源）

Appendix E

Glossary and Translation of Chinese Terms

Adam Hsu 徐紀 – A Chinese martial arts teacher currently residing in California.

An Hui Province 安徽省 – A province in China.

An 按 – Means "pressing downward." One of the common techniques in Chinese martial arts.

Ba Da Zhang 八大掌 – Means "Eight Great Palm." The name of a Baguazhang sequence.

Ba Xing Zhang 八形掌 – Means "Eight Shapes Palm." The name of a Baguazhang sequence.

Ba 八 – Means "Eight."

Bagua Ba Xing Zhang 八卦八形掌 – Means "Bagua Eight Shapes Palm." The name of a Baguazhang sequence.

Bagua Dao 八卦刀 – Means "Bagua Saber." The name of a Baguazhang sequence.

Bagua Gau 八卦鉤 – Means "Bagua Hook." The name of a Baguazhang sequence.

Bagua Guai 八卦枴 – Means "Bagua Crutch." The name of a Baguazhang sequence.

Bagua Jian 八卦劍 – Means "Bagua Sword." The name of a Baguazhang sequence.

Bagua Lian Huan Zhang 八卦連環掌 – Means "Bagua Linking Palm." The name of a Baguazhang sequence.

Bagua Qiang 八卦槍 – Means "Bagua Spear." The name of a Baguazhang sequence.

Bagua Zhuan Xuan Gong 八卦轉旋功 – Means "Bagua Turning-Spinning Gong." The name of a Baguazhang Qigong practice routine.

Baguazhang Dui Lian 八卦掌對練 – Means "Bagua Matching Training." The name of a Baguazhang two-person matching sequence.

Baguazhang 八卦掌 – Means "Eight Trigram Palms." The name of one of the Chinese internal martial styles.

Bai He 白鶴 – Means "White Crane." One of the Chinese southern martial styles.

Ban Yu Bu 半魚步 – Means "half fish stepping." In this stepping, a practitioner will walk following the Taiji symbol, pass through the center to the other end, and finally reverse the circle.

Ban 搬 – Means "to move" or "to twist."

Bao Shi 褒氏 – Lady Bao, who was captured by Emperor You of Zhou and later became his favorite courtesan

Bao 褒 – The name of a tribe in Chinese Zhou dynasty (781-771 B.C.).

Beijing 北京 – Capital of China.

Bi Cheng Xia 碧澄俠 – An ancient Baguazhang master; also called Bi Deng Xia.

Bi Deng Xia 碧燈俠 – An ancient Baguazhang master; also called Bi Cheng Xia.

Bi Yue-Xia 避月俠 – An ancient Baguazhang master.

Cai 採 – Means "to pluck." A common Chinese martial arts technique.

Cangzhou 滄州 – Name of a city in Chinese Hebei province.

Cao Zhong-Sheng 曹鐘升 – An old Baguazhang master.

Ce Zhang 側掌 – One of the eight basic shapes of the palms in Baguazhang.

Chan 纏 – Means "to wrap." A common Chinese martial arts technique.

Chang Chuan (Changquan) 長拳 – Means "Long Range Fist." Chang Chuan includes all northern Chinese long range martial styles.

Chang San-Feng 張三峰 – Chang San-Feng is credited as the creator of Taijiquan during the Song dynasty in China (960-1127 A.D.).

Chang Xiang-San 張詳三 – A well known Chinese martial artist in Taiwan.

Changquan (Chang Chuan) 長拳 – Means "Long Range Fist." Changquan includes all northern Chinese long range martial styles.

Chen Pan-Ling 陳泮嶺 – A well known Baguazhang master.

Chen Style Taijiquan 陳氏太極拳 – A style of Taijiquan.

Chen Wei-Ming 陳微明 – A well know Taiji master in China.

Chen Ziyu (Bill Chen) 陳子渝 – Master Liang Shou-Yu's friend.

Chen's village 陳家溝 – The village where Chen style Taijiquan was developed.

Cheng Gin-Gsao 曾金灶 – Dr. Yang Jwing-Ming's White Crane master.

Cheng Man-Ching 鄭曼青 – A well known Taijiquan master in America.

Cheng Shi Baguazhang 程氏八卦掌 – A style of Baguazhang created by Cheng Ting-Hua.

Cheng Ting-Hua 程庭華 – A well known Baguazhang master.

Cheng village 程家村 – The village where Cheng style Baguazhang was developed.

Cheng Yipeng (Raymond Ching) 程一鵬 – Master Liang Shou-Yu's friend.

Cheng You-Long 程有龍 – The older son of Cheng Ting-Hua, a well known Baguazhang master.

Cheng You-Xin 程有信 – The younger son of Cheng Ting-Hua, a well known Baguazhang master.

Chengdu Athletic Institute 成都體育學院 – Name of an athletic institute located in Chengdu city of Chinese Sichuan province.

Chi (Qi) 氣 The energy pervading the universe, including the energy circulating in the human body.

Chi Shi-Xin 遲世信 – Name of a Baguazhang master.

Chin Na (Qin Na) 擒拿 – Literally means "grab control." A component of Chinese martial arts which emphasizes grabbing techniques, to control the opponent's joints, in conjunction with attacking certain acupuncture cavities.

Chongqian 重慶 – A city located in Sichuan province, China.

Chuan 穿 – Means "to bore." A technique used in Baguazhang.

Chun Qiu Dao 春秋刀 – Means "Spring-Autumn Saber." A long handle Baguazhang saber sequence.

Chuo Jiao 戳腳 – A style of Chinese martial arts which specializes in leg techniques.

Cui Hua 崔華 – A Baguazhang master.

Cui Zhen-Dong 崔振東 – A Baguazhang master.

Da Mo 達摩 – The Indian Buddhist monk who is credited with creating the Yi Jin Jing and Xi Sui Jing while at a Shaolin monastery. His last name was Sardili, and he was also known as Bodhidarma. He was once the prince of a small tribe in southern India.

Da Peng Qigong 大鵬氣功 – Means "Great Roc Qigong." A style of Qigong which was developed in Emei mountain, Sichuan, China.

Dai 帶 – Means "to carry." A common Chinese martial arts technique.

Dan Lu 丹爐 – Means "Elixir Furnace" which implies the Lower Dan Tian.

Dan Tian 丹田 – Means "Elixir Field." Located in the lower abdomen, it is considered the place which is able to store Qi or energy.

Dao 道 – Means the "way" which implies the "natural way."

Di Pan 低盤 – Means "low posture."

Dian Xue 點穴 – Dian means "to point and exert pressure" and Xue means "the cavities." Dian Xue refers to those Qin Na techniques which specialize in attacking acupuncture cavities to immobilize or kill an opponent.

Diao 刁 – Means "to hook." A common Chinese martial arts technique.

Ding 丁 – A Chinese word.

Dong Hai-Chuan 董海川 – A well known Baguazhang master.

Dong Meng-Lin 董夢麟 (碧燈俠，碧澄俠) – Also called Bi Deng-Xia or Bi Cheng Xia. He is credited as the creator of Baguazhang.

Dong Wen-Xou 董文修 – A Baguazhang master.

Du Mai 督脈 – Usually translated Governing Vessel. One of the eight extraordinary vessels.

Dui (☱) 兌 – One of the Eight Trigrams.

Duke Dao 晉悼公 – A Duke in the Chinese Jin dynasty.

Duke Wen of Jin 晉文公 – A Duke in the Chinese Jin dynasty.

Dun Bu 頓步 – Means "pulse stepping." One of the stepping techniques in Baguazhang.

Duo 躲 – Means "to dodge" or "to avoid." A common technique in Chinese martial arts.

Emei Bagua Lian Huan Zhang 峨嵋八卦連環掌 – Means "Emei Bagua Linking Palm." The name of a Emei Baguazhang sequence.

Emei Bagua Mei Hua Zhang 峨嵋八卦梅花掌 – Means "Emei Bagua Plum Flower Palm." The name of a Emei Baguazhang sequence.

Emei Baguazhang 峨嵋八卦掌 – Means "Emei Bagua Palm." The name of a Emei Baguazhang sequence.

Emei Da Peng Gong 峨嵋大鵬功 – Means "Emei Great Roc Gong." A Qigong practice developed in Emei mountain.

Emei Gongfu 峨嵋功夫 – Gongfu developed at Emei mountain.

Emei Long Xing Baguazhang 峨嵋龍形八卦掌 – Means "Emei Dragon Shape Bagua Palm." The name of a Emei Baguazhang sequence.

Emei Mountain 峨嵋山 – A mountain located in Sichuan province, China.

Emei Qingcheng Baguazhang 峨嵋青城八卦掌 – Means "Emei Qingcheng Bagua Palm." The name of a Emei Baguazhang sequence.

Emei Wugong 峨嵋武功 – Martial Gongfu developed at Emei mountain.

Emei Wushu 峨嵋武術 – The martial techniques developed in Emei mountain.

Emei Xian Tian Baguazhang 峨嵋先天八卦掌 – Means "Emei Pre-Heaven Bagua Palm." The name of a Emei Baguazhang sequence.

Emei Xingyi Baguazhang 峨嵋形意八卦掌 – Means "Emei Xingyi Bagua Palm." The name of an Emei Baguazhang sequence.

Emei Yin Yang Baguazhang 峨嵋陰陽八卦掌 – Means "Emei Yin Yang Bagua Palm." The name of an Emei Baguazhang sequence.

Emei You Shen Bagua Lian Huan Zhang 峨嵋游身八卦連環掌 – Means "Emei Swimming Body Bagua Linking Palm." The name of an Emei Baguazhang sequence.

Emei You Shen Baguazhang 峨嵋游身八卦掌 – Means "Emei Swimming Body Bagua Palm." The name of an Emei Baguazhang sequence.

Emei 峨嵋 – Name of a mountain in Sichuan province, China.

Emperor You of Zhou 周幽王 – An emperor in Chinese Zhou dynasty (781-771 B.C.)

Fa Jin 發勁 – Means "emitting Jin." Jin is martial power, in which muscular power is manifested to its maximum from mental concentration and Qi circulation.

Fan Shen Zhang 返身掌 – Means "returning body palm." A set of movements in Baguazhang.

Fan 翻 – To turn over.

Fan Errui 范爾銳 – Master Liang Shou-Yu's friend.

Fei Jiu Gong 飛九宮 – Means "flying Nine Palaces." It is the training of stepping in which a practitioner will swiftly walk through a pattern, which is arranged by the Eight Trigrams, and also the center of the trigrams.

Feng Jun-Yi 馮俊義 – A Baguazhang master.

Feng Ke-Shan 馮克善 – A Baguazhang master.

Fu Hu Bu 伏虎步 – Means "taming the tiger stance." A fundamental stance in Chinese martial arts. It is also called Pu Bu.

Fu Hua-Qiu 傅劍秋 – A Baguazhang master.

Fu Shi Baguazhang 傅氏八卦掌 – Fu Style Baguazhang which was created by Fu Zhen-Song.

Fu Shu-Yun 傅淑雲 – A well known Chinese female martial artist.

Fu Xi 伏羲 – Name of the person credited as the creator of Bagua (Eight Trigrams).

Fu Yong-Hui 傅永輝 – A Baguazhang master whose father is the creator of the Fu Style Baguazhang.

Fu Zhen-Song 傅振嵩 – A well known Baguazhang master who is credited as the creator of the Fu Style Baguazhang.

Gao Pan 高盤 – Means "high posture."

Gao Qi-Shan 高岐山 – A Baguazhang master.

Gao Yi-Sheng 高義盛 – A Baguazhang master.

Gao Zhen-Dong 高振東 – A Baguazhang master.

Gen（☶）艮 – One of the Eight Trigrams.

Gong Bao-Tian 宮寶田 – A Baguazhang master.

Gong Yu-Zhai 宮愚齋 – A Baguazhang master.

Gongfu (Kung Fu) 功夫 – Means "energy-time." Anything which will take time and energy to learn or to accomplish is called Gongfu.

Gau 鉤 – Means "to hook." A common technique in Chinese martial arts.

Gu Dao 穀道 – Means "grain path" which implies the anus.

Gua 挂 – Means "to draw back." A common technique in Chinese martial arts.

Guan Lixuan (L. H. Kwan) 關禮暄 – Master Liang Shou-Yu's friend.

Guang Xu 光緒 – An emperor in Qing dynasty in China (1875-1908 A.D.).

Gun 滾 – Means "to roll." A common technique in Chinese martial arts.

Gung Li Chuan 功力拳 – The name of barehand sequence in Chinese Long Fist martial arts.

Guo Gu-Min 郭古民 – A Baguazhang master.

Guo Meng-Shen 郭夢深 – A Baguazhang master.

Guo Qi-Feng 郭歧鳳 – A Baguazhang master.

Guo Shu-Fan 郭叔蕃 – A Baguazhang master.

Guo Yong-Lu 郭永祿 – A Baguazhang master.

Guo Yun-Shen 郭雲深 – A Baguazhang master.

Guo Zhen-Ya 郭振亞 – A Baguazhang master.

Guo Zhu-Shan 郭鑄山 – A Baguazhang master.

Guo 裹 – Means "to wrap." A technique in Chinese martial arts.

Guoshu 國術 – Abbreviation of "Zhongguo Wushu," which means "Chinese Martial Techniques."

Ha 哈 – A sound which is able to energize a fighter's spirit and energy. The "Ha" sound is commonly used in Chinese martial arts training.

Han Ching-Tang 韓慶堂 – A well known Chinese martial artist, especially in Taiwan in the last forty years. Master Han is also Dr. Yang Jwing-Ming's Long Fist grandmaster.

Han Fu-Shun 韓福順 – A Baguazhang master.

Han Mu-Xia 韓慕俠 – A Baguazhang master.

Han Qi-Ying 韓奇英 – A Baguazhang master.

Hao En-Guang 郝恩光 – A Baguazhang master.

He Jin-Kui 何金奎 – A Baguazhang master.

He 合 – Means "to combine,""to harmonize,""to coordinate," and "to unify."

Hebei Province 河北省 – A province in China.

Hei Liu 黑劉 – Means "black Liu." A nickname of a Baguazhang master.

Hen 哼 – A sound which is commonly used in Chinese martial arts. While making this sound on inhalation, you are able to lead the Qi inward and store it in the Lower Dan Tian, and also bone marrow.

Hen 橫 – Means "sideways." One of the techniques used in Chinese internal martial arts.

Henan 河南 – A province in China. The most famous Shaolin temple is located in Henan province.

Heng Xin 恆心 – Literally "persistent heart." This implies "patience,""endurance," and "perseverance."

Hong Ze Great Master 洪澤大師 – A nickname of one of Master Liang Shou-Yu's Baguazhang masters.

Hou Tian Fa 後天法 – Means "Post-Heaven Techniques." An internal Qigong style known from 550 A.D.

Hou Tian Gua 後天卦 – Literally "Post-Heaven Trigram." This is to correspond with the "Pre-Heaven Trigram." Pre-Heaven Trigram explains the natural phenomena and rules which have already been patterned. The Post-Heaven Trigram explains the derivations of the changes, which can be influenced by many factors such as emotion, luck, and thinking.

Hou Yi 后羿 – A well known archer in Chinese history.

Hsing Yi Chuan (Xingyiquan) 形意拳 – A style of internal Chinese martial arts.

Huang Zhexi 黃哲西 – One of Master Liang Shou-Yu's friends in Canada.

Hu Kou 虎口 – A name of a cavity. It is also called "Hegu" in acupuncture.

Hua Mountain 華山 – A well known mountain in Shanxi province, China.

Huang Bo-Nian 黃柏年 – A well known Chinese martial artist, who graduated from Nanking Central Guoshu Institute.

Huang Guan Dao Ren 黃冠道人 – Means "Yellow Hat Daoist." The nickname of Baguazhang master, Dong Meng-Lin.

Huang 黃 – Means "yellow." A common Chinese family name.

Hubei 湖北 – Literally "Lake North." A province in China.

Huiyin 會陰 – The first acupuncture cavity on the Conceptional Vessel.

Hunan 湖南 – Literally "Lake South." A province in China.

Huo 豁 – To open. One of the Chinese martial techniques.

Huo 火 – Fire. One of the Five Elements.

Ji 擠 – Means "to press." One of the common techniques in Chinese martial arts.

Ji Feng-Xiang 姬鳳祥 – A Baguazhang master.

Jia Dan Tian 假丹田 – Means "false Dan Tian." Taoists believe that the Lower Dan Tian, which is also called Qihai in acupuncture, is not a real Dan Tian, since though it generates the Qi, it does not store it.

Jia Qing 嘉慶 – A title of an emperor's reign in Qing dynasty (1796-1821 A.D.).

Jia Yun-Gao 賈蘊高 – A Baguazhang master.

Jiang Hao-Quan 蔣浩泉 – A Chinese martial artist who is currently residing in California. Master Jiang graduated from Nanking Central Guoshu Institute.

Jiang Hu 江湖 – Literally "rivers lakes." Chinese martial artists often traveled among rivers and lakes. Therefore, it implies "martial society."

Jiang Rong-Qiao 姜容樵 – A Baguazhang and Xingyi master.

Jiang's Baguaz1hang 姜氏八卦掌 – The Baguazhang modified by Master Jiang Rong-Qiao.

Jie 截 – Means "to intercept." A common technique in Chinese martial arts.

Jin Bu 進步 – Advancing. A strategy in Chinese martial arts.

Jin Shao-Feng 金紹峰 – Master Yang Jwing-Ming's White Crane grandmaster.

Jin Yun-Ting 靳雲亭 – A Baguazhang master.

Jin 晉 – A dynasty in Chinese history (265-420 A.D.).

Jin 金 – Metal. One of the Five Elements.

Jin 勁 – Chinese martial power. A combination of "Li" (muscular power) and "Qi."

Jin 進 – Forward. A strategy in Chinese martial arts.

Jing Bian Ji 靖邊記 – Means "Safeguard the Border Record." An informal historical record of Qing dynasty discovered in "Blue House History".

Jing 精 – Essence. One of the three treasures (Jing, Qi, and Shen) in the human body.

Jiquan 極泉 – The name of a cavity which belongs to the Heart Primary Channel.

Jiu Gong Bu 九宮步 – Literally "Nine Palace Stepping." The stepping training in which a Baguazhang practitioner walks, following a set pattern organized by the Eight Trigrams and center.

Jiu Gong Sanpanzhang 九宮三盤掌 – A style of Baguazhang.

Jiu Gong 九宮 – Means "Nine Palace," which is constructed by the Eight Trigrams and the central point.

Jiu Hua Mountain 九華山 – One of the mountains in China located in Anhui province.

Jiulong Baguazhang 九龍八卦掌 – A style of Baguazhang.

Juan 卷 – Wrapping. A technique in Chinese martial arts.

Jun 鈞 – "Jun" was the unit of weight used in earlier times. One Jun equals to 30 catties. A catty is an Asian unit of weight generally equivalent to 1 1/3 pounds.

Kan (☵) 坎 – One of the Eight Trigrams.

Kan Gua 坎卦 – Kan Trigram.

Kan Ling-Feng 闞齡峰 – A Baguazhang master.

Kan Zhong Man 坎中滿 – Means "the center of Kan is full." This implies that in the symbol of Kan, the center is a solid line.

Kao Tao 高濤 – Master Yang Jwing-Ming's first Taijiquan master.

Kao 靠 – Means "to lean against." A Chinese martial arts technique.

King Zhou Wen 周文王 – King Wen in Chinese Zhou dynasty (1122-255 B.C.).

Kong Qi 空氣 – Air.

Kou Bai Bu 扣擺步 – Arcing and swaying stepping. The main stepping techniques in Baguazhang.

Kou 扣 – To pluck or to grab. A Chinese martial arts technique.

Kua 胯 – The hip area, which includes the Nei Kua (internal Kua) and Wai Kua (external Kua). External Kua includes the upper thigh on the external side of the legs and hips. Internal Kua includes the area of the upper thigh on the internal side of legs.

Kun（☷）坤 – One of the Eight Trigrams.

Kung Fu (Gongfu) 功夫 – Means "energy-time." Anything which will take time and energy to learn or to accomplish is called Kung Fu.

Lady Shen 申氏 – The queen of Emperor of You of Zhou (781-771 B.C.)

Lai Zhi-De 來知德 – A scholar who studied Yi Jing (Book of Change).

Lan Yi Wai Shi 藍簃外史 – Lan (blue) Yi (small house attached to a pavilion) Wai Shi (historical novel), a historical novel written in Qing dynasty.

Lan 攔 – To block. A Chinese martial arts technique.

Lan 蘭 – A duke of Zheng during Chinese Spring and Autumn Period (722-481 B.C.).

Lao Ba Zhang 老八掌 – Old Eight Palms. Old traditional Baguazhang eight palms.

Lao Zi 老子 – A renowned philosopher and founder of Daoism (604-531 B.C.).

Laogong 勞宮 – Literally "labor palace." One of the cavities on the Pericardium Primary Qi Channel.

Li（☲）離 – One of the Eight Trigrams.

Li Bai 李白 – Li Bai (701-762 A.D.). One of China's greatest poets during the Tang dynasty.

Li Chang-Ye 李長葉 – A Baguazhang master.

Li Ching-Yuan 李青雲 – A Daoist who is believed to have lived for 250 years in Sichuan, China (1678-1928 A.D.).

Li Cun-Yi 李存義 – A Baguazhang master.

Li Hai-Ting 李海亭 – A Baguazhang master.

Li Han-Zhang 李漢章 – A Baguazhang master.

Li Jian-Hua 李劍華 – A Baguazhang master.

Li Jing-Lin 李景林 – A Baguazhang master.

Li Long-Dao (Dr. Frank Li) 李龍道 – Dr. John Painter's Baguazhang master.

Li Mao-Ching 李茂清 – Master Yang Jwing-Ming's Long Fist master.

Li Qiaodong (Arthur J. Lee) 李橋棟 – Master Liang Shou-Yu's friend.

Li Qing-Wu 李慶五 – A Baguazhang master.

Li Tian-Ji 李天驥 – A Baguazhang master.

Li Wen-Bao 李文豹 – A Baguazhang master.

Li Wen-Biao 李文彪 – A Baguazhang master.

Li Xing-He 李性和 – A Baguazhang master.

Li Yao-Ting 李耀亭 – A Baguazhang master.

Li Ying-Ang 李英昂 – A Baguazhang master.

Li Yu-Lin 李玉琳 – A Baguazhang master.

Li Zhen-Qing 李振清 – A Baguazhang master.

Li Ziming 李子鳴 – A Baguazhang master.

Li-Li 麗麗 – A common name for girl's in China.

Lian Huan Chun Yang Jian 連環純陽劍 – Name of a Bagua Sword Sequence.

Lian Huan Jian 連環劍 – Name of a Bagua Sword Sequence.

Lian Huan Pan Long Gun 連環盤龍棍 – Name of a Bagua Staff Sequence.

Lian Po 廉頗 – Name of an officer in the Chinese Zhao dynasty, during the period of the Warring States (475-222 B.C.).

Liang Dexing (Jeffrey D. S, Liang) 梁德馨 – Master Liang Shou-Yu's uncle, currently residing in Seattle, Washington.

Liang dynasty 梁朝 – A dynasty in Chinese history (502-557 A.D.)

Liang Xiangyong 梁向勇 – Master Liang Shou-Yu's wife.

Liang Zuofeng 梁作風 – Master Liang Shou-Yu's father.

Liang Shou-Yu 梁守渝 – One of the authors in this book.

Liang Tang Yinghua (Eva Liang) 梁唐應華 – Master Liang Shou-Yu's aunt.

Liang Wu 梁武帝 – An Emperor of the Chinese Liang dynasty (502-550 A.D.).

Liang Yi 兩儀 – Two poles, Yin and Yang.

Liang Zheng-Pu 梁振蒲 – A Baguazhang master.

Liang Zhi Xiang 梁芷箱 – Master Liang Shou-Yu's grandfather.

Liangong Shr Ba Fa 練功十八法 – Eighteen techniques of training Gong. One of the martial Qigong trainings.

Liao 撩 – To Scoop. A Chinese martial arts technique.

Lie 例 – Split or rend. A Chinese martial arts technique.

Lien Bu Chuan 連步拳 – One of the Long Fist barehand sequences.

Lin Xiang-Ru 藺相如 – Name of an officer in Chinese Zhao dynasty during the period of the Warring States (475-222 B.C.).

Lin 麟 – Female of a wondrous, fabled animal resembling the deer or unicorn.

Ling Gui-Qing 凌桂青 – A Baguazhang master.

Ling 領 – To lead. A Chinese martial arts technique.

Liu Bao-Zhen 劉寶珍 – A Baguazhang master.

Liu Bin 劉斌 – A Baguazhang master.

Liu De-Kuan 劉德寬 – A Baguazhang master.

Liu Feng-Chun 劉鳳春 – A Baguazhang master.

Liu He Ba Fa 六合八法 – One of the Chinese internal martial arts, its techniques are combined from Taijiquan, Xingyi, and Baguazhang.

Liu Hu-Hai 劉湖海 – A Baguazhang master.

Liu Lao-Qing 劉老清 – A Baguazhang master.

Liu Qing-Fu 劉慶福 – A Baguazhang master.

Liu Wen-Hua 劉文華 – A Baguazhang master.

Liu Xi-Wu 劉錫五 – A Baguazhang master.

Liu Yun-Qiao 劉雲樵 – A Baguazhang master.

Liu Zhen-Zong 劉振宗 – A Baguazhang master.

Long Xing Baguazhang 龍形八卦掌 – Dragon Shape Baguazhang. A style of Baguazhang.

Lu Jiao Dao 鹿角刀 – Deer Hook Saber (Sword). A special unique weapon used in Baguazhang.

Lu Shui-Tian 盧水田 – A Baguazhang master.

Lu Zijian 呂子劍 – A Baguazhang master.

Lu 擺 – Rollback. A Chinese martial arts technique.

Luo Shu 洛書 – The characters supposedly devised by Emperor Yu of the Xia dynasty (2000-1700 B.C.) in imitation of the shell pattern of a divine tortoise in the Lo River.

Ma Gui 馬貴 – A Baguazhang master.

Ma Wei-Qi 馬維祺 – A Baguazhang master.

Ma Yun-Cheng (Bi Yue Xia) 馬雲程 (避月俠) – A Baguazhang master.

Mountain Bei 北山 – A mountain's name. Location unknown.

Mu 木 – Wood. One of the Five Elements.

Nan Yue 南岳 – Name of mountain. Nan Yue is located in Hunan province, China.

Nanking Central Guoshu Institute 南京中央國術館 – A national Chinese martial arts institute organized by the Chinese government at Nanking, Sichuan province, 1928.

Nei Gong 內功 – Means "internal Gongfu," martial arts Qigong.

Nei Jing 內經 – Literally "Inner Classic." One of the oldest Chinese medical books, which includes two portions: "Shuwen" and "Lingshu."

Nei Qi 內氣 – Internal Qi. The internal energy which is circulating in human body.

Ni Chuan 逆穿 – Literally "reverse boring." In "Boring Nine Palace" practice in Baguazhang, a practitioner can walk, following a set path which is called "Shun Chuan," or the reverse path which is called "Ni Chuan."

Ning 擰 – Twisting. A Chinese martial arts technique.

Niu Liang-Chen 牛亮臣 – A Baguazhang master.

Pan 盤 – Pan means "sections." When the body is discussed in Chinese martial society, it is normally divided into three sections. These three sections are called "San Pan" (three sections). San Pan includes the lower section (Xia Pan) from the knees down to the feet, the middle section (Zhong Pan) from the knees up to the solar plexus, and the upper section (Shang Pan) from the solar plexus up to the head.

Pei Xi-Rong 裴錫榮 – A Baguazhang master.

Peng Zhao-Kuang 彭昭曠 – A Baguazhang master.

Peng 棚 – To wardoff. A Chinese martial arts technique.

Pi 劈 – To chop. A Chinese martial arts technique.

Qi (Chi) 氣 – Chinese term for universal energy. A current popular model is that the Qi circulating in the human body is bio-electric in nature.

Qi Shi Er Tui Fa 七十二腿法 – Seventy-two leg techniques.

Qi Wu 祁午 – An officer of the Jin dynasty in the Chinese Spring and Autumn Period (722-481 B.C.). Qi Wu was Qi Xi's son.

Qi Xi 祁奚 – An officer of the Jin dynasty in Chinese Spring and Autumn Period (722-481 B.C.).

Qian (三) 乾 – One of the Eight Trigrams.

Qian Long Xia Jiang Nan 乾隆下江南 – Name of a novel written during the Qing dynasty which described the events of the Emperor Qian Long when he visited Southern China.

Qian Xu 謙虛 – Humility.

Qigong (Chi Kung) 氣功 – The Gongfu of Qi, which means the study of Qi.

Qihai 氣海 – Name of cavity located in the Conceptional Vessel. This cavity is also called "Xia Dan Tian" (Lower Dan Tian) in Daoist society.

Qin Cheng 秦成 – A Baguazhang master.

Qin Na (Chin Na) 擒拿 – Literally means "grab control." A component of Chinese martial arts which emphasizes grabbing techniques, to control the opponent's joints, in conjunction with attacking certain acupuncture cavities.

Qin 秦 – A dynasty in Chinese history (255-206 B.C.).

Qing Dao Guang 清道光 – A title of an emperor's reign in Qing dynasty (1821-1851 A.D.).

Qing dynasty 清朝 – A dynasty in Chinese history (1644-1912 A.D.).

Qing Guang Xu 清光緒 – A title of an emperor's reign in Qing dynasty (1875-1908 A.D.).

Qing Jia Qing 清嘉慶 – A title of an emperor's reign in Qing dynasty (1796-1821 A.D.).

Qingcheng Mountain 青城山 – Name of mountain, located in Sichuan province, China.

Quan Rong 犬戎 – Name of a tribe during Chinese Zhou dynasty (781-771 B.C.).

Quanshu 拳術 – Fist techniques. Means martial arts.

Ren Mai 任脈 – Conceptional Vessel. One of the Eight Extraordinary Vessels.

Ren Nai 忍耐 – Endurance.

Ren Zhi-Cheng 任致誠 – A Baguazhang master.

Ri Yue Qian Kun Jian 日月乾坤劍 – Literally "Sun Moon Qian Kun Sword." It is also called "Lu Jiao Dao" (Deer Hook Saber).

San Chuan 三穿 – Three "borings." A techniques of Baguazhang which the boring technique is applied three times continuously.

San Pan 三盤 – When the body is discussed in Chinese martial society, it is normally divided into three sections. These three sections are called "San Pan" (three sections). San Pan includes the lower section (Xia Pan) from the knees down to the feet, the middle section (Zhong Pan) from the knees up to the solar plexus, and the upper section (Shang Pan) from the solar plexus up to the head. San Pan also means the three different heights of postures: Gao Pan (High Posture), Zhong Pan (Middle Posture), and Di Pan (Low Posture).

San Shi Liu Tui Fa 三十六腿法 – Thirty-Six leg techniques.

Seng Men Baguazhang 僧門八卦掌 – Means "Monk's Family Baguazhang." One of the Emei Baguazhang styles.

Sha Guozheng 沙國政 – A Baguazhang master.

Shan Dong Ji Ning 山東濟寧 – A county in Sandong province, China.

Shan 閃 – Dodge. A Chinese martial arts technique.

Shandong 山東 – A province in China.

Shang Pan 上盤 – Means upper section (Shang Pan) of the body which is from the solar plexus up to the head.

Shang Yun-Xiang 尚雲祥 – A Baguazhang master.

Shanghai Athletic College 上海體育院 – An athletic college located in Shanghai.

Shanghai 上海 – A big city on the east coast of China.

Shao Yu-Sheng 少餘生 – The pen name of an author who wrote the novel "Shaolin Yen Yi."

Shao 梢 – Means "ending."

Shaolin Temple 少林寺 – A monastery located in Henan province, China. The Shaolin Temple is well known because of its martial arts training.

Shaolin Yen Yi 少林演義 – Name of a novel written in Qing dynasty. Shaolin Yen Yi means Historical Drama of Shaolin.

Shaolin 少林 – Young woods. Name of Shaolin Temple.

Shaoyang 少陽 – Less Yang.

Shaoyin 少陰 – Less Yin.

Shen County 深縣 – A county located in Hebei province; the birth place of Master Cheng Ting-Hua.

Shen 神 – Spirit.

Shen 申 – The family name of the queen during Emperor You of Zhou (781-771 B.C.).

Sheng Men Bagua Da Yin 生門八卦打引 – A style of Baguazhang.

Sheng Men Baguazhang 生門八卦掌 – A style of Baguazhang.

Shi Han-Zhang 時漢章 – A Baguazhang master.

Shi Ji-Dong 施繼棟 – A Baguazhang master.

Shi Li-Qing 史立卿 – A Baguazhang master.

Shi Liu 史六 – A Baguazhang master.

Shi Zi Zhang 獅子掌 – Lion Palm. One of the Eight Palms.

Shi 視 – Watching or observing. A martial arts training.

Shu Zhan 叔詹 – An officer of Zhen during China's Spring and Autumn period (722-481 B.C.).

Shuai Jiao 摔交 – Chinese wrestling. Part of Chinese martial arts.

Shui 水 – Water. One of the Five Elements.

Shun Chuan 順穿 – Literally "following boring." In "Boring Nine Palace" practice in Baguazhang, a practitioner can walk, following a set path which is called "Shun Chuan," or a reverse path which is called "Ni Chuan."

Si Ma-Guang 司馬光 – An officer in the Chinese Song dynasty (1019-1086 A.D.).

Si Xiang 四象 – Four phases which are derived from two poles in the Eight Trigrams.

Sichuan 四川 – A province in China.

Song Chang-Rong 宋長榮 – A Baguazhang master.

Song dynasty 宋朝 – A dynasty in Chinese history (960-1127 A.D.).

Song Shi-Rong 宋世榮 – A Baguazhang master.

Song Tie-Lin 宋鐵麟 – A Baguazhang master.

Song Wei-Yi 宋唯一 – A Baguazhang master.

Song Yong-Xiang 宋永祥 – A Baguazhang master.

Su Jing-Tian 蘇景田 – A Baguazhang master.

Sun Cun-Zhou 孫存周 – A Baguazhang master.

Sun Lu-Tang 孫祿堂 – A well known Baguazhang master.

Sun Wu 孫武 – Sun Zi, a strategist during Chinese Spring and Autumn Period (722-481 B.C.), noted for his book, The Art of War.

Sun Xi-Kun 孫錫坤 – A Baguazhang master.

Sun Yong-Sheng 孫永生 – A Baguazhang master.

Tai Mountain 泰山 – Name of mountain located in Sandong province. Tai Mountain is one of the Five Sacred Mountains in China.

Tai Yi Xing Jiu Gong Zhi Fa 太一行九宮之法 – A stepping training in Baguazhang in which a practitioner walks following the "Nine Palace" pattern.

Taiji 太極 – Means 1"grand ultimate." It is this force which generates two poles, Yin and Yang.

Taijiquan (Tai Chi Chuan) 太極拳 – A Chinese internal martial style which based on the theory of Taiji (grand ultimate).

Taipei Xian 台北縣 – The county on the north of Taiwan.

Taipei 台北 – The capital city of Taiwan located on the north of Taiwan.

Taisun Wang – Master Liang Shou-Yu's friend.

Taiwan 台灣 – An island to the south-east of mainland China. Also known as "Formosa."

Taixing 太行 – Name of mountain. Location unknown.

Taiyang 太陽 – Means "great Yang." A terminology used in acupuncture.

Taiyi Huo Long Baguazhang 太乙火龍八卦掌 – A style of Emei Baguazhang.

Taiyin 太陰 – Means "great Yin." A terminology used in acupuncture.

Taizuquan 太祖拳 – A style of Chinese external martial arts.

Tamkang College Guoshu Club 淡江國術社 – A Chinese martial arts club founded by Dr. Yang when he was studying in Tamkang College.

Tamkang 淡江 – Name of a University in Taiwan.

Tang Ni Bu 踏泥步 – Means "muddy stepping." The way that a Baguazhang practitioner walks in training.

Tao Chun-Xiu 陶春秀 – A Baguazhang master.

Teintsin 天津 – A city in China.

Tian Hui 田迴 – A Baguazhang master.

Tian Zhen-Feng 田鎮峰 – A Baguazhang master.

Tiao 挑 – To pick. A Chinese martial arts technique.

Tu 土 – The Earth. One of the Five Elements.

Tui Bu 退步 – Step backward. A strategic movement in Chinese martial arts.

Tui Na 推拿 – Means "to push and grab." A category of Chinese massages for healing and injury treatment.

Tui 退 – Retreat. A strategic movement in Chinese martial arts.

Tui 推 – To push. A Chinese martial arts technique.

Tuo 托 – To hold or to lift. A Chinese martial arts technique.

Wai Dan Chi Kung (Wai Dan Qigong) 外丹氣功 – External Elixir Qigong. In Wai Dan Qigong, a practitioner will generate the Qi to the limbs, and then allow the Qi flow inward to nourish the internal organs.

Wai Men 外門 – External door. When a martial artist attacks his opponent from the opponent's side. This side door is called "external door."

Wang Jun-Chen 王俊臣 – A Baguazhang master.

Wang Jurong 王菊蓉 – A well known Chinese martial artist whose father is Wang Ziping. Wang Ziping was one of the martial arts teachers at Nanking Central Guoshu Institute.

Wang Li-De 王立德 – A Baguazhang master.

Wang Shenhuan (Solen Wong) 王深寰 – Master Liang Shou-Yu's friend.

Wang Shu-Tian 王樹田 – Master Liang Shou-Yu's Baguazhang and Xingyiquan teacher.

Wang Xiang 王祥 – A Baguazhang master.

Wang Zhong-Xian 王仲獻 – A Baguazhang master.

Wang Ziping 王子平 – A very well known master who was the Long Fist style instructor at Nanking Central Guoshu Institute.

Wangwu 王屋 – Name of mountain. Location unknown.

Wei Ji 魏吉 – A Baguazhang master.

Weilu 尾閭 – Tail bone.

Wen An County 文安縣 – A county located in Hebei province; the birth place of Master Dong Hai-Chuan.

Wen Wang 文王 – An emperor of the Zhou dynasty in China (1122 B.C.)

Wilson Chen 陳威伸 – Master Yang Jwing-Ming's friend.

Wu Jun-Shan 吳峻山 – A Baguazhang master.

Wu Meng-Xia 吳孟俠 – A Baguazhang master.

Wu Qi-Shan 吳歧山 – A Baguazhang master.

Wu Wen-Ching 吳文慶 – One of the authors in this book.

Wu Xing Bang 五行棒 – Name of staff sequence in Baguazhang.

Wu Xing San He Zhang 五行三合掌 – Name of barehand sequence in Baguazhang.

Wu Xing Zhen 五行陣 – Five Element tactical deployment of troops, which based on the theory and relationship of mutual generation and conquest of the Five Elements.

Wu Xing 五行 – Five Elements which include Metal, Wood, Water, Fire, and Earth.

Wu Zhao-Feng 吳兆奉 – A Baguazhang master.

Wu 午 – Noon.

Wudang Baguazhang 武當八卦掌 – A style of Baguazhang developed in Wudang mountain.

Wudang Mountain 武當山 – A mountain located in Hubei province, China.

Wude 武德 – The Martial Moralities.

Wugong 武功 – Martial Gongfu.

Wuji 無極 – No extremity.

Wujiquan 無極拳 – A Chinese martial style developed based on the theory of Wuji.

Wushu 武術 – Literally, "martial techniques."

Wuyi 武藝 – Literally, "martial arts."

Xi Sui Jing 洗髓經 – Marrow/Brain Washing Classic. An advanced level of Qigong practice for enlightenment. Da Mo is credited as the creator of this classic.

Xia Pan 下盤 – San Pan includes the lower section (Xia Pan) of the body, which extends from the knees down to the feet.

Xia Zhiquan (Paul Ha) 夏智權 – Master Liang Shou-Yu's friend.

Xian Tian Gua 先天卦 – Pre-Heaven Trigrams. The Eight Trigrams which explains the natural rules and theory.

Xian 西安 – A city located in Shanxi province, China.

Xiao Hai-Bo 肖海波 – A Baguazhang master.

Xiao Jiu Tian 小九天 – Small Nine Heaven. A Qigong style created around 550 A.D.

Xiao 削 – Paring. A Chinese martial arts technique.

Xie Hu 解狐 – An officer in the state of Jin during Spring and Autumn Period (722-481 B.C.).

Xin Yong 信用 – Trust.

Xin 心 – Literally, "heart." Means the mind generated from emotional disturbance.

Xincheng County 新城縣 – A county located in Hebei province, China; the birth place of Master Wang Shu-Tian.

Xingyi 形意 – An abbreviation of Xingyiquan.

Xingyiquan (Hsing Yi Chuan) 形意拳 – One of the best known Chinese internal martial styles created by Marshal Yue Fei during Chinese Song dynasty (1103-1142 A.D.).

Xinzhu Xian 新竹縣 – Birth place of Dr. Yang Jwing-Ming in Taiwan.

Xu Yu-Sheng 許禹生 – A Baguazhang master.

Xu Yue 徐岳 – A Baguazhang master.

Xun 巽 – One of the Eight Trigrams.

Yan De-Hua 閻德華 – A Baguazhang master.

Yang Jwing-Ming 楊俊敏 – One of the authors in this book.

Yang Mai 陽脈 – Yang Vessels.

Yang Mei-Ling 楊美玲 – Master Yang Jwing-Ming's wife.

Yang Ming-San 楊明山 – A Baguazhang master.

Yang Rong-Ben 楊榮本 – A Baguazhang master.

Yang Yao 陽爻 – A solid straight line which is used to symbolize the Yin and Yang, and also the Eight Trigrams.

Yang Yi 陽儀 – Yang pole. One of the two poles, Yin and Yang.

Yang 陽 – Too sufficient. Yang pole.

Yangtze River 揚子江 – The northernmost of the two main rivers in China.

Yi Da Zhuan 易大傳 – Book name, which explains the Yi Jing.

Yi Jin Jing 易筋經 – Muscle/Tendon Changing Classic. One of the two classics written by Da Mo.

Yi Jing 易經 – Book of Changes.

Yi Li 易理 – The theory explained in the Yi Jing.

Yi Xi Ci 易繫辭 – The name of a book which explains the Yi Jing.

Yi Zhi 意志 – Will.

Yi 意 – Wisdom mind. The mind generated from the wise judgement.

Yin Bagua 陰八卦 – The Yin side of Bagua.

Yin De-An 尹德安 – A Baguazhang master.

Yin Family 尹氏 – Yin's family.

Yin fire 陰火 – The fire generated from the Yin sufficient.

Yin Fu 尹福 – A Baguazhang master.

Yin Jin 陰勁 – The Jing which is hidden and cannot be easily seen.

Yin Mai 陰脈 – Yin Vessels.

Yin Shi Baguazhang 尹氏八卦掌 – Yin family Baguazhang. Created by Yin Yu-Zhang.

Yin Yang Baguazhang 陰陽八卦掌 – A style of Baguazhang.

Yin Yang Yu Bu 陰陽魚步 – The Baguazhang stepping training, in which a practitioner walks following the Taiji symbol.

Yin Yang Yu 陰陽魚 – The Taiji symbol, constructed by combination of the teardrop shapes of the Yin and Yang portions to form a circular pattern.

Yin Yang 陰陽 – Two poles or two extremities.

Yin Yao 陰爻 – A broken line which symbolizes Yin.

Yin Yi 陰儀 – Yin Pole.

Yin Yu-Zhang 尹玉璋 – A Baguazhang master, credited as the creator of the Yin style Baguazhang.

Yin 陰 – Deficient. One of the two extremities or two poles.

Yong Gan 勇敢 – Bravery.

Yongquan 湧泉 – Cavity name. Belongs to the Kidney Primary Qi Channel (K-1).

You of Zhou 周幽王 – King of Zhou in Chinese Zhou dynasty.

You Pan 右盼 – Beware of the right. One of the moving strategies in Taijiquan.

You Shen Bagua Lian Huan Zhang 游身八卦連環掌 – Swimming Body Baguazhang Linking Sequence. Name of a barehand Baguazhang sequence.

You Shen Long Xing Baguazhang 游身龍形八卦掌 – Swimming Body Dragon Shape Baguazhang. Name of a barehand Baguazhang sequence.

Yu Bu 魚步 – Fish step. A Baguazhang practitioner steps following the Taiji symbol.

Yu Chang 魚腸 – Fish Intestine. Name of a sword, well known for its sharpness in China.

Yuan Jing 元精 – Original essence.

Yuan-Yang Yue 鴛鴦鉞 – Mandarin Duck Axe. Another name of the Deer Hook Sword.

Za 砸 – Smash. A Chinese martial arts technique.

Zen 忍 – Endurance.

Zhan Shen Qiang 戰身槍 – Battle Body Spear. Name of a Baguazhang spear sequence.

Zhan 黏 – Sticking. A Chinese martial arts technique.

Zhang Chang-Hai 張長海 – A Baguazhang master.

Zhang Jun-Feng 張俊峰 – A Baguazhang master.

Zhang Xian 張憲 – A Baguazhang master.

Zhang Xiang-Yu 張項羽 – A Baguazhang master.

Zhang Yu-Kui 張玉魁 – A Baguazhang master.

Zhang Zhao-Dong 張兆東 – A Baguazhang master.

Zhao Dao-Xin 趙道新 – A Baguazhang master.

Zhao Fei-Zhen 趙飛震 – A Baguazhang master.

Zhao Yun-Long 趙雲龍 – A Baguazhang master.

Zhao 趙 – A country name in the Chinese Warring States Period (475-222 B.C.).

Zhen (☳) 震 – One of the Eight Trigrams.

Zhen Dan Tian 真丹田 – The real Dan Tian, which is located near the center of the gravity.

Zhen Wu Mountain 真武山 – Mountain's name, located in Sichuan province, China.

Zheng Huai-Xian 鄭懷賢 – Master Liang Shou-Yu's Baguazhang and Xingyiquan master.

Zheng Yi 正義 – Righteousness.

Zheng 鄭 – A country in Chinese Spring and Autumn Period (722-481 B.C.).

Zheng 爭 – Struggling. A Chinese martial arts technique.

Zheng Dasun (Taisun Wang) 鄭大蓀 – Master Liang Shou-Yu's friend.

Zhong Cheng 忠誠 – Loyalty.

Zhong Ding 中定 – Centering, means stable and keep the center.

Zhong Gong 中宮 – Central palace. In the "Nine Palace" stepping training, the center location is the central palace.

Zhong Pan 中盤 – The middle section (Zhong Pan) of the body which starts from the knees up to the solar plexus.

Zhou Xiang 周祥 – A Baguazhang master.

Zhou Yi 周易 – Zhou's Yi. Means the Yi Jing explained by Zhou Wen Wang.

Zhou 肘 – Elbow strike. A Chinese martial arts technique.

Zhou 周 – A dynasty in China (1122-255 B.C.).

Zhu Guo-Fu 朱國福 – A Baguazhang master.

Zhu Guo-Xiang 朱國祥 – A Baguazhang master.

Zhu Guo-Zhen 朱國楨 – A Baguazhang master.

Zhu Village 朱家塢村 – A village in which all Zhu families reside.

Zhuan Zhang 轉掌 – Turning palms. Another name of Baguazhang.

Zhuan 轉 – Turning. One of the strategic movements in Chinese martial arts.

Zi Wu Yuan Yang Yue 子午鴛鴦鉞 – Midnight Noon Mandarin Duck Ax. Another name of the Deer Hook Sword.

Zi 子 – Midnight.

Zou 走 – Walk away. One of the strategic movements in Chinese martial arts.

Zuan 鑽 – Drill. A Chinese martial arts technique.

Zun Jing 尊敬 – Respect.

Zuo 坐 – To sit or settle down. Means stabilize in Chinese martial arts.

Zuo Gu 左顧 – Look to the left. One of the strategic movements in Chinese martial arts.

Zuo Wan 坐腕 –
Settle down the wrist. When you use your palm to strike, first your fingers are pointing forward. Right before you reach your opponent, suddenly you settle down your wrist for the strike.

About the Authors

Master Liang Shou-Yu
梁守渝

Master Liang Shou-Yu was born on June 28, 1943 in the city of Chongqian, Sichuan Province, China. When he was six he began his training in Qigong, the art of breathing and internal energy control, under the tutelage of his renowned grandfather, the late Liang Zhi-Xiang. Mr. Liang was taught the esoteric skills of the Emei Mountain sect, including Da Peng Qigong. When he was eight, his grandfather made special arrangements for him to begin training Emei Wushu (martial arts).

In 1959, as a young boy, Mr. Liang began the study of Qin Na and Chinese Shuai Jiao (Wrestling). From 1960 to 1964 he devoted his attention to the systematic research and practice of Wrestling, Wushu, and other special martial power training.

In addition to the advantage of being born to a Wushu family, Mr. Liang also had the chance to come into contact with many of the legendary grandmasters. By the time he was twenty, Mr. Liang had already received instruction from 10 of the most well-known contemporary masters of both Southern and Northern origin, who gladly instructed and inspired this ardent young man. His curiosity inspired him to learn more than one hundred sequences from many different styles. His study of the martial arts has taken him throughout mainland China, having gone to Henan Province to learn Chen style Taijiquan, Hubei Province to learn the Wudang system, and Hunan Province to learn the Nan Yue system.

With his wealth of knowledge, Mr. Liang was inspired to compete in martial arts competitions, in which he was many times gold medalist in China. During his adolescence, Mr. Liang won titles in Chinese wrestling (Shuai Jiao), various other martial arts, and weight lifting.

Through and beyond his college years, Mr. Liang's wide background in various martial arts helped form his present character, and led him to achieve a high level of martial skill. Some of the styles he concentrated on include the esoteric Emei system, Shaolin, Long Fist, Praying Mantis, Chuo Jiao, Xingyi, Baguazhang, Taijiquan, Liu He Ba Fa, Shuai Jiao, Qin Na, vital point striking, many weapons systems, and several kinds of internal Qigong.

Mr. Liang received a university degree in biology and physiology from West-South National University in 1964. However, it was a time of political turmoil, and because of his bourgeois family background, the Communist government sent him to a remote, poverty stricken village to teach high school. Despite this setback, Mr. Liang began to organize Wushu teams in the local community, and he trained numerous farmer-students in Wushu and in wrestling.

Then came a disastrous time in modern Chinese history. During the years of the Cultural Revolution (1966-1974 A.D.), all forms of martial arts and Qigong were suppressed. Because he came from a bourgeoisie family, Mr. Liang was vulnerable to the furious passions and blind madness of the revolutionaries. To avoid conflict with the red guards, he gave up his teaching position. Mr. Liang used this opportunity to tour various parts of the country to discover and visit great masters in Wushu, and to make friends with people who shared his devotion to and love for the art. Mr. Liang went through numerous provinces and large cities, visiting especially the many renowned and revered places where Wushu was created, developed and polished. Among the many places he visited were Emei Mountain, Wudang Mountain, Hua Mountain, Qingcheng Mountain, Chen's village in Henan, the Cangzhou Territory in Hebei Province, Beijing, and Shanghai. In eight years he made many Wushu friends and met many great masters, and his mastery of the techniques and philosophy of the art grew to new horizons.

At the end of the Cultural Revolution, the Chinese government again began to support the martial arts and Qigong, including competitions. There was a general movement to organize and categorize the existing martial and internal arts. Research projects were set up to search out the old masters who remained alive, select their best techniques, and organize their knowledge. It was at this time that the Sichuan government appointed Mr. Liang as a coach for the city, the territory, and the province. So many of his students were among the top martial artists of China that in 1978 Mr. Liang was voted one of the top national coaches since 1949. He also received acclamation from the People's Republic of China Physical Education and Sports Commissions, and often served as judge in national competitions.

After the Cultural Revolution, and despite his many official duties, Mr. Liang continued to participate actively in competitions at the provincial and national level. Between 1974 and 1981 he won numerous medals, including four gold medals. His students also performed superbly in national and provincial open tournaments, winning many medals. Many of these students have now become professional Wushu coaches or college Wushu instructors themselves. Other students have become Wushu trainers in the armed forces, or have become movie actors in Wushu pictures. In 1979, Mr. Liang received several appointments, including a committee membership in the Sichuan Chapter of the China National Wushu Association, and an executive membership of the Wushu Coaches Committee.

1981 marked a new era in the course of Mr. Liang's life, when he first visited Seattle, Washington in the United States. His art impressed every one of the Wushu devotees immediately, and the Wushu and Taiji Club of the University of Washington retained him as a Wushu Coach. In addition, Mr. Liang offered lessons at the Taiji Association in Seattle. The following year, Mr. Liang went north to Vancouver, Canada, where he was appointed Taiji Coach by the Villa Cathy Care Home, and Honorary Chairman and Head Coach by the North American Taiji Athletic Association.

In 1984, Mr. Liang became Chairperson and Wushu Coach for the School of Physical Education of the University of British Columbia. In 1985, he was elected coach of the First Canadian National Wushu Team, which was invited to participate in the First International Wushu Invitational Tournament in Xian, China. Competing against teams from 13 other countries, the Canadian team won third place.

In 1986, Mr. Liang was again elected coach of the Second Canadian National Wushu Team, which competed in the Second International Wushu Invitational Tournament held in the city of Teintsin, China. This time, 28 countries participated, and the Canadian team earned more medals than any other country except the host country itself. Mr. Liang's role and achievements were reported in 14 newspapers and magazines throughout China, and the performances and demonstrations of Mr. Liang and his team were broadcast on the Sichuan television station.

Mr. Liang has not limited his Wushu contributions to Canada. He has given numerous lectures and demonstrations to Wushu professionals and instructors in the United States. Adherents of many disciplines, including Karate, Taiji and others, have benefited from Mr. Liang's personal touch. In addition to instructing in such cities as Houston, Denver, Boston, and New York, Mr. Liang was invited to several cities in Italy for seminars in 1991. Mr. Liang has also judged in the National Wushu Tournament in the United States, and has produced an instructional video program teaching Liangong Shr Ba Fa Qigong in conjunction with the Chinese National Qigong Institute.

Master Liang Shou-Yu

Master Liang Shou-Yu

About the Authors

Dr. Yang Jwing-Ming, Ph.D.
楊俊敏

Dr. Yang Jwing-Ming was born on August 11, 1946, in Xinzhu Xian, Taiwan, Republic of China. He started his Wushu (Gongfu or Kung Fu) training at the age of fifteen under the Shaolin White Crane (Bai He) Master Cheng Gin-Gsao. Master Cheng originally learned Taizuquan from his grandfather when he was a child. When Master Cheng was fifteen years old, he started learning White Crane from Master Jin Shao-Feng, and followed him for twenty-three years until Master Jin's death.

In thirteen years of study (1961-1974 A.D.) under Master Cheng, Dr. Yang became an expert in the White Crane style of Chinese martial arts, which includes both the use of barehands and of various weapons such as saber, staff, spear, trident, two short rods, and many others. With the same master he also studied White Crane Qin Na (or Chin Na), Tui Na and Dian Xue massage, and herbal treatment.

At the age of sixteen, Dr. Yang began the study of Taijiquan (Yang Style) under Master Kao Tao. After learning from Master Kao, Dr. Yang continued his study and research of Taijiquan with several masters and senior practitioners such as Master Li Mao-Ching and Mr. Wilson Chen in Taipei. Master Li learned his Taijiquan from the well-known Master Han Ching-Tang, and Mr. Chen learned his Taijiquan from Master Chang Xiang-San. Dr. Yang has mastered the Taiji barehand sequence, pushing hands, the two-man fighting sequence, Taiji sword, Taiji saber, and Taiji Qigong.

When Dr. Yang was eighteen years old he entered Tamkang College in Taipei Xian to study Physics. In college he began the study of traditional Shaolin Long Fist (Changquan or Chang Chuan) with Master Li Mao-Ching at the Tamkang College Guoshu Club (1964-1968 A.D.), eventually becoming an assistant instructor under Master Li. In 1971 he completed his M.S. degree in Physics at the National Taiwan University, and then served in the Chinese Air Force from 1971 to 1972. In the service, Dr. Yang taught Physics at the Junior Academy of the Chinese Air Force while also teaching Wushu. After being honorably discharged in 1972, he returned to Tamkang College to teach Physics and resume study under Master Li Mao-Ching. From Master Li, Dr. Yang learned Northern style Wushu, which includes both barehand (especially kicking) techniques and numerous weapons.

In 1974, Dr. Yang came to the United States to study Mechanical Engineering at Purdue University. At the request of a few students, Dr. Yang began to teach Gongfu (Kung Fu), which resulted in the founding of the Purdue University Chinese Kung Fu Research Club in the spring of 1975. While at Purdue, Dr. Yang also taught college-credited courses in Taijiquan. In May, 1978 he was awarded a Ph.D. in Mechanical Engineering by Purdue.

In 1980, Dr. Yang moved to Houston to work for Texas Instruments. While in Houston he founded Yang's Shaolin Kung Fu Academy, which was eventually taken over by his student Mr. Jeffery Bolt after Dr. Yang moved to Boston in 1982. Dr. Yang founded Yang's Martial Arts Academy (YMAA) in Boston on October 1, 1982.

In January of 1984 Dr. Yang gave up his engineering career to devote more time to research, writing, and teaching martial arts and Qigong. In March, 1986 he purchased property in the Jamaica Plain area of Boston to use as the headquarters of a new organization - Yang's Martial Arts Association. The organization has continued to expand, and as of July 1st 1989, YMAA has become just one division of Yang's Oriental Arts Association, Inc. (YOAA, Inc). In recent years, YMAA has grown to include three schools in the United States, eleven schools in Poland, three schools in France, one school in Portugal, and one school in Saudi Arabia.

In summary, Dr. Yang has been involved in Chinese Wushu since 1961. During this time, he has spent thirteen years learning Shaolin White Crane (Bai He), Shaolin Long Fist (Changquan), and Taijiquan. Dr. Yang has more than twenty-four years of instructional experience: seven years in Taiwan, five years at Purdue University, two years in Houston, Texas, and eleven years in Boston, Massachusetts.

In addition, Dr. Yang has also been invited to offer seminars around the world to share his knowledge of Chinese martial arts and Qigong. The countries he has visited include Canada, Mexico, France, Italy, Poland, England, Ireland, Portugal, Switzerland, Saudi Arabia, and Germany.

Dr. Yang has published seventeen other volumes on the martial arts and Qigong:

1. *Shaolin Chin Na;* Unique Publications, Inc., 1980.
2. *Shaolin Long Fist Kung Fu;* Unique Publications, Inc., 1981.
3. *Yang Style Tai Chi Chuan;* Unique Publications, Inc., 1981.
4. *Introduction to Ancient Chinese Weapons;* Unique Publications, Inc., 1985.
5. *Chi Kung - Health and Martial Arts;* YMAA Publication Center, 1985.
6. *Northern Shaolin Sword;* YMAA Publication Center, 1985.
7. *Advanced Yang Style Tai Chi Chuan, Vol.1, Tai Chi Theory and Tai Chi Jing;* YMAA Publication Center, 1986.
8. *Advanced Yang Style Tai Chi Chuan, Vol.2, Martial Applications;* YMAA Publication Center, 1986.
9. *Analysis of Shaolin Chin Na;* YMAA Publication Center, 1987.
10. *The Eight Pieces of Brocade;* YMAA Publication Center, 1988.
11. *The Root of Chinese Chi Kung - The Secrets of Chi Kung Training;* YMAA Publication Center, 1989.
12. *Muscle/Tendon Changing and Marrow/Brain Washing Chi Kung - The Secret of Youth;* YMAA Publication Center, 1989.
13. *Hsing Yi Chuan - Theory and Applications;* YMAA Publication Center, 1990.
14. *The Essence of Tai Chi Chi Kung - Health and Martial Arts;* YMAA Publication Center, 1990.
15. *Qigong for Arthritis;* YMAA Publication Center, 1991.
16. *Chinese Qigong Massage - General Massage;* YMAA Publication Center, 1992.
17. *How to Defend Yourself;* YMAA Publication Center, 1992.

Dr. Yang has also published the following videotapes:

1. *Yang Style Tai Chi Chuan and Its Applications;* YMAA Publication Center, 1984.
2. *Shaolin Long Fist Kung Fu - Lien Bu Chuan and Its Applications;* YMAA Publication Center, 1985.
3. *Shaolin Long Fist Kung Fu - Gung Li Chuan and Its Applications;* YMAA Publication Center, 1986.
4. *Shaolin Chin Na;* YMAA Publication Center, 1987.
5. *Wai Dan Chi Kung, Vol. 1 — The Eight Pieces of Brocade;* YMAA Publication Center, 1987.
6. *Chi Kung for Tai Chi Chuan;* YMAA Publication Center, 1990.
7. *Qigong for Arthritis;* YMAA Publication Center, 1991.
8. *Qigong Massage - Self Massage;* YMAA Publication Center, 1992.
9. *Qigong Massage - With a Partner;* YMAA Publication Center, 1992.
10. *Defend Yourself 1 - Unarmed Attack;* YMAA Publication Center, 1992.
11. *Defend Yourself 2 - Knife Attack;* YMAA Publication Center, 1992.

Dr. Yang Jwing-Ming

Dr. Yang Jwing-Ming

About the Authors

Mr. Wu Wen-Ching
吳文慶

Mr. Wu was born in Taiwan, Republic of China in 1964. In 1976 he went to West Africa with his family, where he attended an international school. Mr. Wu graduated as the salutatorian of his high school class.

In 1983 Mr. Wu came to Boston, Massachusetts to attend Northeastern University. It is at this time that Mr. Wu was accepted by Dr. Yang as a student. Mr. Wu's dedicated training helped him excel in Shaolin Long Fist and White Crane Kung Fu, as well as in Yang Style Taijiquan. In five years, Mr. Wu completed the cooperative and academic requirements to receive his BSME Degree with honors, and also qualified as an assistant instructor under Dr. Yang.

After graduation, Mr. Wu began working as a mechanical engineer during the day, and teaching Shaolin Kung Fu and Taijiquan classes at YMAA Headquarters in the evenings. He also continued his advanced training under Dr. Yang's personal guidance.

After years of dedicated training, Mr. Wu proved his moral character, and his martial arts potential in both internal and external styles to Dr. Yang. In May 1989, Mr. Wu was publicly accepted by Dr. Yang as a "disciple."

In 1986, Mr. Wu had the good fortune of being introduced to Master Liang by Dr. Yang. Mr. Wu's martial potential and moral character won the liking of Master Liang. For the last seven years, Master Liang has readily shared much of his vast knowledge with Mr. Wu. Mr. Wu has learned Xingyiquan, Baguazhang, White Ape Sword, and Taijiquan from Master Liang.

With Dr. Yang and Master Liang's encouragement, Mr. Wu competed in eight events in the 1990 United States National Chinese Martial Arts Competition held in Houston, Texas. Mr. Wu was ranked first nationally for every event in which he competed. He was awarded two of the highest awards in the competition: Men's All-Around Internal Style and External Style Grand Champion.

On November 6, 1990, with Dr. Yang's permission, Mr. Wu founded Yang's Martial Arts Association of Rhode Island (YMAA-RI), where he still continues to pass down his lineage of Chinese martial arts. In less than two years, YMAA-RI has established a solid foundation, attracting students from Rhode Island and other neighboring states. During the past three years, Mr. Wu has not only offered his expertise to students at YMAA-RI, but has also traveled to several other states and countries to offer seminars on Taijiquan, Xingyiquan, Baguazhang, and Shaolin Kung Fu. During this time, he also translated a major part of a Traditional Yang Family Style Taijiquan video tape by the fourth and the sixth generation Yang family descendants, and co-authored A Guide to Taijiquan with Master Liang. It is his goal to carry on his teachers' legacy, not only by improving his own ability and understanding, but by benefiting others through his teaching and writing.

Mr. Wu Wen-Ching

Index

BOOKS FROM YMAA (PARTIAL LIST)

ANCIENT CHINESE WEAPONS	B004R/671
ANALYSIS OF SHAOLIN CHIN NA 2ND ED.	B009R/0002
ARTHRITIS—CHINESE WAY OF HEALING & PREVENTION	B015R/426
BACK PAIN RELIEF—CHINESE QIGONG FOR HEALING & PREVENTION	B030R/0258
BAGUAZHANG	B020/300
CHIN NA IN GROUND FIGHTING	B028/493
CHINESE FAST WRESTLING—THE ART OF SAN SHOU KUAI JIAO	B029/37X
CHINESE FITNESS—A MIND / BODY APPROACH	B016/254
CHINESE QIGONG MASSAGE	B021/36X
COMPREHENSIVE APPLICATIONS OF SHAOLIN CHIN NA	B010R/523
EIGHT SIMPLE QIGONG EXERCISES FOR HEALTH, 2ND ED.	B025/353
ESSENCE OF SHAOLIN WHITE CRANE	B014R/639
ESSENCE OF TAIJI QIGONG, 2ND ED.	B065/424
EXPLORING TAI CHI	B056/108
INSIDE TAI CHI	B071/0266
KATA AND THE TRANSMISSION OF KNOWLEDGE	B067/728
LIUHEBAFA FIVE CHARACTER SECRETS	B072/024X
MARTIAL ARTS INSTRUCTION	B066/698
MARTIAL WAY AND ITS VIRTUES	B061/183
MUGAI RYU	B006R/85X
NORTHERN SHAOLIN SWORD, 2ND ED.	B053/99X
PRINCIPLES OF TRADITIONAL CHINESE MEDICINE	B005R/574
QIGONG FOR HEALTH & MARTIAL ARTS 2ND ED.	B058/116
QIGONG FOR LIVING	B068/736
QIGONG MEDITATION - EMBRYONIC BREATHING	B012R/841
QIGONG, THE SECRET OF YOUTH	B011R/507
ROOT OF CHINESE QIGONG, 2ND ED.	B055/884
SHIHAN TE—THE BUNKAI OF KATA	B049/930
TAEKWONDO—ANCIENT WISDOM FOR THE MODERN WARRIOR	B059/221
TAEKWONDO—SPIRIT AND PRACTICE	B032/647
TAI CHI BOOK	B007R/434
TAI CHI THEORY & MARTIAL POWER, 2ND ED.	B008R/442
TAI CHI CHUAN MARTIAL APPLICATIONS, 2ND ED.	B060/23X
TAI CHI WALKING	B022/378
TAIJI CHIN NA	B036/744
TAIJI SWORD, CLASSICAL YANG STYLE	B034/68X
TAIJIQUAN, CLASSICAL YANG STYLE	B063/432
TAIJIQUAN THEORY OF DR. YANG, JWING-MING	B046/892
TRADITIONAL CHINESE HEALTH SECRETS	B069/0029
WAY OF KENDO AND KENJITSU	B045/833
WOMAN'S QIGONG GUIDE	B013R/416
XINGYIQUAN	

VIDEOTAPES FROM YMAA (PARTIAL LIST)

ADVANCED PRACTICAL CHIN NA SERIES	T004/531
ANALYSIS OF SHAOLIN CHIN NA	T007/558
ARTHRITIS—THE CHINESE WAY OF HEALING & PREVENTION	T028/566
BACK PAIN RELIEF—CHINESE QIGONG FOR HEALING & PREVENTION	
CHIN NA IN DEPTH SERIES—COURSES (12 SEPARATE VIDEOS)	
CHINESE QIGONG MASSAGE SERIES (2 SEPARATE VIDEOS)	
COMPREHENSIVE APPLICATIONS OF SHAOLIN CHIN NA (2 SEPARATE VIDEOS)	
DEFEND YOURSELF (2 SEPARATE VIDEOS)	
EMEI BAGUAZHANG SERIES (3 SEPARATE VIDEOS)	T005/54X
EIGHT SIMPLE QIGONG EXERCISES FOR HEALTH 2ND ED.	T006/238
ESSENCE OF TAIJI QIGONG	T050/467
MUGAI RYU	
NORTHERN SHAOLIN SWORD SERIES (3 SEPARATE VIDEOS)	
SHAOLIN KUNG FU BASIC TRAINING SERIES (2 SEPARATE VIDEOS)	
SHAOLIN LONG FIST KUNG FU SERIES (6 SEPARATE VIDEOS)	
SHAOLIN WHITE CRANE GONG FU—BASIC TRAINING SERIES (2 SEPARATE VIDEOS)	
SIMPLIFIED TAI CHI CHUAN—24 & 48 FORMS	T021/329
TAIJI BALL QIGONG SERIES (4 SEPARATE VIDEOS)	T016/408
TAIJI CHIN NA	
TAIJI PUSHING HANDS SERIES (5 SEPARATE VIDEOS)	T053/491
TAIJI SABER	T061/0088
TAIJI & SHAOLIN STAFF - FUNDAMENTAL TRAINING - 1	T031/817
TAIJI SWORD, CLASSICAL YANG STYLE	
TAIJI YIN & YANG SYMBOL STICKING HANDS SERIES (2 SEPARATE VIDEOS)	T030/752
TAIJIQUAN, CLASSICAL YANG STYLE	
WHITE CRANE QIGONG SERIES (2 SEPARATE VIDEOS)	T023/477
WU STYLE TAIJIQUAN	T020/310
XINGYIQUAN—12 ANIMAL FORM	T001/181
YANG STYLE TAI CHI CHUAN	

COMPLETE DVDS FROM YMAA

ANALYSIS OF SHAOLIN CHIN NA (DVD)	DVD012/0231
CHIN NA INDEPTH SERIES—COURSES 1-4/5-8/9-12	DVD008/0037
EIGHT SIMPLE QIGONG EXERCISES FOR HEALTH (DVD)	DVD010/0215
ESSENCE OF TAIJI QIGONG (DVD)	DVD009/0207
SHAOLIN KUNG FU FUNDAMENTAL TRAINING - 1&2 (DVD)	DVD007/661
SHAOLIN LONG FIST KUNG FU - BASIC SEQUENCES (DVD)	DVD006/599
SHAOLIN WHITE CRANE GONG FU BASIC TRAINING 1 & 2	DVD002/645
TAIJIQUAN CLASSICAL YANG STYLE (DVD)	DVD011/0223
TAIJI SWORD, CLASSICAL YANG STYLE (DVD)	DVD003/637
WHITE CRANE HARD & SOFT QIGONG (DVD)	

more products available from...

YMAA Publication Center, Inc. 楊氏東方文化出版中心

4354 Washington Street Roslindale, MA 02131
1-800-669-8892 • ymaa@aol.com • www.ymaa.com